# A HAWAIIAN READER
## Edited by A. Grove Day and Carl Stroven
## With an introduction by James A. Michener

This is a colorful treasure house of the best writings on Hawaii from Captain Cook's arrival to the year of statehood. Some of these pieces are vigorous accounts of plain travelers' adventures and many others are by literary greats. For since Mark Twain's time the islands have been visited and written about by an astonishing array of well-known authors.

Together they provide an informal history of Hawaii from primitive times to the present. A history which covers almost every aspect of a people who were swiftly carried from the Stone Age, through exploitation, to a pivotal position in the last war, in less than two hundred years.

Here are the early voyagers' impressions of the untouched paradise they had discovered and the missionaries' accounts of their stubborn and often successful efforts to bring the word of God and the Mother Hubbard to it. There are stories such as Maugham's of the rapscallion drifters of the Pacific. There are sketches which show Robert Louis Stevenson's ability to capture the magic of native legends; Jack London's iconoclastic view; and Mark Twain's merrier one. Here is Honolulu after Pearl Harbor as James Jones and Marquand saw it. Among the other writers are Charles Warren Stoddard, Austin Strong, Genevieve Taggard, Rupert Brooke, May Sarton, and Kathryn Hulme.

For the first time such a selection of writers who have known and loved Hawaii have been brought together between the covers of a book. They provide a superb way to visit Hawaii without leaving home. Moreover, it is a book for everyone who has been to Hawaii or who is going there.

Mutual Publishing
1127 11th Avenue, Mezz. B
Honolulu, Hawaii 96816
Telephone (808) 732-1709
Fax (808) 734-4094

# WHAT THE REVIEWERS SAY

"By wise selection of material Editors Day and Stroven, English professors at the University of Hawaii, are able in this book of vignettes to highlight Hawaii's history and, even more difficult, to capture the spirit of the periods through which the Islands passed in their transformation from the late Stone Age to a cultured State of the Union."

—Honolulu *Star-Bulletin*

"We are indebted to them for having provided us with a varied and well-balanced fare calculated to suit all tastes, all appetites."

—Honolulu *Advertiser*

"This book is a potpourri of short stories, autobiography, poems, historical accounts, edited expertly in chronological continuity. As entertainment, it is exciting reading — for the scholar, it affords authentic Hawaii."

—Dallas *Morning News*

"If I could have only one book about Hawaii, this would be it."

—Richard Armour

THIS BOOK CONTAINS THE COMPLETE TEXT
OF THE ORIGINAL HARDBOUND EDITION

# A
# HAWAIIAN
# READER

Selected and edited by
A. GROVE DAY and CARL STROVEN

With an introduction by JAMES A. MICHENER

Mutual Publishing Paperback Series
Tales of the Pacific
Honolulu · Hawaii

## ACKNOWLEDGMENTS

GWENFREAD ALLEN: "Bombs Fall on Hawaii: Dec. 7, 1941." Reprinted by permission of the publisher from *Hawaii's War Years* by Gwenfread Allen (Honolulu, University of Hawaii Press, 1950). Copyright 1950 by University of Hawaii Press.

MARTHA BECKWITH (translator): "The Kumulipo: A Hawaiian Creation Chant," translated and edited with commentary by Martha Warren Beckwith, by permission of The University of Chicago Press. Copyright 1951 by the University of Chicago.

SOPHIA CRACROFT: "Two Victorian Ladies Visit Honolulu." Reprinted by permission of the publisher from *The Victorian Visitors* by Alfons L. Korn (Honolulu, University of Hawaii Press, 1958). Copyright 1958 by University of Hawaii Press.

KATHRYN HULME: "Father Damien's Village." First published in *The Atlantic Monthly*, November, 1958. Copyright 1958 by Kathryn Hulme. Reprinted by permission.

JAMES JONES: "The Way It Is." Reprinted from *Harper's Magazine*, June, 1949, by permission of the author.

KATHARINE LUOMALA: "Menehunes, The Little People." Reprinted by permission of the author and the Bernice P. Bishop Museum from *Voices on the Wind: Polynesian Myths and Chants* (Bishop Museum Press, Honolulu). Copyright 1955 by Bernice P. Bishop Museum.

J.P. MARQUAND: "Lunch at Honolulu." From *Thirty Years* by J.P. Marquand, by permission of Little, Brown & Co. Copyright 1945 by John P. Marquand.

WILLIAM MEREDITH: "An Account of a Visit to Hawaii." Reprinted by permission of Alfred A. Knopf, Inc. Also with the permission of the author. Copyright, 1953, 1957 by William Meredith. This poem first appeared in *Poetry*, March, 1953.

THOMAS D. MURPHY: "The AJA's Come Home." Reprinted by permission of the publisher from *Ambassadors in Arms* by Thomas D. Murphy (Honolulu, University of Hawaii Press, 1954). Copyright 1954 by University of Hawaii Press.

MARY PUKUI and MARTHA BECKWITH: "The Marchers of the Night." From *Kepelino's Traditions of Hawaii*, edited by Martha Warren Beckwith (Honolulu, Bernice P. Bishop Museum, 1932). Reprinted by permission of the Museum.

MAY SARTON: "Sukiyaki on the Kona Coast." Reprinted from *The Reporter*, June 27, 1957, by permission of Russell and Volkening, Inc., and of the Reporter Magazine Company. Copyright 1957 by the Reporter Magazine Company.

AUSTIN STRONG: "His Oceanic Majesty's Goldfish." First published in *The Atlantic Monthly*. Copyright 1944 by the Atlantic Monthly Company. Reprinted by permission.

## ISBN 0-935180-07-9

Cover photographs from the Baker-Van Dyke Collection.

Cover design by Bill Fong, the Art Directors.

# EDITORS' NOTE

This anthology contains thirty-seven selections from the work of thirty authors who have written about Hawaii. We have tried to collect here some of the best literature in English concerning this colorful region which has become the Fiftieth State. The chief criteria on which the selections were made are: Does this piece have literary value? Is it interesting? Does it capture in some significant way the spirit of the place and time? Can the work be included without using an excessive amount of space? No passages from the number of highly readable novels written about Hawaii — for example, O. A. Bushnell's *The Return of Lono,* Ruth McKee's *The Lord's Anointed,* and Marjorie Sinclair's *The Wild Wind* — could be included, since the structure of a good novel seldom lends itself to the extraction of a part.

The selections have been arranged in chronological order by date of incident or setting, starting with the discovery of the islands by Captain Cook. Five pieces representing ancient Hawaiian literature and lore have been placed at the end of the book. Each selection is preceded by a brief introduction concerning the author and the particular offering. The texts, written by many hands over almost two hundred years, have not been changed except to modernize the spelling and punctuation. Ellipsis marks in certain nonfiction selections indicate that, for the purpose of condensation, passages have been omitted; ellipsis marks in fiction or poetry are stylistic. A glossary of Hawaiian words that appear in the book is appended.

The editors of this anthology have, in the main, been able to include the selections of their choice. Authors, publishers, and copyright holders are acknowledged in a bibliographic note. We are indebted to Professor A. L. Korn, University of Hawaii, for several helpful suggestions. The hopes of the editors will be fulfilled if the narratives, stories, poems, sketches, journals, and folklore that are here collected arouse in the reader an interest in the richly varied literature of the Hawaiian Islands and in the progress of their people from primitive times to statehood.

A. G. D.
C. S.

University of Hawaii

# CONTENTS

## ANCIENT HAWAII

# INTRODUCTION

It is wonderfully propitious that this book should reach the American public in the same season that Hawaii becomes an integral part of the United States, for we have all too long thought of these glamorous islands as a legendary paradise rather than as the maturing international society which they in fact are. This admirably timed book can thus serve as an introduction of Hawaii to its forty-nine sister states.

No previous territory has ever sought admission to our federal union from such an advanced state of culture as has Hawaii. The islands contain a fine university, one of the world's greatest ethnological museums, an art academy that is astonishing in its riches, a symphony orchestra, and a guild of theatrical players which sends its graduates to Broadway. Best of all, Hawaii has a number of libraries which would be the envy of most states and a population which seems to have an absolute thirst for knowledge. This present book illustrates one facet of the amazing richness of our new state: its interest in literary matters.

Here is offered a garner of the most interesting writing that has so far appeared about Hawaii: the poems, the stories, the recollections, and the adventures. Here one meets the great figures who helped mold the intellectual character of these islands, and here a faithful picture is given of the manner in which people adjusted themselves to a vivid new home.

Under any circumstances I would be happy to commend such a work to the American public, for Hawaii is a land that deserves to be better known, but in the case of *A Hawaiian Reader* I have a special pleasure in writing this introduction. For in a curious way I was connected with the genesis of this anthology.

In early 1959 I was coming to the end of a review of almost everything that had so far been written about Hawaii, and I was delighted with some of the things I had found. One day at close of work the thought came to me that I ought to collect some three dozen samples of the best writing that has been done on Hawaii, prefacing each with a brief explanation of how it had come to be written and what we could deduce from its contents.

Excited by the prospect of doing something useful, I made a brief preliminary sketch of what the book should contain, and then called on my old friend and former collaborator, Professor A. Grove Day of the University of Hawaii.

"I think we should do another book," I announced peremptorily.

"Good," said Day. "On what?"

I explained quickly what I had in mind, and showed him my rough outline. Instead of the joy I expected to diffuse his face, a pronounced scowl appeared, followed by signs of positive embarrassment. It was obvious that he did not think much of my idea, so I defended it vigorously, pointing out: "Hawaii's going to become a state pretty soon, and I think Americans ought to know, from the pens of those who did the building and watched it, what happened there. I think this book is a marvelous idea."

Professor Day gulped and said, "So do I."

"Then why do you seem so hesitant about going ahead with me?" I pressed.

"Because Carl Stroven and I have just done it ourselves," Day confessed. He was right. Their manuscript was virtually finished. The prefaces I had in mind were already written. Everything had been done on almost the exact lines that I, working by myself, had developed. It was an extraordinary case of parallel literary thinking. I looked at Professor Day and laughed.

Now, contrary to popular belief, a professional writer is never disturbed when he hears that someone else equally competent is about to do a book whose vague outlines he has had in mind for some time. There is no professional jealousy involved, for the sensible writer cries: "Thank God! That's one more headache I don't have to worry about." It is a curious fact not widely appreciated by the general public that books and plays and good television programs are not in competition, in the ultimate sense of the word. A layman who sees one good play is likely to want to see another, whereas if his first venture yields a bad play, he is quite apt to have done with the whole business then and there. It is the same with books. A man who reads one good book will want to read another . . . and on the very same subject. Thus good breeds good, and I am constantly delighted when some apparent competitor turns out a fine book in a field that I am interested in, because that means that more people will probably want to read what I myself may later write on the same subject.

When I saw the manuscript I realized that Day and Stroven had completed their job in a markedly better fashion than I would have done. They are without question the two men best qualified in the entire world to edit this particular book. A decade ago they produced *The Spell of the Pacific*, a superb anthology of the best writing in English from the whole Pacific Ocean area. Their knowledge of Hawaiian writings is comprehensive, and their love of the islands excels even my own. They are scholars and they have good literary judgment. My only wish is that half a dozen other books I would vaguely like to write might fall into such capable hands, for then I would both avoid the hard work that lies ahead and see the ideas worked out in book form more effectively than I could have done. Rarely has a man writing the foreword to a book done so with more pleasure than I feel in presenting this work to the public. It is not only timely, a birthday book to a new state; it is also as good as it could possibly be.

Here, then, is the record of a just and forward-moving society. The central passage, it seems to me, is Hiram Bingham's powerful account of his personal battle against the man-of-warsmen. Like Bingham, whose self-righteous, unyielding rectitude gave Hawaii its formative character, this passage is taut and to the point. It tells of the basic struggle that gave birth to American Hawaii: the fight between devout New England missionaries and their seafaring adversaries who were bent upon continuing the corruption of the islands. Hiram Bingham is one of the most difficult great men of history to love, but everyone looking at either Hawaii or the Pacific in general is required either to stand for Bingham, the bigoted Old Testament figure, or for those other Americans who almost destroyed the islands. I have always been for Bingham, and I consider his awkward and unlovely book, *A Residence of Twenty-One Years in the Sandwich Islands*, the most significant volume yet published on the islands. I am glad to see it treated so capably in these pages, for it deserves to be better known.

Another characteristic of this anthology which pleases me intensely is the fact that the editors, through judicious selection of materials, give recognition to the fact that Hawaii's population today is about fifty per cent Oriental in ancestry. One can read dozens of previous books on the islands without ever discovering that fact, yet it was the Chinese who gave the islands much of their nineteenth-century color. It was the Japanese who did the heavy work in building the great plantations, and it has been the Filipinos who have kept the sugar cane and the pineapple growing. Having arrived in the islands as laboring peasants, these Orientals did not produce a literature of their own, but Professors Day and Stroven have included important passages that give them representation.

This leads to a consideration of the most perplexing selection in the anthology, and I think the editors have done a service in bringing this particular passage once more to our attention. Jack London, while writing on the mainland of America, had built for himself a solid reputation as a socialist defender of the underdog, and his works had world-wide acceptance; but when he came to Hawaii and saw at firsthand a population — the Chinese — which had many of the characteristics he had espoused in mainland America, he was completely unable to understand what he saw. In "Chun Ah Chun," reprinted here, and in other stories he not only failed to comprehend what was happening in the Pacific; he actually denigrated an entire body of people, largely on racist grounds. The story, as Day and Stroven properly point out, was founded upon events occurring within a real Chinese family, but is, I fear, a pathetic misreading both of the Chinese and of the spirit that activates Hawaii. I have never understood how Jack London could be one man in California, and such a different man in Hawaii. I still cannot understand how he could be a practicing socialist on the one hand and a race supremacist on the other. Yet the story "Chun Ah Chun" does have a sly warmth and much wit and remains one of the focal works in the London repertoire.

One of the finest services performed by this anthology will be its wider dissemination of Kathryn Hulme's perceptive essay on Hawaii's leper station as it exists today. For years the islands suffered well-deserved rebuke for the unfeeling manner in which their patients were isolated on an inclement bit of coast. Unfortunately, the contumely persisted long after the abuses were corrected, but now Miss Hulme reports the truth . . . and in a most beautiful piece of writing.

The reader may be interested in six passages which I had intended including in my version of the anthology, but which Professors Day and Stroven have correctly excluded because they fall outside the purview of the volume as finally planned. I nevertheless commend them to all who wish to dig more deeply into Hawaiian backgrounds.

In 1826 Captain James Hunnewell brought to Honolulu one of the smallest and least auspicious craft ever to negotiate the Strait of Magellan. His log of that incredible passage, *Journal of the Voyage of the "Missionary Packet,"* should be required reading for the fainthearted.

In 1855 Mrs. Lucy Goodale Thurston, a missionary wife then sixty years old, faced sure death from cancer of the breast. With the fortitude that marked all the early misionaries, she held herself in a chair, without sedatives, for an hour and a half, while a surgeon cut away her entire breast. She conversed with him during the operation, and her later account of what happened in those dreadful hours, which appears in her book, *The Life and Times of Lucy G. Thurston,* could well serve as the spiritual summary of the missionary.

In 1928 Miss Teura Henry published in Hawaii one of the world's most exciting ethnographic works — for the layman at least — *Ancient Tahiti*. It was a reworking of copious notes left by Miss Henry's grandfather, an English missionary long resident in Tahiti. His original manuscript, which must have been an even more sterling work than the one his granddaughter reconstructed, was mysteriously lost en route from Tahiti to Paris, but all who love the Pacific pray that it may someday just as mysteriously reappear. The antecedents of Hawaii are explained in this work, and I consider it the best book ever written in Hawaii.

In 1948 Dr. Elwood C. Zimmerman began publishing a series of learned volumes entitled *Insects of Hawaii,* but before he launched into his erudite material he composed an account of how the Hawaiian Islands were built and how life came to them. In doing so he wrote one of the most striking pieces yet composed about Hawaii.

In 1948 Kathleen Dickenson Mellen, a visitor from North Carolina, began publishing a series of volumes on Hawaii, the first titled *In a Hawaiian Valley*. Portions of it make fine reading for those who want to understand today's Polynesians.

And in 1934 another visitor, Ruth Eleanor McKee, wrote what I consider the best novel yet published about the islands, *The Lord's Anointed*. It has sweep, compassion, and flashes of brilliant writing. It deserves to be better known than it is. Of course, if one is willing to categorize James Jones's *From Here to Eternity* as a Hawaiian novel — I vacillate on doing so — it would have to be termed the islands' foremost work of fiction. Jones' skill in the short story is well represented by the inclusion here of his wartime "The Way It Is."

The present editors have been wise to save for the end of their volume the five selections dealing with the folklore of the islands, for the language of these passages is so alien to the modern world that it might have alienated the casual reader. It was advisable to start with some selection more in the modern mood, like that written by Captain Cook. But actually it is in these older passages that we catch the fundamental spirit upon which Hawaii has been built. All who love Hawaii remain indebted to David Malo, that curious misfitted man who did so much to save his people's records, and to Mary Pukui, who fortunately still lives today, a reservoir of knowledge and of sympathy.

JAMES A. MICHENER

# A HAWAIIAN READER

*No alien land in all the world has any deep strong charm for me but that one, no other land could so longingly and so beseechingly haunt me, sleeping and waking, through half a lifetime, as that one has done. Other things leave me, but it abides; other things change, but it remains the same. For me its balmy airs are always blowing, its summer seas flashing in the sun; the pulsing of its surfbeat is in my ear; I can see its garlanded crags, its leaping cascades, its plumy palms drowsing by the shore, its remote summits floating like islands above the cloud rack; I can feel the spirit of its woodland solitudes, I can hear the plash of its brooks; in my nostrils still lives the breath of flowers that perished twenty years ago.*

*Mark Twain*

JAMES COOK

# THE DISCOVERY OF
# THE HAWAIIAN ISLANDS

Sailing north from Tahiti, bound for the northwest coast of
America on his third voyage to the Pacific, Captain James Cook
discovered the Hawaiian Islands on the morning of January 18,
1778. The first island he sighted was Oahu, then soon afterwards
Kauai and Niihau. He named them the Sandwich Islands, in
honor of the Earl of Sandwich, First Lord of the British Ad-
miralty.

When the *Resolution* and the *Discovery* dropped anchor off
the village of Waimea on Kauai and Captain Cook and his men
went ashore, hundreds of natives had gathered there, marveling
at the great ships and the strange white visitors. They behaved
toward the captains as if they were the highest tabu chiefs or as
if they were gods. Soon, however, the shore became a busy market place. The ships needed fresh provisions; and the Hawaiians,
eager for anything made of iron, brought an abundance of pigs,
taro, and sweet potatoes, which they exchanged for nails. After
two weeks Captain Cook sailed away in a vain attempt to find
a passage over the American continent to the Atlantic Ocean.
He was to return a year later to these islands, the discovery of
which seemed to him "in many respects to be the most important
that had hitherto been made by Europeans throughout the extent of the Pacific Ocean."

IN THE MORNING OF THE 18TH [JANUARY, 1778], AN ISLAND MADE
its appearance, bearing northeast by east; and soon after we saw
more land bearing north and entirely detached from the
former. Both had the appearance of being high land. At noon

1

the first bore northeast by east, half east, by estimation about eight or nine leagues distant. Our latitude at this time was 21° 12' N. and longitude 200° 41' E. We had now light airs and calms, by turns; so that at sunset we were not less than nine or ten leagues from the nearest land.

On the 19th, at sunrise, the island first seen bore east several leagues distant. This being directly to windward, which prevented our getting near it, I stood for the other, which we could reach; and not long after discovered a third island in the direction of west-northwest, as far distant as land could be seen. We had now a fine breeze at east by north; and I steered for the east end of the second island, the nearest part being about two leagues distant.

At this time, we were in some doubt whether or no the land before us was inhabited; but this doubt was soon cleared up by seeing some canoes coming off from the shore toward the ships. I immediately brought to, to give them time to join us. They had from three or six men each; and on their approach we were agreeably surprised to find that they spoke in the language of Otaheite and of the other islands we had lately visited. It required but very little address to get them to come alongside, but no entreaties could prevail upon any of them to come on board. I tied some brass medals to a rope and gave them to those in one of the canoes, who in return tied some small mackerel to the rope as an equivalent. This was repeated; and some small nails or bits of iron, which they valued more than any other article, were given them. For these they exchanged more fish, and a sweet potato — a sure sign that they had some notion of bartering, or at least of returning one present for another. They had nothing else in their canoes except some large gourd shells and a kind of fishing net; but one of them offered for sale the piece of stuff that he wore round his waist, after the manner of the other islands.

These people were of a brown color, and though of the common size were stoutly made. There was little difference in the cast of their color but a considerable variation in their features, some of their visages not being very unlike those of Europeans. The hair of most of them was cropped pretty short; others had it flowing loose; and with a few, it was tied in a bunch on the crown of the head. In all, it seemed to be naturally black; but most of them had stained it, as is the practice of the Friendly Islanders, with some stuff which gave it a brown or burnt color. In general they wore beards. They had no ornaments about their persons, nor did we observe that their ears were perforated; but some were punctured on the hands or near the groin, though in a small degree; and the bits of cloth which they wore were curiously stained with red, black, and white colors. They seemed very mild and had no arms of any kind, if we except some small stones which they had evidently brought for their own defense; and these they threw overboard when they found that they were not wanted. . . .

The next morning we stood in for the land, and were met with several canoes filled with people, some of whom took courage and ventured on board. In the course of my several voyages, I never before met with the natives of any place so much astonished as these people were upon entering a ship. Their eyes were continually flying from object to object; the wildness of their looks and gestures fully expressing their entire ignorance about everything they saw, and strongly marking to us that till now they had never been visited by Europeans nor been acquainted with any of our commodities except iron, which, however, it was plain they had only heard of, or had known it in some small quantity brought to them at some distant period. They seemed only to understand that it was a substance much better adapted to the purposes of cutting or of boring of holes than anything their own country produced. They asked for it by the name of *hamaite,* probably referring to some instrument in the making of which iron could be usefully employed; for they applied that name to the blade of a knife, though we could be certain that they had no idea of that particular instrument; nor could they at all handle it properly. For the same reason they frequently called iron by the name of *toe*, which in their language signifies a hatchet, or rather a kind of adz. On asking them what iron was, they immediately answered, "We do not know. You know what it is, and we only understand it as *toe* or *hamaite*." When we showed them some beads, they asked first what they were, and then whether they should eat them. But on their being told that they were to be hung in their ears, they returned them as useless. They were equally indifferent as to a looking glass which was offered them, and returned it for the same reason; but sufficiently expressed their desire for *hamaite* and *toe*, which they wished might be very large. Plates of earthernware, china cups, and other such things were so new to them that they asked if they were made of wood; but wished to have some, that they might carry them to be looked at on shore. They were in some respects naturally well bred, or at least fearful of giving offense, asking where they should sit down, whether they might spit upon the deck, and the like. Some of them repeated a long prayer before they came on board; and others afterward sung and made motions with their hands, such as we had been accustomed to see in the dances of the islands we had lately visited. There was another circumstance in which they also perfectly resembled those other islanders. At first, on their entering the ship, they endeavored to steal everything they came near; or rather to take it openly, as what we either should not resent or not hinder. We soon convinced them of their mistake; and if they after some time became less active in appropriating to themselves whatever they took a fancy to, it was because they found that we kept a watchful eye over them.

At nine o'clock, being pretty near the shore, I sent three armed boats under the command of Lieutenant Williamson to look for a landing place and for fresh water. I ordered him that if he should find it necessary to land in search of the latter, not to suffer more than one man to go with him out of the boats. Just as they were putting off from the ship, one of the natives having stolen the butcher's cleaver leaped overboard, got into his canoe, and hastened to the shore, the boats pursuing him in vain.

The order not to permit the crews of the boats to go on shore was issued that I might do everything in my power to prevent the importation of a fatal disease into this island, which I knew some of our men labored under, and which, unfortunately, had been already communicated by us to other islands in these seas. With the same view, I ordered all female visitors to be excluded from the ships. Many of them had come off in the canoes. Their size, color, and features did not differ much from those of the men; and though their countenances were remarkably open and agreeable, there were few traces of delicacy to be seen, either in their faces or other proportions. The only difference in their dress was their having a piece of cloth about the body, reaching from near the middle to halfway down the thighs, instead of the *maro* worn by the other sex. They would as readily have favored us with their company on board as the men; but I wished to prevent all connection which might, too probably, convey an irreparable injury to themselves, and through their means to the whole nation. Another necessary precaution was taken by strictly enjoining that no person known to be capable of propagating the infection should be sent upon duty out of the ships. Whether these regulations, dictated by humanity, had the desired effect or not, time only can discover. . . .

While the boats were occupied in examining the coast, we stood on and off with the ships, waiting for their return. About noon Mr. Williamson came back and reported that he had seen a large pond behind a beach near one of the villages, which the natives told him contained fresh water; and that there was an anchoring ground before it. He also reported that he had attempted to land in another place, but was prevented by the natives, who, coming down to the boats in great numbers, attempted to take away the oars, muskets, and, in short, everything that they could lay hold of; and pressed so thick upon him that he was obliged to fire, by which one man was killed. But this unhappy circumstance I did not know till after we had left the island, so that all my measures were directed as if nothing of the kind had happened. Mr. Williamson told me that after the man fell his countrymen took him up, carried him off, and then retired from the boat; but still they made signals for our people to land, which he declined. It did not appear to Mr. Williamson that the natives had any design to kill, or even to hurt, any of his party; but they seemed excited by mere curiosity to get from them what they had, being at the same time ready to give in return anything of their own. . . .

Between three and four o'clock I went ashore with three armed boats, and twelve marines, to examine the water and to try the disposition of the inhabitants, several hundred of whom were assembled on a sandy beach before the village. The very instant I leaped on shore, the collected body of the natives fell flat upon their faces and remained in that very humble posture till by expressive signs I prevailed upon them to rise. They then brought a great many small pigs, which they presented to me, with plantain trees, using much the same ceremonies that we had seen practiced on such occasions at the Society and other islands; and a long prayer being spoken by a single person, in which others of the assembly sometimes joined, I expressed my acceptance of their proffered friendship by giving them in return such presents as I had brought with me from the ship for that purpose. When this introductory business was finished, I stationed a guard upon the beach and got some of the natives to conduct me to the water, which proved to be very good and in a proper situation for our purpose. It was so considerable that it may be called a lake, and it extended farther up the country than we could see. Having satisfied myself about this very essential point and about the peaceable disposition of the natives, I returned on board; and then gave orders that everything should be in readiness for landing and filling our water casks in the morning, when I went ashore with the people employed in that service, having a party of marines with us for a guard, who were stationed on the beach.

As soon as we landed, a trade was set on foot for hogs and potatoes, which the people of the island gave us in exchange for nails and pieces of iron formed into something like chisels. We met with no obstruction in watering; on the contrary, the natives assisted our men in rolling the casks to and from the pool and readily performed whatever we required. Everything thus going on to my satisfaction and considering my presence on the spot as unnecessary, I left the command to Mr. Williamson, who had landed with me, and made an excursion into the country, up the valley, accompanied by Mr. Anderson and Mr. Webber; the former of whom was as well qualified to describe with the pen as the latter was to represent with his pencil, everything we might meet with worthy of observation. A numerous train of natives followed us; and one of them, whom I had distinguished for his activity in keeping the rest in order, I made choice of as our guide. This man from time to time proclaimed our approach; and everyone whom we met fell prostrate upon the ground, and remained in that position till we had passed. This, as I afterward understood, is the mode of paying their respect to their own great chiefs. . . .

At sunset I brought everybody on board, having procured in the course of the day nine tons of water; and, by changes chiefly for nails and pieces of iron, about seventy or eighty pigs, a few fowls, a quantity of potatoes, and a few plantains and taro roots. These people merited our best commendations in this commercial intercourse, never once attempting to cheat us, either ashore or alongside the ships. . . .

Amongst the articles which they brought to barter this day, we could not help taking notice of a particular sort of cloak and cap, which, even in countries where dress is more particularly attended to, might be reckoned elegant. The first are near of the size and shape of the short cloaks worn by the women of England and by the men in Spain, reaching to the middle of the back and tied loosely before. The ground of them is a network

upon which the most beautiful red and yellow feathers are so
closely fixed that the surface might be compared to the thickest
and richest velvet, which they resemble, both as to the feel
and the glossy appearance. The manner of varying the mixture
is very different; some having triangular spaces of red and
yellow alternately; others, a kind of crescent; and some that
were entirely red had a broad yellow border which made them
appear, at some distance, exactly like a scarlet cloak edged with
gold lace. The brilliant colors of the feathers, in those that
happened to be new, added not a little to their fine appearance;
and we found that they were in high estimation with their
owners; for they would not at first part with one of them for
anything that we offered, asking no less a price than a musket.
However, some were afterward purchased for very large nails.
Such of them as were of the best sort were scarce; and it should
seem that they are only used on the occasion of some particular
ceremony or diversion. The cap is made almost exactly like
a helmet, with the middle part, or crest, sometimes of a hand's
breadth; and it sits very close upon the head, having notches
to admit the ears. It is a frame of twigs and osiers, covered
with a network into which are wrought feathers, in the same
manner as upon the cloaks, though rather closer and less diver-
sified, the greater part being red, with some black, yellow, or
green stripes on the sides, following the curve direction of the
crest. These, probably, complete the dress with the cloaks, for
the natives sometimes appeared in both together. . . .

These people are vigorous, active, and most expert swim-
mers; leaving their canoes upon the most trifling occasion,
diving under them, and swimming to others though at a great
distance. It was very common to see women, with infants at the
breast, when the surf was so high that they could not land in
the canoes, leap overboard, and without endangering their little
ones, swim to the shore through a sea that looked dreadful. They
seem to be blessed with a frank, cheerful disposition; and were
I to draw any comparisons, I should say that they are equally
free from the fickle levity which distinguishes the natives of

Otaheite and the sedate cast observable amongst many of those of Tongatabu. They seem to live very sociably in their intercourse with one another; and, except the propensity to thieving, which seems innate in most of the people we have visited in this ocean, they were exceedingly friendly to us. . . .

Though I did not see a chief of any note, there were, however, several, as the natives informed us, who reside upon Atooi, and to whom they prostrate themselves as a mark of submission, which seems equivalent to the *moe* paid to the chiefs of the Friendly Islands, and is here called *haomea* or *moe*. Whether they were at first afraid to show themselves or happened to be absent I cannot say; but after I had left the island, one of these great men made his appearance and paid a visit to Captain Clerke on board the *Discovery*. He came off in a double canoe and, like the king of the Friendly Islands, paid no regard to the small canoes that happened to lie in his way, but ran against or over them, without endeavoring in the least to avoid them. And it was not possible for these poor people to avoid him, for they could not manage their canoes, it being a necessary mark of their submission that they should lie down till he had passed. His attendants helped him into the ship, and placed him on the gangway. Their care for him did not cease then, for they stood round him holding each other by the hands; nor would they suffer anyone to come near him but Captain Clerke himself. He was a young man, clothed from head to foot, and accompanied by a young woman supposed to be his wife. His name was said to be Tamahano. Captain Clerke made him some suitable presents and received from him in return a large bowl supported by two figures of men, the carving of which, both as to the design and execution, showed some degree of skill. This bowl, as our people were told, used to be filled with the kava, or ava (as it is called in Otaheite), which liquor they prepare and drink here, as the other islands in this ocean. Captain Clerke could not prevail upon this great man to go below, nor to move from the place where his attendants had first fixed him. After staying some time in the ship, he was carried again into his canoe and returned to the island, receiving the same honors from all the natives as when he came on board. The next day several messages were sent to Captain Clerke inviting him to return the visit ashore and acquainting him that the chief had prepared a large present on that occasion. But being anxious to get to sea and join the *Resolution,* the captain did not think it advisable to accept of the invitation.

From James Cook and James King, *A Voyage to the Pacific Ocean* ... (London, G. Nicol and T. Cadell, 1784).

JAMES BURNEY

# THE LAST DAYS
# OF CAPTAIN COOK

Captain Cook, on returning to Hawaii from his northern voyage, discovered the remaining large islands of the chain, Maui and Hawaii. While stopping at Kealakekua Bay on the latter island, he was killed by the natives on February 14, 1779.

One of the most interesting and authentic accounts of the events leading to the death of the great navigator is recorded in the private journal of James Burney (1750–1821), who was serving at the time as first lieutenant on the *Discovery*. There are other more finished, dramatized accounts, but perhaps none of these conveys better the sense of direct observation than this unvarnishd, matter-of-fact chronicle. When Cook went ashore to try to retrieve the stolen cutter, no one had reason to imagine that the day might end in tragedy. Then suddenly the situation went out of control, everything began to go wrong, and at the end of a few minutes' sequence of rapid action the captain was dead.

After Cook's death, Burney returned to England, arriving in command of the *Discovery*. Some years later, having served with the East Indies squadron, he retired from the navy and devoted his leisure to writing. (He was a friend of Dr. Johnson and Charles Lamb, and his sister, Fanny Burney, was a novelist of note.) His most important work is a five-volume chronological history of early European voyages in the Pacific.

The following passage from the journal picks up at the time when Captain Cook's two ships, damaged in a storm, were forced to return to Kealakekua Bay after a pleasant sojourn there among the natives, whom Burney, like most early voyagers, calls "Indians."

SATURDAY, FEBRUARY 6, 1779. AT 4 IN THE AFTERNOON A FRESH breeze suddenly sprang up from the NW. The canoes all left us, making towards the land, which was about ten miles distant. In less than an hour the wind increased to a gale and we lost sight of the *Resolution* to the northward of us. At midnight were within three leagues of the south side of Mowwhe. Stood backwards and forwards till morning.

Sunday, 7th. At daylight, not seeing the *Resolution* and the gale continuing, stood back to the SE to get under the lee of Owhyhe. At 1 in the afternoon saw the *Resolution*. Towards evening the weather moderated. All night standing off and on near NW part of Owhyhe.

Monday, 8th. In the morning, being to windward of the *Resolution*, took all the sails in and set our rigging up afresh. Afternoon, running to the southward along the west side of Owhyhe, found a current against us. In the night the *Resolution* hailed us that they had sprung their foremast.

Tuesday, 9th. The *Resolution's* boat came on board and informed us the head of their foremast was so badly sprung as to make it necessary to get the mast out, and that their old leak had broken out afresh, on which accounts Captain Cook was bound back to Karacacooa Bay again, there being no certainty of finding a harbor at Mowwhe, and the road at Atoui too exposed a place for getting a mast out. . . .

Wednesday, 10th. At 2 in the morning, the *Resolution* having made too free with the shore found themselves very near breakers and made signal of danger. Both ships hauled off till near daylight and then ran along shore again. In the forenoon, being moderate weather and in sight of Karacacooa Bay, many canoes came off to us with provisions. The Indians told us that eight men in a double canoe were lost in the bad weather.

Thursday, 11th. At 6 in the morning the *Resolution* anchored in Karacacooa Bay, as did we two hours after, nearly in our old berth, and moored the ship. The natives flocked about us with hogs, vegetables, curiosities, etc. as formerly.

Friday, 12th. The astronomers' tents were erected at the same place as before. A great many canoes arrived in the bay from the northward, Kerrioboo with his followers amongst the rest. He was very inquisitive, as were several of the Owhyhe chiefs, to know the reason of our return, and appeared much dissatisfied with it.

Saturday, 13th. The *Resolution's* foremast was taken out and hauled up on the beach between the tents and the watering place. All the carpenters of both ships were set to work to repair it.

This morning, an Indian snatched away a pair of tongs from the armorer's forge, with which he jumped overboard and put them into a canoe. Our boat was so quick after him that he had not time to get in himself but was seized and brought on board, though the canoe escaped. He was severely flogged and kept in irons till the tongs were sent from the shore to procure his release. Our launch watering on shore this forenoon was much disturbed by the Indians, who threw stones and played other mischievous tricks, which made it necessary to have a guard when she was next sent.

In the afternoon the same unlucky tongs were again stolen and in the same manner by an Indian who jumped overboard and got into a canoe with them. They were fired at with muskets from the ship but without execution, whilst Mr. Edgar, our master, in the small cutter pursued them to the shore near the south point of the bay. Parrear, the Indian chief before mentioned, was in Captain Clerke's cabin when the theft was committed, and immediately left the ship promising to get the tongs restored. At the same time the *Resolution's* pinnace, which was at the tent, seeing the bustle, rowed alongshore and joined in the chase. The thief got first on shore and immediately put the tongs with a chisel and the lid of a harness cask, that had been stolen but not missed, into another canoe, which came out and delivered them to the small cutter. Mr. Edgar then thought of returning to the ship, satisfied with what he had got, but seeing the *Resolution's* pinnace at hand and Captain Cook walking that way from the tents, he thought he might safely venture to seize the canoe in which the thief had landed. For this purpose he got on shore and was pushing her off, when Parrear, to whom it seems the canoe belonged and who probably was the contriver of the theft, laid hold to prevent him, which was resented by one of the pinnace's men, striking Parrear with an oar. A crowd of Indians, who had been by the waterside all the time, and till then quiet, immediately began to throw stones. There being no arms in either boat, the pinnace men were so roughly handled that to avoid the stones they all jumped into the water and swam to some rocks at a little distance. Mr. Edgar and one of our midshipmen, Mr. Vancouver, who were on shore, fared very little better, till Parrear ordered the Indians to desist, and told our people to go on board with the boats. This they would gladly have done but all the pinnace's oars had been taken away. Parrear said he would fetch them, but he was no sooner out of sight than the mob began to throw stones again. Mr. Edgar, on this, attempted to walk towards the tents, expecting to meet Capain Cook, but was prevented by some Indians who said they would lead him to Parrear. He followed these people and soon met Parrear and another man with an oar and a broken one. He was conducted back to the boats and put off, rowing towards the tents.

In their way thither, Parrear overtook them in a canoe and brought Mr. Vancouver's cap, which had been lost in the fray. He then asked if he might come on board the next morning and whether we should hurt him for what had happened. Being promised he should suffer no harm if he came, he went away paddling towards the town of Kavarooa where Kerrioboo lived. Captain Cook, who at the beginning of the disturbance was at the astronomers' tents, ran around alongshore towards the boats with Lieutenant King and two of the marines, but was misled by some of the Indian chiefs, and did not know anything of the ill usage of the boats till he returned to the tents, by which time it was dark and too late to take any notice of it.

Sunday, 14th. At daylight our great cutter, which had been moored to the buoy of the small bower anchor, was missing, and on examining, the rope which fastened her was found to have been cut. This theft was the more easily committed as the boat was left full of water to preserve her from the sun, making the upper part of her gunwale even with the water's edge. Captain Clerke having informed Captain Cook of this, orders were given for our launch and small cutter to go armed to the south point of the bay and prevent any of the sailing canoes going out, but not to molest the small ones.

The *Resolution's* great cutter was sent in chase of a large sailing canoe that was making off; their small cutter was dispatched to guard the west point, whilst Captain Cook himself prepared to go with his pinnace and launch to the town of Kavarooa with an intention to bring Kerrioboo on board. The canoe chased by the *Resolution's* great cutter was not overtaken, but her retreat was cut off in such a manner that she was forced to the nearest shore within the south point of the harbor, where the Indians hauled her up, the cutter not being able to follow for the rocks. Captain Cook, who was then leaving the ship, seeing the canoe ashore, said he was sure she could not escape; and being asked how the cutter was to get her if the natives made resistance, he answered there could be no great difficulty, for he was very positive the Indians would not stand the fire of a single musket. Indeed, so many instances have occurred which have all helped to confirm this opinion that it is not to be wondered at if everybody thought the same.

A little before 8, Captain Cook landed at the town of Kavarooa with Lieutenant Phillips of the Marines, a sergeant, corporal, and seven privates; in all, reckoning himself, eleven. The Indians made a lane for him to march along, having always showed great respect to both captains, however insolent they may have been at times to others. Captain Cook had scarcely got on shore when the boats near the south point of the harbor fired several muskets at some large canoes that were trying to get out, by which an Indian chief named Nooekemar was killed. The first notice we had of this was from two Indians that came off to the ships in a small canoe to complain of it, but finding they were not attended to, they inquired for Captain Cook. Being told he was at the town of Kavarooa, they went thither. About half an hour after this, we heard the firing of muskets on shore, which was followed by the *Resolution's* pinnace and launch firing. With glasses we could see Captain Cook receive a blow from a club and fall off a rock into the water. The ships then fired, but at too great a distance to make certain of any particular mark. The boats soon after came off with an account that Captain Cook and four of the marines were killed and their bodies in possession of the Indians.

The particulars of this misfortune, gathered from those who were on the spot, are as follows. When Captain Cook with his party landed, the Indians made a lane and some of them brought hogs which they offered him. He inquired for Kerrioboo and his two sons; the Indians immediately dispatched messengers and the boys came, who conducted them to Kerrioboo's house.

Having waited some time without, Captain Cook doubted his being there. Lieutenant Phillips went in to see and found Kerrioboo just awakened. He came out to Captain Cook, who after some inquiries appeared perfectly satisfied that Kerrioboo was innocent of the cutter's being stolen, and desired he would go on board with him, to which Kerrioboo readily agreed, and they walked down towards the boats. Kaoowa, the youngest of Kerrioboo's sons, who was a great favorite of Captain Cook, went before and got into the pinnace. When Kerrioboo came near the waterside, two chiefs, and an old woman who was crying, stopped him, and made him sit down. He then seemed irresolute and frightened. At this time our people began to suspect mischief. The marines were stationed on a rock close to the waterside that they might not be surrounded by the natives who were seen to be arming themselves; whilst an old man who seemed to be one of the priesthood was singing to Captain Cook and Kerrioboo, as was thought, to prevent suspicion. Captain Cook then let Kerrioboo go, and said he was not to be forced on board without killing a number of people.

The old chief was immediately taken away and no more seen. Captain Cook likewise was about to give orders for embarking, when he was provoked by the insolence of a man armed with a thick mat and a long spike, at whom he fired with small shot, which neither penetrated the mat nor frightened the Indians as was expected. Another man with an iron spike came near Mr. Phillips, who, suspecting his intentions, drove him back with the butt end of his musket. Two or three stones were then thrown and one of the marines knocked down. Captain Cook, who had a double-barreled gun, immediately fired with ball. The sergeant said he had shot the wrong man, on which he told the sergeant to shoot the right. The Indians gave a general volley of stones and began to close on our people; Captain Cook therefore gave orders for the marines to fire, which they did amongst the crowd and were seconded by the boats. The Indians at first gave back, but directly after, before the marines had time to load again, advanced. Captain Cook called out to take to the boats. The pinnace was near the shore, but ten or twelve yards distant from the rock where the marines stood, and this short space was uneven slippery rocks, so that being pressed upon in their retreat, they were obliged to take to the water. Captain Cook in coming down was struck by an Indian behind him with a staff, on which he turned and beat the man back with his musket. He was again followed and received at the same instant a blow on the head and a stab with a spike in the neck, which tumbled him into the water. Being no swimmer and stunned with the blow, he turned towards the shore again, and a number of Indians surrounded and dragged him on the rocks, where they beat and stabbed him in several places, snatching the daggers from each other out of eagerness to have their share in killing him. Four of the marines were killed, one of them on shore (Thomas Fatchet), whom nobody knew what became of; the other three in the water, James Thomas, corporal, and John Allen and Theophilus Hinks, privates.

The corporal had loaded again, and received a stab in the belly when up to the middle in the water. He fired at the Indian who gave it and directly after fell dead. They were all dragged on shore.

Of those that escaped, the lieutenant of marines was wounded in the shoulder by a spike, the sergeant received a slight wound, and one of the marines, Jackson, was struck in the face with a stone, by which he is in danger of losing an eye. Being unable to swim he would probably have been drowned or fell into the hands of the Indians, had not Lieutenant Phillips jumped overboard out of the pinnace and assisted him. The people in the boats at first had so little apprehensions of any danger from the Indians that when the firing began on shore, the pinnace put close in to the rocks to let Kaoowa land, as he was much frightened and asked to go.

The whole of this affair, from Captain Cook's leaving the *Resolution* to the return of the boats, happened in the short space of one hour. Nine stand of arms with iron ramrods, besides Captain Cook's double-barreled gun and hanger, fell into the hands of the Indians.

On notice of our defeat, the boats stationed near the points of the harbor were recalled and a strong reinforcement sent to Lieutenant King at the tents, and soon after orders to strike them and get the *Resolution's* foremast off. Many Indians being seen assembling to the right of the tents, we kept firing with our great guns to disperse them; and a large party of our people were posted on the marai, which overlooked that part of the beach where the mast lay, to protect those who were busied in launching it.

About 1 everything came off from the shore without any other molestation from the Indians than a few stones, in return for which some of them were shot who ventured nearer than otherwise they would have done, from an idea that their armor (thick mats soaked in water) were musketproof. . . .

The Indians were observed to be very careful of conveying away their dead. Proofs of great courage were shown by two men in carrying off a dead body from within reach of our fire.

At 4 in the afternoon the boats were sent to the town of Kavarooa to demand the dead bodies. On approaching the shore, stones were thrown which fell short. Lieutenant King went in with our small cutter waving a white flag, whilst the other boats lay on their oars. The Indians left off throwing and waved a white flag in return. They had already made a number of little stone breastworks to screen them from our firearms, and during this conference they several times counted our numbers. In answer to the demand, some chiefs said that tomorrow the bodies should be brought, of which word was sent to Captain Clerke. An old man, named Kooaha, whom we have all along taken to be the chief priest, had the confidence to swim off and get into the boat, where he remained some time. He had an iron dagger in his hand. This is the same man who performed the strange ceremonies when Captain Cook landed at our first coming here. The reason given why the bodies were not delivered tonight was that they were carried some distance up into the country.

At another part of the town, however, the Indians made motions which we thought signified they were cut to pieces. And one fellow came to the waterside flourishing Captain Cook's hanger with many tokens of exultation and defiance. Orders soon after came for the boats to return.

After dark, a guard boat was stationed to row round the ship, lest any of the Indians should swim off and attempt to cut the cables. They were very busy on shore all night, making much noise, running about with lights, and howling, as we supposed, over their dead.

From a manuscript in the Mitchell Collection of the Public Library of New South Wales, Sydney, Australia.

THOMAS MANBY

# WITH VANCOUVER
# AT KEALAKEKUA BAY

Thomas Manby (1769–1834) sailed as master's mate with Captain
George Vancouver on the famous British exploring expedition
to the Pacific in the *Chatham* and the *Discovery* in 1791. In his
private journal this young officer wrote with candor and uninhibited detail about his experiences and observations in the Sandwich Islands. The following selection is a lively account of the
memorable visit of three weeks at Kealakekua Bay in 1793, fourteen years after Captain Cook was killed there. It provides vivid
glimpses of King Kamehameha and of events on board and
ashore that are not to be found in the official narrative of the
voyage.

Before the voyage ended Manby was appointed acting lieutenant by Captain Vancouver. Later, he distinguished himself
as the brilliant and daring commander of one ship after another
in the wars with France. In 1825 he was promoted to the rank
of rear admiral.

[FEBRUARY 15, 1793] BY NOON WE HAD APPROACHED WITHIN
five miles of Karakakooah Bay, and had soon after the satisfaction of seeing three canoes paddling toward us. We shortened
sail to let them come up, and were a good deal surprised to find
an Englishman in one of them. The canoes belonged to the
king: on seeing us he hurried off this man to welcome us to the
island and beg our acceptance of seven hogs and some vegetables.

The history of our countryman instantly engaged our attention. When last at Atooi we first learnt that the treacherous Tianna * had seized an American schooner and murdered all the crew but one. From this man we learnt the truth of the report, and that he at that time belonged to an American brig laying in Karakakooah Bay. The natives made an attempt on the brig and would have succeeded had she not cut her cables and stood for sea. This poor fellow happened to be on shore at the time, saw with astonishment his vessel sail without him, and was immediately after made prisoner and doomed to death. The humane chief that saved the life of the schooner's man also preserved this man from destruction and sent him to the king, with whom he has been living ever since exceedingly happy and contented. His name is John Young, a native of Lancashire. All thoughts of returning to his own country he has long since given up. By the natives he is considered as a chief. The sovereign has given him extensive estates well stored with hogs and plantations of all kinds of vegetables. He has a town house near the royal residence and as many wives as his inclination dictates.

From Young we learnt that a general Tabooroora [*kapu loulu*] now existed through the island. It had been in force eight days and would not expire till two more were past. This was unpleasant news, as it precluded both men and women coming afloat. During these days of penance the king and nearly all the chiefs reside in the marai, or place of worship. Animal and vegetable sacrifices are offered every morning to some particular deity. Women at these stated periods are not allowed to quit their houses, or even be seen; and the men lay under very great restrictions. The present Tabooroora is an invocation to the god that presides over fish: it is annually observed at this season of the year, as a notion prevails that were this ceremony neglected, the finny tribe would immediately quit the shores of Owhyee.

While this religious interdiction remains in force it is rigidly attended to, and death is the consequence should anyone dis-

---

* A powerful chief whom Captain Vancouver had met on his visit to Hawaii a year earlier.

obey the mandate of the high priest. A suitable present was sent on shore to the king with our wish of seeing him as soon as possible. In the evening the canoes left us; we stood off and on during the night and found that a strong current drifted us ten miles to the westward during the night. We continued plying near the west point till the 16th, expecting the *Discovery* every moment would heave in sight.

In the afternoon of this day we brought to, to let a squadron of large double canoes join us. As they came from Karakakooah and were paddling with more than common speed, we knew it was some great man approaching. It proved to be his majesty attended by the Englishman and a large retinue of attendance.

He shook hands with us and expressed a good deal of joy at seeing us, and ordered some of his retinue to unload the canoes that held his present, consisting of hogs, pigs, and various kinds of fruit.

Our royal visitor asked many questions about the *Discovery* and appeared to be under great apprehension lest she should go to the other islands in preference to Owhyee. His name is Tomahamaha. He had on a large Chinese dressing gown which is considered as the most valuable piece of attire in his majesty's wardrobe: it belonged to the late King Terrieboo, who received it from Captain Cook a few days before he lost his life.

We offered him wine and brandy; the former he stuck to with evident satisfaction and soon finished his bottle. He sent for his purveyor into the cabin and demanded something to eat. A roasted dog, two fish, and a calabash full of taro pudding were placed before him. In a few minutes the whole of the dog was devoured; the fish, each weighing half a pound, followed the dog, although they were in the same state as when taken from the water — scales, gills, and garbage. His feeding actually disgusted us, and the quantity he consumed would have been a profusion for three moderate men. . . .

He is of large stature and very athletic; his countenance is truly savage, as all his foreteeth are out. The greatest respect is paid to him; as he is beloved by all his subjects, we may certainly pronounce him a good king.

On the morning of the 17th, by sunrise, the vessel was surrounded by canoes, every one freighted with the choicest part of the creation, the female sex. It is them alone that can harmonize the soul, banish sorrows from the mind, and give to mankind true felicity; even the uncivilized brunette in a state of nature can do all this, and convinces that happiness is incomplete without them. In a moment our decks were crowded with young, good-natured girls, whilst the surface of the water around us was covered with some hundreds soliciting admittance. Our bark instantly became a scene of jollity and all was pleasure and delight.

A strong lee current and light winds drifted us some miles off the land; most of the canoes returned to the shore, and soon after we were joined by the *Discovery*.

Captain Vancouver made known his intentions of anchoring in Karakakooah Bay. Both vessels made all sail, but by the perverseness of the winds did not reach it till the 22nd, at night.

Large fires were made on the western point of the bay, and the king sent out some of his large double canoes, who assisted us greatly in towing. At 10 p.m. we anchored in twelve fathoms and moored about half a mile from the shore. On the following morning, long before day broke, canoes began to assemble round us; they flocked into the bay from all parts; by noon you could scarce see the water in any part of the bay, as the canoes formed a complete platform. The number of people then afloat could not be less than thirty thousand. The noise they made is not to be conceived; everybody loudly speaking and being assisted by the musical cries of some scores of hogs and pigs absolutely stunned us on board the brig.

The shores in every direction were lined with people; and such was their curiosity to approach the vessels that many hundreds swam off to us, holding up by one hand a little pig, a fowl, or a bunch of plantains.

In the forenoon the bay became a scene of sad confusion by his majesty embarking with a large retinue to pay his respects to Captain Vancouver. He brought with him an amazing present contained in fourteen double canoes all following each other in an exact line.

The sovereign led the van in one of the largest canoes we ever saw, paddled by forty-six men. The monarch with his squadron passed three times around the vessels before he went alongside the *Discovery*. The exactness of his rowers both in skill, dexterity, and dress, and the appearance of the royal personage standing up in a manly attitude holding a spear in his right hand, had an appearance both splendid and magnificent.

He was robed in a beautiful cloak of yellow feathers that reached from his shoulders to his feet, whilst a feather helmet adorned his head of scarlet, black, and yellow. The usual token of friendship being exchanged by touching noses with Captain Vancouver, his present was ordered on board the ships — consisting of eighty large hogs, pigs, fowls, and all the kinds of fruit and vegetables Owhyee produced.

The cattle greatly delighted him, though it took some time to quiet his fears lest they should bite him. He called them large hogs, and after much persuasion we prevailed on him to go close up to them; at that instant one of the poor animals, turning its head round quickly, so alarmed his majesty that he made a speedy retreat and ran over half of his retinue. His fright was not of long duration and ceased on seeing some of his attendants take them by the horns.

They were sent on shore in his canoes to his village; a chief of consequence and a party of men were appointed to attend them, and very particular orders were given with the sick bull to see him carefully nursed. The four cows were in tolerable condition and had got very tame by being on board. The concourse of people to see them landed was immense; we were a good deal diverted at seeing the terror the whole village was thrown into by one of the cows galloping along the beach and kicking up her heels. Thousands ran for the sea and plunged in; every coconut tree was full in a moment; some jumped down precipices, others scrambled up rocks and houses; in short, not a man would approach for half an hour. The king directed that his two Englishmen should remain on board the vessels during our stay, to regulate the traffic and keep the natives in order. All kinds of refreshments he promised to supply us daily with, and finished his civilities by requesting to hear our wants that he might get them supplied as soon as possible.

He made numerous inquiries about King George, whether he had forgiven them for killing Captain Cook; that dreadful event gave him, he said, frequent uneasiness. The blame was all thrown on Terrieboo, the late king. Tomahamaha was an active performer on that important day. His name at that time was Mahamaha and is mentioned in the narrative of Captain Cook's death by such.

Before he left the ship his two queens came on board with other female relations; they were each presented with ribbons and beads. The royal dames were plump and jolly, very lively and good-humored. The girls on board offered all the trinkets we had given them to these ladies of rank; they received some and enquired after particular sorts of beads. The only clothing they had on was many folds of thin cloth about their waist reaching nearly to the knee; every other part of them remains uncovered, with few ornaments, the principal one a piece of polished bone fastened round their necks with plaited hair. The visitors left the ship a little before sunset, and an unwelcome messenger from the marai proclaimed another vile Tabooroora to take place at the setting of the luminary.

Our female friends instantly left us, with many invectives against the barbarous custom that would now confine them to their habitations for two nights and one day. We parted with them with regret and reluctance; passed thirty dull hours; and received them again in our arms by sunrise on the 24th. The moon being within a day of the full created this religious restriction: it is called the Tabooroora Marai: while it lasts the chiefs and priests reside in the marai, pass their time in prayer, and make offerings to their departed friends. Captain Vancouver directed that no one should go ashore belonging to our vessels, in order to convince them no violation of their laws and customs should take place on our part and that we looked for equal attention and exactness to be observed in everything relating to the ship.

The master of the *Discovery* was sent on shore with the observatory and instruments to regulate the timekeepers. Tomahamaha gave him a small potato garden at the foot of the marai; in this place Captain Cook made his observations and settled the longtitude of the island. A chief and party of men were appointed as guards of the observatory. And as no women could come to the tents, being within the limits of the marai, the considerate king supplied the astronomers with a large house about sixty yards from their residence, where they might entertain their female friends and observe the beauties of Venus whilst the other planets were obscured by clouds.

On the 25th, I paid my first visit to the shore and, of course, to the royal apartments immediately on landing. They are walled round, and consist of four houses. One of the queens received me; she was sitting under the branches of a cloth tree stringing beads, surrounded by twenty attendants, most of whom were cooling the air with fans. She placed me by her, sent for fruit, and ordered some coconuts to be fresh gathered from a neighboring tree. Her majesty amused herself some time in tying and untying my hair, decorating it with feathers, flowers, and other things. She then nearly undressed me to observe my skin. My left leg, that had undergone an operation of tattooing at Otaheite, pleased her greatly. She sent for an old man to come and see it, who examined it attentively for a quarter of an hour; and then a long conversation ensued which produced a great deal of mirth.

The hieroglyphical characters at Otaheite may be known to these people; and as the man who tattooed me knew my disposition and how I was circumstanced at the moment, I conjecture he has imprinted some South Sea mark that will create a smile in most islands in the Pacific Ocean.

After passing an hour in flirtation with this generous queen, some little particulars were exchanged, though by no means criminal, that occasioned her majesty to be called to order by a little deformed wretch who, I was afterwards informed, held a situation of high honor in the royal household. On inquiring from our Englishman I find every woman of distinction is attended by one or more of this humpbacked race in Owhyee; they are responsible for the conduct of the females, and are put to death should she be found in any other arms than those of her husband.

Only two of the houses in the palace yard were considered as the residence of the sovereign; the others were occupied by his retinue. The two appropriated to his use were of equal size and well built, one dedicated to his meals, the other to his slumbers. The sleeping mansion was spread with a great many mats and large piles of the softest cloth; a softer or better bed cannot be formed. The smallness of the door renders their habitations unpleasant by the want of light, and obstructs a more considerable consideration to a tropical climate, that of air. Passing through a small wicket door brought us to the marai, or place of worship. The marai much resembles the square steeple of an English country church in its form; it is built with wood and ornamented with small bunches of cloth. We did not see the inside, but were informed the bones of deceased kings lay in it. It is fenced round with short poles with many human skulls sticking on them, the remains of sacrifices. Close to the marai is a house, the residence of the chief priest, called Tahoona, and before his door stands the great Oroona, or god of Owhyee.

The Oroona is a huge figure cut out of wood to resemble a man's face, with an enormous large mouth, stuck full of teeth, with two large mother-of-pearl eyes. An old man while we were present brought him his dinner; it consisted of a large fish and a bundle of plantains; they were first carried into the marai, underwent some ceremony, and then brought to the Oroona.

The fish they crammed into his mouth and hung the plantains near him. I understand the deity's repast is always consumed before the morning: the idol has the credit, and the priests, no doubt, have the gratification of a good supper every night and laugh at the credulity of the countrymen.

Four little images are ranged near the Oroona; each had an

offering of flesh or fruits, and all decorated with cloth of various colors.

To distort the countenances the artists of these figures particularly attend to, and I believe the deity most deformed in features gains veneration by his hideous appearance. In the marai yard we saw three other houses that held the bones of a great many warriors: they were paled round, but stunk so abominably we could not approach them. The stench arose from hogs, dogs, and fowls in a state of putrefaction; the roof of each sepulcher was filled with them and thronged by large swarms of flies.

When human sacrifices are offered the cruel deed is executed in this place on a place built with stones erected twelve feet from the ground. The miserable victim is dragged to it and the priests are his executioners; his brains are beat out and the body is cut up with shark's-teeth knives. The eyes and bones are dedicated to the Oroona: part of the flesh is consumed by fire and the rest given to the king's fishermen to catch sharks with.

Having seen the contents of the marai yard, we returned to the palace. His majesty was just come in from bathing. He gave us each a mat of fine texture and a piece of cloth. We attended him to see the cattle; they were all in high health but the bull; his death is inevitable. A number of people were closely watching him, keeping off the flies with green boughs. . . .

Having passed a pleasant forenoon, we returned on board to dinner with some chiefs who very willingly partook of our fare. In the evening shortly after dark a double canoe came alongside, which threw our female visitors into the greatest confusion. An elderly woman came on board whom we found to be a captive queen taken prisoner at the island of Mowee about three years ago. This unfortunate lady is treated with the greatest respect. No woman can stand in her presence — which created a droll scene, as our decks were full of girls at the time of her unexpected coming on board. They went about on their hands and knees flying from every place the captive approached, scrambling up and down the ladders of the vessel to the great diversion of our sailors, who for an hour laughed heartily at the confusion of their little favorites. Cranniakooah is the name of this lady; she was very cheerful and requested often to see us when we went on shore. She is restricted from leaving her house in daylight, but may ramble where she pleases at night. A small retinue always attend her; amongst them are two humpbacked. She remained with us two hours and then took her leave.

The duty of both vessels went on very smoothly without anything particular taking place until the 30th, when Tomahamaha came on board early in the morning with the cook's ax and a few other articles that had been stolen from the *Chatham* during the night. An unfortunate girl was the culprit, whom the king had made a close prisoner on shore, saying he would put her to death if the captain wished it. Her friends came on board to intercede in her behalf, urging that she had been invited on board to pass the night with one of the seamen, who had neglected her; and that in revenge she had swam on shore with everything she could find laying loose about the deck.

Tomahamaha wished to inflict some punishment that it might deter others from the like pilfering practices. We resigned her to his disposal, only begging not to be too severe. He left us very much displeased, hurried on shore, and passed immediate sentence on the poor girl. She underwent an everlasting tabu from ever again going afloat, and her father to pay a tribute in hogs for his daughter's dishonesty.

March 1, 1793. The king and his brother Terriemyty came on board to breakfast, and brought some fish just caught, with a canoe full of young coconuts. By the wish of the latter we attended him to the village of Karooah to see his residence. We landed on the spot where Captain Cook received his deadly wound. The man who gave the fatal blow is still living and intends coming to us in a day or two. We remained some time where the scene of horror was committed. A large concourse of natives drew about us, and an old man made a long speech relative to that day of destruction; he wept considerably in the midst of his harangue, as did many others of both sexes. The old orator soon evinced the cause of his grief as his two sons who fell in desperate conflict.

My heart sympathized with his sorrows, and I mingled a sigh with the numerous bystanders that were then in tears for a husband or brother or friend. They lay much of the blame on Terrieboo, the late king, for not attending Captain Cook to his boat after he promised it; although it is related in the narrative he would willingly have gone had not his wives prevented him. The bones of the immortal navigator are placed beneath a heap of stones close to a marai, about a quarter of a mile from the spot of destruction.

The village of Karooah contains about one hundred and fifty houses: it is built on a bed of lava; we saw many spots where the liquid stream retained the exact appearance it had cooled in. Even in these barren spots they contrive to cultivate the cloth tree and have plantations of it without any other protection to the root than a few stones piled round it.

Our walk was very short, as the sun had heated the lava so much that we felt it very plainly through our shoes. We retired to the habitation of our friend, who spread mats in the shade of coconut trees and produced a roasted hog, a dog, and vegetables. The premises of this chief were encompassed with a stone wall six feet high: on one corner stands a small marai with a few images, all of which were well supplied with provisions. Terriemyty is acknowledged to be one of the greatest warriors of Owhyee; he showed us many trophies gained in the battle at Mowee, one of them the skull of a chief he killed by throwing a spear through his body. His skill in throwing the spear greatly surprised us, as he scarce ever missed his mark at thirty yards. . . .

March 4, 1793. The weather having been for some days exceedingly fine enabled us this morning to finish our rigging and report the *Chatham* ready for sea, well stowed with wood and water; and every corner of the vessel full of refreshments. The *Discovery*'s defects being not yet made perfect detains us in the bay; a delay not to be repined at, as the friendly and courteous behavior of the natives has long merited our warmest esteem: they have scarcely given us a single opportunity of finding fault.

The worthy chief Tomahamaha is the watchful sentinel; he has placed his own canoes about the vessels to see that no improprieties are committed, and takes equal care of our friends at the observatory. Two chiefs and a few trusty subjects have charge of the encampment, with positive orders from the sovereign to seize anyone found within the tabued limits.

His majesty came to us almost in tears to relate the death of the bull, which has just expired. The cows are sent in canoes a few miles to the northward, where much better pasturage is to be found. One of the cows being with a calf, we are in hopes the issue will be of the male sex; otherwise our good intentions will be totally defeated unless we have it in our power to augment their stock by a further supply of this valuable animal, should we again return to the Sandwich Islands.

Before we became acquainted with these people we considered them as a ferocious and turbulent set of savages. This character they are by no means entitled to, as they are mild and tractable; uncivilized, unpolished, and in a true state of nature, they possess great courage, and will not tamely bear an insult or an injury. Their few laws are strictly adhered to, and was their code more numerous, I conceive they would abide by them with equal promptitude. To each other they are free, easy, and cheerful, and show more real good nature than I have seen in your better regulated societies. During the whole of my stay I was never witness to a quarrel: they delight in jokes, which were never known to produce an angry brow or uplifted arm.

In the evening of the 5th Tomahamaha, with a large retinue, paid us an unpleasant visit to announce the approaching Tabooroora to take place at sunset, and to last two nights and one day. Many were the importunings to remove this barbarous custom, but all arguments proved ineffectual. The good chief agreed to the absurdity of the ceremony but still insisted he was bound by the laws of his country to follow the religious tenets so strictly attended to by his ancestors. We kept the worthy fellow in conversation to the last moment and tried every expedient to get it removed, but in vain. He remained with us till the journeying sun was sinking in the west and then in haste took his leave. The king's departure was the signal, and in an instant every subject followed his example.

The brunettes expressed considerable disappointment, and plunged into the sea much dejected at being so unexpectedly forced from our society. The poor females undergo a much closer restriction than the men during the existence of the Tabooroora, not being permitted to move without their habitations and secluded from male visitors. At this period they weep and chant songs in honor of those chiefs whose bones are lodged in the marai, or place of worship.

The Englishmen resided one in each of our vessels during our stay and had the sole management of regulating our traffic; having complete knowledge of the language, no trouble ever took place. The situation Tomahamaha had placed them in gives them considerable authority in the islands: and their good conduct, I was happy to see, had gained them the confidence and good will of every inhabitant.

On the 7th, at sunrise, the Tabooroora ceased. Joy and delight were ushered in with the newborn day. In an instant our decks were covered with lovely women. Every tar folded in his arms youth and beauty.

The *Discovery* being ready for sea, it was made known our intention for sailing on the following day. The friendly and generous king heard the intelligence with marked concern: and every islander expressed the greatest sorrow. Tomahamaha begged Captain Vancouver and all the officers to visit him on shore in the afternoon to be spectators of a sham battle in which their warlike exploits would be practiced.

The invitation was accepted, and that something novel might be exhibited on our part, various fireworks were sent to the observatory to be thrown off after the close of the day. After dinner a large party from both vessels assembled at the royal residence, where we found the principal warriors all ready to commence the battle. The beach was chosen as the scene of action: thither we repaired and found a large concourse waiting our arrival. Several large bundles of six-foot spears, blunted at the ends, were piled and soon after distributed to the fighting men.

The king headed his party of fifty: and another chief took the command of an equal number who were to play the enemy.

A shout was given by each party as a signal for battle. They then advanced to about forty yards, trying to provoke each other by threatening gestures and making the most hideous faces imaginable. In my life I never saw such a distortion of countenances and conceived it impossible that human beings could draw features into such a variety of forms. During this time they kept approaching each other, and when arrived at about twenty yards a terrific yell was given and instantly followed by a shower of spears. The adverse party made as quick a return, and the battle became general. Many of them possessed considerable agility as they caught the flying spears before they reached their bodies and instantly returned them with great dexterity. Although their weapons were perfectly blunt, some very awkward blows were given, which always brought blood and tore pieces out of several of their bodies. Tomahamaha kept flying from wing to wing of his division, encouraging his troops and giving the necessary orders, often advancing far in front to brave the power of the enemy. Numerous spears were thrown at him, the whole of which he avoided by falling or jumping. Few of his subjects equalled him in his warlike exploits, as his strength enabled him to throw his javelin an amazing distance and to the greatest nicety.

The stone slingers were stationed in the rear, but did not play their part for fear of annoying the British. The king's opponents kept for some time giving ground, and at last being hard pressed made a speedy retreat behind some old houses where they changed their weapons to long spears of twenty feet in length. With these they rallied, but were as speedily attacked by Tomahamaha's party, who using similar implements, a famous onset now took place which soon gave victory to the king and his adherents.

The mode of treating prisoners was then shown, which completed the sham fight. The vanquished foes who had fallen into the hands of the conquerors were dragged about by the legs and their brains beat out with stones. The body is then cut up with shark's-teeth knives and divided among the warriors, reserving the skull as a trophy for the royal commander. In real battles the party that first gets possession of a man and sacrifices him at a hazard is sure of gaining the honors of the day. Even should their armies amount to thousands, they will not stand their ground after this event, but instantly take refuge in the mountains.

Hostilities having ceased, all the royal family and some of the principal chiefs attended us to the tents and partook with us in bumpers of grog to the health of our beloved sovereign, King George the Third.

Upwards of forty thousand people were assembled around our encampment, waiting with anxiety the approach of dark to behold our performance. The first skyrocket actually staggered them with surprise; as if with one voice a general sound was heard expressive of wonder and amazement. Balloons, flower pots, roman candles, mines, and water rockets astonished them past conception; they could only express the inferiority of Owhyee and praise the prodigies of Britannia. After amusing the gazing multitudes an hour we returned on board, leaving our friends to their meditations.

Early on the 8th, we got off the tents and observatory from the shore and made every preparation for sailing. Tomahamaha and his queens remained with us during the day, frequently urging us to take more hogs and vegetables. The chiefs of the surrounding districts came to us with equal kindness, bringing extensive presents of canoes loaded with every kind of refreshments. They were presented with different trinkets, and the Englishmen were abundantly supplied with a large assortment of implements for cookery, husbandry, carpenter's tools, and almost every article that could be of service to them, besides a large variety of garden seeds. . . .

At 3 a.m. the 9th both vessels weighed and came to sail. Our movement at so early an hour created considerable confusion on board amongst the females: several leaped overboard and swam to shore, although the major part remained free from alarm. The breeze blew very faint off the land, which prevented our clearing the bay before 5 a.m., though aided by all our boats and several canoes who voluntarily offered their services to tow us clear off the shore. At 9 the king and all his family came to the *Discovery*, where they passed two hours in great grief for our departure, and then visited the *Chatham*. The greatest concern was marked on his countenance. In the true language of friendship, he kept continually inquiring if all our wants were gratified, offering hogs and vegetables which some of his canoes were filled with: but our decks were too abundantly thronged to make use of his generous intentions.

The inquiry was made on our part if we could augment his little store by anything we had on board. Every present he declined, but begged a plate, knife, and fork. Of course, he had it, and we learnt he had made a similar request previous to his quitting the *Discovery*. One of his domestics remained on board during our stay in the bay to learn the art of cookery. And now that he was in possession of the requisites for the table, a tolerable cook, and every kind of implement for culinary purposes, the monarch boasted with pride and satisfaction that he should now live like King George.

The breeze from the sea freshing up shortened the visit of our royal friends; they embraced us all round and left the vessel in tears, wishing us success and a speedy return. At this moment our decks were filled with moistened eyes. The pleasing girls of Owhyee bidding adieu to the men they had attached themselves to, general sadness prevailed throughout: and for my part I felt it exceedingly. Macooah, a pretty, good-natured girl who had been a good deal with me, had been weeping all the morning, and as the instant for separation approached her anguish became oppressive. With a bursting heart she implored to go the voyage; but that was impossible, and to part necessary. To divert her attention, a few beads, ribbons, and other trinkets were added to her collection, but her grief was not to

be lessened by such baubles. The poor girl had grown fond; we
parted — I was glad she was gone. Of all sights that sooth
my soul to pity, nothing so effectually does it as a woman in
tears.

From *The Honolulu Mercury,* July and August, 1929.

Otto Von Kotzebue

# A QUEEN OF THE
# SANDWICH ISLANDS

Captain Otto von Kotzebue (1787–1846), a German in the service of the Russian Imperial Navy, on his third voyage to the Pacific, arrived in Honolulu late in 1824. He was received by acquaintances of an earlier visit to the islands — Governor Kinau and the queen dowager, Namahana, one of the widows of King Kamehameha. Queen Namahana, among the first of the great chiefs to accept Christianity, had been taught by the missionaries to wear clothes, to read and write, and to live in a wooden house with European furnishings; but Kotzebue found that, for all these evidences of civilization, her lusty, primitive nature had not been greatly changed.

ON THE MORNING AFTER OUR ARRIVAL, I ROWED ASHORE WITH some of my officers, to pay my respects to the Queen Nomahanna, and on landing was met by the Spaniard Marini, who accompanied us to her majesty as interpreter. On the way I was recognized by several old friends, with whom I had become acquainted on my former visit. They saluted me with a friendly *aloha*. I cannot say there was much room for compliment on any visible improvement in their costume; for they still wore with much self-complacency some ill-assorted portions of European attire.

The residence of Nomahanna lay near the fortress on the seashore: it was a pretty little wooden house of two stories, built in the European style, with handsome large windows, and a balcony very neatly painted. We were received on the

stairs by Chinau, the governor of Wahu, in a curious dishabille.
He could hardly walk from the confinement his feet suffered
in a pair of fisherman's shoes, and his red cloth waistcoat would
not submit to be buttoned, because it had never been intended
for so colossal a frame. He welcomed me with repeated *alohas,*
and led me up to the second floor, where all the arrangements
had a pleasing and even elegant appearance. The stairs were
occupied from the bottom to the door of the queen's apartments,
by children, adults, and even old people, of both sexes, who,
under her majesty's own superintendence, were reading from
spelling books, and writing on slates — a spectacle very honorable to her philanthropy. The governor himself had a spelling
book in one hand, and in the other a very ornamental little
instrument made of bone, which he used for pointing to the
letters. Some of the old people appeared to have joined the
assembly rather for example's sake than from a desire to learn,
as they were studying, with an affectation of extreme diligence,
books held upside down.

The spectacle of these scholars and their whimsical and
scanty attire nearly upset the gravity with which I had prepared
for my presentation to the queen. The doors were, however,
thrown open and I entered, Chinau introducing me as the captain of the newly arrived Russian frigate. The apartment was
furnished in the European fashion, with chairs, tables, and looking glasses. In one corner stood an immensely large bed with
silk curtains; the floor was covered with fine mats, and on these,
in the middle of the room, lay Nomahanna, extended on her
stomach, her head turned towards the door, and her arms supported on a silk pillow. Two young girls, lightly dressed, sat
cross-legged by the side of the queen, flapping away the flies
with bunches of feathers. Nomahanna, who appeared at the utmost not more than forty years old, was exactly six feet two
inches high and rather more than two ells in circumference.
She wore an old-fashioned European dress of blue silk; her
coal-black hair was neatly plaited at the top of a head as round
as a ball; her flat nose and thick projecting lips were certainly
not very handsome, yet was her countenance on the whole pre-

possessing and agreeable. On seeing me, she laid down the psalm book in which she had been reading; and having, with the help of her attendants, changed her lying for a sitting posture, she held out her hand to me in a very friendly manner, with many *alohas,* and invited me to take a seat on a chair by her side.

Her memory was better than my own; she recognized me as the Russian officer who had visited the deceased monarch Tameamea, on the island of O Wahi. On that occasion I had been presented to the queens; but since that time Nomahanna had so much increased in size that I did not know her again. She was aware how highly I esteemed her departed consort; my appearance brought him vividly to her remembrance, and she could not restrain her tears in speaking of his death. "The people," said she, "have lost in him a protector and a father. What will now be the fate of these islands, the God of the Christians only knows." She now informed me with much self-gratulation that she was a Christian, and attended the prayer meeting several times every day. Desirous to know how far she had been instructed in the religion she professed, I inquired through Marini the grounds of her conversion. She replied that she could not exactly describe them, but that the missionary Bingham, who understood reading and writing perfectly well, had assured her that the Christian faith was the best; and that, seeing how far the Europeans and Americans, who were all Christians, surpassed her compatriots in knowledge, she concluded that their belief must be the most reasonable. "If, however," she added, "it should be found unsuited to our people, we will reject it, and adopt another."

Hence it appears that the Christianity of the missionaries is not regarded with the reverence which, in its purity, it is calculated to inspire in the most uncultivated minds. In conclusion, Nomahanna triumphantly informed me that the women might now eat as much pork as they pleased, instead of being, as formerly, limited to dog's flesh. At this observation, an intrusive idea suddenly changed her tone and the expression of her features. With a deep sigh, she exclaimed, "What would

Tameamea say if he could behold the changes which have taken place here? No more gods — no more marais: all are destroyed! It was not so in his time — we shall never have such another king!" Then, while the tears trickled down her cheeks, she bared her right arm and showed me, tattooed on it in the O Wahi language — "Our good King Tameamea died on the 8th of May 1819." This sign of mourning for the beloved monarch, which cannot be laid aside like our pieces of crape, but accompanies the mourner to the grave, is very frequent on the Sandwich Islands, and testifies the esteem in which his memory is held: but it is a still more striking proof of the universal grief for his loss that on the anniversary of his death all his subjects struck out one of their front teeth; and the whole nation have in consequence acquired a sort of whistle in speaking. Chinau had even had the above words tattooed on his tongue, of which he gave me ocular demonstration; nor was he singular in this mode of testifying his attachment. It is surprising that an operation so painful, and which occasions a considerable swelling, should not be attended with worse consequences.

Nomahanna spoke with enthusiasm on the subject of writing. Formerly, she said, she could only converse with persons who were present; now, let them be ever so far distant, she could whisper her thoughts softly to them alone. She promised to write me a letter, in order, she said, that I might prove to every one in Russia that Nomahanna was able to write.

Our conversation was interrupted by the rattling of wheels and the sound of many voices. I looked from the window and saw a little cart to which a number of active young men had harnessed themselves with the greatest complacency. I inquired of Marini what this meant, and was informed that the queen was about to drive to church. An attendant soon after entered and announced that the equipage was ready. Nomahanna graciously proposed my accompanying her; and rather than risk her displeasure by a refusal, I accepted the invitation with many thanks, though I foresaw that I should thus be drawn in as a party to a very absurd spectacle.

The queen now put on a white calico hat decorated with Chinese flowers, took a large Chinese fan in her hand, and, having completed her toilette by drawing on a pair of clumsy sailor's boots, we set out. In descending the stairs, she made a sign that the school was over for the present — an announcement that seemed very agreeable to the scholars, to the old ones especially. At the door below, a crowd had assembled, attracted by curiosity to see me and their queen drive out together. The young men in harness shouted for joy, and patiently waited the signal for the race. Some delay, however, occurred in taking our seats with suitable dignity. The carriage was very small, and my companion very large, so that I was fain to be content with a seat upon the edge, with a very good chance of losing my balance, had not her majesty, to obviate the danger, encircled my waist with her stout and powerful arm, and thus secured me on my seat. Our position, and the contrast presented by our figures, had no doubt a sufficiently comical effect. When we were at length comfortably settled, the Governor Chinau came forth, and with no other addition than a round hat to the costume already described, mounted a meager unsaddled steed, and off we all went at full gallop, the queen taking infinite pains to avoid losing me by the way. The people came streaming from all sides, shouting *"Aloha maita!"* — our team continually increasing, while a crowd behind contended for the honor of helping to push us forward. In this style we drove the whole length of Hanaruro, and in about a quarter of an hour reached the church. . . .

Fourteen days after our arrival, I received a message from Karemaku, who was still at O Tuai. He assured me that he was rejoiced at my coming, stated that he had sent orders to Chinau to supply my ship with the best provisions, and added that having happily concluded the expedition he should soon return to Hanaruro.

Meanwhile, we had no cause to complain of our situation: everything was to be had for money; and Nomahanna overwhelmed us with presents of fat hogs and the finest fish, putting all the fishermen into requisition to provide abundantly for our table. We had all reason to be grateful for her attention and kindness, and are all therefore ready to maintain that she is not only the cleverest and the most learned, but also the best woman in Wahu, as indeed she is considered both by the natives and settlers.

But I can also bear testimony to another qualification, of equal importance in her estimation — she has certainly the greatest appetite that ever came under my observation. I usually visited her in the morning, and was in the habit of finding her extended at full length upon the floor, employed in inditing her letter to me, which appeared to occasion her many a headache. Once, however, I called exactly at dinner time, and was shown into the eating room. She was lying on fine mats before a large looking glass, stretched as usual on her prodigious stomach. A number of Chinese porcelain dishes, containing food of various kinds, were ranged in a semicircle before her, and the attendants were busily employed in handing first one and then another to her majesty. She helped herself with her fingers from each in its turn, and ate most voraciously, whilst two boys flapped away the flies with large bunches of feathers. My appearance did not at all disturb her: she greeted me with her mouth full, and graciously nodded her desire that I should take my seat in a chair by her side, when I witnessed, I think, the most extraordinary meal upon record. How much had passed the royal mouth before my entrance, I will not undertake to affirm; but it took in enough in my presence to have satisfied six men! Great as was my admiration at the quantity of food thus consumed, the scene which followed was calculated to increase it. Her appetite appearing satisfied at length, the queen drew her breath with difficulty two or three times, then exclaimed, "I have eaten famously!" These were the first words her important business had allowed her time to utter. By the assistance of her attendants, she then turned upon her back and made a sign with her hand to a tall, strong fellow, who seemed well practised in his office; he immediately sprang upon her body, and kneaded her as unmercifully with his knees and fists as if she had been a trough of bread. This was done to favor digestion; and her majesty, after groaning a little at this ungentle treatment and taking a short time to recover herself, ordered her royal person to be again turned on the stomach, and recommenced her meal. This account, whatever appearance of exaggeration it may bear, is literally true, as all my officers, and the other gentlemen who accompanied me, will witness.

M. Preuss, who lived in the neighborhood of the lady, frequently witnessed similar meals, and maintains that Nomahanna and her fat hog were the greatest curiosities in Wahu. The latter is in particular favor with the queen, who feeds him almost to death: he is black, and of extraordinary size and fatness: two Kanakas are appointed to attend him, and he can hardly move without their assistance.

Nomahanna is vain of her tremendous appetite. She considers most people too thin, and recommends inaction as an accelerator of her admired *embonpoint* — so various are the notions of beauty. On the Sandwich Islands, a female figure a fathom long and of immeasurable circumference is charming; whilst the European lady laces tightly and sometimes drinks vinegar in order to touch our hearts by her slender and delicate symmetry.

One of our officers obtained the queen's permission to take her portrait. The limner's art is still almost a novelty here; and many persons of rank solicited permission to witness the operation. With the greatest attention, they watched every stroke of the outline, and loudly expressed their admiration as each feature appeared upon the paper. The nose was no sooner traced than they exclaimed — "Now Nomahanna can smell!" When the eyes were finished — "Now she can see!" They expressed especial satisfaction at the sight of the mouth, because it would enable her to eat; and they seemed to have some apprehension that she might suffer from hunger. At this point, Nomahanna became so much interested that she requested to see the picture also: she thought the mouth much too small, and begged that it might be enlarged. The portrait, however, when finished, did not please her; and she remarked rather peevishly — "I am surely much handsomer than that!" ...

According to Nomahanna's request, I sent off an officer with the shallop to fetch her [for a visit to Captain von Kotzebue's ship]. Some hours, however, elapsed before she came, her majesty's toilette having, said my officer, occupied all this time. When at length it was completed, she desired him to give her his arm and conduct her to the shallop. This is another imitation of European customs.

For a lady of the Sandwich Islands, Nomahanna was this day very elegantly attired. A peach-colored dress of good silk, trimmed at the bottom with black lace, covered her majesty's immense figure, which a very broad many-colored sash, with a large bow in the front, divided exactly into two halves. She had a collar round her neck of native manufacture, made of beautiful red and yellow feathers; and on her head a very fine leghorn hat, ornamented with artificial flowers from Canton and trimmed round the edge with a pendant flounce of black lace; her chin lying modestly hidden behind a whole bed of flowers that bloomed on her mountain bosom. In somewhat striking contrast to all this finery were the clumsily accoutered feet, and stout, ill-shaped, brown, unstockinged legs, which the shortness of her majesty's petticoats, proportioned originally to the stature of a European belle, displayed to a rather unsightly extent.

As yet, the shoemaker's craft does not flourish in the Sandwich Islands; so that all the shoes and boots worn there are imported from Europe and America. But as neither of these continents can produce such a pair of feet as those of Queen Nomahanna, the attempt to force them into any ready-made shoes would be hopeless; and her majesty is therefore obliged, if she would not go barefoot, which she does not consider altogether decorous, to content herself with a pair of men's galoshes. Such trifles as these were, however, beneath her notice, and she contemplated her dress with infinite complacency, as a pattern of princely magnificence. In these splendid habiliments, with a parasol in her hand, slowly and with difficulty, she climbed the ship's stairs, on which, with some of my officers, I was in waiting to receive her. On the highest step she endeavored already to give us a proof of her acquaintance with our customs, by making a curtsey, which was intended to accord with the most approved rules of the art of dancing, though the feet, not perfectly tutored in their parts, performed in rather a comic style. In attempting this feat, she lost her balance, and would have fallen into the water, if a couple of strong sailors had not caught her illustrious person in their arms.

She was much delighted with all that she saw on board, especially with my cabin, where the sofa paid dearly for the honor of her approbation — she sat upon it, and broke it down. The portrait of the Emperor Alexander attracted her particular attention; she sat down opposite to it upon the floor, where she could cause no farther destruction, and said, after gazing upon it for some minutes with much interest, *"Maitai, Yeri nue Rukkini!"* (the great Governor of the Russians is beautiful!) She told me that she knew a great deal about Russia. A Sandwich Islander, named Lauri, who in 1819 had made the voyage thither in the Russian ship *Kamtschatka* with Captain Golowin, and had afterwards returned to his own country, had told her many things concerning Petersburg and the Emperor. She said she would have liked to make the voyage herself, but that Lauri's fearful description of the cold had terrified her. He had told her that it was necessary to envelop the body entirely in fur, and that even this would not obviate all danger of losing the nose and ears; that the cold changed the water into a solid substance, resembling glass in appearance, but of so much strength that it was used for a high road, people passing over it in huge chests drawn by horses, without breaking it; that the houses were as high as mountains, and so large that he had walked three days in one of them without coming to the end of it. It was evident that Lauri had stretched a little; but Nomahanna had no notion of incredulity. She approved of our inventions for warming the inside of our houses, and thought that if she were at Petersburg she would not go out at all during the cold weather, but would drive her carriage about the house. She inquired how it could possibly be so warm at one season of the year, and so cold at another. I endeavored to accommodate my answer to her powers of comprehension, and she seemed satisfied.

"Lauri was in the right," she observed; "there are very clever people in Russia." Her acknowledgement of my abilities, however, proved rather inconvenient, for she now overwhelmed me with a host of questions, some of them very absurd, and which to have answered with methodical precision would have required much time and consideration. For instance, she desired me to tell her how much wood must be burnt every year to warm all the countries of the earth? Whether rain enough might not fall, at some time or other, to extinguish all the fires? And whether, by means of such a rain, Wahu might not become as cold as Russia? I endeavored to cut the matter as short as possible and, in order to divert her thoughts to other subjects, set wine before her. She liked it very much, and I therefore presented her with a bottle; but her thirst for knowledge was not thus to be quenched, and during a visit of two hours she asked such incessant questions that I was not a little relieved when at length she proposed to depart. In taking leave she observed, "If I have wine, I must have glasses, or how can I drink it?" So saying, she took the bottle that had been given her in one hand and, with the other, seizing without ceremony the glasses that stood on the table, she went upon deck. There she made a profound curtsey to all present, and again took her seat in the shallop. Thus ended this condescending visit, with the royal appropriation of my wine glasses. Nomahanna had, however, been so liberal to us that she had a right to suppose she would be welcome to them.

From *A New Voyage Round the World* by Otto Von Kotzebue, translated by H. E. Lloyd (London, Henry Colburn & Richard Bentley, 1830).

HIRAM BINGHAM

# MISSIONARIES VS.
# MAN-OF-WARSMEN

The first missionaries to Hawaii arrived aboard the brig *Thaddeus* in 1820, sent out from Boston by the American Board of Commissioners for Foreign Missions. They came at a propitious time. The young King Liholiho and his advisers had just thrown off the old Polynesian religion, with its irksome tabus; and most of his people, bewildered without their gods, listened willingly to the new teachings.

Leader of the "First Company" on the *Thaddeus* was the Reverend Hiram Bingham (1789–1869), son of a Vermont farmer. A young man with a high forehead and a determination verging upon stubbornness, Bingham was destined to spend twenty-one years in active mission work in the islands. The chiefs surrounding the king — including Kalanimoku the prime minister (nicknamed "Billy Pitt"); the queen dowager and regent Kaahumanu; and Governor Boki of Oahu — eagerly heard the Gospel and tried to apply its teachings to their rule over the kingdom.

One change, resented by some shipmasters, was to tighten the control over the troupes of Hawaiian girls who boarded ships in the harbor to entertain lusty sailors. Particularly resentful was "Mad Jack" Percival, captain of the U.S.S. *Dolphin*, which arrived in January, 1826, the first United States warship to visit Honolulu. Bingham's account of the clash of wills and the ensuing rioting of American tars against the missionaries is a dramatic incident from the volume in which he recalls the trials and progress of the mission during its early period.

THE HAWAIIANS HAD HEARD OF THE POWER AND GREATNESS OF

the United States, and though Russia, France, and Great Britain had sent their naval vessels to these islands, yet the inhabitants knew little or nothing of American ships of war, or of the urbanity, intelligence, and elevated character of the United States naval officers. How exceedingly desirable it was that a naval commander from the United States, arriving so soon after Lord Byron's agreeable visit, and especially at a time when hostility was showing itself among both Englishmen and Americans, against the efforts of the best rulers of the islands to restrain crime, should exert a high moral influence for good, or at least not counteract our mission, nor interfere with the municipal or civil regulations of the place.

The *Dolphin* came into the roads on Friday, and into Honolulu Harbor on Saturday, and her commander proposed to the authorities to exchange salutes on the morrow morning. Kalanimoku and Kaahumanu declining such a secular service as unsuitable to the sanctity of the Lord's Day, the former sent this reply, "We keep sacred the Sabbath, and observe the Word of God." The *Dolphin* fired her salute Sabbath morning, which the natives returned from the fort on Monday morning. The little vessel was then put under repair.

Soon the ship *London,* Edwards master, from New York was wrecked on the shores of Lanai. Boki and Lieutenant Percival hastened thither to render assistance; and the latter took in charge, as a matter of honor it was said, the specie of the *London,* not without causing Captain Edwards and himself some trouble about salvage in the sequel.

Returning to Honolulu, he soon made known his views of the restraints on vile women, and asked an audience with the chief rulers on that subject of grievance, which his crew, by a committee, presented to him. Kaahumanu and Kalanimoku proposed to him to write to them if he had aught to say on that matter. Kalanimoku was then too ill for such an interview. Kaahumanu prepared a condescending and conciliatory statement for the commander's information on that subject, as full as he had any right to ask or expect, to meet the strange pretense that an embargo on lewd women, at the islands, was an insult to the U. S. flag! In this statement she maintained "that she had a right to control her own subjects in this matter; that in enforcing the tabu she had not sought for money; that in apprehending and punishing the offending subjects she had done no injustice to other nations, or the foreigners who belonged to other nations; and that while seeking specially to save the nation from vice and ruin, they had been lenient to strangers, though he very well knew that strangers, passing from one country to another, are bound, while they remain in a country, to conform to its laws."

Boki being charged to deliver this said the commander would be *huhu loa,* extremely angry. He delivered it, however, and in reporting to the queen said: "The man-of-war chief says he will not *write,* but will come and have a talk, and if Mr. Bingham comes, he will shoot him; that he was ready to fight, for though his vessel was small, she was just like fire." Seeing Boki wavering, Kaahumanu said, "Let us be firm on the side of the Lord, and follow the Word of God." Boki said, "If we meet the man-of-war chief, and then yield not to his demands, what will be the consequence?" Kaahumanu, alluding to Boki's having taken the eucharist in England or to his standing as a magistrate, replied with dignity, firmness, and consistent principle, "You are a servant of God, and must maintain his cause." Both wept.

On the 22nd of February, Lieutenant Percival obtained an audience at the house of Kaahumanu. She called the little royal pupil from his studies, under my instruction at Kalanimoku's, either that with her he might have the honor of an interview with a representative of the United States, or see how she would manage the matter. As Lieutenant Percival had previously requested me not to be present at the interview, I insert Kaahumanu's account of it, which, in the presence of her Hawaiian friends, she gave to several missionaries, and which accords well with the report of Governor Kahalaia and others present, and with the scenes of the drama which preceded and followed it under our own eyes. Carefully translated, her narrative is as follows:

Percival came to the council and asked, "Who is the king of the country?" I pointed out Kauikeaouli. He asked again, "Who is his guardian?" I replied, "*I.*" He asked further, "Who has the charge of his country?" I replied, "I and my brother, he being under me." He said to me, "You are then king. I also am a chief. You and I are alike. You are the person for me to talk with. By whom are the women tabued? Is it by you?" I replied, "It is by *me.*" He said, "Who is your teacher that has told you that the women must be tabu by the law?" I replied, "It is God." He laughed with contempt. He said, "It was not by *you;* it was by Bingham." I said, "It was by *me.* By Bingham the Word of God is made known to us." He said to me, "Why tabu the women? Take heed. My people will come: if the women are not forthcoming they will not obey my word. Take care of your men, and I will take care of mine. By and by they will come to get women, and if they do not obtain them, they will fight, and my vessel is just like fire." I said, "Why make war upon us without a fault of ours as to restraining our women? We love the Word of God, and therefore hold back our women. Why then would you fight us without cause?" He said, "You formerly attended properly with Kamehameha to the ships, both American and English." I said, "In former time, before the Word of God had arrived here, we were dark-minded, lewd, and murderous; at the present time we are seeking a better way." He denied, and said, "It is not good — it is not good to tabu the women. It is not so in America. Why did you give women to Lord Byron's ship, and deny them to mine? Kamehameha did not show such partiality between English and American vessels." We all denied, and said, "We gave no women to the ship of Lord Byron. That was a tabu ship. But why are you angry with us for laying a tabu on the women of our own country? Had you brought American women with you, and we had tabued them, you might then justly be displeased with us."

Soon after this he applied to Boki to liberate the women that were fast in consequence of the tabu. Boki spoke to me about it, and I informed you. He came the evening before the outrage of the crew, and said to me, "Send and liberate the women. If you still hold them, I myself will liberate them. Why do you do evil to the women?" I said, "It is for *us* to give directions respecting our women — it is for *us* to establish tabus — it is for *us* to bind, to liberate, to impose fines." He said, "The missionaries are not good; they are a company of liars: the women are *not* tabu in America." He snapped his fingers in rage, and clenched his fists, and said, "Tomorrow I will give my men rum"; — probably the daily ration — "look out: they will come for women; and if they do not get them, they will fight. My vessel is just like fire. Declare to me the man that told you the women must be tabu, and my people will pull down his house. If the women are not released from the tabu tomorrow, my people will come and pull down the houses of the missionaries."

There were several other crews in port, of whom many sympathized with this commander and a large part of his crew. On Sunday, the 26th of February, the commander of the *Dolphin* allowed double the usual number of his men to spend the day on shore at Honolulu. The violent among them, and the violent of other crews, attempted to form a coalition to "knock off the tabu."

As we were assembling for worship, in and around the house of Kalanimoku, in the afternoon, several seamen, part of whom belonged to the *Dolphin,* rushed into the spacious hall or saloon in the second story where were Kaahumanu, Kalanimoku, Namahana, and Boki, and a considerable number of others, and with menacing tones and gestures made their demands and threats. "Where are the women? Take off this tabu, and let us have women on board our vessels, or we will pull down your houses. There are a hundred and fifty of us — the tabu must come off: there is no other way." Thus commenced a riot which occupied the time and place of the expected divine service. These were followed by successive squads. One and another dashed in the windows of Kalanimoku's fine hall, breaking some seventy panes along the veranda. Some, I think, did not intend violence; and one of them said to me; "I wish you to take notice who they are that are doing this; we are not *all* engaged in it."

Being apprised of the riot at the place of assemblage, and hearing the crash of the chief's windows, Mrs. Bingham sent to me and requested me to return home; but fearing my compliance would attract the enemy thither, I preferred to stay on the premises of the chief. Seeing soon a party of sailors directing their steps towards my house, and thinking my wife and child

would instantly need my care, without a moment's further
hesitation I made speed by another direction and reached my
door a moment soonest, hoping to enter and lock it and exclude
the mob; but to my disappointment I found myself, as well as
the rioters, excluded. Mrs. Bingham not expecting me, and seeing the seamen approach, had turned the key against them, and
I fell into their hands.

One seized me by the shoulder and exclaimed, "What does
this tabu mean? Here he is: I have got him; come on." Another
pulled me by the skirts. One said, "We are sent here by our
captain." Another dashed in my windows with his club. Some
crossed their clubs around me to confine me.

I called out to the natives for help, but before any arrived, dis-
engaging myself from my assailants, I returned into the chief's
enclosure, whither I was followed. One who pressed me on my
retreat asked to speak to me. Putting my hand on his club, I
said, "Put down your club if you wish me to talk with you."
Coming around me again in the midst of the natives, they desired to know why they could not have women. One of the
*Dolphin's* men, who appeared like an Irishman, brandishing his
knife near my face said, with malignant emphasis. "*You* are
the *man, every* day." Namahana, standing near me, bade him
be quiet.

Fearing that Boki, whose duty it was to defend me, was
unwilling any longer to enforce the tabu or protect the missionaries against riotous foreigners, I looked around to see if
there were any on whom I could rely for immediate help, if
the rioters should strike me, and seeing John Ii, Koa, Nahinu,
and others whom I had instructed, standing but a few yards
from me, I said to them, *"Aole anei oukou malama mia iau?*
Do ye not take care of me?" *"Ke malama nei no makou,"* they
calmly replied; "we *do* take care."

Suddenly one of the *Dolphin's* men struck a spiteful blow
with a club at my head, which was warded off, partly by the
arm of Lydia Namahana, and partly by my umbrella. It was
the signal for resistance, for which the natives had waited.
They sprang upon the rioters; some they seized, disarmed, and

bound, and to some they dealt leveling blows. For one, knocked down senseless like an ox at the slaughter, with a two-hand club near me, I instantly felt the bowels of tenderness move, and entreated the natives not to kill the foreigners.

By this time, Mr. Chamberlain and Mr. Loomis reached the scene of strife, and probably saved the life of one of the fallen sailors, over whom a stone was raised for a dreadful blow. I returned to my house, but had hardly time to correct the report there that the foreigners were killing me, and assure Mrs. Bingham, who had heard the blows, that a kind hand had shielded me from wounds, before a company of sailors approached my premises, broke and rushed through my gate, and hastened towards my door, which I locked against them. One broke in a window; another beat with violence against the door; two applied their strength to force it, and as we looked down from the chamber window, one strangely turning his vengeance on his fellow, like the enemies of Israel, with his heavy club gave him a blow which I feared was fatal, laying him senseless on the earth. He was then lifted from the ground by order of Lieutenant Percival, who with some of his officers came upon the spot about an hour after the riot commenced, and used his cane over some of the turbulent men. One of his crew attempting to force his way into the court of Kalanimoku's house after it had been cleared and closed received on his head a severe cutlass wound from the sentinel at the gate.

In the evening of the same day, the commander waited on the chiefs and reiterated his objections to the tabu, and, while he admitted that the sailors had gone too far, expressed his unwillingness to leave the country till his vessel should enjoy the privileges that had been enjoyed by the vessels of other nations. Governor Boki and Manuia, the commander of the fort, whose effective agency were then essential to the enforcement of the tabu, yielded to its violation in the harbor of Honolulu.

An ambiguous circular, designed either to express regard for the safety and comfort of missionaries, or to palliate the outrage and confirm the prejudice of the seamen, and at the same time guard their heads from heavier blows from a wronged and offended people, was shortly addressed to the several shipmasters in port, though not agreeable to their wishes, and was shown to me by the writer, Lieutenant Percival. He moreover ordered the repair of Kalanimoku's house and mine, and put in irons two men who assailed me with knife and club; and our physician, Dr. Blatchley, applied his skill to heal the wounds of his men.

After a visit of about three months, the *Dolphin* sailed, having obtained the proud name of "the mischief-making man-of-war." With that term was associated the shout of the vile which was heard in the harbor as the first boatload of vile women was seen to pass under its flag. Never did the advocacy of licentiousness or opposition to the tabu appear more odious. While some exulted for a time in the partial triumph, those citizens and subjects of other countries and leading natives, who had been looking for something not less friendly, wise, and honorable in a naval "chief" from the United States than had appeared in Lord Byron, were disappointed. But he that makes the wrath of man to praise him overruled this temporary triumph to the increase of the confidence of some in the Gospel and in its propagators.

From *A Residence of Twenty-One Years in the Sandwich Islands* . . . by Hiram Bingham (New York, Sherman Converse, 1847).

LAURA FISH JUDD

# LEAVES FROM
# A MISSIONARY'S DIARY

The astonishing success of the first missionaries in Hawaii and
the need for additional recruits soon prompted others to follow
to this fertile field for the Lord's work. Among the "Third Company" of missionaries, arriving on the *Parthian* in 1828, was Dr.
Gerrit P. Judd and his young bride, Laura Fish Judd (1804–
1872). The capable, astute physician was to become one of the
most influential men in Hawaii, holding important posts in the
government and helping to guide the little kingdom through
perennial crises. In the selection that follows Laura Judd sets
down in her diary, through observant eyes and in a pleasing
style, her first impressions while becoming adjusted to strange
surroundings and a new way of life.

SHIP *Parthian*, MARCH, 1828. RIGHT BEFORE US, UP IN THE
clouds, and apparently distant but a stone's throw, appears a spot
of beautiful, deep blue, intermingled with dazzling white. It is
land! — the snow-capped summit of Mauna Kea, on the island
of Hawaii. Among the passengers the excitement is intense and
variously expressed; some rush below to their staterooms to
pour out their hearts in gratitude and thanksgiving, others
fear to turn away lest the scene fade or prove a delusion, like
our dreams of homeland; some exhaust their vocabulary in
exclamations of delight; others sit alone in tears and silence.

What wonder that we so long for release from this little
prison house! We have suffered many hardships, often unexpected. The ladies, ten in number, have been obliged to per-

form the drudgery of steward and cabin boy, as the services of these functionaries have been denied us by the captain, although, *mirabile dictu,* he did in his condescension allow his black cook to prepare our food after his, if furnished and conveyed to the ship's galley. We possessed but little practical knowledge of the arts of the cuisine at first, but have sometimes astonished each other and ourselves at our success in producing palatable dishes, and most of all, light bread. These trials of patience and skill will be of use to us in our future housekeeping.

The voyage is now over, but I must run on deck to look again on that deep blue spot. The ship glides along smoothly; the clouds open — the blue space has become a broad mountain; now we see the green valleys and dashing cascades all along the northern shores of the island. The scene reminds one of the pilgrim's land of Beulah. Can anything so fair be defiled by idol worship and deeds of cruelty?

We shall pass the island of Maui tonight, and reach Oahu tomorrow, which will be Sunday. We have packed our baggage in the smallest possible compass, and have everything ready to go ashore on Monday morning. We retire to rest with mingled anticipations of pain and pleasure. For once we regret that tomorrow will be the Sabbath; we look up for guidance — our Heavenly Father will pity us.

Sunday morning, March 30. The island of Oahu, our Ultima Thule, looms up in the distance, displaying gray and red rocky hills, unrelieved by a single shade of green, forbidding enough in aspect. Now we pass the old crater, Diamond Head, and we can see a line of coconut trees stretching gracefully along the sea beach for a mile or more. "Please give me the glass for a moment. There! I see the town of Honolulu, a mass of brown huts, looking precisely like so many haystacks in the country; not one white cottage, no church spire, not a garden nor a tree to be seen save the grove of coconuts. The background of green hills and mountains is picturesque. A host of living, moving beings are coming out of that long, brown building; it must be Mr. Bingham's congregation just dismissed from morning service; they pour out like bees from a hive. I can see their draperies of brown, black, white, pink and yellow native tapa."

Hark! There goes a gun for the pilot; our captain seems somewhat flurried; afraid of the land, perhaps; I surely am not. How I long for a run on those green hills! But patience till tomorrow.

Evening — our last one on board the *Parthian*. We have sung our last evening hymn together. Mutual suffering has created mutual sympathy, and we separate in Christian friendship.

We received a short but welcome visit from Messrs. Bingham, Chamberlain and Goodrich, on their way to hold service on board the ship *Enterprise*. They look careworn and feeble; Mr. W—— said "hungry." They gave us a cordial welcome to their fields of labor, which they describe as "whitening for the harvest." Mr. Goodrich brought some sugar cane and fresh lavender; the fragrance of the latter made me wild with delight. I have been on deck to look at the town and harbor. There are flitting lights among the shipping, but none visible on shore. The houses are windowless, looking dark and dreary as possible. "Here we are to live and labor," said good Dr. Worcester, "until the land is filled with churches, schoolhouses, fruitful fields, and pleasant dwellings." When will it be?

Mission House, March 31. We passed a sleepless night; the vessel being at anchor we missed the accustomed rocking. At nine o'clock this morning we were handed over the ship's side (by our kind and unwearying friend Mr. S——, the mate), into the launch, and were towed ashore, twenty in number, passing quite a fleet of ships, on board of which we saw native men and women.

Landing at the fort we were received by the acting governor, Manuia, a very gentlemanly-looking person, dressed in half military costume. He spoke a little English as he escorted us to the gate, where vehicles were ready to take us to the Mission, a mile distant. These vehicles consisted of a yellow one-horse wagon and two blue handcarts, all drawn by natives, and kindly furnished by the queen regent, Kaahumanu; but I could not be persuaded to ride in such style, and begged to walk with my husband.

We stopped on the way at the door of the royal lady, who joined our procession after welcoming us most cordially to her dominions. She is tall, stately, and dignified; often overbearing in her manner, but with a countenance beaming with love whenever she addresses her teachers. She was dressed in striped satin, blue and pink, with a white muslin shawl and Leghorn bonnet, the latter worn doubtless in compliment to us, as the common headdress is a wreath of feathers or flowers.

We were followed all the way from the landing by a crowd of natives, men, women, and children, dressed and undressed. Many of them wore a sheet of native cloth, tied on one shoulder, not unlike the Roman toga; one had a shirt minus pantaloons, another had a pair of pantaloons minus a shirt; while a large number were destitute of either. One man looked very grand with an umbrella and shoes, the only foreign articles he could command. The women were clad in native costume, the *pa-u,* which consists of folds of native cloth about the hips, leaving the shoulders and waist quite exposed; a small number donned in addition a very feminine garment made of unbleached cotton, drawn close around the neck, which was quite becoming. Their hair was uncombed and their faces unwashed, but all of them were good-natured. Our appearance furnished them much amusement; they laughed and jabbered, ran on in advance, and turned back to peer into our faces. I laughed and cried too, and hid my face for very shame.

We reached the Mission House at last and were ushered into Mr. Bingham's parlor, the walls of which were naked clapboards, except one side newly plastered with lime, made by burning coral stone from the reef. After being presented and welcomed, Mr. Bingham took his hymnbook and selected the hymn commencing: "Kindred in Christ, for His dear sake."

Some of the company had sufficient self-control to join in the singing, but I was choking; I had made great efforts all the morning to be calm, and to control an overflowing heart, but

when we knelt around that family altar, I could no longer sub-
due my feelings.

A sumptuous dinner, consisting of fish, fowl, sweet potatoes,
taro, cucumbers, bananas, watermelons, and sweet water from
a mountain spring had thoughtfully been provided by the
good queen. As we had not tasted fruit or vegetables for
months, it was difficult to satisfy thoroughly *salted* appetites
with fresh food.

Kaahumanu treated us like pet children, examined our eyes
and hair, felt of our arms, criticized our dress, remarking the
difference between our fashions and those of the pioneer ladies,
who still wear short waists and tight sleeves, instead of the present long waists, full skirts, and leg-of-mutton sleeves. She says
that one of our number must belong exclusively to her, and
instruct her women in all domestic matters so that she can
live as we do. As the choice is likely to fall on me, I am well
pleased, for I have taken a great fancy to the old lady.

After dinner she reclined on a sofa and received various
presents sent by friends in Boston. Mr. Bingham read letters
from Messrs. Stewart, Loomis, and Ellis to her. She listened
attentively, her tears flowed freely, and she could only articulate
the native expression *"aloha ino"* (love intense). At four o'clock
she said she was tired, and must go home; accordingly her
retinue were summoned, some twenty in number, one bearing
the kahili (a large feather fly brush and badge of rank), another an umbrella, still another her spittoon, etc., etc. She took
each of us by the hand, and kissed each one in the Hawaiian
style, by placing her nose against our cheeks and giving a sniff,
as one would inhale the fragrance of flowers. After repeating
various expressions of affectionate welcome and pleasure at the
arrival of so many fresh laborers, she seated her immense
stateliness in her carriage, which is a light handcart, painted
turquoise blue, spread with fine mats and several beautiful dam-
ask- and velvet-covered cushions. It was drawn by half a dozen
stout men, who grasped the rope in pairs, and marched off as
if proud of the royal burden. The old lady rides backward, with
her feet hanging down behind the cart, which is certainly a

safe, if not convenient, mode of traveling. As she moved away, waving her hand and smiling, Mrs. Bingham remarked, "We love her very much, although the time is fresh in our memories when she was very unlovely; if she deigned to extend her little finger to us, it was esteemed a mark of distinguished consideration." She was naturally haughty, and was then utterly regardless of the life and happiness of her subjects. What has wrought this great change in her disposition and manner? Let those who deny the efficacy of divine grace explain it, if they can.

Crowds of curious but good-natured people have thronged the premises the whole day; every door and pane of glass has been occupied with peering eyes, to get a glimpse of the strangers. I have shaken hands with hundreds, and exchanged *aloha* with many more. We seem to be regarded as but little lower than the angels, and the implicit confidence of these people in our goodness is almost painful.

The chiefs of both sexes are fine looking, and move about with the easy grace of conscious superiority. Three or four of them, to whom we have been introduced today, visited England in the suite of King Liholiho, and were presented at the Court of St. James's. They dress well, in fine broadcloths and elegant silks, procured in exchange for sandalwood, which is taken to China and sold at an immense profit; fortunes have been made by certain merchants in this traffic (honorable, of course, especially when the hand or foot was used on the scales!). Our captain told us that some of the chiefs had paid eight hundred and a thousand dollars for mirrors not worth fifty.

March 31. Nine o'clock in the evening. Is it enchantment? Can it be a reality that I am on dear mother earth again? A clean, snug little chamber all to ourselves! I can go to the door, and by the light of the moon see the brown village and the distant, dark-green hills and valleys. Strange sounds meet the ear. The ocean's roar is exchanged for the lowing of cattle on the neighboring plains; the braying of donkeys, and the bleating of goats, and even the barking of dogs are music to me.

April 1, 1828. Mrs. Bingham, who is in feeble health, allowed me the privilege of superintending the breakfast this morning, as I am eager to be useful in some way. I arose quite early, and hastened to the kitchen. Judge of my dismay on entering to find a tall, stalwart native man, clad much in the style of John the Baptist in the wilderness, seated before the fire, frying taro. He was covered from head to foot with the unmentionable cutaneous malady common to filth and negligence. I stood aghast, in doubt whether to retire or stand my ground like a brave woman, and was ready to cry with annoyance and vexation. The cook's wife was present, and her keener perceptions read my face; she ordered him out to make his toilet in foreign attire. I suppose travelers in southern Italy become accustomed to this statuesque style, but I am verdant enough to be shocked, and shall use all my influence to increase the sales and use of American cottons.

April 2, 1828. This is my twenty-fourth birthday. Have received our baggage from the ship. Found time to take a stroll with my husband, and on our way visited the grass church, where Mr. Bingham preaches to an audience of two thousand. The building is sadly dilapidated, the goats and cattle having browsed off the thatching, as high as they could reach. The strong trade wind always blowing sweeps through, tossing up the mats, which are spread upon the bare earth, and raising a disagreeable cloud of dust. The church is surrounded by a burying ground, already thickly tenanted. I saw some small graves, where lay sleeping some of the children of the pioneer missionaries.

We looked into some of the native huts, primitive enough in point of furniture; mats, and tapa in one corner for a bed, a few calabashes in another, hardly suggesting a pantry, were all. Their principal article of food is poi, a paste made of baked taro, which they eat with fish, often raw and seasoned with salt. It is the men's employment to cultivate and cook the taro. Housekeeping I should judge to be a very light affair, the manufacture of mats and tapa being almost the sole employment of the women. There are no cold winters to provide for; the continuous summer furnishes food with but little labor, so that the real wants of life are met, in a great degree, without experiencing the original curse pronounced upon the breadwinner.

Such quantities of native presents as we have received today, from the natives coming in procession, each one bearing a gift! Among these were fish, lobsters, bananas, onions, fowls, eggs, and watermelons. In exchange, they expect us to shake hands and repeat *aloha*. Their childish exclamations of delight are quite amusing — as, for example, when they request us to turn around, so that they may examine our dresses and hair behind.

They all express themselves delighted in having a physician among them, and one man said, on being introduced to Dr. Judd, "We are healed."

Her Royal Highness dined with us again today. She had been sending in nice things for the table all the morning, but did not seem quite satisfied, kindly inquiring if there was not something the strangers would like, not on the bill of fare. Mr. Bingham remarked, "You have been very thoughtful today." She looked him in the face, and asked with an arch smile, "Ah, is it today only?" No mother's tenderness could exceed hers toward Mr. and Mrs. Bingham. As she is an Amazon in size, she could dandle any one of us in her lap, as she would a little child, which she often takes the liberty of doing.

April 3, 1828. I visited some sick people with my husband — also called on Lydia Namahana, a sister of Kaahumanu. She is not so tall as her royal sister, but more fleshy. I should like to send home, as a curiosity, one of her green kid gaiters; her ankle measures eighteen inches without exaggeration. She is kind and good, and the wife of a man much younger than herself, Laanui, one of the savants of the nation, who assists in translating the Bible. "Robert," a Cornwall* youth, and his wife, Halakii, reside with these chiefs as teachers. They are exemplary Christians, and have been very useful. I am sorry to say that they are both quite ill of a fever.

Several captains from the whaling fleet have called on us today, who appear very pleasant and friendly. We have also

* The Foreign Mission School at Cornwall, Connecticut, set up to train young American Indians and Polynesians for mission work.

received the compliments of Governor Boki (who was absent on our arrival), requesting an interview at his house at two o'clock p.m. We shook the wrinkles from our best dresses, arrayed ourselves as becomingly as possible, and at the appointed hour were on our way.

The sun was shining in its strength, and we had its full benefit in the half-mile walk to the governor's house. He met us at the gate and escorted us into the reception room in a most courtly manner. There we found Madam Boki, sitting on a crimson-covered sofa, and dressed in a closely fitting silk. She was surrounded by her maids of honor seated on mats, and all wrapped in mantles of gay-colored silk. I counted forty of them, all young, and some pretty. The room was spacious, and furnished with a center table, chairs, a mahogany secretary, etc., all bespeaking a degree of taste and civilization. Madam arose as we were individually presented by name, and curtsied to each. Mr. Bingham was presented with the governor's welcome in writing, which he interpreted to us as follows: "Love to you, Christian teachers, I am glad to meet you. It is doubtless God who sent you hither. I regret that I was at another place when you arrived. — NA BOKI."

I did not think he appeared very hearty in his welcome; time, however, will show. As this was our formal presentation to the magnates of the land, several speeches were made by those present. Kaahumanu presented hers in writing, as follows:

"Peace, good will to you all, beloved kindred. This is my sentiment, love and joy in my heart towards God, for sending you here to help us. May we dwell together under the protecting shadow of his great salvation. May we all be saved by Jesus Christ. — NA ELIZABETA KAAHUMANU."

Governor Boki and lady visited England in King Liholiho's suite in 1823. Kekuanaoa, husband of Kinau, a daughter of Kamehameha I, was also of the favored number received at Buckingham Palace. They would grace any court. The best-looking man in the group was a son of Kaumualii, king of Kauai. He is a captive prince, as his father was conquered by Kamehameha I, and is not allowed to return to his native island. They all appear deeply interested on the subject of religion, and enter earnestly into every plan for the improvement of the people. The schools are under their especial patronage. Today Mrs. Bingham gave us an account of her first presentation at the Hawaiian court seven years ago. It was at the palace of Liholiho, before any of the natives had visited foreign countries. The palace was a thatched building, without floors or windows, and with a door but three feet high. His Majesty's apparel was a few yards of green silk wrapped about his person. Five queens stood at his right hand, two of them his half sisters. After the three foreign ladies had been introduced, the king remarked to the queen nearest him, "These foreigners wish to remain in our kingdom, and teach a new religion. One of their peculiar doctrines is that a man must have but one wife. If they remain, I shall be obliged to send away four of you." "Let it be so," was the prompt answer, "let them remain, and and be it as you say." This was Kamamalu, who accompanied the king to England two years after, and died in London, whom, being the favorite, he retained as his only wife. The other four are happily married to men of rank. They are all of immense proportions, weighing three or four hundred pounds each. I have been silly enough, in my younger days, to regret being so large; I am certainly in the right place now, where beauty is estimated strictly by pounds avoirdupois!

The natives are doing our six months' washing. I have been at the stream to see them. They sit in the water to the waist, soap the clothes, then pound them with smooth stones, managing to make them clean and white in cold water. But the texture of fine fabrics suffers in this rough process. Wood is scarce, being brought from the mountains, without the convenience of roads or beasts of burden.

Mrs. Charlton, wife of the English consul, and Mrs. Taylor, her sister, called on us today. They have been here but a short time, and are the only white ladies in the place, excepting those of the mission. Mrs. Taylor is particularly agreeable.

Visited again our sick friends, Robert and wife, and fear they are not long for earth, as they appear to be in the first stages of rapid consumption. On our way home we called on our friend Kaahumanu, and found her reclining on a divan of clean mats, surrounded by her attendants, who had evidently been reading to her. She was wrapped in a *kihei* of blue silk velvet. This *kihei* is a very convenient article, answering for both wrapper and bedspread, and is made of every variety of material. It is as easy here to take one's bed and walk as it was in Judea.

Kaahumanu insists that we shall live with her; she will give us a house and servants, and I must be called by her name. We do not like to refuse, but the plan is thought to be impracticable, so we propose to have her come and live with us. She has a little adopted daughter, Ruth, whom she wishes me to take and educate as my own. There is certainly before us enough, and we need wisdom to choose wisely between duties to be done, and what is to be left undone.

In conversation with Mr. and Mrs. Bingham today, they related some anecdotes of our good queen-mother in former times. Quite a number of chiefs embraced the new religion, were baptized, and received into the Church, before this haughty personage deigned to notice the foreign teachers at all. It was after a severe illness, during which she had been often visited, and the wants of her suffering body attended to, that her manner softened toward them. The native language had been reduced to writing; a little book containing the alphabet, a few lessons in reading, and some hymns had been printed. Mr. and Mrs. Bingham took a copy of this little book and called on her one evening, hoping and praying to find some avenue to her heart. They found her on her mats, stretched at full length, with a group of portly dames like herself, engaged in a game of cards, of which they were passionately fond. This was the first accomplishment learned from foreigners, and they could play cards well before they had books, paper, pen, or pencil.

The teachers waited patiently until the game was finished; they then requested the attention of her ladyship to a new *pepa* (paper), which they had brought her. (They called cards *pepa*, the same word applying to books.) She turned toward them and asked, "What is it?" They gave her the little spelling book in her own language, explaining how it could be made to talk to her, and some of the words it would speak. She listened, was deeply interested, pushed aside her cards, and was never known to resume them to the day of her death. She was but a few days in mastering the art of reading, when she sent orders for books, to supply all her household. She forsook her follies, and gave her entire energies to the support of schools, and in attendance upon the worship in the sanctuary.

It is no marvel that Mr. and Mrs. B—— looked thin and careworn. Besides the care of her own family, Mrs. B—— boarded and taught English to a number of native and half-caste children and youths. Fancy her, in the midst of these cares, receiving an order from the king to make him a dozen shirts, with ruffled bosoms, followed by another for a whole suit of broadcloth! The shirts were a comparatively easy task, soon finished with the efficient aid of Mrs. Ruggles, who was a host in anything she undertook. But the coat, how were they going to manage that? They were glad to be valued for any accomplishment, and did not like to return the cloth, saying they had never learned to make coats. No, that would not do, so after mature deliberation, Mrs. Ruggles got an old coat, ripped it to pieces, and by it cut one out for His Majesty, making allowance for the larger mass of humanity that was to go into it. Their efforts were successful, and afforded entire satisfaction to the king, who was not yet a connoisseur in the fit of a coat.

A strange scene occurred in the church at the Wednesday lecture of this week. At the close of the usual services, nineteen couples presented themselves at the matrimonial altar, arranged like a platoon of soldiers. As I cannot understand much that is said, I must confine my observations to what I saw. One bride was clad in a calico dress, and a bonnet, procured probably from some half-caste lady who has a foreign husband. The groom wore a blue cloth coat with bright buttons, which, I am informed, is the property of a fortunate holder who keeps it to rent to needy bridegrooms. This coat is always seen on these occasions. Most of the brides wore some article of foreign origin; one sported a nightcap scrupulously clean, but a little ragged, abstracted, perhaps, from the washing of some foreign lady. Another head was bandaged with a white handkerchief, tied on the top of the head in an immense fancy knot, over which was thrown a green veil, bringing down the knot quite on to her nose, almost blinding the poor thing. The scene was so ludicrous I could hardly suppress laughter, especially at the response of "Aye, aye," pronounced loud enough to be heard all over the neighborhood.

There seems to be quite a furor for the marriage service. Mr. Richards, at Lahaina, says he has united six hundred couples in a few months. It is certainly a vast improvement upon the old system of living together like brutes, and it is to be hoped they will find it conducive to much greater happiness. The usual fee to the officiating clergyman is a few roots of taro, or a fowl, a little bundle of onions, or some such article for the table, to the value of twenty-five cents. Cheap matrimony this, even counting the cost of outfit or for the rental of clothes. . . .

April 28, 1828. The grand annual exhibition of all the schools on this island is to be held at the church. Adults compose these schools, as the children are not yet tamed. The people come from each district in procession, headed by the principal man of the land (*konohiki*), all dressed in one uniform color of native cloth. One district would be clad in red, another in bright yellow, another in pure white, another in black or brown. The dress was one simple garment, the *kihei* for men and the *pa-u* for women.

It is astonishing how so many have learned to read with so few books. They teach each other, making use of banana leaves, smooth stones, and the wet sand on the sea beach, as tablets. Some read equally well with the book upside down or sidewise, as four or five of them learn from the same book with one teacher, crowding around him as closely as possible.

The aged are fond of committing to memory, and repeating in concert. One school recited the 103rd Psalm, and another Christ's Sermon on the Mount; another repeated the fifteenth chapter of John, and the Dukes of Esau and Edom. Their power of memory is wonderful, acquired, as I suppose, by the habit of committing and reciting traditions, and the genealogies of their kings and priests.

As yet, only portions of the Bible are translated and printed. These are demanded in sheets still wet from the press. Kaahumanu admires those chapters in Paul's epistles where he greets his disciples by name; she says, "Paul had a great many friends."

The children are considered bright, but too wild to be brought into the schools. We intend, however, to try them very soon.

From *Honolulu: Sketches of the Life, Social, Political, and Religious, in the Hawaiian Islands from 1828 to 1861* by Laura Fish Judd (New York, Anson D. F. Randolph & Company, 1880).

# JAMES J. JARVES

# BETWEEN HEATHENISM
# AND MISSIONARYISM

James Jackson Jarves (1818–1888), born in Boston, son of the manufacturer of "Sandwich glass," arrived in Hawaii in 1837, when he was nineteen. There he spent nearly nine years as a planter, merchant, and editor of a newspaper, the *Polynesian*. In the international rivalry that existed in Honolulu at this period, Jarves was a partisan journalist, supporting the American missionary faction. For one of his articles the French consul challenged him to a duel, and for another he was horsewhipped by the British consul. But he could not be intimidated; and in his writing he continued to oppose French and British influence and urge that the United States take more interest in the affairs of the Pacific kingdom.

After leaving the Islands, Jarves lived most of the rest of his life in Europe, where he became an art critic and collector of Italian paintings. Among his fourteen books three are about Hawaii, including *A History of the Hawaiian or Sandwich Islands* (1843), a volume of travel sketches (1843), and *Kiana* (1857), the first novel with a Hawaiian setting. In the following selection — a chapter from his pseudo-autobiography, written in Florence — Jarves recalls "the extraordinary intermixture of civilization and barbarism" in Honolulu at the time he was there.

LILIBOLU [HONOLULU] WAS A STRANGE PLACE AT THIS DATE [1837]. It was in a transition state between heathenism and missionaryism; and, though the two parties had ceased to fight with carnal, they were none the less bitter with their lingual weapons. To

69

me, coming from America to Lilibolu was like stepping back
from the nineteenth century into the chaotic barbarism of the
Heptarchy. It was a curious experience, and a picture of it
may amuse you.

Conceive a thousand or more thatched huts, looking like
geometrical haystacks, most of them low and filthy in the extreme, scattered higgledy-piggledy over a plain, and along the
banks of a scanty river, surrounded in general with dilapidated
mud walls, and inhabited by a mixed population of curs, pigs,
Shanghai poultry, and unwashed natives, on a footing as to sexes
and conditions, of liberty, fraternity, and equality, that would
have gladdened the heart of the reddest republican, and you
have the ground plan of Lilibolu. Here and there a white
trader, mechanic, or sailor had squatted, taken to himself a
tawny mistress and made to himself a mongrel home, in which
the comforts and conveniences of his motherland were oddly
blended with the necessities and fashions of his adopted country. There were a few shops, stores, and houses, of stone or
wood, Orientalized externally by spacious verandas, and numerous doors and windows, and internally presenting a medley
of native mats and divans, furniture from China, France, or
New England, and merchandise in homeopathic doses from
the four quarters of the globe, all strewed about in sailor-like
prodigality, or assorted with the right-angular and graceless
system of the Yankee peddler.

A few white women had followed their adventurous husbands hither, and, with their Parisian hats and boots, their
rosy faces and boundless hospitality, despite much domestic dis-
comfort, made quite a social oasis amid the general dirt and
barbarism. As the streets or lanes were in general almost im-
passible to their tender feet, on account of the hot, deep dust,
their visits or shoppings were made in little, low four-wheeled
carriages, drawn by natives, who, out of compliment to their
mistresses, consented to mount short-flapped shirts when in
service. A white woman in full toilet was still a sufficient curiosity to attract a crowd; consequently, if one went out, she was
soon surrounded with a cortege of men and maidens, more or

less in a state of nudity, all bent upon studying the fashions with an eagerness proportioned to their own want of clothing. . . .

A few of the chiefs had attempted crude imitations of foreign houses, but most of them were lodged in more ample and better-constructed straw huts than the common sort. Some were really very neat and attractive in their way, and far more convenient and comfortable to their owners than the more ambitious experiments of those who had thrown away their money upon foreign mechanics. The exteriors of these were, in general, more or less dilapidated, and the grounds about them parched and barren. Their interiors presented an incongruous mixture of white and native habits and articles. Huge state beds to look at, and piles of fine cool mats to sleep upon. Chairs and sofas backed rigidly and uselessly against the walls while their owners squatted upon the floors. Velvets and porcelain were snubbed by tapas and calabashes. Fleas and other vermin revelled amid the sweets of cologne and attar of roses. At dinner, you might be served, one day, reclining on the ground, with baked dog or live fish, by your own fingers, from a common wooden platter; and the next, sit comfortably upright at a high table, horrified at the rapacity and awkwardness with which your aristocratic hosts devoured paté de foie gras with the aid of silver forks, and engulfed champagne from the costliest crystal. But everywhere you went you were sure to see, conspicuously displayed, a huge Bible, printed in the native language. It had completely exorcised all other gods, and was held in a degree of reverence and affection which gave it an almost supernatural character. Yet its precepts, though gaining ground, were but indifferently appreciated by many church members. How could it be expected that these sensuous, sensual natures should be suddenly transformed by sermons and threats into missionary asceticism! Their white instructors in taking away their games, dances, festivals, and wars had given them nothing in return as an outlet of their animal energies. A polka or waltz was proscribed as a device of the devil. Theatricals were something worse. Horse races were no better than hell's tournaments. Even smoking was made a capital sin,

and tattooing was the mark of the beast. National songs and
festivals all smacked of eternal damnation. There was absolutely nothing left to the poor native for the indulgence of
his physical forces, or the development of his intellectual, but
that which he hated most, hard labor and theological reading.

In the latter his choice was limited to the Bible, a few
hymns, and elementary schoolbooks. The most rigid principles
of the most rigid of Protestant sects were made the standard of
salvation for the most sensualized of races. The poor native
was to labor to attain to the sanctity of men and women who
rarely smiled and dared not joke; whose intellectual excite-
ments, in general, were preaching and praying; who led lives
of rigid abstinence from all the usual pleasures of life; whose
greatest dissipation was a tea party, enlivened by prayer and
serious discourse; who produced and reared numerous children
in the same straitlaced way; comfortable in their homes and
tables; neat, orderly, and exact in every circumstance; plain,
somber, and tasteless in speech, dress, and deportments; preferring, from principle, the desert side of life to its amenities;
worshiping the Jehovah of Moses — a harsh, retributive, cruel
being, softened only through the sufferings of the innocent and
pure Jesus, who was equally God and his son, and yet neither
were able to give salvation, except through the capricious inter-
vention of a third god, called the Holy Ghost, and these three
were one god — such, in brief, were the examples and doctrines of Christianity the astonished Polynesian had presented
to him to replace his own effete religious system. On the other
hand, he had before him the careless lives of numerous white
visitors or settlers, who resembled the missionaries in nothing
but color. They neither prayed nor preached. They smoked,
drank, and were merry, after the desires of their own flesh.
They took to themselves wives or mistresses, as interest or
passion dictated. They labored for money, but spent it freely.
Some were renegade sailors, to whom the change from a fore-
castle to this sensuous climate and sensuous people was a paradise. Others were of every grade of life, from the honest,
industrious mechanic, seeking a competency to take him back

to his own village, amid the granite hills of New England, where his constant Susan impatiently awaited him, to the intelligent merchant or educated stranger, who, in visiting these shores, brought with him the enterprise, refinement, and experience which made him a valuable citizen at home.

Between the bigoted missionary and the profane, licentious renegade, most likely an escaped Botany Bay convict, there being every gradation of intelligence and morals, society was kept from the open warfare or anarchy into which the two extremes would otherwise have forced it. The missionary was, in fact, a far more useful and agreeable man than his catechism would indicate; and the trader was not so bad a man as the missionary would make him out to be. Both were necessary ingredients in the social reorganization. The one, it is true, protested against and would annihilate the entire past, because it was born of his mortal enemy, heathenism. The other served to keep alive and give play to the inborn instincts of human nature, slowly and surely refining them to the conditions of civilized life; and the missionary, on his part, as he better learned his mission, fought less uncompromisingly against humanity, seeking to purify its impulses, and direct them to loftier ends.

When I arrived, a fierce hostility was raging between the two parties. The Guelf and Ghibelline factions of Italy were more bloody, but not more sincere in their mutual opposition and denunciations. The missionaries were by far the most powerful. They not only represented the progressive moral principles of this strange society, but were bound together by a sincere zeal and piety, against which their opponents could only offer a sort of skirmishing opposition of outwardly selfish interests, or dubious pleasures. They had, besides, the great advantage of being the actual government.

When the missionaries landed on these islands, the old form of religion, with its idol worshipers, had almost quietly died out, from the twofold cause of its own lost vitality and the skepticism of the people, derived from intercourse with white traders. The result was as unbridled a licentiousness and tyranny as a sensualized race and omnipotent oligarchy could devise. Such influence as their old religion had when it represented to a certain extent conservative or restraining ideas was now gone, and the aborigines were abandoned to the anarchy of their passions, curbed only by the selfish interests of a tyrannical government. Social corruption, under the patronage of infidelity, was, in fact, holding its last saturnalia.

In the height of this revolution, the missionaries arrived, and began their preaching. Even the lowest class of whites had come to revolt at the horrible orgies and scenes of violence they had witnessed; so they rather welcomed than otherwise the newcomers. Soon, some of the chiefs, wearied of their debaucheries, were attracted. Two classes of converts came quickly to them: the best minds, which gladly availed themselves of a newer and pure knowledge; and those that having gone to one extreme of folly and wickedness were anxious to expiate it by going to the other extreme of faith and virtue. These two made the new religion fashionable. It speedily became a state power, and after its kind, owing to the zeal and ignorance of the new converts, an ecclesiastical despotism, which would have been almost as intolerable, in the end, as the old order of things, had it not been for the greater enlightenment of some of the missionaries, and the continual opposition of the foreign population to the extreme measures the chiefs sought to impose upon their people for the forcible furtherance of Christianity. The leaven of foreign opposition and example derived from the white settlers alone prevented the reign of the saints from being absolute. As it was, the enactments which attended their ascendancy were of the most arbitrary character, having for their object not only to root out every vestige of heathen ideas and customs but to compel every inhabitant to an observance of laws whose spirit was derived almost exclusively from the Mosaic dispensation.

No people ever underwent a more forcible and thorough outward change than these unfortunate aborigines, in less than a score of years. There was some resistance and fighting, at the first, resulting from the expiring force of the old in contact with the new faith. But, as soon as the latter was fully adopted by the chiefs, their people acquiesced, and upon the whole welcomed a moral reaction, which exchanged the violence and degradation of excessive sensuality for the order, strictness, and sobriety of their new religion. They gave up, though at first not without a murmur, their dances and songs, their feastings and licentious revelries, their games, and even their tattooings, the superfluous wives and drunken debaucheries — all that was in itself harmless as well as what was vicious which belonged to their former belief — and in exchange accepted the Bible, meetinghouse, schoolroom, and prayer circle, and loyally sustained their chiefs in their inquisitorial spread of new ideas. The external reform soon became as extreme as the previous undisguised vice.

One who frequented only missionary circles would have concluded that Puritanism had revived in Polynesia. Many of their chiefs and their retinues were sincerely pious, and, considering their antecedents, exceedingly exemplary in their deportment. With but few exceptions, the people at large devoutly conformed in their external conduct to the new order of things. But it would have been contrary to their common sense to have accepted the outward for the true view.

The same extraordinary intermixture of civilization and barbarism that was to be observed in their household effects was equally perceptible in their morals, apart from the restraint of missionary vision. Within sound of one of Watts' hymns, as sung by a native choir, the curious visitor would be cautiously conducted into the premises of a high chief, who was surreptitiously indulging himself in witnessing wanton dances by young, half-clad maidens, followed by scenes not to be described.

A little further off, he might hear through the open windows of a merchant's house the enlivening notes of waltz or cracovienne. Nearer by, the monotonous tones of natives, earnestly praying to Jehovah, would strike his ear, interrupted, perhaps, by the profane and vulgar mirth of groggy sailors ashore on a spree, but kept like wild animals chafing within the limits of some white man's enclosure, from which they and their female companions could sally forth only at the risk of being arrested by native constables, greedy to collect the fines imposed upon drunkenness or debauchery. Should he wander into one of those huts so recently the scene of a devotion, its owner — a church member, perhaps a deacon — would not unlikely welcome him in the spirit of the former hospitality of his race, and inquire if it would be agreeable to him to have a female to share his couch. Possibly the next day he would meet the same woman at hard labor on the public highways, betrayed by a spy, and condemned to an infamous punishment for indulging in what in her early youth she had been taught to consider as a virtue, but which now was very properly denounced as a vice. . . .

I cannot give better an idea of the state of morals among this race at this period than in the words often used by themselves: "Me mikonaree here," pointing to the head; "*aole* mikonaree," no missionary here, designating the rest of the body. Brass joined to clay they indeed were.

From *Why and What Am I? The Confessions of an Enquirer* by James J. Jarves (Boston, Philips, Sampson and Co., 1857).

F. A. OLMSTED

# BULLOCK HUNTERS
# OF THE KOHALA RANGE

Cowboys are hardly what one would expect to find on a Pacific
island. The history of the cattle industry in Hawaii, however,
goes back to 1793, when George Vancouver gave King Kamehameha some longhorns from Santa Barbara, California. The
king placed a tabu upon killing the herds which grazed on the
island of Hawaii. They increased and ran wild for some years,
laying waste to the forests and damaging the taro patches of
the villagers. An American from Massachusetts, John Palmer
Parker, settled at Waimea in 1815 to take care of the royal herds
and market the hides. This was the origin of the immense Parker
Ranch of today, one of the largest under the American flag.

Francis Allyn Olmsted (1819–1844), while a student at Yale,
was advised for his health to seek a more temperate climate. He
went as a passenger on a whale ship which cruised in the Pacific.
The bullock hunters described by Olmsted after he had visited
the Waimea region in 1840 foreshadowed the Hawaiian cowboys of today. The Hawaiians, taught by Spanish *vaqueros*
brought from California, soon excelled in the riding and roping
arts. Even now, the native word for cowboy is *paniolo*, from
*español* or Spaniard.

THE FIRST THING WE ATTENDED TO, UPON LANDING, WAS TO MAKE
immediate preparations for a walk to Waimea, a settlement
among the mountains about fifteen miles from the coast. The
impossibility of procuring any accommodations for the night
obliged us to set off on the Sabbath, much against our wishes.
A couple of natives were engaged by my comrades to transport

77

their baggage, although it had been expressly told me that it was to be left behind, and forwarded the next day. When I requested a delay of a few minutes, until a native could be engaged by me, I was answered by two of the party setting off without me, which compelled me to seize one or two necessary articles and hurry along after them. It was most intolerably hot; the sun was blazing down in all his intensity, while scarcely a breath of wind mitigated his ardor. In addition to this, contrary to my repeated suggestions, the party were so impatient to proceed that they did not provide themselves with any water, and were it not for a pineapple we had with us, I should have suffered extremely from thirst. For the first eight miles the heat was very oppressive, and a thick woolen jacket together with a heavy pea jacket strapped to my back by no means contributed to my comfort. About nine miles from Kawaihae, a cold rain came driving down from the mountains, and instantly checked the perspiration that was flowing from me in streams, so that before I had walked more than a mile or two farther, I was seized with violent rheumatic pains. . . .

It was now growing dark, and I had been revolving in my mind how I should spend the night in the native huts which were scattered along the road, as the severe pain I experienced seemed to forbid any farther exertion.

About eight o'clock, we came up with a collection of thatched houses, towards the principal one of which we directed our steps, which was a store belonging to Mr. French of Honolulu. Here a novel scene presented itself to us. In front of the door, a bright fire was blazing in a cavity in the earthen floor, displaying in strong light the dark features, of the natives congregated around it in their grotesque attitudes. Immediately back of these, a group of fine-looking men, in a peculiar costume, were leaning against the counter of the store. Some of them were Spaniards from California, and they were all attired in the poncho, an oblong blanket of various brilliant colors, having a hole in the middle through which the head is thrust. The pantaloons are open from the knee downwards on the outside, with a row of dashing gilt buttons along the outside seam. A pair of boots armed with prodigiously long spurs completed their costume. They were "bullock hunters," employed in capturing the wild bullocks that roam the mountains, and had just returned from an expedition of eight or ten days, in which they had been very successful.

After a delicious cup of tea and some excellent beefsteaks, we adjourned to our place for spending the night, about three quarters of a mile distant. Grimes took it upon himself to be the pilot, but after stumbling about among the bogs, and being exposed to a cold wind and rain for more than half an hour, we were obliged to return and get a native for our guide. Our bed consisted of layers of thick mats, upon which the usual bedding was spread out. The beds of the natives are nothing more than several large mats laid one upon the other, making a slight elevation above the floor, as in the present instance. The chiefs, not infrequently, take fifteen or twenty of these mats for a bed, the area of which is sometimes ten or twelve feet square. . . .

Our principal object in taking the walk was to witness the marking of a lot of cattle that had been driven down from the mountains not long since. Great numbers of wild bullocks are caught in the mountains every year by the hunters. The lasso, the principal instrument in their capture, is made of braided thongs, upon one end of which is a ring forming a slip noose, which is thrown with astonishing precision around any part of the animal. Even while at full gallop in pursuit, the hunter grasps his lasso, and giving it two or three twirls around his head with the right hand throws it unerringly and entangles his victim by the horns or limbs. And now, be wary for thy life, bold hunter; for the savage animal is maddened with terror. See, he turns upon his pursuer, with eyeballs glaring with fire and his frame quivering with rage. But the well-trained horse springs to one side, and braces himself, while the unwieldy animal plunges forward, but is suddenly brought up by the lasso, and falls with a heavy momentum on the ground. Again he rises, and tears the ground with his hoofs, and loudly roars; then doubly furious, comes down upon his pursuer, but is again

avoided and again dashed upon the ground. Exhausted by repeated shocks like these, his fury is subdued and he allows himself to be secured to a tame bullock, which soon removes all
his ferocity.

The bullocks of the mountains were till within a year or
two very numerous and savage, so that traveling among the
mountains was attended with great danger. For their capture,
a mode frequently resorted to by the hunters was to dig deep
pits and cover them over with underbrush and dirt. A very
melancholy casualty occurred three or four years since among
the mountains. A gentleman named Douglas, of distinguished
attainments as a naturalist, was engaged in a scientific expedition to the volcano. He had nearly accomplished the objects of
his excursion when he met with an awful fate. As he was leaving
an encampment where he had spent the night, he was particularly cautioned respecting three bullock pits that lay along
the path he was expecting to take. He mistook the directions
given him, it is presumed, for the first that was seen of him
afterwards was when he was discovered by some natives, in one
of the bullock pits under the feet of a savage bull, who was
trampling upon him and goring him in the most terrific manner! The bull was very soon killed, and the mangled body of
the unfortunate naturalist drawn out, but life had long since
become extinct.

The Spanish saddle is of very different construction from the
saddles of our country in general use, and to myself is far
preferable. It rises very high before and behind, rendering
it much easier for the rider, especially in ascending or descending hills. The pommel is surmounted by a large flat knot,
termed the "loggerhead," from which the lasso of the hunter
depends. A pair of large wooden stirrups with a broad piece
of leather before each, to protect the feet in traversing a region
where the bushes grow thickly together, are also peculiarities
of the Spanish saddle. Their horses are governed with powerful
bits, such as would be intolerable to our horses, and are allowed free rein, which seemed very strange to me, who had
always been accustomed to see the equestrian exhausting the

strength of his arms to keep his horse from stumbling. With us, a pull upon either rein teaches the horse which way we would have him go, whereas with the Spanish horse, the reins are gently pressed against that side of the neck in the direction in which he is to turn. The bullocks to be marked were driven into a pen towards which we directed our steps. They were noble animals, and had been tamed by tying them singly with tame cattle for a time. I had here some slight exhibition of the skill with which the lasso is thrown. One of the bullocks was selected from the herd, and in an instant the lasso was firmly entangled around his horns or legs, and he was thrown down and pinioned. The burning brand was then applied, and after sundry bellowings and other indications of disapprobation, the poor animal was released. There were not far from forty bullocks marked on this occasion, intended for the *Clementine,* in her trip down to Honolulu, fellow passengers of your humble servant. They are there put into pasture, to be fattened for the supply of ships visiting Honolulu in the fall season.

From *Incidents of a Whaling Voyage* by F. A. Olmsted (New York, D. Appleton and Company, 1841).

Sophia Cracroft

# TWO VICTORIAN LADIES
# VISIT HONOLULU

A middle-aged English lady with a sharp eye and abundant zest for new scenes and experiences toured the Hawaiian Islands in the summer of 1861. She was Sophia Cracroft (1816–1892), a niece of the renowned Arctic explorer Sir John Franklin and the lifelong companion of his remarkable wife, Lady Jane Franklin. When it was learned definitely in 1859 that Sir John, who had gone in search of the Northwest Passage in 1845, had perished with his men on the northern ice, the two ladies embarked on travels which in time brought them to Honolulu during the reign of young Kamehameha IV and his part-English wife Emma. The charming queen was friendly, and it was her pleasure to entertain these two genteel visitors from her grandfather's country.

Miss Cracroft's letters home, recently published for the first time in a volume by Professor A. L. Korn of the University of Hawaii, contain vivid, entertaining, and sometimes acid sketches not only of court life and the principal persons in the government, but also of such matters as the education system and the amusements of the town. Punahou School, described in the selection that follows, had been founded twenty years earlier by the missionaries, and is still the best-known private school in Hawaii. The Colonel Kalakaua mentioned was destined to be king of Hawaii from 1874 to 1891; his sister became Queen Liliuokalani, who ruled from 1891 until her deposition in 1893. The Dr. Judd referred to was a medical missionary and a leader of the American colony in Honolulu. He was the husband of Laura Fish Judd, a portion of whose diary appears earlier in this collection.

TUESDAY, MAY 21, 1861. WE SET OFF AT TEN O'CLOCK TO SEE THE schools, and drove at once to the Palace, round the front, to a separate wing behind, in which are the private apartments. The queen is so modest and respectful that it is difficult to make her accept the position due to her; but my aunt refused to enter the carriage first, and insists that she shall walk first.

Mr. Allen, the chancellor, accompanied us. The king saw us off and has a council today upon questions of finance, his great trouble, as the revenue is diminishing year by year, owing to the falling off of the whaling trade. It is expected, however, that this will be for the ultimate good of the community even in a commercial sense, as the people will adopt other means of support than the furnishing of whale ships with supplies. The king, however, looked anxious and preoccupied, as well he might be.

We drove first to a little school of about forty children — girls and boys, all or mostly orphans, white or of mixed blood, in age from eight or nine to perhaps fifteen; some of the boys may have been as old. They are taught in English; the Hawaiian language is not allowed within the walls of the enclosure. Mr. Ingraham is, of course, an American, with the usual bad pronunciation of his race — for instance, a boy pronouncing "promontory" rightly was corrected and enjoined to say "prom-on*tory*." It is a primary school and payment is altogether voluntary. The children answered questions in geography and arithmetic and recited in poetry and prose, but I must say it was not easy to understand what they were repeating. Mr. Ingraham is assisted with the girls in sewing, etc., by a half-caste Hawaiian, Miss Chapman, who teaches them to sing in a childlike way.

From this primary school we drove to the Punahou College, a missionary school of the highest class, in which the children of the missionaries and other foreigners receive their education. They have as principals Mr. and Mrs. Mills, who have had charge for some years of a similar institution in Ceylon, and are highly esteemed, having it is said much improved upon the training formerly given. They have assistants, but chiefly Mr.

Alexander, son of a former missionary, who is considered an excellent classic and mathematician.

We were received at the door by Mr. and Mrs. Mills, and my aunt having insisted that once and for all the queen and not she should have precedence, we followed her to a large room in which the pupils were arranged on benches — girls on one side, boys on the other — in front of a raised platform on which were chairs for us. Many of the pupils were grown up and there were only two or three little girls. We were received with singing, all standing up, after which they fluttered down into their seats, the young ladies looking rather like a parterre (not closely packed, however: there is generally plenty of room given in these hot countries) as they were evidently in their best — short sleeves being not uncommon even in the morning here, with young people.

The boys were first brought forward in algebra, mathematics, Latin, and Greek, we must suppose to their own credit; but that is a point I do not feel able to give you any opinion upon! Then we were asked what the young ladies should be called upon to show off in — but the selection was quickly made for us: botany — which we have since learned to be a strong point in their training as amended from old times, under Mrs. Mills's rule. There were but few who did not stand up in this class. The questions were put by Mrs. Mills, and the young ladies answered in turn with perfect glibness as to the natural and Linnean systems, the structure of plants (with minute details), in the very words of a book — proving the excellence of their memories and the interest they took in the subject (from which exercise I drew the conclusion, not for the first time, that the study of botany would suit me less than most other subjects).

Having already paid a pretty long visit, we were going away when we were requested with much earnestness to let them show their calisthenic exercises. All but two or three girls walked out of the room by the door we had entered, set up singing in the passage and came in again in file, marched about here and there and separated into figures — a chain — joining hands and leaving off. Each change of figure was set to music

and accompanied by themselves, with a different song to each
change. We had "I'd Be a Butterfly," "We're a-Noddin'," 
with other hackneyed tunes of questionable taste, with words to
suit — sometimes they set forth the "beauty and grace" of the
performers, others had a pastoral turn, some trilled of garlands as typified by the fair Presbyterians before us! They did
not jig, nor waltz, nor was the polka indulged in, but if ever
the Lord was cheated, it was here!

Mr. Mills remarked to me how prettily they went through
the exercise, and I really could not help answering: "Very
much so indeed, but it is *dancing*." He did not look angry,
which he really might have been excused for doing, but answered: "We like to give the children ease and grace of movement, and they enjoy these exercises very much!" Since then,
in a newspaper report of the yearly examinations at this college,
the afore-described "calisthenics" are (with complete com-
mendation) dubbed "Presbyterian dancing."

I ought to have said that the young men and boys did part
of the looking on. There were also several ladies present; and
after this they were all introduced — Mrs. Cooke in particular,
who with her husband had kept the school for chief's children,
where the king was educated as well as others (girls as well as
boys) of the same rank. We did not perceive anything remarkable about her; but she is much respected by her former
pupils, more so than her husband is. The queen was very cordial
to her (she used to receive some lessons at the establishment,
though she never lived there I think) and her manner to all the
ladies was charming in its perfect simplicity and kindness. All
were delighted to see her and begged she would come again,
which she promised to do with great readiness and spoke of the
great pleasure she had in coming. We were introduced to some
more of the missionaries' wives, of whom there is a great gathering in Honolulu just now with their husbands, for the conference.

We afterwards went to Mr. and Mrs. Mills's private residence, and saw some curiosities they brought from Ceylon. They
seem sensible people and have done much good here in the

college, we hear. The college lies about a mile and a half beyond the town, nearly under the hills and back from the seashore. Amongst the pupils was Mrs. Judd's youngest daughter, a girl of fifteen or sixteen with a heavy, large figure, whose "grace and beauty" certainly did *not* shine in the mazy turns and airy movements of the "calisthenics."

Here ended our first day's labor of inspection. On our return we received a message from the king, who had decided during our absence upon attending an exhibition in biology to be given this evening in the theater, and desired Mr. Wyllie to invite us to go down to the Palace and join their party. The operator is a passenger by a ship going from Australia to California, and a professional biologist, Professor Bushell.

We accepted the invitation and went down again to the Palace in the evening and thence to the theater with the king and queen, attended by several gentlemen and ladies. Our friend Colonel Kalakaua was the A.D.C. on duty — his sister (as pure Hawaiian as himself, in reality as well as in appearance) being next to the queen — my aunt and I next to the king, in front of the stage, of which we had an excellent view. Mr. Bushell had already held three exhibitions, and it was the fame of these which made the king desirous of seeing what could be done.

He began by inviting people to come on the stage to be experimented upon, and from the front row below, which was filled with medical men, Dr. Judd started up and ascended the stage amidst great applause. The whole number was about twenty and all were more or less known to the audience — some were natives, but the great majority white, and very respectable-looking persons. After going through the usual process, certain individuals on whom it had no effect were dismissed while others were retained, among them a young man on whom it had extraordinary power — the higher phenomena being developed.

This over, Mr. Bushell selected Dr. Judd as his next subject and proceeded to show off his power over him. We heard whispered speculations whether "the doctor" were acting or *really* under the influence. At last he stopped short and said he did not feel anything: that he had never been under any influence and, farther, that he did not believe that any could be exerted unless the subject participated with the operator. He did not *say*, but he implied, that on his part it was participation with what Mr. Bushell wished to show rather than an exhibition of real sensations. You can imagine the effect of such a proceeding. All around us seemed to feel, as we did, that Dr. Judd acted a very unworthy and undignified part in pretending to show phenomena, and we sympathized with the professor, who fairly complained that he had not called for *deception*, but on the contrary wished for nothing but the truth, having come alone among perfect strangers to exhibit facts of frequent and common occurrence in Europe. He did not wish anyone to feign symptoms which in most cases he knew to be real, though he was well aware that there were many persons not susceptible of mesmeric influence.

He behaved really very well under great provocation, and his remonstrances and reflections upon Dr. Judd were perfectly justifiable and made in good taste. You can imagine the effect of such an episode upon the assembly, every one of whom knew Dr. Judd intimately. Many said to us that it was "just like the doctor — he never cared or wished to do a thing openly and never minded being found out!"

*We* were not surprised after having heard so many instances of his secret working in the politics of this country, in the crisis of annexation so very nearly effected by him, in the settlement of the basis of the representation of the people, and other public questions of vital importance. He did not seem disturbed by what had taken place, but remained in his seat on the stage during the remainder of the proceedings (which, I may add, could not *possibly fail* to convince him that some persons may be extraordinarily influenced). But as he came down to go away, we heard a slight (and well-deserved) hiss. We passed him riding home on our way back to Mr. Wyllie's in the queen's open carriage — but he did not speak.

From *The Victorian Visitors* by Alfons L. Korn (Honolulu, University of Hawaii Press, 1958).

M ARK  T WAIN

# EQUESTRIAN EXCURSION
# TO DIAMOND HEAD

Samuel Langhorne Clemens (1835–1910) was not yet famous as
"Mark Twain" when in 1866 he spent four months in Hawaii as
a roving reporter for the Sacramento *Weekly Union.*

An insatiable sightseer, Mark rode around the islands on a
hack horse, covering many aspects of Hawaiian life for his newspaper. After a month in Honolulu he went to the island of Maui,
visiting Iao Valley and the enormous crater of Haleakala. He
then took a schooner to the Kona Coast on the island of Hawaii,
and climbed around the Kilauea volcano district.

For the rest of his life, Mark Twain remembered Hawaii as
"the loveliest fleet of islands that lies anchored in any ocean."
His visit also gave him a new and lucrative profession, for his
famous lecture on the Hawaiian Islands was his star turn for
seven years. As late as 1884 Mark Twain began to write a novel
with a Hawaiian setting.

The following account of a trip to Waikiki and Diamond
Head in the horse-and-buggy days of Hawaii foreshadows Mark
Twain's fame as America's foremost humorist.

I AM PROBABLY THE MOST SENSITIVE MAN IN THE KINGDOM OF
Hawaii tonight — especially about sitting down in the presence
of my betters. I have ridden fifteen or twenty miles on horseback
since 5 P.M., and to tell the honest truth, I have a delicacy
about sitting down at all. I am one of the poorest horsemen in
the world, and I never mount a horse without experiencing a
sort of dread that I may be setting out on that last mysterious
journey which all of us must take sooner or later, and I never

88

come back in safety from a horseback trip without thinking of my latter end for two or three days afterward. This same old regular devotional sentiment began just as soon as I sat down here five minutes ago.

An excursion to Diamond Head and the King's Coconut Grove was planned today — time, 4:30 P.M. — the party to consist of half a dozen gentlemen and three ladies. They all started at the appointed hour except myself. I was at the Government Prison, and got so interested in its examination that I did not notice how quickly the time was passing. Somebody remarked that it was twenty minutes past five o'clock, and that woke me up. It was a fortunate circumstance that Captain Phillips was there with his "turn-out," as he calls a top-buggy that Captain Cook brought here in 1778, and a horse that was here when Captain Cook came. Captain Phillips takes a just pride in his driving and in the speed of his horse, and to his passion for displaying them I owe it that we were only sixteen minutes coming from the prison to the American Hotel — a distance which has been estimated to be over half a mile. But it took some awful driving. The Captain's whip came down fast, and the blows started so much dust out of the horse's hide that during the last half of the journey we rode through an impenetrable fog, and ran by a pocket compass in the hands of Captain Fish, a whaler captain of twenty-six years' experience, who sat there through that perilous voyage as self-possessed as if he had been on the euchre-deck of his own ship, and calmly said, "Port your helm — port," from time to time, and "Hold her a little free — steady — so-o," and "Luff — hard down to starboard!" and never once lost his presence of mind or betrayed the least anxiety by voice or manner. When we came to anchor at last, and Captain Phillips looked at his watch and said, "Sixteen minutes — I told you it was in her! that's over three miles an hour!" I could see he felt entitled to a compliment, so I said I had never seen lightning go like that horse. And I never had.

The landlord of the American said the party had been gone nearly an hour, but that he could give me my choice of several

horses that could easily overtake them. I said, never mind — I
preferred a safe horse to a fast one — I would like to have an
excessively gentle horse — a horse with no spirit whatever —
a lame one, if he had such a thing. Inside of five minutes I was
mounted, and perfectly satisfied with my outfit. I had no time
to label him "This is a horse," and so if the public took him
for a sheep I cannot help it. I was satisfied, and that was the
main thing. I could see that he had as many fine points as
any man's horse, and I just hung my hat on one of them, behind
the saddle, and swabbed the perspiration from my face and
started. I named him after this island, "Oahu" (pronounced
O-wa-hoo). The first gate he came to he started in; I had
neither whip nor spur, and so I simply argued the case with
him. He firmly resisted argument, but ultimately yielded to insult and abuse. He backed out of the gate and steered for another one on the other side of the street. I triumphed by my
former process. Within the next six hundred yards he crossed
the street fourteen times and attempted thirteen gates, and in
the meantime the tropical sun was beating down and threatening to cave the top of my head in, and I was literally dripping
with perspiration and profanity. (I am only human and I was
sorely aggravated. I shall behave better next time.) He quit
the gate business after that and went along peaceably enough,
but absorbed in meditation. I noticed this latter circumstance,
and it soon began to fill me with the gravest apprehension.
I said to myself, this malignant brute is planning some new
outrage, some fresh deviltry or other — no horse ever thought
over a subject so profoundly as this one is doing just for
nothing. The more this thing preyed upon my mind the more
uneasy I became, until at last the suspense became unbearable
and I dismounted to see if there was anything wild in his eye
— for I had heard that the eye of this noblest of our domestic
animals is very expressive. I cannot describe what a load
of anxiety was lifted from my mind when I found that he
was only asleep. I woke him up and started him into a faster
walk, and then the inborn villainy of his nature came out again.
He tried to climb over a stone wall, five or six feet high. I saw

that I must apply force to this horse, and that I might as well begin first as last. I plucked a stout switch from a tamarind tree, and the moment he saw it, he gave in. He broke into a convulsive sort of a canter, which had three short steps in it and one long one, and reminded me alternately of the clattering shake of the great earthquake, and the sweeping plunging of the *Ajax* in a storm. . . .

This is a good time to drop in a paragraph of information. There is no regular livery stable in Honolulu, or, indeed, in any part of the kingdom of Hawaii; therefore, unless you are acquainted with wealthy residents (who all have good horses), you must hire animals of the vilest description from the Kanakas. Any horse you hire, even though it be from a white man, is not often of much account, because it will be brought in for you from some ranch, and has necessarily been leading a hard life. If the Kanakas who have been caring for him (inveterate riders they are) have not ridden him half to death every day themselves, you can depend upon it they have been doing the same thing by proxy, by clandestinely hiring him out. At least, so I am informed. The result is that no horse has a chance to eat, drink, rest, recuperate, or look well or feel well, and so strangers go about the islands mounted as I was today.

In hiring a horse from a Kanaka, you must have all your eyes about you, because you can rest satisfied that you are dealing with as shrewd a rascal as ever patronized a penitentiary. You may leave your door open and your trunk unlocked as long as you please, and he will not meddle with your property; he has no important vices and no inclination to commit robbery on a large scale; but if he can get ahead of you in the horse business, he will take a genuine delight in doing it. This trait is characteristic of horse jockeys the world over, is it not? He will overcharge you if he can; he will hire you a fine-looking horse at night (anybody's — maybe the king's, if the royal steed be in convenient view), and bring you the mate to my Oahu in the morning, and contend that it is the same animal. If you raise a row, he will get out by saying it was not himself who made the bargain with you, but his brother, "who went out in the country this morning." They have always got a "brother" to shift the responsibility upon. A victim said to one of these fellows one day:

"But I know I hired the horse of you, because I noticed that scar on your cheek."

The reply was not bad: "Oh, yes — yes — my brother all same — we twins!"

A friend of mine, J. Smith, hired a horse yesterday, the Kanaka warranting him to be in excellent condition. Smith had a saddle and blanket of his own, and he ordered the Kanaka to put these on the horse. The Kanaka protested that he was perfectly willing to trust the gentleman with the saddle that was already on the animal, but Smith refused to use it. The change was made; then Smith noticed that the Kanaka had changed only the saddles, and had left the original blanket on the horse; he said he forgot to change the blankets, and so, to cut the bother short, Smith mounted and rode away. The horse went lame a mile from town, and afterward got to cutting up some extraordinary capers. Smith got down and took off the saddle, but the blanket stuck fast to the horse — glued to a procession of raw sores. The Kanaka's mysterious conduct stood explained.

Another friend of mine bought a pretty good horse from a native, a day or two ago, after a tolerably thorough examination of the animal. He discovered today that the horse was as blind as a bat, in one eye. He meant to have examined that eye, and came home with a general notion that he had done it; but he remembers now that every time he made the attempt his attention was called to something else by his victimizer. . . .

I wandered along the sea beach on my steed Oahu around the base of the extinct crater of Leahi, or Diamond Head, and a quarter of a mile beyond the point I overtook the party of ladies and gentlemen and assumed my proper place — that is, in the rear — for the horse I ride always persists in remaining in the rear in spite of kicks, cuffs and curses. I was satisfied as long as I could keep Oahu within hailing distance of the cavalcade — I knew I could accomplish nothing better even if Oahu were Norfolk himself.

We went on — on — on — a great deal too far, I thought, for people who were unaccustomed to riding on horseback, and who must expect to suffer on the morrow if they indulged too freely in this sort of exercise. Finally we got to a point which we were expecting to go around in order to strike an easy road home; but we were too late; it was full tide and the sea had closed in on the shore. Young Henry McFarlane said he knew a nice, comfortable route over the hill — a short cut — and the crowd dropped into his wake. We climbed a hill a hundred and fifty feet high, and about as straight up and down as the side of a house, and as full of rough lava blocks as it could stick — not as wide, perhaps, as the broad road that leads to destruction, but nearly as dangerous to travel, and apparently leading in the same general direction. I felt for the ladies, but I had no time to speak any words of sympathy, by reason of my attention being so much occupied by Oahu. The place was so steep that at times he stood straight up on his tiptoes and clung by his forward toenails, with his back to the Pacific Ocean and his nose close to the moon — and thus situated we formed an equestrian picture which was as uncomfortable to me as it may have been picturesque to the spectators. You may think I was afraid, but I was not. I knew I could stay on him as long as his ears did not pull out.

It was great relief to me to know that we were all safe and sound on the summit at last, because the sun was just disappearing in the waves, night was abroad in the land, candles and lamps were already twinkling in the distant town, and we gratefully reflected that Henry had saved us from having to go back around that rocky, sandy beach. But a new trouble arose while the party were admiring the rising moon and the cool, balmy night breeze, with its odor of countless flowers, for it was discovered that we had got into a place we could not get out of — we were apparently surrounded by precipices — our pilot's chart was at fault, and he could not extricate us, and so we had the prospect before us of either spending the night in the admired night breeze, under the admired moon, or of clambering down the way we came, in the dark. However, a Kanaka came along presently and found a first-rate road for us down an almost imperceptible decline, and the party set out on a cheerful gallop again, and Oahu struck up his miraculous canter once more. The moon rose up, and flooded mountain and valley and ocean with silvery light, and I was not sorry we had lately been in trouble, because the consciousness of being safe again raised our spirits, and made us more capable of enjoying the beautiful scene than we would have been otherwise. I never breathed such a soft, delicious atmosphere before, nor one freighted with such rich fragrance. A barber shop is nothing to it.

Gaily laughing and talking, the party galloped on, and with set teeth and bouncing body I clung to the pommel and cantered after. Presently we came to a place where no grass grew — a wide expanse of deep sand. They said it was an old battleground. All around everywhere, not three feet apart, the bleached bones of men gleamed white in the moonlight. We picked up a lot of them for mementos. I got quite a number of arm bones and leg bones — of great chiefs, maybe, who had fought savagely in that fearful battle in the old days, when blood flowed like wine where we now stood — and wore the choicest of them out on Oahu afterward, trying to make him go. All sorts of bones could be found except skulls; but a citizen said, irreverently, that there had been an unusual number of "skull hunters" there lately — a species of sportsmen I had never heard of before. . . .

Nothing whatever is known about this place — its story is a secret that will never be revealed. The oldest natives make no pretense of being possessed of its history. They say these bones were here when they were children. They were here when their grandfathers were children — but how they came here, they can only conjecture. Many people believe this spot to be an ancient battleground, and it is usual to call it so; and they believe that these skeletons have lain for ages just where their proprietors fell in the great fight. Other people believe that Kamehameha I fought his first battle here. On this point, I have heard a story, which may have been taken from one of the numerous books which have been written concerning these islands — I do not know where the narrator got it. He said that when Kamehameha (who was at first merely a subordinate chief on the island of Hawaii), landed here, he brought a large army with him, and encamped at Waikiki. The Oahuans marched against him, and so confident were they of success that they readily acceded to a demand of their priests that they should draw a line where these bones now lie, and take an oath that, if forced to retreat at all, they would never retreat beyond this boundary. The priests told them that death and everlasting punishment would overtake any who violated the oath, and the march was resumed. Kamehameha drove them back step by step; the priests fought in the front rank and exhorted them both by voice and inspiriting example to remember their oath — to die, if need be, but never cross the fatal line. The struggle was manfully maintained, but at last the chief priest fell, pierced to the heart with a spear, and the unlucky omen fell like a blight upon the brave souls at his back; with a triumphant shout the invaders pressed forward — the line was crossed — the offended gods deserted the despairing army, and, accepting the doom their perjury had brought upon them, they broke and fled over the plain where Honolulu stands now — up the beautiful Nuuanu Valley — paused a moment, hemmed in by precipitous mountains on either hand and the frightful precipice of the Pari (pronounced *Pally;* intelligent natives claim that there is no *r* in the Kanaka alphabet) in front, and then were driven over — a sheer plunge of six hundred feet!

The story is pretty enough, but Mr. Jarves' excellent history says the Oahuans were intrenched in Nuuanu Valley; that Kamehameha ousted them, routed them, pursued them up the valley and drove them over the precipice. He makes no mention of our boneyard at all in his book.

There was a terrible pestilence here in 1804 which killed great numbers of the inhabitants, and the natives have legends of others that swept the islands long before that; and therefore many persons now believe that these bones belonged to victims of one of these epidemics who were hastily buried in a great pit. It is by far the most reasonable conjecture, because

Jarves says that the weapons of the islanders were so rude and inefficient that their battles were not often very bloody. If this was a battle it was astonishingly deadly, for in spite of the depredations of "skull hunters," we rode a considerable distance over ground so thickly strewn with human bones that the horses' feet crushed them, not occasionally, but at every step.

Impressed by the profound silence and repose that rested over the beautiful landscape, and being, as usual, in the rear, I gave voice to my thoughts. I said:

"What a picture is here slumbering in the solemn glory of the moon! How strong the rugged outlines of the dead volcano stand out against the clear sky! What a snowy fringe marks the bursting of the surf over the long, curved reef! How calmly the dim city sleeps yonder in the plain! How soft the shadows lie upon the stately mountains that border the dream-haunted Manoa Valley! What a grand pyramid of billowy clouds towers above the storied Pari! How the grim warriors of the past seem flocking in ghostly squadrons to their ancient battlefield again — how the wails of the dying well up from the — "

At this point the horse called Oahu deliberately sat down in the sand. Sat down to listen, I suppose. Never mind what he heard. I stopped apostrophizing and convinced him that I was not a man to allow Contempt of Court on the part of a horse. I broke the backbone of a chief over his rump and set out to join the cavalcade again.

Very considerably fagged out we arrived in town at 9 o'clock at night, myself in the lead — for when my horse finally came to understand that he was homeward bound and hadn't far to go, he threw his legs wildly out before and behind him, depressed his head and laid his ears back, and flew by the admiring company like a telegram. In five minutes he was far away ahead of everybody.

From Sacramento, California, *Weekly Union*, April 28, 1866.

# MARK TWAIN

# A VISIT
# TO THE VOLCANO

Travelers for more than a century have vied with each other in trying to paint word pictures of the beauties and terrors of Kilauea Volcano on the island of Hawaii, in what is now a part of Hawaii National Park. One of the best accounts is that by Mark Twain, describing his visit to the volcano in 1866. Although the fire pit of Halemaumau was not in violent eruption at the time he saw it, the sight was enough to awe even that inveterate humorist into writing in a more serious vein than usual.

WE GOT BACK TO THE SCHOONER IN GOOD TIME, AND THEN SAILED down to Kau, where we disembarked and took final leave of the vessel. Next day we bought horses and bent our way over the summer-clad mountain terraces, toward the great volcano of Kilauea. We made nearly a two days' journey of it, but that was on account of laziness. Toward sunset on the second day, we reached an elevation of some four thousand feet above sea level, and as we picked our careful way through billowy wastes of lava long generations ago stricken dead and cold in the climax of its tossing fury, we began to come upon signs of the near presence of the volcano — signs in the nature of ragged fissures that discharged jets of sulphurous vapor into the air, hot from the molten ocean down in the bowels of the mountain.

Shortly the crater came into view. I have seen Vesuvius since, but it was a mere toy, a child's volcano, a soup kettle, compared to this. Mount Vesuvius is a shapely cone thirty-six hundred feet high; its crater an inverted cone only three hundred feet deep, and not more than a thousand feet in diameter, if as much as that; its fires meager, modest, and docile. But here was a vast, perpendicular, walled cellar, nine hundred feet deep in some places, thirteen hundred in others, level-floored, and *ten miles in circumference!* Here was a yawning pit upon whose floor the armies of Russia could camp, and have room to spare.

Perched upon the edge of the crater, at the opposite end from where we stood, was a small lookout house — say three miles away. It assisted us, by comparison, to comprehend and appreciate the great depth of the basin — it looked like a tiny martin-box clinging at the eaves of a cathedral. After some little time spent in resting and looking and ciphering, we hurried on to the hotel.

By the path it is half a mile from the Volcano House to the lookout house. After a hearty supper we waited until it was thoroughly dark and then started to the crater. The first glance in that direction revealed a scene of wild beauty. There was a heavy fog over the crater and it was splendidly illuminated by the glare from the fires below. The illumination was two miles wide and a mile high, perhaps; and if you ever, on a dark night and at a distance, beheld the light from thirty or forty blocks of distant buildings all on fire at once, reflected strongly against overhanging clouds, you can form a fair idea of what this looked like.

A colossal column of cloud towered to a great height in the air immediately above the crater, and the outer swell of every one of its vast folds was dyed with a rich crimson luster, which was subdued to a pale rose tint in the depressions between. It glowed like a muffled torch and stretched upward to a dizzy height toward the zenith. I thought it just possible that its like had not been seen since the children of Israel wandered on their long march through the desert so many centuries ago over a path illuminated by the mysterious "pillar of fire." And I was sure that I now had a vivid conception of what the majestic "pillar of fire" was like, which almost amounted to a revelation.

Arrived at the little thatched lookout house, we rested our elbows on the railing in front and looked abroad over the wide crater and down over the sheer precipice at the seething fires beneath us. The view was a startling improvement on my daylight experience. I turned to see the effect on the balance of the company, and found the reddest-faced set of men I almost ever saw. In the strong light every countenance glowed like red-hot iron, every shoulder was suffused with crimson and shaded rearward into dingy, shapeless obscurity! The place below looked like the infernal regions and these men like half-cooled devils just come up on a furlough.

I turned my eyes upon the volcano again. The "cellar" was tolerably well lighted up. For a mile and a half in front of us and half a mile on either side, the floor of the abyss was magnificently illuminated; beyond these limits the mists hung down their gauzy curtains and cast a deceptive gloom over all that made the twinkling fires in the remote corners of the crater seem countless leagues removed — made them seem like the campfires of a great army far away. Here was room for the imagination to work! You could imagine those lights the width of a continent away — and that hidden under the intervening darkness were hills, and winding rivers, and weary wastes of plain and desert — and even then the tremendous vista stretched on, and on, and on! — to the fires and far beyond! You could not compass it — it was the idea of eternity made tangible — and the longest end of it made visible to the naked eye!

The greater part of the vast floor of the desert under us was as black as ink, and apparently smooth and level; but over a mile square of it was ringed and streaked and striped with a thousand branching streams of liquid and gorgeously brilliant fire! It looked like a colossal railroad map of the State of Massachusetts done in chain lightning on a midnight sky. Imagine it — imagine a coal-black sky shivered into a tangled network of angry fire!

Here and there were gleaming holes a hundred feet in diameter, broken in the dark crust, and in them the melted lava — the color of a dazzling white just tinged with yellow — was boiling and surging furiously; and from these holes branched numberless bright torrents in many directions, like the spokes of a wheel, and kept a tolerably straight course for a while and then swept round in huge rainbow curves, or made a long succession of sharp worm-fence angles, which looked precisely like the fiercest jagged lightning. These streams met other streams, and they mingled with and crossed and recrossed each other in every conceivable direction, like skate tracks on a popular skating ground. Sometimes streams twenty or thirty feet wide flowed from the holes to some distance without dividing — and through the opera glasses we could see that they ran down small, steep hills and were genuine cataracts of fire, white at their source, but soon cooling and turning to the richest red, grained with alternate lines of black and gold. Every now and then masses of the dark crust broke away and floated slowly down these streams like rafts down a river. Occasionally, the molten lava flowing under the superincumbent crust broke through — split a dazzling streak, from five hundred to a thousand feet long, like a sudden flash of lightning, and then acre after acre of the cold lava parted into fragments, turned up edgewise like cakes of ice when a great river breaks up, plunged downward and were swallowed in the crimson cauldron. Then the wide expanse of the "thaw" maintained a ruddy glow for a while, but shortly cooled and became black and level again. During a "thaw," every dismembered cake was marked by a glittering white border which was superbly shaded inward by aurora borealis rays, which were a flaming yellow where they joined the white border, and from thence toward their points tapered into glowing crimson, then into a rich, pale carmine, and finally into a faint blush that held its own a moment and then dimmed and turned black. Some of the stream preferred to mingle together in a tangle of fantastic circles, and then they looked something like the confusion of ropes one sees on a ship's deck when she has just taken in sail and dropped anchor — provided one can imagine those ropes on fire.

Through the glasses, the little fountains scattered about looked very beautiful. They boiled, and coughed, and spluttered, and discharged sprays of stringy red fire — of about the consistency of mush, for instance — from ten to fifteen feet into the air, along with a shower of brilliant white sparks — a quaint and unnatural mingling of gouts of blood and snowflakes!

We had circles and serpents and streaks of lightning all twined and wreathed and tied together, without a break throughout an area more than a mile square (that amount of ground was covered, though it was not strictly "square"), and it was with a feeling of placid exultation that we reflected that many years had elapsed since any visitor had seen such a splendid display — since any visitor had seen anything more than the now snubbed and insignificant "North" and "South" lakes in action. We had been reading old files of Hawaiian newspapers and the "Record Book" at the Volcano House, and were posted.

I could see the North Lake lying out on the black floor away off in the outer edge of our panorama, and knitted to it by a web-work of lava streams. In its individual capacity it looked very little more respectable than a schoolhouse on fire. True, it was about nine hundred feet long and two or three hundred wide, but then, under the present circumstances, it necessarily appeared rather insignificant, and besides it was so distant from us.

I forgot to say that the noise made by the bubbling lava is not great, heard as we heard it from our lofty perch. It makes three distinct sounds — a rushing, a hissing, and a coughing or puffing sound, and if you stand on the brink and close your eyes, it is no trick at all to imagine that you are sweeping down a river on a large low-pressure steamer, and that you hear the hissing of the steam about her boilers, the puffing from her escape pipes and the churning rush of the water abaft her wheels. The smell of sulphur is strong, but not unpleasant to a sinner.

We left the lookout house at ten o'clock in a half cooked condition, because of the heat from Pele's furnaces, and, wrapping up in blankets, for the night was cold, we returned to our hotel.

The next night was appointed for a visit to the bottom of the crater, for we desired to traverse its floor and see the "North Lake" (of fire) which lay two miles away, toward the further wall. After dark half a dozen of us set out, with lanterns and native guides, and climbed down a crazy, thousand-foot pathway in a crevice fractured in the crater wall, and reached the bottom in safety.

The eruption of the previous evening had spent its force and the floor looked black and cold; but when we ran out upon it we found it hot yet, to the feet, and it was likewise riven with crevices which revealed the underlying fires gleaming vindictively. A neighboring cauldron was threatening to overflow, and this added to the dubiousness of the situation. So the native guides refused to continue the venture, and then everybody deserted except a stranger named Marlette. He said he had been in the crater a dozen times in daylight and believed he could find his way through it at night. He thought that a run of three hundred yards would carry us over the hottest part of the floor and leave us our shoe soles. His pluck gave me backbone. We took one lantern and instructed the guides to hang the other to the roof of the lookout house to serve as a beacon for us in case we got lost, and then the party started back up the precipice and Marlette and I made our run. We skipped over the hot floor and over the red crevices with brisk dispatch and reached the cold lava safe but with pretty warm feet. Then we took things leisurely and comfortably, jumping tolerably wide and probably bottomless chasms, and threading our way through picturesque lava upheavals with considerable confidence. When we got fairly away from the cauldrons of boiling fire, we seemed to be in a gloomy desert, and a suffocatingly dark one, surrounded by dim walls that seemed to tower to the sky. The only cheerful objects were the glinting stars high overhead.

By and by Marlette shouted "Stop!" I never stopped quicker in my life. I asked what the matter was. He said we were out of the path. He said we must not try to go on till we found it again, for we were surrounded with beds of rotten lava through which we could easily break and plunge down a thousand feet. I thought eight hundred would answer for me, and was about to say so when Marlette partly proved his statement by accidentally crushing through and disappearing to his armpits. He got out and we hunted for the path with the lantern. He said there was only one path, and that it was but vaguely defined. We could not find it. The lava surface was all alike in the lantern light. But he was an ingenious man. He said it was not the lantern that had informed him that we were out of the path, but his *feet*. He had noticed a crisp grinding of fine lava-needles under his feet, and some instinct reminded him that in the path these were all worn away. So he put the lantern behind him, and began to search with his boots instead of his eyes. It was good sagacity. The first time his foot touched a surface that did not grind under it he announced that the trail was found again; and after that we kept up a sharp listening for the rasping sound, and it always warned us in time.

It was a long tramp, but an exciting one. We reached the North Lake between ten and eleven o'clock, and sat down on a huge overhanging lava-shelf, tired but satisfied. The spectacle presented was worth coming double the distance to see. Under us, and stretching away before us, was a heaving sea of molten fire of seemingly limitless extent. The glare from it was so blinding that it was some time before we could bear to look upon it steadily. It was like gazing at the sun at noonday, except that the glare was not quite so white. At unequal distances all around the shores of the lake were nearly white-hot chimneys or hollow drums of lava, four or five feet high, and up through them were bursting gorgeous sprays of lava-gouts and gem spangles, some white, some red, and some golden — a ceaseless bombardment, and one that fascinated the eye with its unapproachable splendor. The more distant jets, sparkling up through an intervening gossamer veil of vapor, seemed miles away; and the further the curving ranks of fiery fountains receded, the more fairylike and beautiful they appeared.

Now and then the surging bosom of the lake under our noses would calm down ominously and seem to be gathering strength for an enterprise; and then all of a sudden a red dome of lava of the bulk of an ordinary dwelling would heave itself aloft like an escaping balloon, then burst asunder, and out of its heart would flit a pale green film of vapor, and float upward and vanish in the darkness — a released soul soaring homeward from captivity with the damned, no doubt. The crashing plunge of the ruined dome into the lake again would send a world of seething billows lashing against the shores and shaking the foundations of our perch. By and by, a loosened mass of the hanging shelf we sat on tumbled into the lake, jarring the surroundings like an earthquake and delivering a suggestion that may have been intended for a hint, and may not. We did not wait to see.

We got lost again on our way back, and were more than an hour hunting for the path. We were where we could see the beacon lantern at the lookout house at the time, but thought it was a star, and paid no attention to it. We reached the hotel at two o'clock in the morning, pretty well fagged out.

Kilauea never overflows its vast crater, but bursts a passage for its lava through the mountainside when relief is necessary, and then the destruction is fearful. About 1840 it rent its overburdened stomach and sent a broad river of fire careering down to the sea, which swept away forests, huts, plantations, and everything else that lay in its path. The stream was *five miles broad,* in places, and *two hundred feet deep,* and the distance it traveled was forty miles. It tore up and bore away acre-patches of land on its bosom like rafts — rocks, trees, and all intact. At night the red glare was visible a hundred miles at sea; and at a distance of forty miles fine print could be read at midnight. The atmosphere was poisoned with sulphurous vapors and choked with falling ashes, pumice stones, and cinders; countless columns of smoke rose up and blended together in a tumbled canopy that hid the heavens and glowed with a ruddy flush reflected from the fires below; here and there jets of lava sprung hundreds of feet into the air and burst into rocket-sprays that returned to earth in a crimson rain; and all the while the laboring mountain shook with nature's great palsy, and voiced its distress in moanings and the muffled booming of subter-ranean thunders.

Fishes were killed for twenty miles along the shore, where the lava entered the sea. The earthquakes caused some loss of human life, and a prodigious tidal wave swept inland, carrying everything before it and drowning a number of natives. The devastation consummated along the route traversed by the river of lava was complete and incalculable. Only a Pompeii and a Herculaneum were needed at the foot of Kilauea to make the story of the eruption immortal.

From *Roughing It* by Mark Twain (Hartford, Connecticut, American Publishing Company, 1872).

# CHARLES WARREN STODDARD

# THE HOUSE OF THE SUN

Charles Warren Stoddard (1843–1909), one of the circle of young San Francisco writers that included Bret Harte, Mark Twain, and Ambrose Bierce, first visited Hawaii in 1864, when he was twenty-one. The happy vagabondage of this early experience remained in his memory and lured him back several times again, once to stay for four years. Published as *South-Sea Idyls* (1873), the charming sketches he wrote about his carefree days in the islands prompted Robert Louis Stevenson to observe, "There are but two writers who have touched the South Seas with genius, both Americans: Melville and Charles Warren Stoddard." And William Dean Howells called his writings "graceful shapes, careless, beautiful, with a kind of undying youth in them."

In the selection that follows Stoddard describes a ride on muleback into the immense extinct crater of Mount Haleakala, or the House of the Sun (so called because there the demigod Maui is supposed in the legend to have snared the sun in his net).

MY HAWAIIAN ORACLE, KAHELE, HAVING POSED HIMSELF IN COMpact and chubby grace, awaited his golden opportunity, which was not long a-coming. I sat on the steps of L——'s veranda, and yawned frightfully, because life was growing tedious, and I did not know exactly what to do next. L——'s house was set in the nicest kind of climate, at the foot of a great mountain, just at that altitude where the hot air stopped dancing, though it was never cool enough to shut a door, or to think of wearing a hat for any other purpose than to keep the sun out of one's eyes. L——'s veranda ran out into vacancy as blank as cloudless sky and shadowless sea could make it; in fact, all that the eye found to rest upon was the low hill jutting off from one corner of the house beyond a jasmine in blossom; and under the hill a flat-sailed schooner rocking in a calm. I think there was nothing else down the slope of the mountain but tangled yellow grass, that grew brown and scant as it crept into the torrid zone, a thousand feet below us, and there it had not the courage to come out of the earth at all; so the picture ended in a blazing beach, with warm waves sliding up and down it, backed by blue-watery and blue-airy space for thousands and thousands of miles.

Why should not a fellow yawn over the situation? especially as L——— was busy and could not talk much, and L———'s books were as old as the hills and a good deal dryer.

Having yawned, I turned toward Kahele, and gnashed my teeth. The little rascal looked knowing; his hour had come. He fired off in broken English, and the effect was something like this:

"Suppose we sleep in House of the Sun — we make plenty good sceneries?"

"And where is that?" quoth I.

Kahele's little lump of a nose was jerked up toward the great mountain at the back of L———'s house. "Haleakala!" cried he, triumphantly, for he saw he had resurrected my interest in life, and he felt that he had a thing or two worth showing, a glimpse of which might content me with this world, dull as I found it just then. "Haleakala — the House of the Sun — up before us," said Kahele.

"And to get into the Sun's House?"

"Make a good climb up, and go in from the top!"

Ha! to creep up the roof and drop in at the skylight: this were indeed a royal adventure. "How long would it take?"

Kahele waxed eloquent. That night we should sleep a little up on the slope of the mountain, lodging with the haoles (foreigners) among the first clouds; in the morning we should surprise the sun in the turrets of his temple; then down — down — down into the crater, that had been strewn with ashes for a thousand years. After that, out on the other side, toward the sea, where the trade winds blew, and the country was fresh and fruitful. The youngster sweated with enthusiasm while he strove to make me comprehend the full extent of the delights pertaining to this journey; and, as he finished, he made a rapid flank movement toward the animals, staked a few rods away.

It was not necessary that I should consent to undertake this expedition. He was eager to go, and he would see that I enjoyed myself when I went; but go I must, now that he had made up my mind for me. I confess, I was as wax in that climate. Yet, why not take this promising and uncommon tour? The charm of travel is to break new paths. I ceased to yawn any further over life. Kahele went to the beasts and began saddling them. L——'s hospitality culminated in a bottle of cold, black coffee, and a hamper of delicious sandwiches, such as Mrs. L—— excels in. I had nothing to do but go. It did look like a conspiracy; but, as I never had the moral courage to fight against anything of that sort, I got into the saddle and went.

Turning for a moment toward the brute's tail, overcome with conflicting emotions, I said:

"Adieu, dear L——, thou picture of boisterous industry! Adieu, Mrs. L——, whose light is hid under the bushel of thy lord; but, as it warms him, it is all right, I suppose, and thy reward shall come to thee some day, I trust! By-by, multitudes of little L——s, tumbling recklessly in the back yard, crowned with youth and robust health and plenty of flaxen curls! Away, Kahele! for it is toward evening, and the clouds are skating along the roof of the House of the Sun. Sit not upon the order of your going, but strike spurs at once — and away!"

It was thus that I relieved myself. The prospect of fresh adventure intoxicated me. I do not believe I could have been bought off after that enlivening farewell. The air of the highlands was charged with electricity. I bristled all over with new life. I wanted to stand up in my saddle and fly.

It seemed the boy had engaged a special guide for the crater — one accustomed to feeling his way through the bleak hollow, where any unpracticed feet must have surely gone astray. Kahele offered him a tempting bonus to head our little caravan at once, though it goes sorely against the Hawaiian grain to make up a mind inside of three days. Kahele managed the financial department, whenever he had the opportunity, with a liberality worthy of a purse ten times as weighty as mine; but as he afterward assured me, that guide was a fine man, and a friend of his whom it was a pleasure and a privilege to serve.

Of course, it was all right, since I couldn't help myself; and we three pulled up the long slopes of Haleakala, while the clouds multiplied, as the sun sank, and the evening grew awfully still. Somewhere up among the low-hanging mist there was a house full of haoles, and there we proposed to spend the night. We were looking for this shelter with all our six eyes, while we rode slowly onward, having scarcely uttered a syllable for the last half hour. You know there are some impressive sorts of solitude that seal up a fellow's lips; he can only look about him in quiet wonderment, tempered with a fearless and refreshing trust in that Providence who has enjoined silence. Well, this was one of those times; and right in the midst of it Kahele sighted a smoke wreath in the distance. To me it looked very like a cloud, and I ventured to declare it such; but the youngster frowned me down, and appealed to the special guide for further testimony. The guide declined to commit himself in the matter of smoke or mist, as he ever did on all succeeding occasions, being a wise guide, who knew his own fallibility. It *was* smoke! — a thin, blue ribbon of it, uncoiling itself from among the branches of the overhanging trees, floating up and up and tying itself into double bowknots, and then trying to untie itself, but perishing in the attempt.

In the edge of the grove we saw the little white cottage of the haoles; and, not far away, a campfire, with bright red flames dancing around a kettle, swung under three stakes with their three heads together. Tall figures were moving about the camp, looking almost like ghosts, in the uncertain glow of the fire; and toward these lights and shadows we jogged with satisfaction, scenting supper from afar.

"Halloo!" said we, with voices that did not sound very loud, up in that thin atmosphere.

"Halloo!" said they, with the deepest unconcern, as though they had been through the whole range of human experiences, and there was positively nothing left for them to get excited over.

Some of their animals whinnied in a fashion that drew a response from ours. A dog barked savagely, until he was spoken to, and then was obliged to content himself with an occasional whine. Some animal — a sheep, perhaps — rose up in the trail before us, and plunged into the bush, sending our beasts back on their haunches with fright. A field cricket lifted up his voice and sang; and then a hundred joined him; and then ten thousand times ten thousand swelled the chorus, till the mountains were alive with singing crickets.

"Halloo, stranger! Come in and stop a bit, won't you?" That was our welcome from the chief of the camp, who came a step or two forward, as soon as we had ridden within range of the campfire.

And we went in unto them, and ate of their bread, and drank of their coffee, and slept in their blankets — or tried to sleep — and had a mighty good time generally.

The mountaineers proved to be a company of California miners, who had somehow drifted over the sea, and, once on that side, they naturally enough went into the mountains to cut wood, break trails, and make themselves useful in a rough, out-of-door fashion. They had for companions and assistants a few natives, who, no doubt, did the best they could, though the Californians expressed considerable contempt for the "lazy devils, who were fit for nothing but to fiddle on a jew's-harp."

We ate of a thin, hot cake, baked in a frying pan over that campfire; gnawed a boiled bone fished out of the kettle swung under the three sticks; drank big bowls of coffee, sweetened with coarse brown sugar and guiltless of milk; and sat on the floor all the while, with our legs crossed, like so many Turks and tailors. We went to our blankets as soon as the campfire had smothered itself in ashes, though meanwhile Jack, chief of the camp, gathered himself to windward of the flames, with his hips on his heels and his chin on his knees, smoking a stubby pipe and talking of flush times in California. He was one of those men who could and would part with his last quarter, relying upon nature for his bed and board. He said to me, "If you can rough it, hang on a while — what's to drive you off?" I could rough it: the fire was out, the night chilly; so we turned in under blue blankets with a fuzz on them like moss, and, having puffed out the candle — that lived long enough to avenge its death in a houseful of villainous smoke — we turned over two or three times apiece and, one after another, fell asleep. At the farther side of the house lay the natives, as thick as sheep in a pen, one of them a glossy black fellow, as sleek as a eunuch, born in the West Indies, but whose sands of life had been scattered on various shores. This sooty fellow twanged a quaint instrument of native workmanship, and twanged with uncommon skill. His art was the life of that savage community at the other end of the house. Again and again, during the night, I awoke and heard the tinkle of his primitive harp, mingled with the ejaculations of delight wrung from the hearts of his dusky and sleepless listeners.

Once only was that midnight festival interrupted. We all awoke suddenly and simultaneously, though we scarcely knew why; then the dog began to mouth horribly. My blanket-fellows — beds we had none — knew there was mischief brewing, and rushed out with their guns cocked. Presently the dog came in from the brush, complaining bitterly, and one of the miners shot at a rag fluttering among the bushes. In the morning we found a horse gone, and a couple of bullet holes in a shirt spread out to dry. As soon as the excitement was over, we returned to the blankets and the floor. The eunuch tuned his harp anew, and, after a long while, dawn looked in at the sun-curtained window, with a pale, gray face, freckled with stars.

Kahele saw it as soon as I did, and was up betimes. I fancy he slept little or none that night, for he was fond of music, and especially fond of such music as had made the last few hours more or less hideous. Everybody rose with the break of day, and there was something to eat long before sunrise, after which our caravan, with new vigor, headed for the summit.

Wonderful clouds swept by us; sometimes we were lost for a moment in their icy depths. I could scarcely see the tall ears of my mule when we rode into those opaque billows of vapor that swept noiselessly along the awful heights we were scaling. It was a momentary but severe bereavement, the loss of those ears and the head that went with them, because I cared not to ride saddles that seemed to be floating in the air. What was Prince Firouz Schah to me, or what was I to the Princess of Bengal, that I should do this thing?

There are pleasanter sensations than that of going to heaven on horseback; and we wondered if we should ever reach the point where we could begin to descend again to our natural level, and talk with people infinitely below us just then. Ten thousand perpendicular feet in the air; our breath short; our animals weak in the knees; the ocean rising about us like a wall of sapphire, on the top of which the sky rested like a cover — we felt as though we were shut in an exhausted receiver, the victims of some scientific experiment for the delectation of the angels. We were at the very top of the earth. There was nothing on our side of it nearer to Saturn than the crown of our heads. It was deuced solemn, and a trifle embarrassing. It was as though we were personally responsible for the planet during the second we happened to be uppermost in the universe. I felt unequal to the occasion in that thin, relaxing atmosphere. The special guide, I knew, would shirk this august investiture, as he shirked everything else, save only the watchful care of my collapsing *porte-monnaie*. Kahele, perhaps, would represent us to the best of his ability — which was not much beyond an amazing capacity for food and sleep, coupled with cheek for at least two of his size. There is danger in delay, saith the copybook; and while we crept slowly onward toward the rim of the crater, the sun rose, and we forgot all else save his glory. We had reached the mouth of the chasm. Below us yawned a gulf whose farther walls seemed the outlines of some distant island, within whose depths a sea of cloud was satisfied to ebb and flow, whose billows broke noiselessly at the base of the somber walls among whose battlements we clung like insects. I wonder that we were not dragged into that awful sea, for strange and sudden gusts of wind swept past us, coming from various quarters, and rushing like heralds to the four corners of the heavens. We were far above the currents that girdle the lower earth, and seemed in a measure cut off from the life that was past. We lived and breathed in cloudland. All our pictures were of vapor; our surroundings changed continually. Forests laced with frost; silvery, silent seas; shores of agate and of pearl; blue, shadowy caverns; mountains of light, dissolving and rising again transfigured in glorious resurrection, the sun tinging them with infinite color. A flood of radiance swept over the mysterious picture — a deluge of blood-red glory that came and went like a blush; and then the mists faded and fled away, and gradually we saw the deep bed of the crater, blackened, scarred, distorted — a desert of ashes and cinders shut in by sooty walls; no tinge of green, no suggestion of life, no sound to relieve the imposing silence of that literal death of nature. We were about to enter the guest chamber of the House of the Sun. If we had been spirited away to the enchanted cavern of some genie, we could not have been more bewildered. The cloud world had come to an untimely end, and we were left alone among its blackened and charred ruins. That magician, the sun, hearing the approach of spies, had transformed his fairy palace into a bare and uninviting wilderness. But we were destined to explore it, notwithstanding; and our next move was to dismount and drive our unwilling animals over into the abyss. The angle of our descent was too near the perpendicular to sound like truth, in print. I will not venture to give it; but I remember that our particular guide and his beast were under foot, while Kahele and his beast were overhead, and I and my beast, sandwiched between, managed to survive the double horror of being buried in the debris that rained down upon us from the tail end of the caravan, and slaying the unfortunate leaders ahead with the multitude of rocks we sent thundering down the cliff. A moving avalanche of stones and dust gradually brought us to the bed of the crater, where we offered thanks in the midst of an ascending cloud of cinders, every soul of us panting with exhaustion, and oozing like a saturated sponge. The heat was terrific; shelter there was none; L——'s coffee was all that saved us from despair. Before us stretched miles and miles of lava, looking like scorched piecrust; two thousand feet above us hung heavy masses of baked masonry, unrelieved by any tinge of verdure. To the windward there was a gap in the walls, through which forked tongues of mist ran in, but curled up and over the ragged cliffs, as though the prospect were too uninviting to lure them farther. It behooved us to get on apace, for life in the deserted House of the Sun was, indeed, a burden, and moreover there was some danger of our being locked in. The wind might veer a little, in which case an ocean of mist would deluge the crater, shutting out light and heat, and bewildering the pilgrim so that escape were impossible. The lodestone bewitched the compass in that fixed sea, and there were no beacons and no sounding signals to steer by. Across the smooth, hard lava occasional traces of a trail were visible, like scratches upon glass. Close to the edges of this perilous path yawned chasms. Sometimes the narrow way led over a ridge between two sandy hollows, out of which it was almost impossible to return, if one false step should plunge you into its yielding vortex. There was a long pull toward afternoon, and a sweltering camp about 3 P.M., where we finished L——'s lunch, and were not half satisfied. Even the consoling weed barely sustained our fainting spirits, for we knew that the more tedious portion of the journey was yet to come.

The windward vestibule wound down toward the sea, a wild gorge through which the molten lava had poured its destructive flood. There it lay, a broad, uneven pass of dead, black coals — clinkers, as ragged and sharp as broken glass — threaded by one beaten track a few inches in breadth. To lose this trail were to tear the hoofs from your suffering beasts in an hour or two, and to lacerate your own feet in half the time. Having refreshed ourselves on next to nothing, we pressed for-

ward. Already the shadows were creeping into the House of
the Sun, and as yet we had scarcely gained the mouth of the pass.
As we rode out from the shelter of a bluff, a cold draft struck us
like a wave of the sea. Down the bleak, winding chasm we saw
clouds approaching, pale messengers that travel with the trade
wind and find lodgment in the House of the Sun. They were
hastening home betimes, and had surprised us in the passage.
It was an unwelcome meeting. Our particular guide ventured
to assume an expression of concern, and cautiously remarked
that we were *pilikia* — that is, in trouble! For once he was
equal to an emergency; he knew of a dry well close at hand;
we could drop into it and pass the night, since it was impossible
to feel our way out of the crater through clouds almost as
dense as cotton. Had we matches? No. Had we dry sticks? Yes, in
the well, perhaps, Kahele could make fire without phosphorus,
and we could keep warm till morning, and then escape from
the crater as early as possible. After much groping about, in
and out of clouds, we found the dusty well and dropped into it.
Ferns — a few of them — grew about its sides; a dwarfed tree,
rejoicing in four angular branches, as full of mossy elbows as
possible, stood in the center of our retreat, and at the roots of
this miserable recluse the Kanakas contrived to grind out a
flame by boring into a bit of decayed wood with a dry stick
twirled rapidly between their palms. Dead leaves, dried moss,
and a few twigs made a short-lived and feeble fire for us. Darkness had come upon the place. We watched the flaming daggers
stab the air fitfully, and finally sheathe themselves for good. We
filled our shallow cave with smoke that drove us into the mouth
of it, from time to time, to keep from strangulation. We saw
our wretched beasts shaking with cold; we saw the swift, be-
lated clouds hurrying onward in ghostly procession; we could
do nothing but shudder and return to our dismal bed. No
cheerful cricket blew his shrill pipe, like a policeman's whistle;
the sea sang not for us with its deep, resounding voice; the
Hawaiian harp was hushed. A stone, loosened by some restless
lizard, rattled down the cliff; a goat, complaining of the cold,
bleated once or twice. The wind soughed; the dry branches

of our withering tree sawed across each other; these were our comforters during that almost endless night.

Once the heavens were opened to us. Through the rent in the clouds we saw a great shoulder of the cliff above us, bathed in moonlight. A thousand grotesque shadows played over the face of it. Pictures came and went — a palimpsest of mysteries. Gargoyles leered at us from under the threatening brows of the bluff; and a white specter, shining like a star, stood on the uppermost peak, voiceless and motionless — some living creature lost in admiration of the moon. Then the sky fell on us, and we were routed to our solitary cave.

There is a solitude of the sea that swallows up hope; the despairing spirit hangs over a threatening abyss of death; yet above it and below it there are forms of life rejoicing in their natural element. But there is a solitude of the earth that is more awful; in it Death taunts you with his presence, yet delays to strike. At sea, one step, and the spirit is set at liberty — the body is entombed forever. But alas! within the deserts of the earth no sepulcher awaits the ashes of him who has suffered, and naught but the winds or the foul-feeding vultures shall cleanse that bleaching skeleton where it lies.

We tried to sleep on our stony pillows. Kahele woke and found the guide and me dozing; later, the guide roused himself to the discovery that Kahele and I were wrapped in virtuous unconsciousness. Anon I sat up among the rocks, listened to the two natives breathing heavily, and heard the wind sighing over the yawning mouth of our cavern. I heard the beasts stamping among the clinkers, and covered my head again with the damp blanket, and besieged sleep. Then we all three started from our unrefreshing dreams, and lo! the clouds were rising and fleeing away, and a faint, rosy light over the summit peaks looked like sunrise; so we rose and saddled the caravan, and searched about us for the lost trail. Hour after hour we drew nearer to the mouth of the crater. Our progress was snaillike; each one of us struck out for himself, having lost confidence in the cunning of the other. From small elevations we took our reckoning, and he who got the farthest toward the sea lifted up his voice in triumph, and was speedily joined by the rest of the party.

At last we came upon the bluffs that overhang the green shores of the island. We were safely out of the Sun's Tabernacle, but not yet free to pass into the lowly vales of the earth. Again and again we rode to the edges of the cliffs, whose precipitous walls forbade our descent. Sometimes we clung to the bare ribs of the mountain, where a single misstep might have sent us headlong into the hereafter. Frequently we rejoiced in a discovery that promised well; but anon a sheltered chasm unveiled its hideous depths, or an indigo-jungle laid hold of us and cut us off in that direction.

Below us lay the verdant slopes of Kaupo. From their dried-grass houses flocked the natives, looking like ants and their hills. They watched us for hours with amused interest. Now and then they called to us with faint and far-off voices — suggestions that were lost to us, since they sounded like so many bird-notes floating in the wind. All day we saw the little village lying under us temptingly peaceful and lazy. Clouds still hung below us: some of them swept by, pouring copious drops, that drove our audience within doors for a few moments; but the rain was soon over, the sun shone brighter than ever, the people returned to watch us, and the day waned. We surprised flock upon flock of goats in their rocky retreats; but they dispersed in all directions like quicksilver, and we passed on. About dusk we got into the grassy land, and thanked God for deliverance.

Here Kahele's heart rejoiced. Here, close by the little chapel of Kaupo, he discovered one whom he proclaimed his grandfather; though, judging from the years of the man, he could scarcely have been anything beyond an uncle. I was put to rest in a little stone cell, where the priests sleep when they are on their mission to Kaupo. A narrow bed, with a crucifix at the foot of it, a small window in the thick wall, with a jug of water in the corner thereof, and a chair with a game leg, constituted the furnishment of the quaint lodging. Kahele rushed about to see old friends — who wept over him — and was very long absent, whereat I waxed wroth, and berated him roundly; but the poor fellow was so charmingly repentant that I forgave him all, and more too, for I promised him I would stay three days, at least, with his uncle-grandfather, and give him his universal liberty for the time being.

From the open doorway I saw the long sweep of the mountains, looking cool and purple in the twilight. The ghostly procession of the mists stole in at the windward gap; the afterglow of the evening suffused the front of the chapel with a warm light, and the statue of the Virgin above the chapel door — a little faded with the suns of that endless summer, a little mildewed with the frequent rains — the statue looked down upon us with a smile of welcome. Some youngsters, as naked as day-old nest birds, tossed a ball into the air; and when it at last lodged in the niche of the Virgin, they clapped their hands, half in merriment and half in awe, and the games of the evening ended. Then the full moon rose; a cock crew in the peak of the chapel, thinking it daybreak, and the little fellows slept, with their spines curved like young kittens. By and by the moon hung, round and mellow, beyond the chapel cross, and threw a long shadow in the grass; and then I went to my cell and folded my hands to rest, with a sense of blessed and unutterable peace.

From *South-Sea Idyls* by Charles Warren Stoddard (Boston, James R. Osgood and Company, 1873).

ISABELLA BIRD


# TWO HAWAIIAN
# HOUSEHOLDS ON THE
# HAMAKUA COAST

She shocked other Victorian ladies by riding unchaperoned through remote parts of the islands. A small woman astride a mule and wearing the native *pa-u* or voluminous split skirt, Isabella Bird (1832–1904) gathered material for her observant and charming letters to her sister in Scotland in 1873.

Miss Bird, first woman fellow of the Royal Geographical Society, had a zest for fresh experiences and an eye for depicting scenes and events which are still enjoyed by other visitors who discover her entertaining volume. On the present excursion she had set out from Hilo to follow the gashed Hamakua Coast to the tremendous gulch of Waipio on the northern shore of the island of Hawaii. She was accompanied only by a sixteen-year-old Hawaiian guide named Kaluna and an English-speaking Hawaiian girl of seventeen named Deborah, who had been recently married to a haole employee of a sugar plantation. And, since there was not a single inn along the way, Miss Bird made up her mind to lodge in the grass-roofed houses of Hawaiians on her road.


TOWARDS AFTERNOON TURBID-LOOKING CLOUDS LOWERED OVER THE sea, and by the time we reached the worst pali of all, the south side of Laupahoehoe, they burst on us in torrents of rain accompanied by strong wind. This terrible precipice takes one entirely by surprise. Kaluna, who rode first, disappeared so suddenly that I thought he had gone over. It is merely a dangerous broken ledge, and besides that it looks as if there were only foothold for a goat; one is dizzied by the sight of the foaming ocean immediately below, and when we actually reached the bottom, there was only a narrow strip of shingle between the stupendous cliff and the resounding surges, which came up as if bent on destruction. The path by which we descended looked a mere thread on the side of the precipice. I don't know what the word beetling means, but if it means anything bad, I will certainly apply it to that pali.

A number of disastrous-looking native houses are clustered under some very tall palms in the open part of the gulch, but it is a most wretched situation; the roar of the surf is deafening, the scanty supply of water is brackish, there are rumors that leprosy is rife, and the people are said to be the poorest on Hawaii. We were warned that we could not spend a night comfortably there, so wet, tired, and stiff, we rode on another six miles to the house of a native called Bola-Bola, where we had been instructed to remain. The rain was heavy and ceaseless, and the trail had become so slippery that our progress was much retarded. It was a most unpropitious-looking evening, and I began to feel the painful stiffness arising from prolonged fatigue in saturated clothes. I indulged in various imaginations as we rode up the long ascent leading to Bola-Bola's, but this time they were not of sofas and tea, and I never aspired to anything beyond drying my clothes by a good fire, for at Hilo some people had shrugged their shoulders, and others had laughed mysteriously at the idea of our sleeping there, and some had said it was one of the worst of native houses.

A single glance was enough. It was a dilapidated frame house, altogether forlorn, standing unsheltered on a slope of the mountain, with one or two yet more forlorn grass piggeries, which I supposed might be the cookhouse, and eating house near it.

A prolonged *har-r-r-ouche* from Kaluna brought out a man with a female horde behind him, all shuffling into clothes as we approached, and we stiffly dismounted from the wet saddles in which we had sat for ten hours, and stiffly hobbled up into the littered veranda, the water dripping from our clothes, and squeezing out of our boots at every step. Inside there was one room about eighteen by fourteen feet, which looked as if the people had just arrived and had thrown down their goods promiscuously. There were mats on the floor, not over clean, and half the room was littered and piled with mats rolled up, boxes, bamboos, saddles, blankets, lassos, coconuts, kalo roots, bananas, quilts, pans, calabashes, bundles of hard poi in ti leaves, bones, cats, fowls, clothes. A frightful old woman, looking like a relic of the old heathen days, with bristling gray hair cut short, her body tattooed all over, and no clothing but a ragged blanket huddled round her shoulder; a girl about twelve, with torrents of shining hair, and a piece of bright green calico thrown round her; and two very good-looking young women in rose-colored chemises, one of them holding a baby, were squatting and lying on the mats, one over another, like a heap of savages.

When the man found that we were going to stay all night he bestirred himself, dragged some of the things to one side, and put down a shakedown of pulu (the silky covering of the fronds of one species of tree fern), with a sheet over it, and a gay quilt of orange and red cotton. There was a thin printed muslin curtain to divide off one half of the room, a usual arrangement in native houses. He then helped to unsaddle the horses, and the confusion of the room was increased by a heap of our wet saddles, blankets, and gear. All this time the women lay on the floor and stared at us.

Rheumatism seemed impending, for the air up there was chilly, and I said to Deborah that I must make some change in my dress, and she signed to Kaluna, who sprang at my soaked boots and pulled them off, and my stockings too, with a savage alacrity which left it doubtful for a moment whether he had not also pulled off my feet! I had no means of making any further change except putting on a wrapper over my wet clothes.

Meanwhile the man killed and boiled a fowl, and boiled

some sweet potato, and when these untempting viands and a calabash of poi were put before us, we sat round them and ate, I with my knife, the others with their fingers. There was coffee in a dirty bowl. The females had arranged a row of pillows on their mat, and all lay face downwards, with their chins resting upon them, staring at us with their great brown eyes, and talking and laughing incessantly. They had low sensual faces, like some low order of animal. When our meal was over, the man threw them the relics, and they soon picked the bones clean. It surprised me that after such a badly served meal the man brought a bowl of water for our hands, and something intended for a towel.

By this time it was dark, and a stone, deeply hollowed at the top, was produced, containing beef fat and a piece of rag for a wick, which burned with a strong flaring light. The women gathered themselves up and sat round a large calabash of poi, conveying the sour paste to their mouths with an inimitable twist of the fingers, laying their heads back and closing their eyes with a look of animal satisfaction. When they had eaten they lay down as before, with their chins on their pillows, and again the row of great brown eyes confronted me. Deborah, Kaluna, and the women talked incessantly in loud, shrill voices till Kaluna uttered the word *auwe* with a long, groaning intonation, apparently signifying weariness, divested himself of his clothes, and lay down on a mat alongside our shakedown, upon which we let down the dividing curtain and wrapped ourselves up as warmly as possible.

I was uneasy about Deborah, who has had a cough for some time, and consequently took the outside place under the window, which was broken, and presently a large cat jumped through the hole and down upon me, followed by another and another, till five wild cats had effected an entrance, making me a steppingstone to ulterior proceedings. Had there been a sixth I think I could not have borne the infliction quietly. Strips of jerked beef were hanging from the rafters, and by the light which was still burning I watched the cats climb up stealthily, seize on some of these, descend, and disappear through the window, making me a steppingstone as before, but with all their craft they let some of the strips fall, which awoke Deborah, and next I saw Kaluna's magnificent eyes peering at us under the curtain. Then the natives got up, and smoked and ate more poi at intervals, and talked, and Kaluna and Deborah quarreled, jokingly, about the time of night she told me, and the moon through the rain clouds occasionally gave us delusive hopes of dawn, and I kept moving my place to get out of the drip from the roof, and so the night passed. I was amused all the time, though I should have preferred sleep to such nocturnal diversions. It was so new, and so odd, to be the only white person among eleven natives in a lonely house, and yet to be as secure from danger and annoyance as in our own home.

At last a pale dawn did appear, but the rain was still coming down heavily, and our poor animals were standing dismally with their heads down and their tails turned towards the wind. Yesterday evening I took a change of clothes out of the damp saddlebags, and put them into what I hoped was a dry place, but they were soaked, wetter even than those in which I had been sleeping, and my boots and Deborah's were so stiff that we gladly availed ourselves of Kaluna's most willing services. The mode of washing was peculiar: he held a calabash with about half a pint of water in it, while we bathed our faces and hands, and all the natives looked on and tittered. This was apparently his idea of politeness, for no persuasion would induce him to put the bowl down on the mat, and Deborah evidently thought it was proper respect. We had a repetition of the same viands as the night before for breakfast, and, as before, the women lay with their chins on their pillows and stared at us.

The rain ceased almost as soon as we started, and though it has not been a bright day, it has been very pleasant. There are no large gulches on today's journey. The track is mostly through long grass, over undulating uplands, with parklike clumps of trees, and thickets of guava and the exotic sumach. Different ferns, flowers, and vegetation, with much less luxuriance and little water, denoted a drier climate and a different soil.

We moved on in single file at a jog trot wherever the road admitted of it, meeting mounted natives now and then, which led to a delay for the exchange of *nuhou* [gossip]; and twice we had to turn into the thicket to avoid what here seems to be considered a danger. There are many large herds of semi-wild bullocks on the mountains, branded cattle, as distinguished from the wild or unbranded, and when they are wanted for food, a number of experienced *vaqueros* on strong, shod horses go up, and drive forty or fifty of them down. We met such a drove bound for Hilo, with one or two men in front and others at the sides and behind, uttering loud shouts. The bullocks are nearly mad with being hunted and driven, and at times rush like a living tornado, tearing up the earth with their horns. As soon as the galloping riders are seen and the crooked-horned beasts, you retire behind a screen. There must be some tradition of someone having been knocked down and hurt, for reckless as the natives are said to be, they are careful about this, and we were warned several times by travelers whom we met that there were "bullocks ahead." The law provides that the *vaqueros* shall station one of their number at the head of a gulch to give notice when cattle are to pass through.

We jogged on again till we met a native who told us that we were quite close to our destination; but there were no signs of it, for we were still on the lofty uplands, and the only prominent objects were huge headlands confronting the sea. I got off to walk, as my mule seemed footsore, but had not gone many yards when we came suddenly to the verge of a pali, about a thousand feet deep, with a narrow, fertile valley, and a yet higher pali on the other side, both abutting perpendicularly on the sea. I should think the valley is not more than three miles long, and it is walled in by high, inaccessible mountains. It is, in fact, a gulch on a greatly enlarged scale. The prospect below us was very charming, a fertile region perfectly level, protected from the sea by sandhills, watered by a winding stream, and bright with fishponds, meadow lands, kalo patches, orange and coffee groves, figs, breadfruit, and palms. There were a number of grass houses, and a native church with a spire, and another up the valley testified to the energy and aggressiveness of Rome. We saw all this from the moment we reached the pali; and it enlarged, and the detail grew upon us with every yard of the laborious descent of broken, craggy track, which is the only mode of access to the valley from the outer world. I got down on foot with difficulty; a difficulty much increased by the long rowels of my spurs, which caught on the rocks and entangled my dress, the simple expedient of taking them off not having occurred to me!

A neat frame house, with large stones between it and the river, was our destination. It belongs to a native named Halemanu, a great man in the district, for, besides being a member of the legislature, he is deputy sheriff. He is a man of property, also; and though he cannot speak a word of English, he is well educated in Hawaiian, and writes an excellent hand. I brought a letter of introduction to him from Mr. Severance, and we were at once received with every hospitality, our horses cared for, and ourselves luxuriously lodged. We walked up the valley before dark to get a view of the cascade, and found supper ready on our return. This is such luxury after last night. There is a very light, bright sitting room, with papered walls, and manila matting on the floor, a round center table with books and a photograph album upon it, two rocking chairs, an office desk, another table and chairs, and a Canadian lounge. I can't imagine in what way this furniture was brought here. Our bedroom opens from this, and it actually has a four-post bedstead with mosquito bars, a lounge and two chairs, and the floor is covered with native matting. The washing apparatus is rather an anomaly, for it consists of a basin and crash towel placed in the veranda, in full view of fifteen people. The natives all bathe in the river.

Halemanu has a cookhouse and native cook, and an eating room, where I was surprised to find everything in foreign style — chairs, a table with a snow-white cover, and table napkins, knives, forks, and even saltcellars. I asked him to eat with us, and he used a knife and fork quite correctly, never, for instance, putting the knife into his mouth. I was amused to see him after-

wards, sitting on a mat among his family and dependents, helping himself to poi from a calabash with his fingers. He gave us
for supper delicious river fish fried, boiled kalo, and Waipio
coffee with boiled milk.

It is very annoying only to be able to converse with this man
through an interpreter; and Deborah, as is natural, is rather
unwilling to be troubled to speak English, now that she is
among her own people. After supper we sat by candlelight in
the parlor, and he showed me his photograph album. At eight he
took a large Bible, put on glasses, and read a chapter in Hawaiian; after which he knelt and prayed with profound reverence
of manner and tone. Towards the end I recognized the Hawaiian
words for "Our Father." Here in Waipio there is something
pathetic in the idea of this Fatherhood, which is wider than
the ties of kin and race. Even here not one is a stranger, an
alien, a foreigner! And this man, so civilized and Christianized,
only now in middle life, was, he said, "a big boy when the
first teachers came," and may very likely have witnessed horrors in the heiau, or temple, close by, of which little is left
now.

This bedroom is thoroughly comfortable. Kaluna wanted to
sleep on the lounge here, probably because he is afraid of *akuas*,
or spirits, but we have exiled him to a blanket on the parlor
lounge.

From *The Hawaiian Archipelago: Six Months Among the Palm Groves, Coral
Reefs, and Volcanoes of the Sandwich Islands* by Isabella Bird (London, John
Murray, 1875).

R.  L.  STEVENSON

# THE ISLE OF VOICES

Among the famous authors who have visited Hawaii and written
about it is Robert Louis Stevenson (1850–1894). In 1888 he and
his American wife chartered the yacht *Casco* and cruised in the
South Seas for two years. They spent five months in Hawaii in
1889 and became close friends of the reigning King Kalakaua
and his sister, Liliuokalani, who was destined to be the last of the
Hawaiian monarchs. The Stevensons joined the social circle
around Iolani Palace and in turn entertained the genial king on
the *Casco*.

R.L.S. toured the Kona region of the island of Hawaii and
also Molokai. He spent eight days at the leper settlement, where
he collected information about the recently deceased Father
Joseph Damien de Veuster, Belgian priest-martyr whom Stevenson afterward defended in his fiery "Open Letter to the Rev.
Doctor Hyde." The idea for Stevenson's novel *The Wrecker*
(1892) came to him from a report in a Honolulu newspaper of a
shipwreck on Midway Island. Other writings dealing with Hawaii
include travel sketches in *The Eight Islands* (1896) and stories
in *Island Nights' Entertainments* (1893).

The following tale, like the author's better-known story "The
Bottle Imp," deals with the supernatural and combines an Oriental myth with a Pacific island setting.

KEOLA WAS MARRIED WITH LEHUA, DAUGHTER OF KALAMAKE, THE
wise man of Molokai, and he kept his dwelling with the father
of his wife. There was no man more cunning than that prophet;
he read the stars, he could divine by the bodies of the dead, and
by means of evil creatures: he could go alone into the highest parts of the mountain, into the region of the hobgoblins, and

there he would lay snares to entrap the spirits of ancient.

For this reason no man was more consulted in all the King-dom of Hawaii. Prudent people bought, and sold, and married, and laid out their lives by his counsels; and the king had him twice to Kona to seek the treasures of Kamehameha. Neither was any man more feared: of his enemies, some had dwindled in sickness by the virtue of his incantations, and some had been spirited away, the life and the clay both, so that folk looked in vain for so much as a bone of their bodies. It was rumored that he had the art or the gift of the old heroes. Men had seen him at night upon the mountains, stepping from one cliff to the next; they had seen him walking in the high forest, and his head and shoulders were above the trees.

This Kalamake was a strange man to see. He was come of the best blood in Molokai and Maui, of a pure descent; and yet he was more white to look upon than any foreigner: his hair the color of dry grass, and his eyes red and very blind, so that "Blind as Kalamake, that can see across tomorrow" was a byword in the islands.

Of all these doings of his father-in-law, Keola knew a little by the common repute, a little more he suspected, and the rest he ignored. But there was one thing troubled him. Kala-make was a man that spared for nothing, whether to eat or to drink or to wear; and for all he paid in bright new dollars. "Bright as Kalamake's dollars" was another saying in the Eight Isles. Yet he neither sold, nor planted, nor took hire — only now and then for his sorceries — and there was no source conceivable for so much silver coin.

It chanced one day Keola's wife was gone upon a visit to Kaunakakai, on the lee side of the island, and the men were forth at sea fishing. But Keola was an idle dog, and he lay in the veranda and watched the surf beat on the shore and the birds fly about the cliff. It was a chief thought with him always — the thought of the bright dollars. When he lay down to bed he would be wondering why they were so many, and when he woke at morn he would be wondering why they were all new; and the thing was never absent from his mind. But this day of all days he made sure in his heart of some discovery. For it seems he had observed the place where Kalamake kept his treasure, which was a lockfast desk against the parlor wall, under the print of Kamehameha the Fifth, and a photograph of Queen Victoria with her crown; and it seems again that, no later than the night before, he found occasion to look in, and behold! the bag lay there empty. And this was the day of the steamer; he could see her smoke off Kalaupapa; and she must soon arrive with a month's goods, tinned salmon and gin, and all manner of rare luxuries for Kalamake.

"Now if he can pay for his goods today," Keola thought, "I shall know for certain that the man is a warlock, and the dollars come out of the devil's pocket."

While he was so thinking, there was his father-in-law behind him, looking vexed.

"Is that the steamer?" he asked.

"Yes," said Keola. "She has but to call at Pelekunu, and then she will be here."

"There is no help for it then," returned Kalamake, "and I must take you in my confidence, Keola, for the lack of anyone better. Come here within the house."

So they stepped together into the parlor, which was a very fine room, papered and hung with prints, and furnished with a rocking chair, and a table and a sofa in European style. There was a shelf of books besides, and a family Bible in the midst of the table, and the lockfast writing desk against the wall; so that anyone could see it was the house of a man of substance.

Kalamake made Keola close the shutters of the windows, while he himself locked all the doors and set open the lid of the desk. From this he brought forth a pair of necklaces, hung with charms and shells, a bundle of dried herbs, and the dried leaves of trees, and a green branch of palm.

"What I am about," said he, "is a thing beyond wonder. The men of old were wise; they wrought marvels, and this among the rest; but that was at night, in the dark, under the fit stars and in the desert. The same will I do here in my own house and under the plain eye of day."

So saying, he put the Bible under the cushion of the sofa so

that it was all covered, brought out from the same place a mat
of a wonderfully fine texture, and heaped the herbs and leaves
on sand in a tin pan. And then he and Keola put on the necklaces and took their stand upon the opposite corners of the
mat.

"The time comes," said the warlock; "be not afraid."

With that he set flame to the herbs, and began to mutter and
wave the branch of palm. At first the light was dim because of
the closed shutters; but the herbs caught strongly afire, and the
flames beat upon Keola, and the room glowed with the burning:
and next the smoke rose and made his head swim and his eyes
darken, and the sound of Kalamake muttering ran in his ears.
And suddenly, to the mat on which they were standing came a
snatch or twitch, that seemed to be more swift than lightning.
In the same wink the room was gone and the house, the breath
all beaten from Keola's body. Volumes of light rolled upon his
eyes and head, and he found himself transported to a beach
of the sea, under a strong sun, with a great surf roaring: he and
the warlock standing there on the same mat, speechless, gasping
and grasping at one another, and passing their hands before
their eyes.

"What was this?" cried Keola, who came to himself the first,
because he was the younger. "The pang of it was like death."

"It matters not," panted Kalamake. "It is now done."

"And in the name of God where are we?" cried Keola.

"That is not the question," replied the sorcerer. "Being
here, we have matter in our hands, and that we must attend to.
Go, while I recover my breath, into the borders of the wood,
and bring me the leaves of such and such a herb, and such and
such a tree, which you will find to grow there plentifully —
three handfuls of each. And be speedy. We must be home again
before the steamer comes; it would seem strange if we had
disappeared." And he sat on the sand and panted.

Keola went up the beach, which was of shining sand and
coral, strewn with singular shells; and he thought in his
heart —

"How do I not know this beach? I will come here again and
gather shells."

In front of him was a line of palms against the sky; not like the palms of the Eight Islands, but tall and fresh and beautiful, and hanging out withered fans like gold among the green, and he thought in his heart —

"It is strange I should not have found this grove. I will come here again, when it is warm, to sleep." And he thought, "How warm it has grown suddenly!" For it was winter in Hawaii, and the day had been chill. And he thought also, "Where are the gray mountains? And where is the high cliff with the hanging forests and the wheeling birds?" And the more he considered, the less he might conceive in what quarter of the islands he was fallen.

In the border of the grove, where it met the beach, the herb was growing, but the tree farther back. Now, as Keola went toward the tree, he was aware of a young woman who had nothing on her body but a belt of leaves.

"Well!" thought Keola, "they are not very particular about their dress in this part of the country." And he paused, supposing she would observe him and escape; and, seeing that she still looked before her, stood and hummed aloud. Up she leaped at the sound. Her face was ashen; she looked this way and that, and her mouth gaped with the terror of her soul. But it was a strange thing that her eyes did not rest upon Keola.

"Good day," said he. "You need not be so frightened; I will not eat you." And he had scarce opened his mouth before the young woman fled into the bush.

"These are strange manners," thought Keola. And, not thinking what he did, ran after her.

As she ran, the girl kept crying in some speech that was not practiced in Hawaii, yet some of the words were the same, and he knew she kept calling and warning others. And presently he saw more people running — men, women, and children, one with another, all running and crying like people at a fire. And with that he began to grow afraid himself, and returned to Kalamake, bringing the leaves. Him he told what he had seen.

"You must pay no heed," said Kalamake. "All this is like a dream and shadows. All will disappear and be forgotten."

"It seems none saw me," said Keola.

"And none did," replied the sorcerer. "We walk here in the broad sun invisible by reason of these charms. Yet they hear us; and therefore it is well to speak softly, as I do."

With that he made a circle round the mat with stones, and in the midst he set the leaves.

"It will be your part," said he, "to keep the leaves alight, and feed the fire slowly. While they blaze (which is but for a little moment) I must do my errand; and before the ashes blacken, the same power that brought us carries us away. Be ready now with the match; and do you call me in good time, lest the flames burn out and I be left."

As soon as the leaves caught, the sorcerer leaped like a deer out of the circle, and began to race along the beach like a hound that has been bathing. As he ran he kept stooping to snatch shells: and it seemed to Keola that they glittered as he took them. The leaves blazed with a clear flame that consumed them swiftly; and presently Keola had but a handful left, and the sorcerer was far off, running and stooping.

"Back!" cried Keola. "Back! The leaves are near done."

At that Kalamake turned, and if he had run before, now he flew. But fast as he ran, the leaves burned faster. The flame was ready to expire when, with a great leap, he bounded on the mat. The wind of his leaping blew it out; and with that the beach was gone, and the sun and the sea, and they stood once more in the dimness of the shuttered parlor, and were once more shaken and blinded; and on the mat betwixt them lay a pile of shining dollars. Keola ran to the shutters; and there was the steamer tossing in the swell close in.

The same night Kalamake took his son-in-law apart, and gave him five dollars in his hand.

"Keola," said he, "if you are a wise man (which I am doubtful of) you will think you slept this afternoon on the veranda, and dreamed as you were sleeping. I am a man of few words, and I have for my helpers people of short memories."

Never a word more said Kalamake, nor referred again to that affair. But it ran all the while in Keola's head — if he were lazy before he would now do nothing.

"Why should I work," thought he, "when I have a father-in-law who makes dollars of sea shells?"

Presently his share was spent. He spent it all upon fine clothes. And then he was sorry:

"For," thought he, "I had done better to have bought a concertina, with which I might have entertained myself all day long." And then he began to grow vexed with Kalamake.

"This man has the soul of a dog," thought he. "He can gather dollars when he pleases on the beach, and he leaves me to pine for a concertina! Let him beware: I am no child, I am as cunning as he, and hold his secret." With that he spoke to his wife Lehua, and complained of her father's manners.

"I would let my father be," said Lehua. "He is a dangerous man to cross."

"I care that for him!" cried Keola; and snapped his fingers. "I have him by the nose. I can make him do what I please." And he told Lehua the story.

But she shook her head.

"You may do what you like," said she; "but as sure as you thwart my father, you will be no more heard of. Think of this person and that person; think of Hua, who was a noble of the House of Representatives, and went to Honolulu every year; and not a bone or a hair of him was found. Remember Kamau, and how he wasted to a thread, so that his wife lifted him with one hand. Keola, you are a baby in my father's hands; he will take you with his thumb and finger and eat you like a shrimp."

Now Keola was truly afraid of Kalamake, but he was vain too; and these words of his wife incensed him.

"Very well," said he, "if that is what you think of me, I will show how much you are deceived." And he went straight to where his father-in-law was sitting in the parlor.

"Kalamake," said he, "I want a concertina."

"Do you indeed?" said Kalamake.

"Yes," said he, "and I may as well tell you plainly, I mean to have it. A man who picks up dollars on the beach can certainly afford a concertina."

"I had no idea you had so much spirit," replied the sorcerer. "I thought you were a timid, useless lad, and I cannot describe how much pleased I am to find I was mistaken. Now I begin to think I may have found an assistant and successor in my difficult business. A concertina? You shall have the best in Honolulu. And tonight, as soon as it is dark, you and I will go and find the money."

"Shall we return to the beach?" asked Keola.

"No, no!" replied Kalamake; "you must begin to learn more of my secrets. Last time I taught you to pick shells; this time I shall teach you to catch fish. Are you strong enough to launch Pili's boat?"

"I think I am," returned Keola. "But why should we not take your own, which is afloat already?"

"I have a reason which you will understand thoroughly before tomorrow," said Kalamake. "Pili's boat is the better suited for my purpose. So, if you please, let us meet there as soon as it is dark; and in the meanwhile let up keep our own counsel, for there is no cause to let the family into our business."

Honey is not more sweet than was the voice of Kalamake, and Keola could scarce contain his satisfaction.

"I might have had my concertina weeks ago," thought he, "and there is nothing needed in this world but a little courage."

Presently after he espied Lehua weeping, and was half in a mind to tell her all was well.

"But no," thinks he; "I shall wait till I can show her the concertina; we shall see what the chit will do then. Perhaps she will understand in the future that her husband is a man of some intelligence."

As soon as it was dark, father and son-in-law launched Pili's boat and set the sail. There was a great sea, and it blew strong from the leeward; but the boat was swift and light and dry, and skimmed the waves. The wizard had a lantern, which he lit and held with his finger through the ring; and the two sat in the stern and smoked cigars, of which Kalamake had always a provision, and spoke like friends of magic and the great sums of money which they could make by its exercise, and what they should buy first, and what second; and Kalamake talked like a father.

Presently he looked all about, and above him at the stars, and back at the island, which was already three parts sunk under the sea, and he seemed to consider ripely his position.

"Look!" says he, "there is Molokai already far behind us, and Maui like a cloud; and by the bearing of these three stars I know I am come where I desire. This part of the sea is called the Sea of the Dead. It is in this place extraordinarily deep, and the floor is all covered with the bones of men, and in the holes of this part gods and goblins keep their habitation. The flow of the sea is to the north, stronger than a shark can swim, and any man who shall here be thrown out of a ship it bears away like a wild horse into the uttermost ocean. Presently he is spent and goes down, and his bones are scattered with the rest, and the gods devour his spirit."

Fear came on Keola at the words, and he looked, and by the light of the stars and the lantern the warlock seemed to change.

"What ails you?" cried Keola, quick and sharp.

"It is not I who am ailing," said the wizard; "but there is one here very sick."

With that he changed his grasp upon the lantern, and behold! as he drew his finger from the ring, the finger stuck and the ring was burst, and his hand was grown to be of the bigness of three.

At that sight Keola screamed and covered his face.

But Kalamake held up the lantern. "Look rather at my face!" said he — and his head was huge as a barrel; and still he grew and grew as a cloud grows on the mountain, and Keola sat before him screaming, and the boat raced on the great seas.

"And now," said the wizard, "what do you think about that concertina? and are you sure you would not rather have a flute? No?" says he; "that is well, for I do not like my family to be changeable of purpose. But I begin to think I had better get out of this paltry boat, for my bulk swells to a very unusual degree, and if we are not the more careful, she will presently be swamped."

With that he threw his legs over the side. Even as he did so, the greatness of the man grew thirty-fold and forty-fold as swift as sight or thinking, so that he stood in the deep seas to the armpits, and his head and shoulders rose like a high isle, and the swell beat and burst upon his bosom, as it beats and breaks against a cliff. The boat ran still to the north, but he reached out his hand, and took the gunwale by the finger and thumb, and broke the side like a biscuit, and Keola was spilled into the sea. And the pieces of the boat the sorcerer crushed in the hollow of his hand and flung miles away into the night.

"Excuse me for taking the lantern," said he; "for I have a long wade before me, and the land is far, and the bottom of the sea uneven, and I feel the bones under my toes."

And he turned and went off walking with great strides; and as often as Keola sank in the trough he could see him no longer; but as often as he was heaved upon the crest, there he was striding and dwindling, and he held the lamp high over his head, and the waves broke white about him as he went.

Since first the islands were fished out of the sea there was never a man so terrified as this Keola. He swam indeed, but he swam as puppies swim when they are cast in to drown, and know not wherefore. He could but think of the hugeness of the swelling of the warlock, of that face which was as great as a mountain, of those shoulders that were broad as an isle, and of the seas that beat on them in vain. He thought, too, of the concertina, and shame took hold upon him; and of the dead man's bones, and fear shook him.

Of a sudden he was aware of something dark against the stars that tossed, and a light below, and a brightness of the cloven sea; and he heard speech of men. He cried out aloud and a voice answered; and in a twinkling the bows of a ship hung above him on a wave like a thing balanced, and swooped down. He caught with his two hands in the chains of her, and the next moment was buried in the rushing seas, and the next hauled on board by seamen.

They gave him gin and biscuit and dry clothes, and asked him how he came where they found him, and whether the light which they had seen was the lighthouse Lae o Ka Laau. But Keola knew white men are like children and only believe their own stories; so about himself he told them what he pleased, and as for the light (which was Kalamake's lantern) he vowed he had seen none.

This ship was a schooner bound for Honolulu and then to trade in the low islands; and by a good chance for Keola she had lost a man off the bowsprit in a squall. It was no use talking. Keola durst not stay in the Eight Islands. Word goes so quickly, and all men are so fond to talk and carry news, that if he hid in the north end of Kauai or in the south end of Kau, the wizard would have wind of it before a month, and he must perish. So he did what seemed the most prudent, and shipped sailor in the place of the man who had been drowned.

In some ways the ship was a good place. The food was extraordinarily rich and plenty, with biscuits and salt beef every day, and pea soup and puddings made of flour and suet twice a week, so that Keola grew fat. The captain also was a good man, and the crew no worse than other whites. The trouble was the mate, who was the most difficult man to please Keola had ever met with, and beat and cursed him daily, both for what he did and what he did not. The blows that he dealt were very sore, for he was strong; and the words he used were very unpalatable, for Keola was come of a good family and accustomed to respect. And what was the worst of all, whenever Keola found a chance to sleep, there was the mate awake and stirring him up with a rope's end. Keola saw it would never do; and he made up his mind to run away.

They were about a month out from Honolulu when they made the land. It was a starry night, the sea was smooth as well as the sky fair; it blew a steady trade; and there was the island on the weather bow, a ribbon of palm trees lying flat along the sea. The captain and the mate looked at it with the night glass, and named the name of it, and talked of it, beside the wheel where Keola was steering. It seemed it was an isle where no traders came. By the captain's way, it was an isle besides where no man dwelt; but the mate thought otherwise.

"I don't give one cent for the directory," said he. "I've been past here one night in the schooner *Eugenie;* it was just such a night as this; they were fishing with torches, and the beach was thick with lights like a town."

"Well, well," says the captain, "it's steep-to, that's the great point; and there ain't any outlying dangers by the chart, so we'll just hug the lee side of it. — Keep her romping full, don't I tell you!" he cried to Keola, who was listening so hard that he forgot to steer.

And the mate cursed him, and swore that Kanaka was for no use in the world, and if he got started after him with a belaying pin, it would be a cold day for Keola.

And so the captain and mate lay down on the house together, and Keola was left to himself.

"This island will do very well for me," he thought; "if no traders deal there, the mate will never come. And as for Kalamake, it is not possible that he can ever get as far as this."

With that he kept edging the schooner nearer in. He had to do this quietly, for it was the trouble with these white men, and above all with the mate, that you could never be sure of them; they would be all sleeping sound, or else pretending, and if a sail shook they would jump to their feet and fall on you with a rope's end. So Keola edged her up little by little, and kept all drawing. And presently the land was close on board, and the sound of the sea on the sides of it grew loud.

With that the mate sat up suddenly upon the house.

"What are you doing?" he roars. "You'll have the ship ashore!"

And he made one bound for Keola, and Keola made another clean over the rail and plump into the starry sea. When he came up again, the schooner had payed off her true course, and the mate stood by the wheel himself, and Keola heard him cursing. The sea was smooth under the lee of the island; it was warm besides, and Keola had his sailor's knife, so he had no fear of sharks. A little way before him the trees stopped; there was a break in the line of the land like the mouth of a harbor; and the tide, which was then flowing, took him up and carried him through. One minute he was without, and the next within: had floated there in a wide shallow water, bright with ten thousand stars, and all about him was the ring of the land, with its string of palm trees. And he was amazed, because this was a kind of island he had never heard of.

The time of Keola in that place was in two periods — the period when he was alone, and the period when he was there with the tribe. At first he sought everywhere and found no man; only some houses standing in a hamlet, and the marks of fires. But the ashes of the fires were cold and the rains had washed them away; and the winds had blown, and some of the huts were overthrown. It was here he took his dwelling; and he made a fire drill, and a shell hook, and fished and cooked his fish, and climbed after green coconuts, the juice of which he drank, for in all the isle there was no water. The days were long to him, and the nights terrifying. He made a lamp of coco shell, and drew the oil of the ripe nuts, and made a wick of fiber; and when evening came he closed up his hut, and lit his lamp, and lay and trembled till morning. Many a time he thought in his heart he would have been better in the bottom of the sea, his bones rolling there with the others.

All this while he kept by the inside of the island, for the huts were on the shore of the lagoon, and it was there the palms grew best, and the lagoon itself abounded with good fish. And to the outer side he went once only, and he looked but the once at the beach of the ocean, and came away shaking. For the look of it, with its bright sand, and strewn shells, and strong sun and surf, went sore against his inclination.

"It cannot be," he thought, "and yet it is very like. And how do I know? These white men, although they pretend to know where they are sailing, must take their chance like other people. So after all we may have sailed in a circle, and I may be quite near to Molokai, and this may be the very beach where my father-in-law gathers his dollars."

So after that he was prudent, and kept to the land side.

It was perhaps a month later when the people of the place arrived — the fill of six great boats. They were a fine race of men, and spoke a tongue that sounded very different from the tongue of Hawaii, but so many of the words were the same that it was not difficult to understand. The men besides were very courteous, and the women very towardly; and they made Keola welcome, and built him a house, and gave him a wife; and, what surprised him the most, he was never sent to work with the young men.

And now Keola had three periods. First he had a period of being very sad, and then he had a period when he was pretty merry. Last of all came the third, when he was the most terrified man in the four oceans.

The cause of the first period was the girl he had to wife. He was in doubt about the island, and he might have been in doubt about the speech, of which he had heard so little when he came there with the wizard on the mat. But about his wife there was no mistake conceivable, for she was the same girl that ran from him crying in the wood. So he had sailed all this way, and might as well have stayed in Molokai; and had left home and wife and all his friends for no other cause but to escape his enemy, and the place he had come to was that wizard's hunting ground, and the shore where he walked invisible. It was at this period when he kept the most close to the lagoon side, and, as far as he dared, abode in the cover of his hut.

The cause of the second period was talk he heard from his wife and the chief islanders. Keola himself said little. He was never so sure of his new friends, for he judged they were too civil to be wholesome, and since he had grown better acquainted with his father-in-law the man had grown more cautious. So he told them nothing of himself, but only his name and descent, and that he came from the Eight Islands, and what fine islands they were; and about the king's palace in Honolulu, and how he was a chief friend of the king and the missionaries. But he put many questions and learned much. The island were he was was called the Isle of Voices; it belonged to the tribe, but they made their home upon another, three hours' sail to the southward. There they lived and had their permanent houses, and it was a rich island, where were eggs and chickens and pigs, and ships came trading with rum and tobacco. It was there the schooner had gone after Keola deserted; there, too, the mate had died, like the fool of a white man as he was. It seems, when the ship came, it was the beginning of the sickly season in that isle; when the fish of the lagoon are poisonous, and all who eat of them swell up and die. The mate was told of it; he saw the boats preparing, because in that season the people leave that island and sail to the Isle of Voices; but he was a fool of a white man, who would believe no stories but his own, and he caught one of these fish, cooked it and ate it, and swelled up and died, which was good news to Keola. As for the Isle of Voices, it lay solitary the most part of the year; only now and then a boat's crew came for copra, and in the bad season, when the fish at the main isle were poisonous, the tribe dwelt there in a body. It had its name from a marvel, for it seemed the sea side of it was all beset with invisible devils; day and night you heard them talking one with another in strange tongues; day and night little fires blazed up and were extinguished on the beach; and what was the cause of these doings no man might conceive. Keola asked them if it were the same in their own island where they stayed, and they told him no, not there; nor yet in any other of some hundred isles that lay all about them in that sea; but it was a thing peculiar to the Isle of Voices. They told him also that these fires and voices were ever on the sea side and in the seaward fringes of the wood, and a man might dwell by the lagoon two thousand years (if he could live so long) and never be any way troubled; and even on the sea side the devils did no harm if let alone. Only once a chief had cast a spear at one of the voices, and the same night he fell out of a coconut palm and was killed.

Keola thought a good bit with himself. He saw he would be all right when the tribe returned to the main island, and right enough where he was, if he kept by the lagoon, yet he had a mind to make things righter if he could. So he told the high chief he had once been in an isle that was pestered the same way, and the folk had found a means to cure that trouble.

"There was a tree growing in the bush there," says he, "and it seems these devils came to get the leaves of it. So the people of the isle cut down the tree wherever it was found, and the devils came no more."

They asked what kind of tree this was, and he showed them the tree of which Kalamake burned the leaves. They found it hard to believe, yet the idea tickled them. Night after night the old men debated it in their councils, but the high chief (though he was a brave man) was afraid of the matter, and reminded them daily of the chief who had cast a spear against the voices and was killed, and the thought of that brought all to a stand again.

Though he could not yet bring about the destruction of the trees, Keola was well enough pleased, and began to look about him and take pleasure in his days; and, among other things, he was the kinder to his wife, so that the girl began to love him greatly. One day he came to the hut, and she lay on the ground lamenting.

"Why," said Keola, "what is wrong with you now?"

She declared it was nothing.

The same night she woke him. The lamp burned very low, but he saw by her face she was in sorrow.

"Keola, she said, "put your ear to my mouth that I may whisper, for no one must hear us. Two days before the boats begin to be got ready, go you to the sea side of the isle and lie in a thicket. We shall choose that place beforehand, you and I; and hide food; and every night I shall come near by there singing. So when a night comes and you do not hear me, you shall know we are clean gone out of the island, and you may come forth again in safety."

The soul of Keola died within him.

"What is this?" he cried. "I cannot live among devils. I will not be left behind upon this isle. I am dying to leave it."

"You will never leave it alive, my poor Keola," said the girl; "for to tell you the truth, my people are eaters of men; but this they keep secret. And the reason they will kill you before we leave is because in our island ships come, and Donat-Kima-ran comes and talks for the French, and there is a white trader there in a house with a veranda, and a catechist. O, that is a fine place indeed! The trader has barrels filled with flour; and a French warship once came in the lagoon and gave everybody wine and biscuit. Ah, my poor Keola, I wish I could take you there, for great is my love to you, and it is the finest place in the seas except Papeete."

So now Keola was the most terrified man in the four oceans. He had heard tell of eaters of men in the south islands, and the thing had always been a fear to him; and here it was knocking at his door. He had heard besides, by travelers, of their practices, and how when they are in a mind to eat a man they cherish and fondle him like a mother with a favorite baby. And he saw this must be his own case; and that was why he had been housed, and fed, and wived, and liberated from all work; and why the old men and the chiefs discoursed with him like a person of weight. So he lay on his bed and railed upon his destiny; and the flesh curdled on his bones.

The next day the people of the tribe were very civil, as their way was. They were elegant speakers, and they made beautiful poetry, and jested at meals, so that a missionary must have died laughing. It was little enough Keola cared for their fine ways; all he saw was the white teeth shining in their mouths, and his gorge rose at the sight; and when they were done eating, he went and lay in the bush like a dead man.

The next day it was the same, and then his wife followed him.

"Keola," she said, "if you do not eat, I tell you plainly you will be killed and cooked tomorrow. Some of the old chiefs are murmuring already. They think you are fallen sick and must lose flesh."

With that Keola got to his feet, and anger burned in him.

"It is little I care one way or the other," said he. "I am between the devil and the deep sea. Since die I must, let me die the quickest way; and since I must be eaten at the best of it, let me rather be eaten by hobgoblins than by men. Farewell," said he, and he left her standing, and walked to the sea side of that island.

It was all bare in the strong sun; there was no sign of man, only the beach was trodden, and all about him as he went the voices talked and whispered, and the little fires sprang up and burned down. All tongues of the earth were spoken there; the French, the Dutch, the Russian, the Tamil, the Chinese. Whatever land knew sorcery, there were some of its people whispering in Keola's ear. That beach was thick as a cried fair, yet no man seen; and as he walked he saw the shells vanish before him, and no man to pick them up. I think the devil would have been afraid to be alone in such a company: but Keola was past fear and courted death. When the fires sprang up, he charged for them like a bull. Bodiless voices called to and fro; unseen hands poured sand upon the flames; and they were gone from the beach before he reached them.

"It is plain Kalamake is not here," he thought, "or I must have been killed long since."

With that he sat him down in the margin of the wood, for he was tired, and put his chin upon his hands. The business before his eyes continued: the beach babbled with voices, and the fires sprang up and sank, and the shells vanished and were renewed again even while he looked.

"It was a by-day when I was here before," he thought, "for it was nothing to this."

And his head was dizzy with the thought of these millions and millions of dollars, and all these hundreds and hundreds of persons culling them upon the beach and flying in the air higher and swifter than eagles.

"And to think how they have fooled me with their talk of mints," says he, "and that money was made there, when it is clear that all the new coin in all the world is gathered on these sands! But I will know better the next time!" said he.

And at last, he knew not very well how or when, sleep fell on Keola, and he forgot the island and all his sorrows.

Early the next day, before the sun was yet up, a bustle woke him. He awoke in fear, for he thought the tribe had caught him napping; but it was no such matter. Only, on the beach in front of him, the bodiless voices called and shouted one upon another, and it seemed they all passed and swept beside him up the coast of the island.

"What is afoot now?" thinks Keola. And it was plain to him it was something beyond ordinary, for the fires were not lighted nor the shells taken, but the bodiless voices kept posting up the beach, and hailing and dying away; and others following, and by the sound of them these wizards should be angry.

"It is not me they are angry at," thought Keola, "for they pass me close."

As when hounds go by, or horses in a race, or city folks coursing to a fire, and all men join and follow after, so it was now with Keola; and he knew not what he did, nor why he did it, but there, lo and behold! he was running with the voices.

So he turned one point of the island, and this brought him in view of a second; and there he remembered the wizard trees to have been growing by the score together in a wood. From this point there went up a hubbub of men crying not to be described; and by the sound of them, those that he ran with shaped their course for the same quarter. A little nearer, and there began to mingle with the outcry the crash of many axes. And at this a thought came at last into his mind that the high chief had consented; that the men of the tribe had set to cutting down these trees; that word had gone about the isle from sorcerer to sorcerer, and these were all now assembling to defend their trees. Desire of strange things swept him on. He posted with the voices, crossed the beach, and came into the borders of the wood, and stood astonished. One tree had fallen, others were part hewed away. There was the tribe clustered. They were back to back, and bodies lay, and blood flowed among their feet. The hue of fear was on all their faces: their voices went up to heaven shrill as a weasel's cry.

Have you seen a child when he is all alone and has a wooden sword, and fights, leaping and hewing with the empty air? Even so the man-eaters huddled back to back, and heaved up their axes, and laid on, and screamed as they laid on, and behold! no man to contend with them! only here and there

Keola saw an ax swinging over against them without hands; and time and again a man of the tribe would fall before it, clove in twain or burst asunder, and his soul sped howling.

For a while Keola looked upon this prodigy like one that dreams, and then fear took him by the midst as sharp as death, that he should behold such doings. Even in that same flash the high chief of the clan espied him standing, and pointed and called out his name. Thereat the whole tribe saw him also, and their eyes flashed, and their teeth clashed.

"I am too long here," thought Keola, and ran further out of the wood and down the beach, not caring whither.

"Keola!" said a voice close by upon the empty sand.

"Lehua! is that you?" he cried, and gasped, and looked in vain for her; but by the eyesight he was stark alone.

"I saw you pass before," the voice answered; "but you would not hear me. — Quick! get the leaves and the herbs, and let us flee."

"You are there with the mat?" he asked.

"Here, at your side," said she. And he felt her arms about him. — "Quick! the leaves and the herbs, before my father can get back!"

So Keola ran for his life, and fetched the wizard fuel: and Lehua guided him back, and set his feet upon the mat, and made the fire. All the time of its burning the sound of the battle towered out of the wood; the wizards and the man-eaters hard at fight; the wizards, the viewless ones, roaring out aloud like bulls upon a mountain, and the men of the tribe replying shrill and savage out of the terror of their souls. And all the time of the burning, Keola stood there and listened, and shook, and watched how the unseen hands of Lehua poured the leaves. She poured them fast, and the flame burned high, and scorched Keola's hands; and she speeded and blew the burning with her breath. The last leaf was eaten, the flame fell, and the shock followed, and there were Keola and Lehua in the room at home.

Now, when Keola could see his wife at last he was mighty pleased, and he was mighty pleased to be home again in

Molokai and sit down beside a bowl of poi — for they make no poi on board ships, and there was none in the Isle of Voices — and he was out of the body with pleasure to be clean escaped out of the hands of the eaters of men. But there was another matter not so clear, and Lehua and Keola talked of it all night and were troubled. There was Kalamake left upon the isle. If, by the blessing of God, he could but stick there, all were well; but should he escape and return to Molokai, it would be an ill day for his daughter and her husband. They spoke of his gift of swelling, and whether he could wade that distance in the seas. But Keola knew by this time where that island was — and that is to say, in the Low or Dangerous Archipelago. So they fetched the atlas and looked upon the distance in the map, and by what they could make of it, it seemed a far way for an old gentleman to walk. Still, it would not do to make too sure of a warlock like Kalamake, and they determined at last to take counsel of a white missionary.

So the first one that came by, Keola told him everything. And the missionary was very sharp on him for taking the second wife in the low island; but for all the rest, he vowed he could make neither head nor tail of it.

"However," says he, "if you think this money of your father's ill gotten, my advice to you would be, give some of it to the lepers and some to the missionary fund. And as for this extraordinary rigmarole, you can not do better than keep it to yourselves."

But he warned the police at Honolulu that, by all he could make out, Kalamake and Keola had been coining false money, and it would not be amiss to watch them.

Keola and Lehua took his advice, and gave many dollars to the lepers and the fund. And no doubt the advice must have been good, for from that day to this Kalamake had never more been heard of. But whether he was slain in the battle by the trees, or whether he is still kicking his heels upon the Isle of Voices, who shall say?

From *Island Nights' Entertainments* by R. L. Stevenson (London, Cassell & Company, Ltd., 1893).

R. L. STEVENSON

# TO PRINCESS KAIULANI

Stevenson's most congenial friends during his sojourn at Waikiki in 1889 were A. S. Cleghorn, a fellow Scot who had become a successful merchant in Honolulu, and his thirteen-year-old daughter Kaiulani. Cleghorn had married Princess Miriam Likelike, sister of the reigning King Kalakaua, and their daughter was later declared heir-apparent. R.L.S. used to stroll over to the Cleghorn estate of Ainahau and talk with father and daughter under a spreading banyan tree, not far from the site of the towering Princess Kaiulani Hotel of today. To her he related stories of Scotland and the Pacific, and she responded with the wit and charm of her nature. When she seemed loath to leave her islands and visit Europe, he tried to tell her how she would make new friends and bring brightness there. Then he inscribed the following lines in her red-plush album.

> Forth from her land to mine she goes,
> The island maid, the island rose,
> Light of heart and bright of face:
> The daughter of a double race.
> Her islands here, in southern sun,
> Shall mourn their Kaiulani gone,
> And I, in her dear banyan shade,
> Look vainly for my little maid.
>
> But our Scots islands far away
> Shall glitter with unwonted day,
> And cast for once their tempests by
> To smile in Kaiulani's eye.

*Written in April to Kaiulani in the April of her age; and at Waikiki, within easy walk of Kaiulani's banyan! When she comes to my land and her father's, and the rain beats upon the window (as I fear it will), let her look at this page; it will be like a weed gathered and pressed at home; and she will remember her own islands, and the shadow of the mighty tree; and she will hear the peacocks screaming in the dusk and the wind blowing in the palms; and she will think of her father sitting there alone.* — R.L.S.

From *Ballads and Other Poems,* Collected Works of Robert Louis Stevenson, Thistle Edition (New York, Scribner, 1897).

AUSTIN STRONG

# HIS OCEANIC MAJESTY'S GOLDFISH

One of the most delightful stories ever written about Hawaii in the days of King Kalakaua is the following reminiscence of childhood by Austin Strong (1881–1957). Born in San Francisco, he was a child when his parents took him on a sojourn to Honolulu. His father was Joseph Strong, an artist, and his mother was Isobel Osbourne Strong, stepdaughter of Robert Louis Stevenson. Later, when his parents were divorced, Austin and his mother lived with the Stevensons in Samoa until the author's death. After attending Wellington College in New Zealand, Strong went to New York, where he became first a landscape architect and afterwards a successful playwright.

THE LARGE MUSTACHE WAS MY FATHER, THE BEAUTIFUL DARK eyes my mother. I was aware of tears, champagne glasses, laughing speeches, and farewell shouts as we stood at the ship's rail looking back at Meiggs Wharf and the receding city of San Francisco.

Our heavy sails turned to iron as the northeast wind struck them with a howl, sending the tiny schooner scudding through the Golden Gate to breast the angry Pacific waiting outside to pounce on us. Suddenly everything went mad; screaming sea gulls were blown high; the vessel leaped into the air and fell on her side, half capsized by a knockdown flaw, her lee rail disappearing under a wash of green water and foaming suds. The young couple fell to the deck clutching their small son.

150

They laughingly held me between them as we all three slid down the careening deck to be rescued in the nick of time by grinning brown sailors smelling of tar, coconut oil, and chewing tobacco. One of them, at the request of my mother, tied a double bowline around my waist, making the end fast to a ring bolt on the white deck.

Here I was tethered, a none too safe prisoner, every day for fourteen terrifying days. Tied to that slanting, heaving floor, which was half under water the whole length of the ship, I was buffeted, jerked off my feet, stung by flying spray, deafened by the never ending roar of the wind and sea.

Green waters full of iridescent bubbles snatched at my feet when they swept by, leaving long damp stains on the deck. The winds blew up my sleeves, whipping my hair in all directions. Everywhere there was wild excitement — banging of blocks, angry shouts, sudden rushings of the crew to take in or let out the main and jib sheets. No one had to tell me that our lives were in the four hands of the two struggling men at the wheel and that the angel with the dark wings was hovering over our masts.

The large mustache would prick my cheek as my father brought his reassuring face close to mine, while my mother held me safe, and together they would sing to keep fear away from me. I would look into the eyes of my mother, searching for any sign of anxiety in the clear, quiet depths, and finding none I would breathe again, feeling the iron band about my heart relax. I caught the infection of their happiness and we would all laugh together for no reason at all.

They were filled with high hope, for riches and honors lay ahead of us. No wonder they were gay, for had not our good rich friend commissioned my father to go to Honolulu to paint a picture of the volcano Mauna Loa in full eruption? And hadn't they an important letter of introduction to a real king who sat on a real throne, wore a real crown, and lived in a real palace, His Oceanic Majesty, King Kalakaua of the Hawaiian Archipelago?

Since we were too poor to afford tickets on a Pacific liner, our benefactor had given us free passage on one of his trading schooners, the *Consuelo*, and these two babes in the wood, with their solemn offspring, were blown at last around Diamond Head under the lee of Punchbowl into the breathless heat of Honolulu Harbor, dangerous seas now far behind, fame and fortune beckoning us from the shores.

A long, graceful boat manned by singing natives in uniform shot out from the king's boathouse. She was dazzling white, with a canvas awning the length of her and a gilded crown on either side of her bow. This was the royal barge coming alongside with tossed oars to row us ashore in state.

We went to live in a wooden cottage that might have been taken from a child's picture book. It was set back from Fort Street, almost lost in a fragrant garden of big leaves and strange-looking flowers. Young attachés and their wives from all the legations annexed my parents with joy, and our wide veranda fairly glistened with naval gold lace from the British, French, Russian, and Chilean men-of-war. My gay parents must have been a godsend to those exiles of every nationality.

I lived to the tune of their laughter and endless parties, but in spite of belonging to the king's set, in spite of my father's success as an artist, I was not happy. The children who lived on our street looked down their noses at me.

It was the fashion in those days to have at the entrances of one's driveway half a tub constantly filled by a pipe with fresh water for the horses. The rich people had handsome tubs painted with bright colors at their gates and, to add to their prestige, their tubs were alive with goldfish. Ours was old and unpainted, a shabby affair with rusty hoops, and, alas, contained no fish. The neighboring children made faces at me and with an ancient malice insisted that we were too poor to have goldfish in our disreputable tub. It troubled me that my hilarious parents had no idea that we were losing face with our neighbors' children, but boylike I kept my suffering to myself.

One day the Japanese attachés from the legation across the way came over for lunch. They were dressed like dark butterflies in their national costume. I stood on the outer edge of the veranda and overheard them telling about the beautiful double-tailed goldfish the Emperor of Japan had just sent to King Kalakaua and how they had emptied them officially that morning into the lily pond of the royal Kapiolani Park. They told my mother these sacred fish were very rare and belonged to the royal family of Japan.

My heart skipped a beat; I was stabbed by a sudden overwhelming desire. In one moment I had become a thief. From then on I saw nothing but an imperial fish swimming in our battered tub, giving face to my carefree parents and despair to my enemies.

Kapiolani Park was out of town near Waikiki, and it cost five cents to go there in the mule-car. Finding I had ten cents in my tin-can bank, I dashed up to the friendly old Chinese groceryman at the head of our street and for five cents bought a ball of red, white, and blue string. I then took two bright new pins from my Portuguese nurse's sewing basket and plunged into action.

This was my first adventure alone into the great out-of-doors away from the safe and protected area under my nurse's eye. With a pounding heart I hailed the mule-car, a wide open-air affair with a cool covering of white canvas and bobbing tassels. It was driven by a barefoot Kanaka with a sleepy face. I held up a timid finger and to my astonishment I was obeyed — the car stopped at my command. I felt important and apologetic at the same time when I found I was the only passenger, for it was the hot, buzzy time of the afternoon when everyone retires for a siesta.

With one wheel flat and squeaking, we swayed and bumped along through the deserted city, down freshly watered avenues kept in perpetual twilight by the shade of flowering trees overhead. The air was filled with the stinging scent of roasting coffee and burnt sugar, while over all hung the redoubtable smell of distant Chinatown, that potent mixture of teeming humanity, rotting fish, sandalwood, and incense.

I heard a warning voice within as I paid my carfare with my last remaining nickel. It whispered, "How are you going to come back with no money?" But I shut my ears tight, and going forward with a pounding heart, I sat close to the driver as we came out of the city into the blinding white road which ran along the shore.

"Want to drive?" he asked, smiling through an enormous yawn as he held out the reins. I clutched the stiff hot leathers while the driver disappeared inside, curled up on the bench, and promptly fell asleep. This was my first meeting with responsibility. Though my bare feet were being burned alive by the heat of the sun on the platform, I stood motionless.

The mule, with his large ears encased in netted fly-bags, feeling the hand of inexperience, promptly relaxed and reduced his speed to a crawl. He dragged us at a snail's pace along the edge of the beach and I could see the lines on lines of charging surf running white over the hidden reefs. To the left I could see half-naked Chinese, with their big cone-shaped hats, working like animated mushrooms, thigh-deep in mud, planting rice in the flat watery fields against a background of green mountains.

We crept along until at last the mule stopped of himself, poked his head around his stern, whisked a fly away with his tail, and looked at me with distaste. The driver woke with a start, shouting automatically as if I were a full carload of passengers: "All out for Kapiolani Park!"

I thanked him politely as he lifted me down in front of the entrance to the Park and I asked him to read me a freshly painted sign at the side of the gates. He slowly read the words: "Fishing in the Park is strictly prohibited and will be punished with the full severity of the law. — KALAKAUA, REX."

I stood rooted to the ground as the driver, with a sleepy grin, drove the bobbing mule-car around a curve and out of sight, leaving me with my ball of twine, my pins, and my pockets empty of money. I stood for a time stunned. "Full severity of the law" meant only one thing when a king caught you. Your head was chopped off on a block of wood in the Tower of London and popped into a basket. Slowly I drew half circles in the dust with my big toe, waiting for my heart to quiet down.

By fine degrees courage returned to me. It came first in the shape of curiosity. I edged my way slowly through the gates, tiptoeing out of the blinding heat into the chill cathedral gloom of the Park. I saw two Chinese gardeners sweeping the driveway. Again I stood still for a long time. Finding they paid no attention to me, I took a few cautious steps farther in and once more became rooted to the ground, for there, quite near me, squatting on his haunches, was a half-naked Chinese with the face of a joss-house mask. He was cutting the grass with an evil-looking scimitar. Standing still until he had worked himself out of sight round a tree, I dashed off the roadway across the lawn into a beautiful Chinese garden with gray stone lanterns, pagodas, and frog-faced lions goggle-eyed with ferocity.

I came to a pond filled with water lilies, the edges of their enormous pads neatly turned up, like little fences. A moon-bridge arched over the still water and I climbed the slippery incline, which is very steep until the circle flattens out on top; here I lay on my stomach, quaking. Guilt had laid a cold hand on me. I was a robber in a royal domain.

Placing my straw hat beside me and slowly raising my head, I looked carefully about for sign of a human being, but apparently this garden was a place apart. It was empty of life save for one pink flamingo who stared at me suspiciously. I peered down into the pool below and saw a small white object which stared up at me with frightened eyes. It was my own face reflected among the lilies.

Then I saw them! I couldn't believe my good luck. I had found them at last, the noble goldfish of the Emperor of Japan. Prodigious fellows, obviously aristocrats of high degree, wearing feathery fins and tails like court trains, trailing clouds of glory.

Quickly I bent a pin, and fastening it to the end of my red, white, and blue string I lowered it, hand over hand, into the liquid crystal below. The leisurely fish, as bright as porcelain, glided haughtily past my pin, not deigning to notice it. Why I thought a fish would swallow my baitless hook I do not know. It was a triumph of hope over experience, however, for after I had lain patiently on my stomach for a long time the miracle happened!

A large, dignified grand duke of a goldfish, attracted by the brightness of my pin, made the stupid mistake of thinking it was something good to eat. He slowly opened his bored face and swallowed it. A hard tug nearly toppled me off the bridge. I hauled up the sacred fish and soon had him indignantly flopping beside me, where he spat out the hook with disdain and would have flopped off the bridge had I not covered him with my straw hat. Again I peered around, now guilty in fact, for the deed was done.

The flamingo was still there, standing motionless on one leg, staring at me with an unblinking, accusing eye. In panic I hastily stuffed the fish into the crown of my hat, and jamming it on my head, with the victim struggling inside, I flew with the heels of terror out into the open road.

To my dismay I found the day almost spent as I ran before a following wind; the whole sky was afire with a red sunset which threw my gigantic shadow like a dancing hobgoblin far ahead of me on the wide road.

The awful voice spoke to me again. "There, what did I tell you? You have no money, so now you have an all-night walk in the dark."

But my only thought was how to keep my fish alive until I got him in our tub. I saw a wide irrigation ditch, which fed the paddy fields with water, running by the side of the road. Slipping down the bank, I removed my hat, and holding the fish by his golden tail, I plunged him into the water, arguing that to a fish this was like a breath of air to a suffocated man.

I held him under until he grew lively again and then I went on my interminable journey, running fast along the road, slipping down to the side of the ditch to souse my imperial highness until he revived enough for the next lap. I don't know how many times I did this, or how many hundred feet I had advanced along the way, but my legs began to ache and my head swam with weariness and wet fish. Then suddenly I was in the midst of warning shouts, angry men's voices, stamping horses, jingling harness, military commands — a carriage had nearly run over me.

I was too young to know about palace revolutions and the necessity for armed escorts. I only knew I was terrified to find myself surrounded by grave men on horseback. An officer leaped from his saddle and stood before me.

I had the presence of mind to jam my prize under my hat as I was led to a shining C-spring victoria which smelled of elegance, varnish, polished leather, and well-groomed horses.

In it rode a fine figure of a man, calm and immaculate in white ducks and pipe-clayed shoes. He sat in noble repose, his strong face, his hands, and his clothes dyed crimson by the tropical sunset. My heart began to jump about, for I recognized the face which was stamped on all the silver coins of his island realm. He wore his famous hat made of woven peacock quills as fine as straw, with its broad band of tiny sea shells. He eyed me gravely as I stood in the road before him, wet to the skin, with muddy hands and feet, my fish violently protesting under my hat. Would he order his soldiers to execute me on the spot?

"Why, it's Mrs. Strong's little boy!" the deep voice was saying. "What are you doing so far away from home?"

I was speechless.

"Your mother must be very anxious. Come, get in and I'll take you home."

The officer deposited me, dirty and damp, on the spotless cushion beside the king. An order rang out and away we dashed, a fine cavalcade with outriders galloping ahead and men on horseback thundering behind.

His Majesty began to question me tactfully, trying, as is the way with kings, to put his guest at ease, but the fish was too much on my mind and head. I realized it would soon die if I held my tongue, but if I told, what would be my punishment?

Try as I might, I couldn't hold back unmanly tears. The king removed his cigar in concern.

"Are you in pain, Austin?" he asked. I began to shake all over in an agony of indecision. "Won't you tell me what's the matter?"

I heard another and a craven voice blurting out of me.

"Oh, please don't cut off my head!" it cried.

The king replied gravely, "I have no intention of cutting off your head."

Removing my hat, I showed him his gift from the Emperor of Japan. The king raised a hand, the cavalcade came to a halt, again the officer was alongside. The king cried, "Stop at the nearest horse trough. Be quick!"

Away we flew, the king with his arm about me, trying vainly to comfort me as I saw my fish growing weaker and weaker. At last we drew up in front of a native hut. I jumped out and plunged my fish into an overflowing horse trough while the king and his men looked on with polite interest. A native was sent running for a large calabash, and the fish was put in it, his sacred life spared, his dignity restored.

I was rolled home in triumph, fast asleep against His Majesty's protecting shoulder, to be roused by shouts of laughter from my relieved parents, who were astounded by my royal return. They watched me with puzzled faces as, struggling with sleep, I staggered away from them to empty my golden prize into our tub.

No one ever knew why I stole that fish; wild horses couldn't drag an explanation from me. I woke very early the next day and crept out through the cool shadows of the morning across the wet lawn in my bare feet and peered anxiously into our tub. There, sure enough, was the grand duke swimming proudly in our shabby barrel, restoring face to my parents and raising their social standing in the society of my enemies.

There is no moral to this story — in fact it is a most unmoral one, for later that morning a smart equerry on horseback, dressed in a glistening uniform, dismounted before our gate.

He came bearing a large gilt-bordered envelope on which was stamped the crown of Hawaii.

It was a royal grant to one Master Austin Strong, giving him permission to fish in Kapiolani Park for the rest of his days. It was signed "KALAKAUA, REX."

From *The Atlantic Monthly*, May, 1944.

JACK LONDON

# KOOLAU THE LEPER

Bound on an adventurous cruise to the South Seas in their forty-three-foot ketch *Snark*, Jack London (1876–1916) and his wife Charmian sailed into Pearl Harbor in the spring of 1907. During a four-month sojourn, while the *Snark* was being refitted for its farther voyage, Jack London fell in love with the ways of Hawaii; and in 1915, at the height of fame, he returned to spend nearly a year as a resident of Honolulu. He took part in the social life of the town, he helped to revive the royal sport of surfboard riding, and he listened with a writer's interest to the tales and gossip about the island families. What he heard and saw on these two visits supplied him with material for two volumes of short stories set in Hawaii, *The House of Pride* (1912) and *On the Makaloa Mat* (1919).

Among the best of all Jack London's short stories is "Koolau the Leper," based upon an actual episode, a tragic clash between the forces of the law and an unfortunate Hawaiian who desperately resisted an attempt to send him to the isolated leper station on the island of Molokai.

"BECAUSE WE ARE SICK THEY TAKE AWAY OUR LIBERTY. WE HAVE obeyed the law. We have done no wrong. And yet they would put us in prison. Molokai is a prison. That you know. Niuli, there, his sister was sent to Molokai seven years ago. He has not seen her since. Nor will he ever see her. She must stay there until she dies. This is not her will. It is not Niuli's will. It is the will of the white men who rule the land. And who are these white men?

"We know. We have it from our fathers and our fathers' fathers. They came like lambs, speaking softly. Well might they

160

speak softly, for we were many and strong, and all the islands
were ours. As I say, they spoke softly. They were of two kinds.
The one kind asked our permission, our gracious permission, to
preach to us the word of God. The other kind asked our permission, our gracious permission, to trade with us. That was
the beginning. Today all the islands are theirs, all the land, all
the cattle — everything is theirs. They that preached the word
of God and they that preached the word of Rum have fore-
gathered and become great chiefs. They live like kings in houses
of many rooms, with multitudes of servants to care for them.
They who had nothing have everything, and if you, or I, or any
Kanaka be hungry, they sneer and say, 'Well, why don't you
work? There are the plantations.' "

Koolau paused. He raised one hand, and with gnarled and
twisted fingers lifted up the blazing wreath of hibiscus that
crowned his black hair. The moonlight bathed the scene in silver. It was a night of peace, though those who sat about him
and listened had all the seeming of battle-wrecks. Their faces
were leonine. Here a space yawned in a face where should have
been a nose, and there an arm stump showed where a hand had
rotted off. They were men and women beyond the pale, the
thirty of them, for upon them had been placed the mark of the
beast.

They sat, flower-garlanded, in the perfumed, luminous night,
and their lips made uncouth noises and their throats rasped
approval of Koolau's speech. They were creatures who once
had been men and women. But they were men and women no
longer. They were monsters — in face and form grotesque
caricatures of everything human. They were hideously maimed
and distorted, and had the seeming of creatures that had been
racked in millenniums of hell. Their hands, when they possessed them, were like harpy-claws. Their faces were the mis-
fits and slips, crushed and bruised by some mad god at play
in the machinery of life. Here and there were features which
the mad god had smeared half away, and one woman wept
scalding tears from twin pits of horror, where her eyes once
had been. Some were in pain and groaned from their chests.

Others coughed, making sounds like the tearing of tissue. Two were idiots, more like huge apes marred in the making, until even an ape were an angel. They mowed and gibbered in the moonlight, under crowns of drooping, golden blossoms. One, whose bloated earlobe flapped like a fan upon his shoulder, caught up a gorgeous flower of orange and scarlet and with it decorated the monstrous ear that flip-flapped with his every movement.

And over these things Koolau was king. And this was his kingdom — a flower-throttled gorge, with beetling cliffs and crags, from which floated the blattings of wild goats. On three sides the grim walls rose, festooned in fantastic draperies of tropic vegetation and pierced by cave entrances — the rocky lairs of Koolau's subjects. On the fourth side the earth fell away into a tremendous abyss, and, far below, could be seen the summits of lesser peaks and crags, at whose bases foamed and rumbled the Pacific surge. In fine weather a boat could land on the rocky beach that marked the entrance of Kalalau Valley, but the weather must be very fine. And a cool-headed mountaineer might climb from the beach to the head of Kalalau Valley, to this pocket among the peaks where Koolau ruled; but such a mountaineer must be very cool of head, and he must know the wild-goat trails as well. The marvel was that the mass of human wreckage that constituted Koolau's people should have been able to drag its helpless misery over the giddy goat trails to this inaccessible spot.

"Brothers," Koolau began.

But one of the mowing, apelike travesties emitted a wild shriek of madness, and Koolau waited while the shrill cachinnation was tossed back and forth among the rocky walls and echoed distantly through the pulseless night.

"Brothers, is it not strange? Ours was the land, and behold, the land is not ours. What did these preachers of the word of God and the word of Rum give us for the land? Have you received one dollar, as much as one dollar, any one of you, for the land? Yet it is theirs, and in return they tell us we can go to work on the land, their land, and that what we produce by our toil shall be theirs. Yet in the old days we did not have to work. Also, when we are sick, they take away our freedom."

"Who brought the sickness, Koolau?" demanded Kiloliana, a lean and wiry man with a face so like a laughing faun's that one might expect to see the cloven hoofs under him. They were cloven, it was true, but the cleavages were great ulcers and livid putrefactions. Yet this was Kiloliana, the most daring climber of them all, the man who knew every goat trail and who had led Koolau and his wretched followers into the recesses of Kalalau.

"Ay, well questioned," Koolau answered. "Because we would not work the miles of sugar cane where once our horses pastured, they brought the Chinese slaves from overseas. And with them came the Chinese sickness — that which we suffer from and because of which they would imprison us on Molokai. We were born on Kauai. We have been to the other islands, some here and some there, to Oahu, to Maui, to Hawaii, to Honolulu. Yet always did we come back to Kauai. Why did we come back? There must be a reason. Because we love Kauai. We were born here. Here we have lived. And here shall we die — unless — unless — there be weak hearts amongst us. Such we do not want. They are fit for Molokai. And if there be such, let them not remain. Tomorrow the soldiers land on the shore. Let the weak hearts go down to them. They will be sent swiftly to Molokai. As for us, we shall stay and fight. But know that we will not die. We have rifles. You know the narrow trails where men must creep, one by one. I, alone, Koolau, who was once a cowboy on Niihau, can hold the trail against a thousand men. Here is Kapahei, who was once a judge over men and a man with honor, but who is now a hunted rat, like you and me. Hear him. He is wise."

Kapahei arose. Once he had been a judge. He had gone to college at Punahou. He had sat at meat with lords and chiefs and the high representatives of alien powers who protected the interests of traders and missionaries. Such had been Kapahei. But now, as Koolau had said, he was a hunted rat, a creature outside the law, sunk so deep in the mire of human horror that he was above the law as well as beneath it. His face was featureless, save for gaping orifices and for the lidless eyes that burned under hairless brows.

"Let us not make trouble," he began. "We ask to be left alone. But if they do not leave us alone, then is the trouble theirs, and the penalty. My fingers are gone, as you see." He held up his stumps of hands that all might see. "Yet have I the joint of one thumb left, and it can pull a trigger as firmly as did its lost neighbor in the old days. We love Kauai. Let us live here, or die here, but do not let us go to the prison of Molokai. The sickness is not ours. We have not sinned. The men who preached the word of God and the word of Rum brought the sickness with the coolie slaves who work the stolen land. I have been a judge. I know the law and the justice, and I say to you it is unjust to steal a man's land, to make that man sick with the Chinese sickness, and then to put that man in prison for life."

"Life is short, and the days are filled with pain," said Koolau. "Let us drink and dance and be happy as we can."

From one of the rocky lairs calabashes were produced and passed around. The calabashes were filled with the fierce distillation of the root of the ti plant; and as the liquid fire coursed through them and mounted to their brains, they forgot that they had once been men and women, for they were men and women once more. The woman who wept scalding tears from open eye-pits was indeed a woman apulse with life as she plucked the strings of an ukulele and lifted her voice in a barbaric love-call such as might have come from the dark forest depths of the primeval world. The air tingled with her cry, softly imperious and seductive. Upon a mat, timing his rhythm to the woman's song, Kiloliana danced. It was unmistakable. Love danced in all his movements, and, next, dancing with him on the mat, was a woman whose heavy hips and generous breast gave the lie to her disease-corroded face. It was a dance of the living dead, for in their disintegrating bodies life still loved and longed. Ever the woman whose sightless eyes ran scalding tears chanted her love-cry, ever the dancers danced of love in the warm night, and ever the calabashes went around till in all their brains were maggots crawling of memory and desire. And with the woman on the mat danced a slender maid whose face was beautiful and unmarred, but whose twisted arms that rose and fell marked the disease's ravage. And the two idiots, gibbering and mouthing strange noises, danced apart, grotesque, fantastic, travestying love as they themselves had been travestied by life.

But the woman's love-cry broke midway, the calabashes were lowered, and the dancers ceased, as all gazed into the abyss above the sea, where a rocket flared like a wan phantom through the moonlit air.

"It is the soldiers," said Koolau. "Tomorrow there will be fighting. It is well to sleep and be prepared."

The lepers obeyed, crawling away to their lairs in the cliff, until only Koolau remained, sitting motionless in the moonlight, his rifle across his knees, as he gazed far down to the boats landing on the beach.

The far head of Kalalau Valley had been well chosen as a refuge. Except Kiloliana, who knew back trails up the precipitous walls, no man would win to the gorge save by advancing across a knife-edged ridge. This passage was a hundred yards in length. At best, it was a scant twelve inches wide. On either side yawned the abyss. A slip, and to right or left the man would fall to his death. But once across he would find himself in an earthly paradise. A sea of vegetation laved the landscape, pouring its green billows from wall to wall, dripping from the cliff lips in great vine masses, and flinging a spray of ferns and air plants into the multitudinous crevices. During the many months of Koolau's rule, he and his followers had fought with this vegetable sea. The choking jungle, with its riot of blossoms, had been driven back from the bananas, oranges, and mangoes that grew wild. In little clearings grew the wild arrowroot; on stone terraces, filled with soil scrapings, were the taro patches and the melons; and in every open space where the sunshine penetrated were papaya trees burdened with their golden fruit.

Koolau had been driven to this refuge from the lower valley by the beach. And if he were driven from it in turn, he knew of gorges among the jumbled peaks of the inner fastnesses where he could lead his subjects and live. And now he lay with his rifle beside him, peering down through a tangled screen of foliage at the soldiers on the beach. He noted that they had large guns with them, from which the sunshine flashed as from mirrors. The knife-edged passage lay directly before him. Crawling upward along the trail that led to it he could see tiny specks of men. He knew they were not the soldiers, but the police. When they failed, then the soldiers would enter the game.

He affectionately rubbed a twisted hand along his rifle barrel and made sure that the sights were clean. He had learned to shoot as a wild-cattle hunter on Niihau, and on that island his skill as a marksman was unforgotten. As the toiling specks of men grew nearer and larger, he estimated the range, judged the deflection of the wind that swept at right angles across the line of fire, and calculated the chances of overshooting marks that were so far below his level. But he did not shoot. Not until they reached the beginning of the passage did he make his presence known. He did not disclose himself, but spoke from the thicket.

"What do you want?" he demanded.

"We want Koolau, the leper," answered the man who led the native police, himself a blue-eyed American.

"You must go back," Koolau said.

He knew the man, a deputy sheriff, for it was by him that he had been harried out of Niihau, across Kauai, to Kalalau Valley, and out of the valley to the gorge.

"Who are you?" the sheriff asked.

"I am Koolau, the leper," was the reply.

"Then come out. We want you. Dead or alive, there is a thousand dollars on your head. You cannot escape."

Koolau laughed aloud in the thicket.

"Come out!" the sheriff commanded, and was answered by silence.

He conferred with the police, and Koolau saw that they were preparing to rush him.

"Koolau," the sheriff called. "Koolau, I am coming across to get you."

"Then look first and well about you at the sun and sea and sky, for it will be the last time you behold them."

"That's all right, Koolau," the sheriff said soothingly. "I know you're a dead shot. But you won't shoot me. I have never done you any wrong."

Koolau grunted in the thicket.

"I say, you know, I've never done you any wrong, have I?" the sheriff persisted.

"You do me wrong when you try to put me in prison," was the reply. "And you do me wrong when you try for the thousand dollars on my head. If you will live, stay where you are."

"I've got to come across and get you. I'm sorry. But it is my duty."

"You will die before you get across."

The sheriff was no coward. Yet was he undecided. He gazed into the gulf on either side, and ran his eyes along the knife-edge he must travel. Then he made up his mind.

"Koolau," he called.

But the thicket remained silent.

"Koolau, don't shoot. I am coming."

The sheriff turned, gave some orders to the police, then started on his perilous way. He advanced slowly. It was like walking a tight rope. He had nothing to lean upon but the air. The lava rock crumbled under his feet, and on either side the dislodged fragments pitched downward through the depths. The sun blazed upon him, and his face was wet with sweat. Still he advanced, until the halfway point was reached.

"Stop!" Koolau commanded from the thicket. "One more step and I shoot."

The sheriff halted, swaying for balance as he stood poised above the void. His face was pale, but his eyes were determined. He licked his dry lips before he spoke.

"Koolau, you won't shoot me. I know you won't."

He started once more. The bullet whirled him half about. On his face was an expression of querulous surprise as he reeled to the fall. He tried to save himself by throwing his body across the knife-edge; but at that moment he knew death. The next moment the knife-edge was vacant. Then came the rush, five policemen, in single file, with superb steadiness, running along the knife-edge. At the same instant the rest of the posse opened fire on the thicket. It was madness. Five times Koolau pulled the trigger, so rapidly that his shots constituted a rattle. Changing his position and crouching low under the bullets that were biting and singing through the bushes, he peered out. Four of the police had followed the sheriff. The fifth lay across the knife-edge, still alive. On the farther side, no longer firing, were the surviving police. On the naked rock there was no hope for them. Before they could clamber down Koolau could have picked off the last men. But he did not fire, and, after a conference, one of them took off a white undershirt and waved it as a flag. Followed by another, he advanced along the knife-edge to their wounded comrade. Koolau gave no sign, but watched them slowly withdraw and become specks as they descended into the lower valley.

Two hours later, from another thicket, Koolau watched a body of police trying to make the ascent from the the opposite side of the valley. He saw the wild goats flee before them as they climbed higher and higher, until he doubted his judgment and sent for Kiloliana, who crawled in beside him.

"No, there is no way," said Kiloliana.

"The goats?" Koolau questioned.

"They come over from the next valley, but they cannot pass to this. There is no way. Those men are not wiser than goats. They may fall to their deaths. Let us watch."

Side by side they lay among the morning-glories, with the yellow blossoms of the hau dropping upon them from overhead, watching the motes of men toil upward, till the thing happened, and three of them, slipping, rolling, sliding, dashed over a cliff lip and fell sheer half a thousand feet.

Kiloliana chuckled.

"We will be bothered no more," he said.

"They have war guns," Koolau made answer. "The soldiers have not yet spoken."

In the drowsy afternoon, most of the lepers lay in their rock dens asleep. Koolau, his rifle on his knees, fresh-cleaned and ready, dozed in the entrance to his own den. The maid with the twisted arm lay below in the thicket and kept watch on the knife-edge passage. Suddenly Koolau was startled wide awake by the sound of an explosion on the beach. The next instant the atmosphere was incredibly rent asunder. The terrible sound frightened him. It was as if all the gods had caught the envelope of the sky in their hands and were ripping it apart as a woman rips apart a sheet of cotton cloth. But it was such an immense ripping, growing swiftly nearer. Koolau glanced up apprehensively, as if expecting to see the thing. Then high up on the cliff overhead the shell burst in a fountain of black smoke. The rock was shattered, the fragments falling to the foot of the cliff.

Koolau passed his hand across his sweaty brow. He was terribly shaken. He had no experience with shellfire, and this was more dreadful than anything he had imagined.

"One," said Kapahei, suddenly bethinking himself to keep count.

A second and a third shell flew screaming over the top of the wall, bursting beyond view. Kapahei methodically kept the count. The lepers crowded into the open space before the caves. At first they were frightened, but as the shells continued their flight overhead the leper folk became reassured and began to admire the spectacle. The two idiots shrieked with delight, prancing wild antics as each air-tormenting shell went by. Koolau began to recover his confidence. No damage was being done. Evidently they could not aim such large missiles at such long range with the precision of a rifle.

But a change came over the situation. The shells began to fall short. One burst below in the thicket by the knife-edge. Koolau remembered the maid who lay there on watch, and ran down to see. The smoke was still rising from the bushes when he crawled in. He was astounded. The branches were splintered and broken. Where the girl had lain was a hole in the ground. The girl herself was in shattered fragments. The shell had burst right on her.

First peering out to make sure no soldiers were attempting the passage, Koolau started back on the run for the caves. All the time the shells were moaning, whining, screaming by, and the valley was rumbling and reverberating with the explosions. As he came in sight of the caves, he saw the two idiots cavorting about, clutching each other's hands with their stumps of fingers. Even as he ran, Koolau saw a spout of black smoke rise from the ground, near to the idiots. They were flung apart bodily by the explosion. One lay motionless, but the other was dragging himself by his hands toward the cave. His legs trailed out helplessly behind him, while the blood was pouring from his body. He seemed bathed in blood, and as he crawled he cried like a little dog. The rest of the lepers, with the exception of Kapahei, had fled into the caves.

"Seventeen," said Kapahei. "Eighteen," he added.

This last shell had fairly entered into one of the caves. The explosion caused all the caves to empty. But from the particular cave no one emerged. Koolau crept in through the pungent, acrid smoke. Four bodies, frightfully mangled, lay about. One of them was the sightless woman whose tears till now had never ceased.

Outside, Koolau found his people in a panic and already beginning to climb the goat trail that led out of the gorge and on among the jumbled heights and chasms. The wounded idiot, whining feebly and dragging himself along on the ground by his hands, was trying to follow. But at the first pitch of the wall his helplessness overcame him and he fell back.

"It would be better to kill him," said Koolau to Kapahei, who still sat in the same place.

"Twenty-two," Kapahei answered. "Yes, it would be a wise thing to kill him. Twenty-three — twenty-four."

The idiot whined sharply when he saw the rifle leveled at him. Koolau hesitated, then lowered the gun.

"It is a hard thing to do," he said.

"You are a fool, twenty-six, twenty-seven," said Kapahei. "Let me show you."

He arose and, with a heavy fragment of rock in his hand, approached the wounded thing. As he lifted his arm to strike, a shell burst full upon him, relieving him of the necessity of the act and at the same time putting an end to his count.

Koolau was alone in the gorge. He watched the last of his people drag their crippled bodies over the brow of the height and disappear. Then he turned and went down to the thicket where the maid had been killed. The shellfire still continued, but he remained; for far below he could see the soldiers climbing up. A shell burst twenty feet away. Flattening himself into the earth, he heard the rush of the fragments above his body. A shower of hau blossoms rained upon him. He lifted his head to peer down the trail, and sighed. He was very much afraid. Bullets from rifles would not have worried him, but this shell fire was abominable. Each time a shell shrieked by he shivered and crouched; but each time he lifted his head again to watch the trail.

At last the shells ceased. This, he reasoned, was because the soldiers were drawing near. They crept along the trail in single file, and he tried to count them until he lost track. At any rate, there were a hundred or so of them — all come after Koolau the leper. He felt a fleeting prod of pride. With war guns and rifles, police and soldiers, they came for him, and he was only one man, a crippled wreck of a man at that. They offered a thousand dollars for him, dead or alive. In all his life he had never possessed that much money. The thought was a bitter one. Kapahei had been right. He, Koolau, had done no wrong. Because the haoles wanted labor with which to work the stolen land, they had brought in the Chinese coolies, and with them had come the sickness. And now, because he had caught the sickness, he was worth a thousand dollars — but not to himself. It was his worthless carcass, rotten with disease or dead from a bursting shell, that was worth all that money.

When the soldiers reached the knife-edged passage, he was prompted to warn them. But his gaze fell upon the body of the murdered maid, and he kept silent. When six had ventured on the knife-edge, he opened fire. Nor did he cease when the knife-edge was bare. He emptied his magazine, reloaded, and emptied it again. He kept on shooting. All his wrongs were blazing in his brain, and he was in a fury of vengeance. All down the goat trail the soldiers were firing, and though they lay flat and sought to shelter themselves in the shallow inequalities of the surface, they were exposed marks to him. Bullets whistled and thudded about him, and an occasional ricochet sang sharply through the air. One bullet ploughed a crease through his scalp, and a second burned across his shoulder blade without breaking the skin.

It was a massacre, in which one man did the killing. The soldiers began to retreat, helping along their wounded. As Koolau picked them off he became aware of the smell of burnt meat. He glanced about him at first, and then discovered that it was his own hands. The heat of the rifle was doing it. The leprosy had destroyed most of the nerves in his hands. Though his flesh burned and he smelled it, there was no sensation.

He lay in the thicket, smiling, until he remembered the war guns. Without doubt they would open up on him again, and this time upon the very thicket from which he had inflicted the damage. Scarcely had he changed his position to a nook behind a small shoulder of the wall where he had noted that no shells fell, than the bombardment recommenced. He counted the shells. Sixty more were thrown into the gorge before the war guns ceased. The tiny area was pitted with their explosions, until it seemed impossible that any creature could have survived. So the soldiers thought, for, under the burning afternoon sun, they climbed the goat trail again. And again the knife-edged passage was disputed, and again they fell back to the beach.

For two days longer Koolau held the passage, though the soldiers contented themselves with flinging shells into his retreat. Then Pahau, a leper boy, came to the top of the wall at the back of the gorge and shouted down to him that Kiloliana, hunting goats that they might eat, had been killed by a fall, and that the women were frightened and knew not what to do. Koolau called the boy down and left him with a spare gun with which to guard the passage.

Koolau found his people disheartened. The majority of them were too helpless to forage food for themselves under such forbidding circumstances, and all were starving. He selected two women and a man who were not too far gone with the disease, and sent them back to the gorge to bring up food and mats. The rest he cheered and consoled until even the weakest took a hand in building rough shelters for themselves.

But those he had dispatched for food did not return, and he started back for the gorge. As he came out on the brow of the wall, half a dozen rifles cracked. A bullet tore through the fleshy part of his shoulder, and his cheek was cut by a sliver of rock where a second bullet smashed against the cliff. In the moment that this happened, and he leaped back, he saw that the gorge was alive with soldiers. His own people had betrayed him. The shellfire had been too terrible, and they had preferred the prison of Molokai.

Koolau dropped back and unslung one of his heavy cartridge belts. Lying among the rocks, he allowed the head and shoulders of the first soldier to rise clearly into view before pulling the trigger. Twice this happened, and then, after some delay, in place of a head and shoulders a white flag was thrust above the edge of the wall.

"What do you want?" he demanded.

"I want you, if you are Koolau the leper," came the answer.

Koolau forgot where he was, forgot everything, as he lay and marvelled at the strange persistence of these haoles who would have their will though the sky fell in. Aye, they would have their will over all men and all things, even though they died in getting it. He could not but admire them, too, what of that will in them that was stronger than life and that bent all things to their bidding. He was convinced of the hopelessness of his struggle. There was no gainsaying that terrible will of the haoles. Though he killed a thousand, yet would they rise like the sands of the sea and come upon him, ever more and more. They never knew when they were beaten. That was their fault and their virtue. It was where his own kind lacked. He could see, now, how the handful of the preachers of God and the preachers of Rum had conquered the land. It was because —

"Well, what have you got to say? Will you come with me?"

It was the voice of the invisible man under the white flag. There he was, like any haole, driving straight toward the end determined.

"Let us talk," said Koolau.

The man's head and shoulders arose, then his whole body. He was a smooth-faced, blue-eyed youngster of twenty-five, slender and natty in his captain's uniform. He advanced until halted, then seated himself a dozen feet away.

"You are a brave man," said Koolau wonderingly. "I could kill you like a fly."

"No, you couldn't," was the answer.

"Why not?"

"Because you are a man, Koolau, though a bad one. I know your story. You kill fairly."

Koolau grunted, but was secretly pleased.

"What have you done with my people?" he demanded. "The boy, the two women, and the man?"

"They gave themselves up, as I have now come for you to do."

Koolau laughed incredulously.

"I am a free man," he announced. "I have done no wrong. All I ask is to be left alone. I have lived free, and I shall die free. I will never give myself up."

"Then your people are wiser than you," answered the young captain. "Look — they are coming now."

Koolau turned and watched the remnant of his band approach. Groaning and sighing, a ghastly procession, it dragged its wretchedness past. It was given to Koolau to taste a deeper bitterness, for they hurled imprecations and insults at him as they went by; and the panting hag who brought up the rear halted, and with skinny, harpy-claws extended, shaking her snarling death's head from side to side, she laid a curse upon him. One by one they dropped over the lip edge and surrendered to the hiding soldiers.

"You can go now," said Koolau to the captain. "I will never give myself up. That is my last word. Good-by."

The captain slipped over the cliff to his soldiers. The next moment and without a flag of truce, he hoisted his hat on his scabbard, and Koolau's bullet tore through it. That afternoon they shelled him out from the beach, and as he retreated into the high inaccessible pockets beyond, the soldiers followed him.

For six weeks they hunted him from pocket to pocket, over the volcanic peaks and along the goat trails. When he hid in the lantana jungle, they formed lines of beaters, and through lantana jungle and guava scrub they drove him like a rabbit. But ever he turned and doubled and eluded. There was no cornering him. When pressed too closely, his sure rifle held them back and they carried their wounded down the goat trails to the beach. There were times when they did the shooting as his brown body showed for a moment through the underbrush. Once, five of them caught him on an exposed goat trail between pockets. They emptied their rifles at him as he limped and climbed along his dizzy way. Afterward they found bloodstains and knew that he was wounded. At the end of six weeks they gave up. The soldiers and police returned to Honolulu, and Kalalau Valley was left to him for his own, though headhunters ventured after him from time to time and to their own undoing.

Two years later, and for the last time, Koolau crawled into a thicket and lay down among the ti leaves and wild ginger blossoms. Free he had lived, and free he was dying. A slight drizzle of rain began to fall, and he drew a ragged blanket about the distorted wreck of his limbs. His body was covered with an oilskin coat. Across his chest he laid his Mauser rifle, lingering affectionately for a moment to wipe the dampness from the barrel. The hand with which he wiped had no fingers left upon it with which to pull the trigger.

He closed his eyes, for, from the weakness in his body and the fuzzy turmoil in his brain, he knew that his end was near. Like a wild animal he had crept into hiding to die. Half conscious, aimless and wandering, he lived back in his life to his early manhood on Niihau. As life faded and the drip of the rain grew dim in his ears, it seemed to him that he was once more in the thick of the horse-breaking, with raw colts rearing and bucking under him, his stirrups tied together beneath, or charging madly about the breaking corral and driving the helping cowboys over the rails. The next instant, and with seeming naturalness, he found himself pursuing the wild bulls of the upland pastures, roping them and leading them down to the valleys. Again the sweat and dust of the branding pen stung his eyes and bit his nostrils.

All his lusty, whole-bodied youth was his, until the sharp pangs of impending dissolution brought him back. He lifted his monstrous hands and gazed at them in wonder. But how? Why? Why should the wholeness of that wild youth of his change to this? Then he remembered, and once again, and for a moment, he was Koolau, the leper. His eyelids fluttered wearily down and the drip of the rain ceased in his ears. A prolonged trembling set up in his body. This, too, ceased. He half lifted his head, but it fell back. Then his eyes opened, and did not close. His last thought was of his Mauser, and he pressed it against his chest with his folded, fingerless hands.

From *The House of Pride* by Jack London (New York, The Macmillan Company, 1912).

JACK LONDON

# CHUN AH CHUN

This tale of the success of an Asian immigrant who came to the
Melting Pot of the Pacific was, like many of London's stories of
Hawaii, broadly based upon the life of an actual person — Chun
Ah Fong, a young mandarin merchant who arrived in the islands
in 1849. Ah Fong married a girl who was descended from
Hawaiian chiefs, whose grandfather was a British sea captain, and
whose father was a Yankee sugar planter. Ah Fong made a fortune
in business, and with his sixteen children founded the most remarkable of Honolulu's cosmopolitan families. In Jack London's
short story, however, since it is fiction and not biography, there
are notable differences between the real Chun Ah Fong and the
Chun Ah Chun created as a fictional character.

THERE WAS NOTHING STRIKING IN THE APPEARANCE OF CHUN
Ah Chun. He was rather undersized, as Chinese go, and the
Chinese narrow shoulders and spareness of flesh were his. The
average tourist, casually glimpsing him on the streets of Honolulu, would have concluded that he was a good-natured little
Chinese, probably the proprietor of a prosperous laundry or
tailor shop. In so far as good nature and prosperity went, the
judgment would be correct, though beneath the mark; for Ah
Chun was as good-natured as he was prosperous, and of the
latter no man knew a tithe of the tale. It was well known that
he was enormously wealthy, but in his case "enormous" was
merely the symbol for the unknown.

Ah Chun had shrewd little eyes, black and beady and so
very little that they were like gimlet holes. But they were wide
apart, and they sheltered under a forehead that was patently

177

the forehead of a thinker. For Ah Chun had his problems, and had had them all his life. Not that he ever worried over them. He was essentially a philosopher, and whether as coolie, or multimillionaire and master of many men, his poise of soul was the same. He lived always in the high equanimity of spiritual repose, undeterred by good fortune, unruffled by ill fortune. All things went well with him, whether they were blows from the overseer in the cane field or a slump in the price of sugar when he owned those cane fields himself. Thus, from the steadfast rock of his sure content he mastered problems such as are given to few men to consider, much less to a Chinese peasant.

He was precisely that — a Chinese peasant, born to labor in the fields all his days like a beast, but fated to escape from the fields like the prince in a fairy tale. Ah Chun did not remember his father, a small farmer in a district not far from Canton; nor did he remember much of his mother, who had died when he was six. But he did remember his respected uncle, Ah Kow, for him had he served as a slave from his sixth year to his twenty-fourth. It was then that he escaped by contracting himself as a coolie to labor for three years on the sugar plantations of Hawaii for fifty cents a day.

Ah Chun was observant. He perceived little details that not one man in a thousand ever noticed. Three years he worked in the field, at the end of which time he knew more about canegrowing than the overseers or even the superintendent, while the superintendent would have been astounded at the knowledge the weazened little coolie possessed of the reduction processes in the mill. But Ah Chun did not study only sugar processes. He studied to find out how men came to be owners of sugar mills and plantations. One judgment he achieved early, namely, that men did not become rich from the labor of their own hands. He knew, for he had labored for a score of years himself. The men who grew rich did so from the labor of the hands of others. That man was richest who had the greatest number of his fellow creatures toiling for him.

So, when his term of contract was up, Ah Chun invested

his savings in a small importing store, going into partnership with one Ah Yung. The firm ultimately became the great one of "Ah Chun & Ah Yung," which handled anything from India silks and ginseng to guano islands and blackbird brigs. In the meantime, Ah Chun hired out as cook. He was a good cook, and in three years he was the highest-paid chef in Honolulu. His career was assured, and he was a fool to abandon it, as Dantin, his employer, told him; but Ah Chun knew his own mind best, and for knowing it was called a triple fool and given a present of fifty dollars over and above the wages due him.

The firm of Ah Chun & Ah Yung was prospering. There was no need for Ah Chun longer to be a cook. There were boom times in Hawaii. Sugar was being extensively planted, and labor was needed. Ah Chun saw the chance, and went into the labor-importing business. He brought thousands of Cantonese coolies into Hawaii, and his wealth began to grow. He made investments. His beady black eyes saw bargains where other men saw bankruptcy. He bought a fishpond for a song, which later paid five hundred per cent and was the opening wedge by which he monopolized the fish market of Honolulu. He did not talk for publication, nor figure in politics, nor play at revolutions, but he forecast events more clearly and farther ahead than did the men who engineered them. In his mind's eye he saw Honolulu a modern, electric-lighted city at a time when it straggled, unkempt and sand-tormented, over a barren reef of uplifted coral rock. So he bought land. He bought land from merchants who needed ready cash, from impecunious natives, from riotous traders' sons, from widows and orphans and the lepers deported to Molokai; and, somehow, as the years went by, the pieces of land he had bought proved to be needed for warehouses, or office buildings, or hotels. He leased, and rented, sold and bought, and resold again.

But there were other things as well. He put his confidence and his money into Parkinson, the renegade captain whom nobody would trust. And Parkinson sailed away on mysterious voyages in the little *Vega*. Parkinson was taken care of until he died, and years afterward Honolulu was astonished when the news leaked out that the Drake and Acorn guano islands had been sold to the British Phosphate Trust for three quarters of a million. Then there were the fat, lush days of King Kalakaua, when Ah Chun paid three hundred thousand dollars for the opium license. If he paid a third of a million for the drug monopoly, the investment was nevertheless a good one, for the dividends bought him the Kalakau Plantation, which, in turn, paid him thirty per cent for seventeen years and was ultimately sold by him for a million and a half.

It was under the Kamehamehas, long before, that he had served his own country as Chinese consul — a position that was not altogether unlucrative; and it was under Kamehameha IV that he changed his citizenship, becoming an Hawaiian subject in order to marry Stella Allendale, herself a subject of the brown-skinned king, though more of the Anglo-Saxon blood ran in her veins than of Polynesian. In fact, the random breeds in her were so attenuated that they were valued at eighths and sixteenths. In the latter proportion was the blood of her great-grandmother, Paahao — the Princess Paahao, for she came of the royal line. Stella Allendale's great-grandfather had been a Captain Blunt, an English adventurer who took service under Kamehameha I and was made a tabu chief himself. Her grandfather had been a New Bedford whaling captain, while through her own father had been introduced a remote blend of Italian and Portuguese which had been grafted upon his own English stock. Legally a Hawaiian, Ah Chun's spouse was more of any one of three other nationalities.

And into this conglomerate of the races, Ah Chun introduced the Mongolian mixture. Thus, his children by Mrs. Ah Chun were one thirty-second Polynesian, one-sixteenth Italian, one-sixteenth Portuguese, one-half Chinese, and eleven thirty-seconds English and American. It might well be that Ah Chun would have refrained from matrimony if he could have foreseen the wonderful family that was to spring from this union. It was wonderful in many ways. First, there was its size. There

were fifteen sons and daughters, mostly daughters. The sons had
come first, three of them, and then had followed, in unswerving
sequence, a round dozen of girls. The blend of the races was
excellent. Not alone fruitful did it prove, for the progeny, without exception, was healthy and without blemish. But the most
amazing thing about the family was its beauty. All the girls
were beautiful — delicately, ethereally beautiful. Mama Ah
Chun's rotund lines seemed to modify papa Ah Chun's lean
angles, so that the daughters were willowy without being
lathy, round-muscled without being chubby. In every feature
of every face were haunting reminiscences of Asia, all manip-
ulated over and disguised by old England, New England,
and South of Europe. No observer, without information, would
have guessed the heavy Chinese strain in their veins; nor could
any observer, after being informed, fail to note immediately
the Chinese traces.

As beauties, the Ah Chun girls were something new. Nothing
like them had been seen before. They resembled nothing so
much as they resembled one another, and yet each girl was
sharply individual. There was no mistaking one for another.
On the other hand, Maud, who was blue-eyed and yellow-
haired, would remind one instantly of Henrietta, an olive
brunette with large, languishing dark eyes and hair that was
blue-black. The hint of resemblance that ran through them all,
reconciling every differentiation, was Ah Chun's contribution.
He had furnished the groundwork upon which had been traced
the blended patterns of the races. He had furnished the slim-
boned Chinese frame, upon which had been builded the delica-
cies and subtleties of Saxon, Latin, and Polynesian flesh.

Mrs. Ah Chun had ideas of her own to which Ah Chun
gave credence, though never permitting them expression when
they conflicted with his own philosophic calm. She had been
used all her life to living in European fashion. Very well. Ah
Chun gave her a European mansion. Later, as his sons and
daughters grew able to advise, he built the bungalow, a spacious,
rambling affair, as unpretentious as it was magnificent. Also,

as time went by, there arose a mountain house on Tantalus, to which the family could flee when the "sick wind" blew from the south. And at Waikiki he built a beach residence on an extensive site so well chosen that later on, when the United States government condemned it for fortification purposes, an immense sum accompanied the condemnation. In all his houses were billiard and smoking rooms and guest rooms galore, for Ah Chun's wonderful progeny was given to lavish entertainment. The furnishing was extravagantly simple. Kings' ransoms were expended without display — thanks to the educated tastes of the progeny.

Ah Chun had been liberal in the matter of education. "Never mind expense," he had argued in the old days with Parkinson when that slack mariner could see no reason for making the *Vega* seaworthy; "you sail the schooner, I pay the bills." And so with his sons and daughters. It had been for them to get the education and never mind the expense. Harold, the eldest-born, had gone to Harvard and Oxford; Albert and Charles had gone through Yale in the same classes. And the daughters, from the eldest down, had undergone their preparation at Mills Seminary in California and passed on to Vassar, Wellesley, or Bryn Mawr. Several, having so desired, had had the finishing touches put on in Europe. And from all the world Ah Chun's sons and daughters returned to him to suggest and advise in the garnishment of the chaste magnificence of his residences. Ah Chun himself preferred the voluptuous glitter of Oriental display; but he was a philosopher, and he clearly saw that his children's tastes were correct according to Western standards.

Of course, his children were not known as the Ah Chun children. As he had evolved from a coolie laborer to a multimillionaire, so had his name evolved. Mama Ah Chun had spelled it A'Chun, but her wiser offspring had elided the apostrophe and spelled it Achun. Ah Chun did not object. The spelling of his name interfered no whit with his comfort nor his philosophic calm. Besides, he was not proud. But when his children arose to the height of a starched shirt, a stiff collar, and a frock coat, they did interfere with his comfort and calm. Ah Chun would have none of it. He preferred the loose-flowing robes of China, and neither could they cajole nor bully him into making the change. They tried both courses, and in the latter one failed especially disastrously. They had not been to America for nothing. They had learned the virtues of the boycott as employed by organized labor, and he, their father, Chun Ah Chun, they boycotted in his own house, Mama Achun aiding and abetting. But Ah Chun himself, while unversed in Western culture, was thoroughly conversant with Western labor conditions. An extensive employer of labor himself, he knew how to cope with its tactics. Promptly he imposed a lockout on his rebellious progeny and erring spouse. He discharged his scores of servants, locked up his stables, closed his house, and went to live in the Royal Hawaiian Hotel, in which enterprise he happened to be the heaviest stockholder. The family fluttered distractedly on visits about with friends, while Ah Chun calmly managed his many affairs, smoked his long pipe with the tiny silver bowl, and pondered the problem of his wonderful progeny.

This problem did not disturb his calm. He knew in his philosopher's soul that when it was ripe he would solve it. In the meantime he enforced the lesson that, complacent as he might be, he was nevertheless the absolute dictator of the Achun destinies. The family held out for a week, then returned, along with Ah Chun and the many servants, to occupy the bungalow once more. And thereafter no question was raised when Ah Chun elected to enter his brilliant drawing room in blue silk robe, wadded slippers, and black silk skullcap with red button peak, or when he chose to draw at his slender-stemmed silver-bowled pipe among the cigarette- and cigar-smoking officers and civilians on the broad verandas or in the smoking room.

Ah Chun occupied a unique position in Honolulu. Though he did not appear in society, he was eligible anywhere. Except among the Chinese merchants of the city, he never went out; but he received, and he was always the center of his household and the head of his table. Himself peasant-born Chinese, he presided over an atmosphere of culture and refinement second to none in all the islands. Nor were there any in all the islands too proud to cross his threshold and enjoy his hospitality. First of all, the Achun bungalow was of irreproachable tone. Next, Ah Chun was a power. And, finally, Ah Chun was a moral paragon and an honest businessman. Despite the fact that business morality was higher than on the mainland, Ah Chun outshone the businessmen of Honolulu in the scrupulous rigidity of his honesty. It was a saying that his word was as good as his bond. His signature was never needed to bind him. He never broke his word. Twenty years after Hotchkiss, of Hotchkiss, Morterson Company, died, they found among mislaid papers a memorandum of a loan of thirty thousand dollars to Ah Chun. It had been incurred when Ah Chun was privy counsellor to Kamehameha IV. In the bustle and confusion of those heyday, money-making times, the affair had slipped Ah Chun's mind. There was no note, no legal claim against him, but he settled in full with the Hotchkiss' Estate, voluntarily paying a compound interest that dwarfed the principal. Likewise, when he verbally guaranteed the disastrous Kakiku Ditch Scheme, at a time when the least sanguine did not dream a guarantee necessary — "Signed his check for two hundred thousand without a quiver, gentlemen, without a quiver," was the report of the secretary of the defunct enterprise, who had been sent on the forlorn hope of finding out Ah Chun's intentions. And on top of the many similar actions that were true of his word, there was scarcely a man of repute in the islands that at one time or another had not experienced the helping financial hand of Ah Chun.

So it was that Honolulu watched his wonderful family grow up into a perplexing problem and secretly sympathized with him, for it was beyond any of them to imagine what he was going to do with it. But Ah Chun saw the problem more clearly than they. No one knew as he knew the extent to which he was an alien in his family. His own family did not guess it. He saw

that there was no place for him amongst this marvelous seed
of his loins, and he looked forward to his declining years and
knew that he would grow more and more alien. He did not
understand his children. Their conversation was of things that
did not interest him and about which he knew nothing. The
culture of the West had passed him by. He was Asiatic to the last
fiber, which meant that he was heathen. Their Christianity was
to him so much nonsense. But all this he would have ignored as
extraneous and irrelevant, could he have but understood the
young people themselves. When Maud, for instance, told him
that the housekeeping bills for the month were thirty thousand
— that he understood, as he understood Albert's request for
five thousand with which to buy the schooner yacht *Muriel*
and become a member of the Hawaiian Yacht Club. But it was
their remoter, complicated desires and mental processes that
obfuscated him. He was not slow in learning that the mind of
each son and daughter was a secret labyrinth which he could
never hope to tread. Always he came upon the wall that divides
East from West. Their souls were inaccessible to him, and by
the same token he knew that his soul was inaccessible to them.

Besides, as the years came upon him, he found himself hark-
ing back more and more to his own kind. The reeking smells
of the Chinese quarter were spicy to him. He sniffed them with
satisfaction as he passed along the street, for in his mind they
carried him back to the narrow tortuous alleys of Canton swarm-
ing with life and movement. He regretted that he had cut off
his queue to please Stella Allendale in the prenuptial days,
and he seriously considered the advisability of shaving his crown
and growing a new one. The dishes his highly paid chef con-
cocted for him failed to tickle his reminiscent palate in the way
that the weird messes did in the stuffy restaurant down in the
Chinese quarter. He enjoyed vastly more a half-hour's smoke
and chat with two or three Chinese chums than to preside at
the lavish and elegant dinners for which his bungalow was
famed, where the pick of the Americans and Europeans sat at
the long table, men and women on equality, the women with
jewels that blazed in the subdued light against white necks and

arms, the men in evening dress, and all chattering and laughing over topics and witticisms that, while they were not exactly Greek to him, did not interest him nor entertain.

But it was not merely his alienness and his growing desire to return to his Chinese fleshpots that constituted the problem. There was also his wealth. He had looked forward to a placid old age. He had worked hard. His reward should have been peace and repose. But he knew that with his immense fortune peace and repose could not possibly be his. Already there were signs and omens. He had seen similar troubles before. There was his old employer, Dantin, whose children had wrested from him, by due process of law, the management of his property, having the Court appoint guardians to administer it for him. Ah Chun knew, and knew thoroughly well, that had Dantin been a poor man, it would have been found that he could quite rationally manage his own affairs. And old Dantin had had only three children and half a million, while he, Chun Ah Chun, had fifteen children and no one but himself knew how many millions.

"Our daughters are beautiful women," he said to his wife, one evening. "There are many young men. The house is always full of young men. My cigar bills are very heavy. Why are there no marriages?"

Mama Achun shrugged her shoulders and waited.

"Women are women and men are men — it is strange there are no marriages. Perhaps the young men do not like our daughters."

"Ah, they like them well enough," Mama Chun answered; "but you see, they cannot forget that you are your daughters' father."

"Yet you forgot who my father was," Ah Chun said gravely. "All you asked was for me to cut off my queue."

"The young men are more particular than I was, I fancy."

"What is the greatest thing in the world?" Ah Chun demanded with abrupt irrelevance.

Mama Achun pondered for a moment, then replied: "God."

He nodded. "There are gods and gods. Some are paper,

some are wood, some are bronze. I use a small one in the office for a paperweight. In the Bishop Museum are many gôds of coral rock and lava stone."

"But there is only one God," she announced decisively, stiffening her ample frame argumentatively.

Ah Chun noted the danger signal and sheered off.

"What is greater than God, then?" he asked. "I will tell you. It is money. In my time I have had dealings with Jews and Christians, Mohammedans and Buddhists, and with little black men from the Solomons and New Guinea who carried their god about them, wrapped in oiled paper. They possessed various gods, these men, but they all worshipped money. There is that Captain Higginson. He seems to like Henrietta."

"He will never marry her," retorted Mama Achun. "He will be an admiral before he dies — "

"A rear admiral," Ah Chun interpolated. "Yes, I know. That is the way they retire."

"His family in the United States is a high one. They would not like it if he married . . . if he did not marry an American girl."

Ah Chun knocked the ashes out of his pipe and thoughtfully refilled the silver bowl with a tiny pleget of tobacco. He lighted it and smoked it out before he spoke.

"Henrietta is the oldest girl. The day she marries I will give her three hundred thousand dollars. That will fetch that Captain Higginson and his high family along with him. Let the word go out to him. I leave it to you."

And Ah Chun sat and smoked on, and in the curling smoke-wreaths he saw take shape the face and figure of Toy Shuey — Toy Shuey, the maid of all work in his uncle's house in the Cantonese village, whose work was never done and who received for a whole year's work one dollar. And he saw his youthful self arise in the curling smoke, his youthful self who had toiled eighteen years in his uncle's field for little more. And now he, Ah Chun, the peasant, dowered his daughter with three hundred thousand years of such toil. And she was but one daughter of a dozen. He was not elated at the thought. It struck him that it was a funny, whimsical world, and he chuckled aloud and startled Mama Achun from a revery which he knew lay deep in the hidden crypts of her being where he had never penetrated.

But Ah Chun's word went forth, as a whisper, and Captain Higginson forgot his rear-admiralship and his high family and took to wife three hundred thousand dollars and a refined and cultured girl who was one thirty-second Polynesian, one-sixteenth Italian, one-sixteenth Portuguese, eleven thirty-seconds English and Yankee, and one-half Chinese.

Ah Chun's munificence had its effect. His daughters became suddenly eligible and desirable. Clara was the next, but when the Secretary of the Territory formally proposed for her, Ah Chun informed him that he must await his turn, that Maud was the oldest and that she must be married first. It was shrewd policy. The whole family was made vitally interested in marrying off Maud, which it did in three months, to Ned Humphreys, the United States immigration commissioner. Both he and Maud complained, for the dowry was only two hundred thousand. Ah Chun explained that his initial generosity had been to break the ice, and that after that his daughters could not expect otherwise than to go more cheaply.

Clara followed Maud, and thereafter, for a space of two years, there was a continuous round of weddings in the bungalow. In the meantime Ah Chun had not been idle. Investment after investment was called in. He sold out his interests in a score of enterprises, and step by step, so as not to cause a slump in the market, he disposed of his large holdings in real estate. Toward the last he did precipitate a slump and sold at sacrifice. What caused this haste were the squalls he saw already rising above the horizon. By the time Lucille was married, echoes of bickerings and jealousies were already rumbling in his ears. The air was thick with schemes and counter schemes to gain his favor and to prejudice him against one or another or all but one of his sons-in-law. All of which was not conducive to the peace and repose he had planned for his old age.

He hastened his efforts. For a long time he had been in correspondence with the chief banks in Shanghai and Macao. Every steamer for several years carried away drafts drawn in favor on one Chun Ah Chun, for deposit in those Far Eastern banks. The drafts now became heavier. His two youngest daughters were not yet married. He did not wait, but dowered them with a hundred thousand each, which sums lay in the Bank of Hawaii, drawing interest and awaiting their wedding days. Albert took over the business of the firm of Ah Chun & Ah Yung, Harold, the eldest, having elected to take a quarter of a million and go to England to live. Charles, the youngest, took a hundred thousand, a legal guardian, and a course in a Keeley institute. To Mama Achun was given the bungalow, the mountain house on Tantalus, and a new seaside residence in place of the one Ah Chun sold to the government. Also, to Mama Achun was given half a million in money well invested.

Ah Chun was now ready to crack the nut of the problem. One fine morning when the family was at breakfast — he had seen to it that all his sons-in-law and their wives were present — he announced that he was returning to his ancestral soil. In a neat little homily he explained that he had made ample provision for his family, and he laid down various maxims that he was sure, he said, would enable them to dwell together in peace and harmony. Also, he gave business advice to his sons-in-law, preached the virtues of temperate living and safe investments, and gave them the benefit of his encyclopedic knowledge of industrial and business conditions in Hawaii. Then he called for his carriage, and, in the company of the weeping Mama Achun, was driven down to the Pacific Mail steamer, leaving behind him a panic in the bungalow. Captain Higginson clamored wildly for an injunction. The daughters shed copious tears. One of their husbands, an ex-Federal judge, questioned Ah Chun's sanity, and hastened to the proper authorities to inquire into it. He returned with the information that Ah Chun had appeared before the commission the day before, demanded an examination, and passed with flying colors. There was nothing to be done, so they went down and said good-by to the little old man, who waved farewell from the promenade deck as the big steamer poked her nose seaward through the coral reef.

But the little old man was not bound for Canton. He knew his own country too well, and the squeeze of the mandarins, to venture into it with the tidy bulk of wealth that remained to him. He went to Macao. Now Ah Chung had long exercised the power of a king and he was as imperious as a king. When he landed at Macao and went into the office of the biggest European hotel to register, the clerk closed the book on him. Chinese were not permitted. Ah Chun called for the manager and was treated with contumely. He drove away, but in two hours he was back again. He called the clerk and manager in, gave them a month's salary, and discharged them. He had made himself the owner of the hotel; and in the finest suite he settled down during the many months the gorgeous palace in the suburbs was building for him. In the meantime, with the inevitable ability that was his, he increased the earnings of his big hotel from three per cent to thirty.

The troubles Ah Chun had flown began early. There were sons-in-law that made bad investments, others that played ducks and drakes with the Achun dowries. Ah Chun being out of it, they looked at Mama Ah Chun and her half million, and, looking, engendered not the best of feeling toward one another. Lawyers waxed fat in the striving to ascertain the construction of trust deeds. Suits, cross-suits, and counter-suits cluttered the Hawaiian courts. Nor did the police courts escape. There were angry encounters in which harsh words and harsher blows were struck. There were such things as flowerpots being thrown to add emphasis to winged words. And suits for libel arose that dragged their way through the courts and kept Honolulu agog with excitement over the revelations of the witnesses.

In his palace, surrounded by all dear delights of the Orient, Ah Chun smokes his placid pipe and listens to the turmoil overseas. Each mail steamer, in faultless English, typewritten on an American machine, a letter goes from Macao to Honolulu, in which, by admirable texts and precepts, Ah Chun advises his family to live in unity and harmony. As for himself, he is out of it all and well content. He has won peace and repose. At times he chuckles and rubs his hands, and his slant little black eyes twinkle merrily at the thought of the funny world. For out of all his living and philosophizing that remains to him — the conviction that it is a very funny world.

From *The House of Pride* by Jack London (New York, The Macmillan Company, 1912).

UNA HUNT DRAGE

# THE PALI, A SHARK,
# AND A HOUSE PARTY

Una Hunt Drage, then Una Clarke, spent six wonderful months in Hawaii in 1901, when in her early twenties she was the house guest of Cordelia Carter, her closest friend. The two girls had grown up together in Washington while "Cordie's" father was the minister from Hawaii to the United States. In Honolulu the Carters, one of the patrician families, wealthy and influential, were able to give their young *malihini* visitor an experience of Hawaiian hospitality at its best. She was plunged at once into the social whirl of the town, meeting new people and situations, with eager response to all she saw and did. From her diary and letters, fifty years after they were written, she compiled a most engaging but little-known book, *Hawaii Deluxe* — "a mosaic of the impressions and experiences of a young girl who, never having traveled beyond the Eastern States, was thrown into the welter of Honolulu with its mixed races and violent contrasts, ranging from naked children in grass huts to luxurious homes where the ladies were dressed by Worth."

THE PALI IS THE FIRST PLACE THE ONE-DAY STOPOVER TOURISTS go to see, but usually don't, as it showers almost continuously in the mountains at this season. However, they hopefully drive to the pass, crowded into a procession of four-horse mountain wagons.

I had been here over two months without seeing it, but one morning when Cordie and I were taking our usual ride up Nuuanu Valley, on reaching the foothills the clouds suddenly lifted, showing the peaks beyond in clear sunshine; and Cordie said, "Now is your chance for the Pali," so we galloped straight into the mountainside through a rift in the cliff where the road mounts a canyon-like passage between towering rocky walls which drip at every cranny with waterfalls, called "bridal veils," because the wind sucking through the gorge blows them to a fine mist that never reaches the ground, but sprays the white flowers and maidenhair ferns covering the rocks, the white film over green film, like a bride's veil over her bouquet as she goes up the aisle.

The effect was so exquisite that it was not until Deaconess slacked her pace that I looked ahead and saw that a huge mass of rock blocked the road. But Cordie's horse made a right-angled turn around its corner, Deaconess meekly following. I was almost blinded, for without any warning, we had left the prison twilight of the pass and were in dazzling sunshine of limitless space. It was like sudden death and finding oneself in Heaven, for we perched on the narrow ledge of a precipice with a sheer drop of hundreds of feet to the plain, lying below us, spread like a vast carpet patterned in every imaginable color of forests, ponds, and farms, scallop-edged by surf breaking on coral reefs, like white fringe against the far-horizoned indigo sea.

I gasped, amazed as Cortez "silent on a peak in Darien" — or however the quotation goes — but that gives the idea. The horses, their heads held high, braced back and sniffed the trade wind which sucked through the pass in a half gale.

Cordie, thrilled by my thrill, said, "Now you see why I wouldn't bring you until you could get the full effect."

Dismounting, we looked down beyond the overhanging ledge on which we stood and she told me how, when Oahu was last invaded by chiefs from the other islands, Kamehameha, who called himself king of the whole group, chased the local army up Nuuanu Valley until they came to the Pali, when, rather than surrender, the hundreds of Oahu warriors, shouting and brandishing their spears as they jumped, threw themselves over the cliff, hurtling down from the dark mountain shadow into the blazing sunshine like huge tropic birds, the gorgeous feather capes of the chieftains flapping like wings as they twisted and whirled in the air before being dashed to death on the rocks below.

Even their conquerors were awed by such a glorious death and composed a chant of commemoration, which is often sung at native *luaus*. Human bones are still to be found, if one hunts among the bushes, ghastly proofs that it is not a legend, but true local history. George has several skulls which he picked up himself.

The splendor of the story, combined with peering down from such a height, made me so lightheaded that I felt it was only the pressure of the wind which held me back from flinging myself over also, and to get my mental and physical balance, turned aside to the bridle path which zigzags down a sloping declivity. It looked so rough and steep that I wondered how I could possibly make it when we go to visit the Swanzys and Judds, who have ranches on that side of the island, for one false step by Deaconess would mean eternity for me. Cordie said it was not as bad as it looked, for even a light buggy could be driven down. Agnes always went that way, but she herself felt safer on a horse. I agree with her and must trust to Deaconess, who has sense if she lacks sensibility.

Dick dined with us last night and was furious that I had been to the Pali without him, as he wanted to see my face when the view burst upon me. He said it had knocked him sky-high. I did not say so, but I was glad that he was not there. As it is, I can treasure my own undistracted impression as one of my most tremendous experiences.

When he is with us, landscapes usually take second place and we seem actors rehearsing in front of a painted backdrop left up by mistake, with Dick in the role of hero, while Cordie and I alternate as the heroine. The competition between us is getting more and more in earnest, and so is he — with both of us! We still can't tell which of us he likes best. He told Cordie she reminded him of the Venus de Milo, but he said that I had the loveliest hair he had ever seen, so it is rather a tossup, though Cordie thinks mine is the sort of compliment she would rather have from a beau — which unfortunately he is not. Helen calls him our cavalier, which is more like it, but too high-flown.

The other day I felt so low in my mind I was afraid I really was falling in love with him, but Miss Jewell said I looked yellow and gave me a Seidlitz powder, which was so effective that I decided it was liver and not love.

We all keep having tropic liver attacks which the natives lay to the kona wind, but the doctor, who is English, calls them intestinal grippe or food poisoning and prescribes calomel. Though obliged to live here because he has had tuberculosis, he detests the tropics and gets around them professionally by pretending that human beings are the same everywhere and that Honolulu is medically a replica of his home town, Liverpool, where people get "a chill on the liver." George says he gives calomel for everything from leprosy to a stroke of paralysis. A man who had his leg broken by being run over protested when the doctor, after setting the bone, dosed him with calomel, but he was squelched by the answer, "You must have been sluggish or you would have got out of the way in time!"

The lepers fill him with such horror that he ships them at once to Molokai; and the law compels him to quarantine scarlet fever and cholera, but beyond that he ignores infection — measles and whooping cough are dismissed as natural childish illnesses, and the sooner they have them the better. When Miss Jewell mentioned tropical microbes, he exploded, "New-fangled notions! These liver attacks aren't catching and neither is food poisoning," and she had to admit that they are not, but she is worried by our having them so often, and makes us drink boiled water.

She has no faith in the doctor, who is supposed to be the best one out here, as his only examinations are feeling the patient's pulse and looking at the tongue when he makes his visits, which are stately affairs; for no matter what the thermometer may be, he is always dressed in the regulation black coat and striped trousers that he wore in England. He is a nice man in himself, and Mrs. Carter is a different person after he has been to see her. He is very kind and always cheerful, which is remarkable as he is nagged by a complaining wife who shudders at lizards, cockroaches, and spiders. They neither of them can see any beauty in this county. "Too glary" is their only comment, a verdict echoed by many of the English, who usually add the words "outlandish." Even our nice Triplets hate it because it is not England. They all sniff at Canada, and take their short holidays in California, which seems inconsistent.

My courage in riding down the Pali trail was tested sooner than I had expected, for Mrs. Swanzy asked Cordie, Dick, and myself to a spur-of-the-moment weekend house party at Kualoa to help entertain two young men from Boston who were visiting Will Castle. She is a cousin of the Carters of whom we see a lot. Her husband is the head of the big English trading company for which the Triplets work, and they live in the nearest they can get to an English style with Chinese servants, even on their ranch where we are now staying.

I was thankful when we came thought the Pali pass to find there was such a gale blowing that I felt it would blow me back to the top if I fell off when we went over the edge of the steep trail. I only got one squint, as my eyes began to water from the wind. So it was going it blind with a vengeance when, with no warning, Deaconess seemed to step off into space and I only saved myself from pitching over her head by hugging her around the neck with both arms.

At Dick's yell from behind me, "Lie back in your stirrups!" I straightened up and opened my eyes. The angle was not as bad as it had looked from the top, so I relaxed, putting my weight near the horse's tail, and hoped for the best. Deaconess almost stood on her head in one place, but she was so sure-footed that she barely jolted me. At the foot of the cliff there was a small stream, and instead of splashing across the ford, to my amazement I found myself flying through the air like a bird, but still safe in the saddle, which seemed to have heaved up with me in it like lifting a person in a chair, for Deaconess jumps as smoothly as she gallops.

"Well, I never!" I heard Cordie exclaim.

"Una certainly has guts," Dick said.

"They are not my guts!" I called back, "they are Deaconess'!"

The other two horses sedately waded the ford, watched out of the corner of her eye by Deaconess, as they slipped on the wet stones while she took a leisurely drink.

I looked up at the Pali and was flabbergasted that I had ever come down what looked like a perpendicular wall; and when a string of pack mules appeared coming over the top, I expected them to pitch down like the Oahu warriors, but they nimbled their way like mountain goats in spite of being top-heavy with tent-shaped packs twice their own size, plus their drivers perched on top.

The road from there crossed the plain to the shore and wound around two bays, where the sea inside the reefs was even more beautiful than at Waikiki, with more patches of amber and dark purple enhancing the pale blue and green. As this is the trade wind side of the island, the colors are crisper, with headlands of bright red rocks, and the soil where it has been ploughed was the same color, but most of the fields were green with crops of sugar cane. I can't get used to there being no regular planting season — they may be sowing seed in one field and harvesting in the next.

The mountain tops were clear of cloud, sharp and saw-edged like Japanese prints, with the same deep blue and purple that is almost black from the koa which grows on the shady side, while the sunny side is covered with yellow-green kukui trees.

I was very stiff when we arrived as it was my longest ride, but Mrs. Swanzy had a native woman ready to massage us. It is an old art called lomi-lomi, and she rubbed and kneaded me so thoroughly that I was all right the next day.

Our teammates, Walter Dillingham and Tarn McGrew, sent word that they couldn't come because of a polo match, so to replace them the Triplets rode over late in the afternoon with Mr. Will Castle and his two Harvard classmates, Mr. Nichols and Mr. Cabot, both from Boston, who scarcely left Cordie's side after they heard that her eldest sister is the wife of a well-known Bostonian — seven men to two girls was doing pretty well, I thought.

That evening we did the English house-party act, wearing full evening dress for dinner, but as there was a moon we risked our clothes and went Hawaiian, sitting on the beach, singing college songs and "Ben Bolt" to the accompaniment of Dick's mandolin.

It is so much cooler here I don't have that clammy feeling or have to change my underclothes several times a day, which is a relief. I wore Jack Galt's beads with great effect — the red during the day with white muslin; the shells with my blue gauze for dinner.

The house is a one-story affair of wood, added to at various times at any convenient angle. There are century-old bread-fruit trees at both sides, the group making a triangular base for a mountain which rises straight behind the house. In front, instead of a lawn and garden, there is a grassy plain where the horses graze, which stretches to the beach, where we bathe in a huge pool enclosed by coral walls, extending to and taking in part of the outside reef. It is one of the queer circular pools about a quarter of a mile wide where they fattened fish for the ancient chiefs. Beyond the reef is the open ocean, with a procession of grotesquely shaped islands, which seem to move in the heat haze, looking like rearing monsters of half-wrecked vessels still afloat.

Saturday, as we were bathing, fortunately all of us on the way in to shore, one of the Swanzy children who was on the beach shrieked, "Shark!" I looked over my shoulder and saw the unmistakable triangular fin raised above a gap where the top of the reef had crumbled, making a channel deep enough at high tide for one to slither over. He charged straight at us, his mouth wide open, and got so close I could see the saw-edged teeth.

Mr. Swanzy called, "Scatter in different directions!" We began frantically swimming at various tangents and soon were in shallow water where we could wade but no shark could swim. When I knew I was safe and dared look back, he was still swimming, humped up half out of the shoal water, enormous and savage, but was evidently in difficulties, for he soon began thrashing about in a mixture of sand and water, floundering to get back to a depth where he could float.

"Gee!" Dick said when we'd got to the beach, "I know how Jonah felt just before he was gobbled by the whale."

"You girls watch him and see that he doesn't get away," Mr. Swanzy said. He and the other man then rushed to the house where the native ranch workers live. They brought them back with them, Mr. Swanzy, Will Castle, and several of the Kanakas brandishing real fishing spears tied to ropes like harpoons, while the others had improvised spears by binding knives to bamboo poles. The shark was still floundering in the shallows, so they waded as near him as they dared, but had to be very nippy to keep out of reach of his jaws and his flail-like tail, while the rest of us threw stones and yelled to drive him close to the reef, where they could stand in safety to spear him.

The tide had gone down rapidly and the top of the reef was already clear, so even when he got into deeper water and could swim, there was no escape. He was penned like a bull in a ring. It was rather like a bullfight when the men began to slash at him with their knives, while he lashed this way and that, streaming blood and snapping first at one, then turning wide-jawed toward another of his tormenters. At last they managed to drive him close to the reef, where the rest of the men, who were strung along in a line on top of the rocks, lunged and speared in earnest, so intent that several of them came near being washed over into the real ocean outside, where other sharks were probably lurking by the surge of water he splashed up in darting at them.

It was terribly exciting to watch and seemed ages before they gradually wore him out and he sank to the bottom of the pool blowing up bubbles of blood. When they finally dragged him to the beach by their ropes he was stuck full of harpoons and knives like a pincushion. Safely landed and too weak to more than gasp, he was finally killed by cutting his spine with an ax. More natives had gathered to share him out — they will have a grand feast tonight. To them and the Chinese, anything that swims seems to be edible. The next tide washed away all the gory traces, so that there was no smell even on the beach; but that afternoon the ocean failed to attract us, and we bathed in an ice-cold pool in the stream that flows down the mountain-side.

The next day was even more momentous — for me — as Will Castle saved my life. We bathed again in the ocean pool, where one can wade out and swim for a quarter of a mile to where the wall joins the reef and walk back on it, for at high tide it is only covered with water up to my waist, except for a few gaps where the rock had crumbled, across which one has to swim.

The water was still so roily with seaweed and small marine objects, animal and vegetable, stirred up by the shark hunt that it was impossible to see the reef as usual, so we had to feel our way with our feet. Being the slowest swimmer of the lot, I was the last one to swim so far and struck the wall without any trouble, for I had noticed that it was in line with the end of Mokolii, the queerest of the outside islands. The other bath-ers were straggling back to the house, and seeing me waist-high out of the water, Mr. Swanzy called, "Don't hurry. Take your time. It's rough going."

As the last person disappeared, I felt alone in an alien world, all the gaiety of the morning quenched as a cloud hid the sun, turning the pool to a murky gray where unknown horrors lurked, while on the ocean side I kept an eye out for the fin of a shark. It was awful, for a stem of kelp coiling around my leg might be an octopus tentacle, and there were unseen scuttling and crawling objects, some hard and others soft, some that pricked and some that stung, which brushed against my feet. I stumbled along the rough coral, getting more and more nervous, until I suddenly stepped into a void and went under, having struck one of the gaps. When I came up, I was no longer aligned with Mokolii, and the other islands seemed to have shifted their places, so I ducked my head under to try and find the other end of the wall, but the water was too clogged to see more than a hand's length around me, so I could only guess at the right direction, but guessed wrong, for after swimming much farther than the width of any possible gap I was still beyond my depth, with no sign of the wall, so I swam this way and that, hoping to cut across it, and began to get flustered on top of feeling awfully tired.

From water level, only the roof of the house was visible and I knew it was too far away for anyone to hear me even if I yelled, and as the beach was completely hidden, I had no idea that Will Castle was there sunning himself behind a rock, so I did not try to call for help. I was terribly scared, for the harder I struggled to swim the weaker I got until, from sheer exhaustion, I sank again. Will Castle, happening to stand up at that moment, saw me as I went down, and knowing that I was nowhere near the wall, realized my danger and plunged in, calling out as I came up, "Just float on your back. I am coming to get you!"

I flopped over and though my waterlogged bathing suit dragged me down, found that I could still float and lay gasping, my head just out of water until, swimming fast, Will Castle reached me.

"Put your arms around my neck," he ordered, "and don't clutch!"

I was too tired to help and fortunately had sense enough not to try, for I should only have hampered him; so half carrying me on his back, he began towing me toward shore. He is a superb swimmer, and his calm, cool Harvard manner was what I needed to give me the strength to hold on until we got near enough in shore for my feet to touch bottom. I tried to stand, but was too weak, so he picked me up in his arms, carried me through the shallows, and laid me down on the beach. After a few moments resting, I said, "I'm all right now."

"I guess you'll make it," he said, helping me to my feet.

I found that I was able to walk, with his arm around my waist and mine around his shoulder, and so we arrived at the house, affectionately intertwined, to the blank amazement of the others, who were all sitting on the *lanai*. Dick said he expected us to announce our engagement, but was astonished that a Harvard man could be such a fast worker. They were all horrified and conscience-stricken when they realized what had happened and that none of them had stayed to look after me. No one had missed me, for some of the party had come out earlier and Dick and Cordie thought I was among them, and Mr. Swanzy thought I had made good time on the wall as I was not in sight when he looked out after dressing.

Brandy was poured down my throat and I was soon all right, but spent the rest of the day on a long chair on the *lanai,* being read to aloud by relays of young men. I never before felt so like a heroine, but at the same time hated myself for not having had the sense to try to float and stay floating until I was missed, for a person can stay up all day in that buoyant water. I just panicked.

The shark hunt of the day before was responsible, for it was high tide, and though I didn't see a fin, I wondered if a small one might not have wriggled through the reef — even a six-foot shark can nip off a foot — so each time a swirl of seaweed had brushed against my legs I paddled frantically to get away, wondering if it had teeth or tentacles.

Even when I thought I was drowning I never once reviewed my past life as people are supposed to do. I am finding that real life is quite different from novels, for I ought to feel romantic about Will Castle, but don't. Nor does he about me.

From *Hawaii Deluxe* by Una Hunt Drage (Honolulu, privately printed, 1952).

GENEVIEVE TAGGARD

# THE PLAGUE

Genevieve Taggard (1894–1948) lived in Hawaii for eighteen
years, from the age of two until she was twenty, a period of time
in which her father taught in the public schools on the island of
Oahu. The experiences of these early years and the island images
were an ineradicable part of the mind and imagination of the
writer she later became. "Yes," she once wrote, "the outline of
trees, and the fruit you risk your neck for, and the insects you
kill and fear, and the kinds of child hardship and toil you per-
form and endure, these make a childhood — and the subtle
difference of memory. One glance at me, and if you are subtle
enough you can tell that I used to eat live minnows. . . . "

After she left Hawaii and was graduated from the University
of California, Genevieve Taggard went east and became an editor,
a poet (she published twelve volumes of poetry), and a teacher
of literature and writing at Mount Holyoke, at Bennington, and
at Sarah Lawrence colleges. She never returned to the islands.

ONE EVENING MY FATHER CAME IN LATE TO SUPPER JUST AS WE
had lighted the kerosene lamp and put it in the middle of the
cleared dining table. He had been off seeing the superintendent about building the new school.

"Hayashida is sick," said my mother, "and wants to see you
before you go to bed."

My father took a little hand lamp and went out into the
tropic blackness, down the latticed walk to Hayashida's little
whitewashed house, where he lived with Kiko. The screen
door banged after him, and he was gone a long time, while I
watched the mealy damp baby moths who came under the lamp
shade and got cooked on the kerosene surface of the silver

lamp. Then the screen door closed lightly, and my father came back holding his lamp up.

"Mama," he said as he blew out the light and stood some distance from us, "Hayashida has a bubo under his arm as big as an egg."

He washed himself with kerosene and called up the doctor on the telephone, sitting down as he waited for a connection. Mother sent us to bed. We didn't know what a bubo was.

The next day the doctors — about four of them and several health officials — came to see Hayashida. They told my father to say that Hayashida had measles and dismiss the school indefinitely. This my father did, because he had to, although he hated to stand up before all his schoolchildren and tell a lie. Hayashida besides being our Japanese boy was the janitor of the school. He had swept it out on Monday afternoon just before he was taken sick.

The neighbors knew what they knew — the measles story wasn't very convincing. The doctors went in and out of the little whitewashed house where Hayashida lived, and Kiko could be seen standing limp against one window — all her lovely oiled hair pressed against the glass. We children loved Hayashida and Kiko. He was a big rawboned Japanese, gaunt and yellow, and very merry. He had come to us right off a plantation when he couldn't speak any English. Only Kiko could speak, because she had been a silkworm girl in Tokyo. Under the lattice of the passion vine over our door they stood beside each other and wished to come and work for us. Hayashida took care of our huge garden and the lawn; he clipped the hedges and swept the walks, and all afternoon long, while he ran the sprinklers and changed them, he kept our swings going too, and carried us around on his shoulders. Once a centipede crawled up inside his blue denim pants and he caught hold of the cloth and called to us to look while he squeezed it to death, so that it wouldn't bite him. He also sang very sweet songs to himself in a high silly voice all the time he worked.

Now, with a great bang, we were overridden with doctors

who tramped into our house and brushed past us children as if we didn't even exist.

"You've got to fumigate," said one. "How solid is this house anyway?" and he poked at the new wallpaper and made a hole. "I thought so — built out of sticks," he said.

I wanted to yell at him for that; to bang him on the head; to tell him to get out of my house. While some of the strange men were talking to my mother, the same one who had broken the paper went over and yanked down the curtains. "Take down all the hangings," he ordered my father.

Then the death wagon came for Hayashida. They carried him out with masks over their faces and gloves on, and little Kiko walked sorrowfully after him in a kimono which she had ceased to wear since she lived with us. Now she reverted to a kimono, and carried a few belongings in a little handkerchief. She sat at his head in the wagon, and a few children were there to see what was happening. My father tried not to cry; so did we all. Hayashida was going for good. No one ever got well of the plague.

"Good-by, Hayashida," said my father, "you have been a good boy with us."

Hayashida sat up in the wagon.

"Will you take care of Kiko if I die, Mr. Taggard?"

"Yes, Hayashida."

So he went away. The doctors hurried him off to the receiving station and he was put in quarantine. Now two health officials fastened on us.

"Take your children and go away for three or four days while we fumigate. Go anywhere. There is no danger. You haven't been exposed. Go visit friends. Don't let anybody know. There mustn't be a scare. This is only the sixth case. We must keep it quiet."

"I won't go to a friend's house," replied my indignant mother. "Where shall we go? There isn't a place in the world."

"You've got to get out for about four days," they said savagely, wishing she wouldn't quibble with them.

I started to take down some dresses.

"Little girl," one of them bawled at me. "Don't touch those things. Get out of the house in the fresh air. You can't take anything with you."

So we went, headachy and driven, forlorn in our old clothes, about four o'clock, knowing that all the neighbors down the long road to the streetcar were looking out from behind the doors and whispering that there was Plague in our family.

The streetcars go very fast in the islands, because there are such long stretches. They are open — a row of seats and a roof. On these flying platforms you go across rice fields and wait at switches for the other car; you climb a hill with a drone, and then branch off into Palama where the Japanese live.

At four o'clock on a school day it seemed strange to be riding through Palama. Dimly, the reason for this ride — the distinction of having Plague in the family, the awful importance of an event that seizes you the way a cat does a rat, the very great satisfaction of having something happen that is huge and terrible, that may end in darker, grimmer events — all this was in our minds as we went through Palama, looking at the Japanese and Chinese, the children, the withered women in their flat-chested black sateen coats and earringed ears. On all the faces that turned up to our car as it danged its bell through the crowded streets and down across the bridge, I extended the now gently painful knowledge that Hayashida would die, that our house would be fumigated, and that my head ached and my feet were cold.

On we went through Honolulu, past the hardware store where the Sherwin Williams paint folders were tucked in little boxes — (we always helped ourselves to the little booklets with their shiny inches of blue and tan); past our little church looking brown and dusty on a weekday with the shutters closed and the bougainvillea vine next it blooming cerise in the heat; past the Palace, the Opera House, the statue of Kamehameha, where the idiot Portuguese boy stood all day, worshipping and rubbing his hands; past the rich people's houses on the way to Waikiki.

Waikiki was our heaven always. It was always reserved for

the greatest occasions of joy. A sharp turn — our car was running wildly over the swamp in the stiff breeze from the sea, with Diamond Head lifted up, brown as a niggertoe nut, running parallel with our track. Another curve and wind and a switch, and the smell of salt, and the first turn of a wave, between two hedges as we started up again, running headlong into Diamond Head — headlong for the place where the water came into the arm of the old brown-purple mountain.

(Oh, the sea, the sea, the sea, the sea, the waves; the high clouds; the bright water, the crazy foam on the surf away out, the blue limpid lovely empty water. Oh, the sea.) So I cried to myself, and got up to stand on the seat.

"Sit down," said my mother wearily. She had a headache, I could tell.

We sat fixed, waiting for the great joy of seeing it suddenly, as we knew we would — the mountain, the surf running in with its arched neck and blowing mane, the dizzy blue water level on the sand. There it was. Oh, sea, sea. My brother and sister wouldn't sit still. My father cheered up, and lifted his head and his dreamy gaze to focus on it; my mother sat dully, because her head ached so. I could tell, by the narrowed slits of her eyes. She didn't look. The sun hit the water and the sunlight hit you as it shot off the surface. Black things danced in the air. It hurt between the eyes to look at it.

We got off at the Waikiki Inn and my mother and father hurried ahead. We ran for the sand.

They came out of the office in a minute, looking very embarrassed and troubled and trying to look untroubled. A Japanese boy led them to a little cottage under some vines and unlocked the door. My mother looked in and then came down to get us.

"You can't go in the water today. I'm sorry. Get out right away. You look like little wild children. You mustn't get wet," she said in a lower tone when we came, holding up our skirts to our waists, all wet-legged from the first tumbled wave. "Mother doesn't dare let you get in the water. One of us may have it."

With that her face looked so terrified and in such dull pain that we came limping in, letting down our dresses, and picking up our shoes and stockings. As we walked away from sand to grass lawn, the sea talked and roared and mumbled and swished at our backs. We didn't dare even turn around.

That night I was sick. The black dots in the air turned to balls of fire; the terrible sunlight on the water, the terrible water we couldn't go in, that became noisy torment, throbbing like the heart in illness; fever that took the bones and broke them and wrenched the stomach. My mother was sick too. We were sick together. The others slept. I lay under the thick mosquito net as if I were as wide as the Pacific Ocean and the fever took one arm off to the east, the other to the west; my legs stretched into dimness, I gazed flat upward, fixed, at some immensity — I immense, and facing immensity. The kerosene lamp purred on the table, a yellow torment. My mother sat retching with a sick headache. Now and then she would come and bow her head on the bed outside the mosquito net and say, "Oh, Genevieve, will this night never be over?" and then she would vomit again.

The sea rose outside in a great wind. A hard tropic tree scratched and clanged on the iron roof of the cottage. It was utterly black except for the torment of the little flame in the lamp. The ocean broke outside so near, the same wave sounds as in daylight, but so interminable at night, and no one to hear it, but us, me and my mother. The waves hit the shore like a blow on a wound; the lamp burned in its chimney stifling the air, never wiggling, just burning. Horror, the black death!

She fanned me and called out that I was her first born, and rubbed the wet hair from my head and chafed my feet. Her hand on my legs made them limited again at the bottom of the bed, not so long that they had no feet as a moment before. "Oh, mother, will this night never end?"

It ended — fear and a sick headache and a little fever — that was all. And I did not die except in some experience of the mind.

From *transition* (Paris), no. 5, August, 1927.

GENEVIEVE TAGGARD

# HIAWATHA IN HAWAII

When her father was taken ill, Genevieve Taggard left high
school before she was graduated and took a job as a substitute
teacher in a plantation school on Oahu. "I had a roomful of
fifty," she recalled, "and fifty is a lot to make mind in a drowsy,
warm, chalk-dusted schoolroom. . . . And I was only eighteen
and didn't have any idea how to bang them into shape." But
when the Department of Public Instruction commanded that
her school put on "the damn Hiawatha play," she capably —
if somewhat reluctantly — met the challenge.

AH HOP AND AH PAU WERE TWO LITTLE CHINESE-HAWAIIAN BOYS
in my school when I was teaching the fourth grade on a plantation. "Pau" is the Hawaiian word for *stop;* fathers usually
name the thirteenth or fifteenth child Pau. I loved Ah Hop and
I loved Ah Pau; sometimes one, sometimes the other. They
were both adorable little boys; and they nearly drove me mad
trying to make them mind and behave.

I had a roomful of fifty; and fifty is a lot to make mind in a
drowsy, warm, chalk-dusted schoolroom. They squirmed in
their seats, they poked their toes through the cracks of the seats
of the children in front; they brought centipedes without nippers. They were terrible.

Ah Pau had a face like a little bad Puck. He was about
as tall as my desk and wore little long trousers of blue denim
and clean shirts. His face was golden and he had half-moon
eyes. His father and his mother were both Chinese-Hawaiian.
I think he really was a thirteenth child.

Ah Hop was very different. He was stocky and round-headed. And he never looked at me without a look of shyness and hurt crossing his face. His eyes were black, and his hair stiff and black. He liked me very much although he shuffled in and out of the schoolroom with his eyes always on the floor and only moved his lips when I said, "Good morning." But once, when I sat at the desk with my head in my hand waiting for the blackboards to be erased, I caught sight through my fingers of a shy black piercing eye looking at me with concern.

But they were both as bad as they could be. And I was only eighteen and didn't have any idea how to bang them into shape. The rest of the children were so dull that I could bring them in and turn them out and make them spell and add by moving my arms and ringing the bell on the desk. I rang it, then I said, "One," and they turned toward the aisle; I said "Two," and they rose up behind each other; I said "Three, mark time, mark," and they scuffed their feet and began to file out onto the veranda, where they broke lines and whooped off to the playground.

Across the road in the tangle of lantana and algarroba trees a forlorn soda-water works chugged, bottling soda pop. The pump went all day, out there in the wilderness, with an irregular rhythm; the pop went away in trucks to the railroad; the plant was run by a Japanese and the soda was salty in spite of its rich syrup because all the water around there was salty. All day that soda works annoyed me with its erratic tune of chug-chugging that had a pause I could never calculate. And its being the only other thing away out there away from everybody (except the railroad station) and the fact that I kept thinking all the time that the soda, after all that work, used salty water — made it an accompaniment to my teaching job, and a funny one, too.

I went in to think over teaching, and Ah Hop and Ah Pau. That morning I had got a letter from the Department of Public Instruction, commanding me to give an entertainment at the school for which I was to charge an admission of ten cents which, when collected, I was to turn over to the Department of

Public Instruction, with greetings, for the Christmas Fund at the Molokai Leper Settlement. The Department further stated that I was to give a dramatization of *Hiawatha* made from the poem by Henry Wadsworth Longfellow, the children's poet, and that I could get the sewing class to make the costumes.

The Department of Public Instruction further stated that it was sending as a gift to our little school a plaster bust of the children's poet which I could get the boys' carpentering class to make a shelf for and which I could use to illustrate my talks on Saint Longfellow.

All this I could do.

The next day the station agent brought up the box with the plaster bust in it. The children said, "Ah-h-h-h-h," and "Ahwey," over and over, at the sight. I stayed after school and put up the shelf myself with a hammer borrowed from the soda works, because there was no boys' carpentering class.

Then I took the damn *Hiawatha* play home and read it. The next morning, smirking as little as possible, I gave a speech, ending up by saying that Hiawatha was a good boy and never hurt living things and never cut the nippers off centipedes (joke for me) and behaved very well in all his social relationships, and *therefore,* since both Ah Hop and Ah Pau were exactly right for the Hiawatha part and would look very nice in an imitation leather costume, I would give the part to the boy who was the kindest to dumb things and to fellow pupils and me, also, the teacher. And on that speech we lived peaceably for some time; almost two days.

And then Ah Pau decided it wasn't worth it, and broke for his old diversions and brought a pocketful of grasshoppers in after recess and let them loose into the starched back of the little Japanese girl in front of him. I put him in a seat by himself and gave him up.

Ah Hop had the part — by elimination — and besides he had been very good. A nervous black eye told me he wanted to be Hiawatha more than anything. I measured him and went home to make the beaded costumes for the play since there was no girls' sewing class. That was Friday.

Monday morning an impassive and unhappy face came up to the desk before school began, two bare feet shuffled the floor, Ah Hop twisted one finger and poked the backs of the books.

"No can be Hiawatha," he announced.

"Why, Ah Hop?"

"My papa no like."

"Why?"

"He say no good."

"Why?"

"He say me watch rice fields."

"Oh, you have to go home after school and scare off the rice birds?"

"Yes."

"Too bad, Ah Hop."

"Me no like."

"I'm sorry."

So Ah Pau got it after all. And how he crowed triumph! How he strutted, announced his lines, made grimaces at stoic Ah Hop — how he loved getting it by not trying at all! Never have the wordy lines of Saint Longfellow been more unctuously pronounced than as Ah Pau said them, with a bad pidgin English accent. And when the costume got done at last, how he twirled in his finery, half-moon eyes gleaming, to make Ah Hop see just how much, by his bad luck, he had missed.

One day, coming in at noon I found the plaster bust minus a nose and a very tidy little pencilled mustache marked on top of the plaster one. There were prints of bare feet on the bottom of a chair; I knew the villain. I knew, I thought, just how long Ah Pau had been planning to de-nose the children's poet. But what could I do? It was the afternoon of the performance and nobody but the villain knew the lines.

And so the villain had his day, as villains do, and nobody noticed the noseless bust elevated over our heads. I hoped to attend to that on Monday. The Japanese mothers and fathers came that night and sat, slightly larger children, in the little seats before the little desks; the Chinese mothers and fathers stayed away as they always did; the Chinese-Hawaiian parents were all there, but they had to sit on the floor between the aisles because they were too big to squeeze into the seats. We had cut down a lot of prickly keawe trees to represent the forest of murmuring pines; we had made a wigwam and an imitation fire with red paper to represent flame. And there was Ah Pau in his imitation leather costume and his pidgin accent.

So the play began and everybody loved it. The kerosene lamps smoked up to the ceiling and smudged their tin reflectors. Old Nokomis said her say and Hiawatha answered in hexameters, bobbing his feathered head. Ah Hop was not there.

He couldn't stand his rival's triumph, I said to myself, but I had thought he would come, in his stoic way, and look on, very surly under a frown. He hadn't even come. I was sorry.

And just then I noticed a flattened nose against the windowpane and, when I stole out to the veranda, there he was, watching like a cat every move Ah Pau was making. He probably couldn't have played the part half so well. "Ah Hop," I said, taking hold of him. He started and then looked down at his feet, overcome.

"Look here, Ah Hop, wouldn't your father let you be Hiawatha, or was there another reason? Did you lie to me?"

"Yes, Ma'am."

"That was just a story then?"

"Yes, Ma'am."

"Why didn't you want to be Hiawatha?"

"I want," he said getting very tight around the mouth.

"What happened then?"

"I swear," he said laconically.

(In the Islands the children call any dirty word "swearing" and the missionaries have made swearing the cardinal sin. You can lie, steal, play hooky and take the nose off Longfellow and still be forgiven.)

So I said, "Oh, Ah Hop, I am so ashamed."

"I no can help," he cried desperately. "I no like swear."

He looked at me a moment to size me up — whether or not I would understand.

Then:

"Hiawatha never swear," he announced.

Well, I saw the point.

"So you told me your father wouldn't let you."

"Yea."

"What did you say?" I demanded.

His head sank low on his little breast. He shook it slowly.

"Come, Ah Hop. You've got to tell me what you said."

"No."

"Is it too bad?"

"Yea."

It probably was, I commented to myself.

Suddenly he looked up at me. "I hear the men on the railroad say it all the time." A long pause. "Ah Pau make a song about me when he no can be Hiawatha and everybody sing, and I say . . . *Beat it! Beat it!*"

From *The Bookman*, July, 1929.

GENEVIEVE TAGGARD

# THE LUAU

Having grown up in Hawaii, where her playmates were the
children of various races, Genevieve Taggard held a deep conviction, often evident in her writing, that all races, being one
humanity, are "of one skin." In the following fine poem she turns
from her adult world "where race is war" to a happy memory of
childhood in Kalihi Valley, where the island children possessed
the fruits of the earth in friendly communion.

Odor of algarroba, lure of release.
The smell of red lehua and the crisp scent of maile . . .
These words and images will help you after a little.
Hypnotic words emerge and bloom in the mind,
Anaesthetic names . . . Dry buzz of bees
Who make a honey eaten at early breakfast
From a comb like a broken coral . . .
Do dreams foretell the honey? Break the spell.

So I come home in the valley of Kalihi,
My bare feet on hard earth, hibiscus with stamen-tongue
Twirled in my fingers like a paper windmill,
A wheel of color, crimson, the petals large,
Kiss of the petal, tactile, light, intense . . .

Now I am back again. I can touch the children:
My human race, in whom was a human dwelling,
Whose names are all the races — of one skin.
For so our games ran tacit, without blur.

What brings me back with giant steps to them?
What was the feast that woke this fabulous thirst?
What was the summer fruit we found and ate
Boldly, with the children of Adam?

A game and a daily search
In the harvest of trees. We played a parable.
We possessed a valley, devoured the juicy, dense
Jewels of appetite hung in fresco sweeps,
In garlands and in fountains toward the sea.
Mangoes of golden flesh, with turpentine
Peel and odor. Cut plums of inky stain
And the pucker of persimmons. Dates to be got
By stepping up a tree trunk. Coconuts
With custard centers. Rose and custard apple,
Eugenia, pink, lemon and little orange,
Guava seedy and tart, and the hidden poha,
And the sacklike fig, to be ripped, to be seen, to be tasted.
How rasping sweet the suck of sugar cane —
Papaya and banana taken for granted.

With giant steps, in sleep and troubled pain
I return to the fabulous feast, the old communion,
With bodiless hunger and thirst. Why have I come
Away from the adult world where race is war?

Here we are dipping and passing the calabash
In the ceremony of friends; I also;
But in frenzy and pain distort
The simple need, knowing how blood is shed:

                                        *To sit together*

*Drinking the blue ocean, eating the sun*
*Like a fruit . . .*

From *Origin: Hawaii* by Genevieve Taggard (Honolulu, Donald Angus, 1947). "The Luau" first appeared under the title "Fructus" in *Poetry Quarterly* (London), Winter, 1946–1947.

RUPERT BROOKE

# WAIKIKI

No other poet who wrote about the South Seas possessed the genius of Rupert Brooke (1887-1915). In 1913 this young Englishman set out on a year of travel in the United States and afterward sojourned in Hawaii, Samoa, Fiji, New Zealand, and Tahiti. It was his happiest period. Less than a year after the outbreak of World War I, Brooke died of blood poisoning on his way to the Dardanelles campaign.

During a short stay in Honolulu, Brooke wrote "Waikiki," one of his finest sonnets. He suggests here the differences between Hawaii and other regions of romance, yet hints that there is a certain universality in legends of love and pain.

Warm perfumes like a breath from vine and tree
    Drift down the darkness. Plangent, hidden from eyes,
    Somewhere an ukulele thrills and cries
And stabs with pain the night's brown savagery.
And dark scents whisper; and dim waves creep to me,
    Gleam like a woman's hair, stretch out, and rise;
    And new stars burn into the ancient skies,
Over the murmurous soft Hawaiian sea.

And I recall, lose, grasp, forget again,
    And still remember, a tale I have heard, or known,
An empty tale, of idleness and pain,
    Of two that loved — or did not love — and one
Whose perplexed heart did evil, foolishly,
A long while since, and by some other sea.

*Waikiki, 1913*

From *The Collected Poems of Rupert Brooke* (New York, Dodd, Mead & Company, 1915).

# W. Somerset Maugham

# HONOLULU

During World War I, William Somerset Maugham (1874 —)
was a British secret agent playing the role of an author living in
neutral countries. He arrived in New York early in 1916 on
his way to Russia, hoping to help keep that nation in the war
and prevent the Bolsheviks from seizing power. Since his health
was poor, Maugham got permission to travel through the South
Pacific on his way to Asia. On this first trip to the South Seas,
he found material for some of his finest short stories and a novel,
*The Moon and Sixpence.*

Maugham's introduction to the Pacific islands was Honolulu,
which he visited presumably in mid-1916. He inspected "Chinatown," the waterfront, and the red-light district of Iwilei, which
he later mentioned in his celebrated story "Rain."

The following story of the effect of an evil Polynesian infliction
upon a white man in love with a brown girl shows the combination of irony and narrative suspense for which Maugham is celebrated.

THE WISE TRAVELER TRAVELS ONLY IN IMAGINATION. AN OLD
Frenchman (he was really a Savoyard) once wrote a book
called *Voyage autour de ma Chambre.* I have not read it and
do not even know what it is about, but the title stimulates my
fancy. In such a journey I could circumnavigate the globe. An
eikon by the chimneypiece can take me to Russia with its great
forests of birch and its white, domed churches. The Volga is
wide, and at the end of a straggling village, in the wineshop,
bearded men in rough sheepskin coats sit drinking. I stand
on the little hill from which Napoleon first saw Moscow and
I look upon the vastness of the city. I will go down and see the

people whom I know more intimately than so many of my friends, Alyosha, and Vronsky, and a dozen more. But my eyes fall on a piece of porcelain and I smell the acrid odors of China. I am borne in a chair along a narrow causeway between the padi fields, or else I skirt a tree-clad mountain. My bearers chat gaily as they trudge along in the bright morning and every now and then, distant and mysterious, I hear the deep sound of a monastery bell. In the streets of Peking there is a motley crowd and it scatters to allow passage to a string of camels, stepping delicately, that bring skins and strange drugs from the stony deserts of Mongolia. In England, in London, there are certain afternoons in winter when the clouds hang heavy and low and the light is so bleak that your heart sinks, but then you can look out of your window, and you see the coconut trees crowded upon the beach of a coral island. The sand is silvery and when you walk along in the sunshine it is so dazzling that you can hardly bear to look at it. Overhead the mynah birds are making a great to-do, and the surf beats ceaselessly against the reef. Those are the best journeys, the journeys that you take at your own fireside, for then you lose none of your illusions.

But there are people who take salt in their coffee. They say it gives it a tang, a savor, which is peculiar and fascinating. In the same way there are certain places, surrounded by a halo of romance, to which the inevitable disillusionment which you must experience on seeing them gives a singular spice. You had expected something wholly beautiful and you get an impression which is infinitely more complicated than any that beauty can give you. It is like the weakness in the character of a great man which may make him less admirable but certainly makes him more interesting.

Nothing had prepared me for Honolulu. It is so far away from Europe, it is reached after so long a journey from San Francisco, so strange and so charming associations are attached to the name, that at first I could hardly believe my eyes. I do not know that I had formed in my mind any very exact picture of what I expected, but what I found caused me a great surprise. It is a typical western city. Shacks are cheek by jowl with stone mansions; dilapidated frame houses stand next door to smart stores with plate-glass windows; electric cars rumble noisily along the streets; and motors, Fords, Buicks, Packards, line the pavement. The shops are filled with all the necessities of American civilization. Every third house is a bank and every fifth the agency of a steamship company.

Along the streets crowd an unimaginable assortment of people. The Americans, ignoring the climate, wear black coats and high, starched collars, straw hats, soft hats, and bowlers. The Kanakas, pale brown, with crisp hair, have nothing on but a shirt and a pair of trousers; but the half-breeds are very smart with flaring ties and patent-leather boots. The Japanese, with their obsequious smile, are neat and trim in white duck, while their women walk a step or two behind them, in native dress, with a baby on their backs. The Japanese children, in bright-colored frocks, their little heads shaven, look like quaint dolls. Then there are the Chinese. The men, fat and prosperous, wear their American clothes oddly, but the women are enchanting with their tightly-dressed black hair, so neat that you feel it can never be disarranged, and they are very clean in their tunics and trousers, white, or powder blue, or black. Lastly there are the Filipinos, the men in huge straw hats, the women in bright yellow muslin with great puffed sleeves.

It is the meeting place of East and West. The very new rubs shoulders with the immeasurably old. And if you have not found the romance you expected you have come upon something singularly intriguing. All these strange people live close to each other, with different languages and different thoughts; they believe in different gods and they have different values; two passions alone they share, love and hunger. And somehow as you watch them you have an impression of extraordinary vitality. Though the air is so soft and the sky so blue, you have, I know not why, a feeling of something hotly passionate that beats like a throbbing pulse through the crowd. Though the native policeman at the corner, standing on a platform, with a white club to direct the traffic, gives the scene an air of respectability, you cannot but feel that it is a respectability only of the surface; a little below there is darkness and mystery. It gives you just that thrill, with a little catch at the heart, that you have when at night in the forest the silence trembles on a sudden with the low, insistent beating of a drum. You are all expectant of I know not what.

If I have dwelt on the incongruity of Honolulu, it is because just this, to my mind, gives its point to the story I want to tell. It is a story of primitive superstition, and it startles me that anything of the sort should survive in a civilization which, if not very distinguished, is certainly very elaborate. I cannot get over the fact that such incredible things should happen, or at least be thought to happen, right in the middle, so to speak, of telephones, tramcars, and daily papers. And the friend who showed me Honolulu had the same incongruity which I felt from the beginning was its most striking characteristic.

He was an American named Winter and I had brought a letter of introduction to him from an acquaintance in New York. He was a man between forty and fifty, with scanty black hair, gray at the temples, and a sharp-featured, thin face. His eyes had a twinkle in them and his large horn spectacles gave him a demureness which was not a little diverting. He was tall rather than otherwise and very spare. He was born in Honolulu and his father had a large store which sold hosiery and all such goods, from tennis racquets to tarpaulins, as a man of fashion could require. It was a prosperous business and I could well understand the indignation of Winter *père* when his son, refusing to go into it, had announced his determination to be an actor. My friend spent twenty years on the stage, sometimes in New York, but more often on the road, for his gifts were small; but at last, being no fool, he came to the conclusion that it was better to sell sock-suspenders in Honolulu than to play small parts in Cleveland, Ohio. He left the stage and went into the business. I think after the hazardous existence he had lived so long, he thoroughly enjoyed the luxury of driving a large car and living in a beautiful house near the golf course, and I am quite sure, since he was a man of parts, he managed the

222 A HAWAIIAN READER

business competently. But he could not bring himself entirely to break his connection with the arts and since he might no longer act he began to paint. He took me to his studio and showed me his work. It was not at all bad, but not what I should have expected from him. He painted nothing but still life, very small pictures, perhaps eight by ten; and he painted very delicately, with the utmost finish. He had evidently a passion for detail. His fruit pieces reminded you of the fruit in a picture by Ghirlandajo. While you marveled a little at his patience, you could not help being impressed by his dexterity. I imagine that he failed as an actor because his effects, carefully studied, were neither bold nor broad enough to get across the footlights.

I was entertained by the proprietary, yet ironical air with which he showed me the city. He thought in his heart that there was none in the United States to equal it, but he saw quite clearly that his attitude was comic. He drove me round to the various buildings and swelled with satisfaction when I expressed a proper admiration for their architecture. He showed me the houses of rich men.

"That's the Stubbs' house," he said. "It cost a hundred thousand dollars to build. The Stubbs are one of our best families. Old man Stubbs came here as a missionary more than seventy years ago."

He hesitated a little and looked at me with twinkling eyes through his big round spectacles.

"All our best families are missionary families," he said. "You're not very much in Honolulu unless your father or your grandfather converted the heathen."

"Is that so?"

"Do you know your Bible?"

"Fairly," I answered.

"There is a text which says: The fathers have eaten sour grapes and the children's teeth are set on edge. I guess it runs differently in Honolulu. The fathers brought Christianity to the Kanaka and the children jumped his land."

"Heaven helps those who help themselves," I murmured.

"It surely does. By the time the natives of this island had embraced Christianity they had nothing else they could afford to embrace. The kings gave the missionaries land as a mark of esteem, and the missionaries bought land by way of laying up treasure in heaven. It surely was a good investment. One missionary left the business — I think one may call it a business without offense — and became a land agent, but that is an exception. Mostly it was their sons who looked after the commercial side of the concern. Oh, it's a fine thing to have a father who came here fifty years ago to spread the faith."

But he looked at his watch.

"Gee, it's stopped. That means it's time to have a cocktail."

We sped along an excellent road, bordered with red hibiscus, and came back into the town.

"Have you been to the Union Saloon?"

"Not yet."

"We'll go there."

I knew it was the most famous spot in Honolulu and I entered it with a lively curiosity. You get to it by a narrow passage from King Street, and in the passage are offices, so that thirsty souls may be supposed bound for one of these just as well as for the saloon. It is a large square room, with three entrances, and opposite the bar, which runs the length of it, two corners have been partitioned off into little cubicles. Legend states that they were built so that King Kalakaua might drink there without being seen by his subjects, and it is pleasant to think that in one or other of these he may have sat over his bottle, a coal-black potentate, with Robert Louis Stevenson. There is a portrait of him, in oils, in a rich gold frame; but there are also two prints of Queen Victoria. On the walls, besides, are old line engravings of the eighteenth century, one of which, and heaven knows how it got there, is after a theatrical picture by De Wilde; and there are oleographs from the Christmas supplements of the *Graphic* and the *Illustrated London News* of twenty years ago. Then there are advertisements of whisky, gin, champagne, and beer; and photographs of baseball teams and of native orchestras.

The place seemed to belong not to the modern, hustling world that I had left in the bright street outside, but to one that was dying. It had the savor of the day before yesterday. Dingy and dimly lit, it had a vaguely mysterious air and you could imagine that it would be a fit scene for shady transactions. It suggested a more lurid time, when ruthless men carried their lives in their hands, and violent deeds diapered the monotony of life.

When I went in the saloon was fairly full. A group of businessmen stood together at the bar, discussing affairs, and in a corner two Kanakas were drinking. Two or three men who might have been storekeepers were shaking dice. The rest of the company plainly followed the sea; they were captains of tramps, first mates, and engineers. Behind the bar, busily making the Honolulu cocktail for which the place was famous, served two large half-castes in white, fat, clean-shaven, and dark-skinned, with thick, curly hair and large bright eyes.

Winter seemed to know more than half the company, and when we made our way to the bar a little fat man in spectacles, who was standing by himself, offered him a drink.

"No, you have one with me, Captain," said Winter.

He turned to me.

"I want you to know Captain Butler."

The little man shook hands with me. We began to talk, but, my attention distracted by my surroundings, I took small notice of him, and after we had each ordered a cocktail we separated. When we had got into the motor again and were driving away, Winter said to me:

"I'm glad we ran up against Butler. I wanted you to meet him. What did you think of him?"

"I don't know that I thought very much of him at all," I answered.

"Do you believe in the supernatural?"

"I don't exactly know that I do." I smiled.

"A very queer thing happened to him a year or two ago. You ought to have him tell you about it."

"What sort of thing?"

Winter did not answer my question.

"I have no explanation of it myself," he said. "But there's no doubt about the facts. Are you interested in things like that?"

"Things like what?"

"Spells and magic and all that."

"I've never met anyone who wasn't."

Winter paused for a moment.

"I guess I won't tell you myself. You ought to hear it from his own lips so that you can judge. How are you fixed up for tonight?"

"I've got nothing on at all."

"Well, I'll get hold of him between now and then and see if we can't go down to his ship."

Winter told me something about him. Captain Butler had spent all his life on the Pacific. He had been in much better circumstances than he was now, for he had been first officer and then captain of a passenger boat plying along the coast of California, but he had lost his ship and a number of passengers had been drowned.

"Drink, I guess," said Winter.

Of course there had been an inquiry, which had cost him his certificate, and then he drifted further afield. For some years he had knocked about the South Seas, but he was now in command of a small schooner which sailed between Honolulu and the various islands of the group. It belonged to a Chinese to whom the fact that his skipper had no certificate meant only that he could be had for lower wages, and to have a white man in charge was always an advantage.

And now that I had heard this about him I took the trouble to remember more exactly what he was like. I recalled his round spectacles and the round blue eyes behind them, and so gradually reconstructed him before my mind. He was a little man, without angles, plump, with a round face like the full moon and a little fat round nose. He had fair short hair, and he was red-faced and clean shaven. He had plump hands, dimpled on the knuckles, and short fat legs. He was a jolly soul, and the tragic experience he had gone through seemed to have left him unscarred. Though he must have been thirty-four or thirty-five he looked much younger. But after all I had given him but a superficial attention, and now that I knew of this catastrophe, which had obviously ruined his life, I promised myself that when I saw him again I would take more careful note of him. It is very curious to observe the differences of emotional response that you find in different people. Some can go through terrific battles, the fear of imminent death and unimaginable horrors and preserve their soul unscathed, while with others the trembling of the moon on a solitary sea or the song of a bird in a thicket will cause a convulsion great enough to transform their entire being. Is it due to strength or weakness, want of imagination or instability of character? I do not know. When I called up in my fancy that scene of shipwreck, with the shrieks of the drowning and the terror, and then later, the ordeal of the inquiry, and the harsh things he must have read of himself in the papers, the shame and the disgrace, it came to me with a shock to remember that Captain Butler had talked with the frank obscenity of a schoolboy of the Hawaiian girls and of Iwilei, the red-light district, and of his successful adventures. He laughed readily, and one would have thought he could never laugh again. I remembered his shining, white teeth; they were his best feature. He began to interest me, and thinking of him and of his gay insouciance I forgot the particular story, to hear which I was to see him again. I wanted to see him rather to find out if I could a little more what sort of man he was.

Winter made the necessary arrangements and after dinner we went down to the waterfront. The ship's boat was waiting for us and we rowed out. The schooner was anchored some way across the harbor, not far from the breakwater. We came alongside, and I heard the sound of a ukulele. We clambered up the ladder.

"I guess he's in the cabin," said Winter, leading the way.

It was a small cabin, bedraggled and dirty, with a table against one side and a broad bench all round upon which slept, I supposed, such passengers as were ill-advised enough to travel

in such a ship. A petroleum lamp gave a dim light. The ukulele
was being played by a native girl and Butler was lolling on the
seat, half lying, with his head on her shoulder and an arm round
her waist.

"Don't let us disturb you, Captain," said Winter, facetiously.

"Come right in," said Butler, getting up and shaking hands
with us. "What'll you have?"

It was a warm night, and through the open door you saw
countless stars in a heaven that was still almost blue. Captain
Butler wore a sleeveless undershirt, showing his fat white arms,
and a pair of incredibly dirty trousers. His feet were bare, but
on his curly head he wore a very old, a very shapeless felt
hat.

"Let me introduce you to my girl. Ain't she a peach?"

We shook hands with a very pretty person. She was a good
deal taller than the captain, and even the Mother Hubbard,
which the missionaries of a past generation had, in the interests of decency, forced on the unwilling natives, could not con-
ceal the beauty of her form. One could not but suspect that age
would burden her with a certain corpulence, but now she was
graceful and alert. Her brown skin had an exquisite trans-
lucency and her eyes were magnificent. Her black hair, very
thick and rich, was coiled round her head in a massive plait.
When she smiled in a greeting that was charmingly natural, she
showed teeth that were small, even, and white. She was certainly a most attractive creature. It was easy to see that the
capain was madly in love with her. He could not take his eyes
off her; he wanted to touch her all the time. That was very
easy to understand; but what seemed to me stranger was that
the girl was apparently in love with him. There was a light in
her eyes that was unmistakable, and her lips were slightly
parted as though in a sigh of desire. It was thrilling. It was
even a little moving, and I could not help feeling somewhat in
the way. What had a stranger to do with this lovesick pair? I
wished that Winter had not brought me. And it seemed to me
that the dingy cabin was transfigured and now it seemed a fit
and proper scene for such an extremity of passion. I thought I

should never forget that schooner in the harbor of Honolulu, crowded with shipping, and yet, under the immensity of the starry sky, remote from all the world. I liked to think of those lovers sailing off together in the night over the empty spaces of the Pacific from one green, hilly island to another. A faint breeze of romance softly fanned my cheek.

And yet Butler was the last man in the world with whom you would have associated romance, and it was hard to see what there was in him to arouse love. In the clothes he wore now he looked podgier than ever, and his round spectacles gave his round face the look of a prim cherub. He suggested rather a curate who had gone to the dogs. His conversation was peppered with the quaintest Americanisms, and it is because I despair of reproducing these that, at whatever loss of vividness, I mean to narrate the story he told me a little later in my own words. Moreover he was unable to frame a sentence without an oath, though a good-natured one, and his speech, albeit offensive only to prudish ears, in print would seem coarse. He was a mirth-loving man, and perhaps that accounted not a little for his successful amours; since women, for the most part frivolous creatures, are excessively bored by the seriousness with which men treat them, and they can seldom resist the buffoon who makes them laugh. Their sense of humor is crude. Diana of Ephesus is always prepared to fling prudence to the winds for the red-nosed comedian who sits on his hat. I realized that Captain Butler had charm. If I had not known the tragic story of the shipwreck I should have thought he had never had a care in his life.

Our host had rung the bell on our entrance and now a Chinese cook came in with more glasses and several bottles of soda. The whisky and the captain's empty glass stood already on the table. But when I saw the Chinese I positively started, for he was certainly the ugliest man I had ever seen. He was very short, but thick-set, and he had a bad limp. He wore a singlet and a pair of trousers that had been white, but were now filthy, and, perched on a shock of bristly, gray hair, an old tweed deerstalker. It would have been grotesque on any Chi-

nese, but on him it was outrageous. His broad, square face was
very flat as though it had been bashed in by a mighty fist,
and it was deeply pitted with smallpox; but the most revolting
thing in him was a very pronounced harelip which had never
been operated on, so that his upper lip, cleft, went up in an
angle to his nose, and in the opening was a huge yellow fang.
It was horrible. He came in with the end of a cigarette at
the corner of his mouth, and this, I do not know why, gave him
a devilish expression.

He poured out the whisky and opened a bottle of soda.

"Don't drown it, John," said the captain.

He said nothing, but handed a glass to each of us. Then he
went out.

"I saw you lookin' at my Chink," said Butler, with a grin on
his fat, shining face.

"I should hate to meet him on a dark night," I said.

"He sure is homely," said the captain, and for some reason
he seemed to say it with a peculiar satisfaction. "But he's fine
for one thing, I'll tell the world; you just have to have a drink
every time you look at him."

But my eyes fell on a calabash that hung against the wall over
the table, and I got up to look at it. I had been hunting for an
old one and this was better than any I had seen outside the
museum.

"It was given me by a chief over on one of the islands," said
the captain, watching me. "I done him a good turn and he
wanted to give me something good."

"He certainly did," I answered.

I was wondering whether I could discreetly make Captain
Butler an offer for it. I could not imagine that he set any store
on such an article, when, as though he read my thoughts, he
said:

"I wouldn't sell that for ten thousand dollars."

"I guess not," said Winter. "It would be a crime to sell it."

"Why?" I asked.

"That comes into the story," returned Winter. "Doesn't it,
Captain?"

"It surely does."

"Let's hear it then."

"The night's young yet," he answered.

The night distinctly lost its youth before he satisfied my curiosity, and meanwhile we drank a great deal too much whisky while Captain Butler narrated his experiences of San Francisco in the old days and of the South Seas. At last the girl fell asleep. She lay curled up on the seat, with her face on her brown arm, and her bosom rose and fell gently with her breathing. In sleep she looked sullen, but darkly beautiful.

He had found her on one of the islands in the group among which, whenever there was cargo to be got, he wandered with his crazy old schooner. The Kanakas have little love for work, and the laborious Chinese, the cunning Japs, have taken the trade out of their hands. Her father had a strip of land on which he grew taro and bananas and he had a boat in which he went fishing. He was vaguely related to the mate of the schooner, and it was he who took Captain Butler up to the shabby little frame house to spend an idle evening. They took a bottle of whisky with them and the ukulele. The captain was not a shy man and when he saw a pretty girl he made love to her. He could speak the native language fluently and it was not long before he had overcome the girl's timidity. They spent the evening singing and dancing, and by the end of it she was sitting by his side and he had his arm around her waist. It happened that they were delayed on the island for several days and the captain, at no time a man to hurry, made no effort to shorten his stay. He was very comfortable in the snug little harbor and life was long. He had a swim round his ship in the morning and another in the evening. There was a chandler's shop on the waterfront where sailormen could get a drink of whisky, and he spent the best part of the day there, playing cribbage with the half-caste who owned it. At night the mate and he went up to the house where the pretty girl lived and they sang a song or two and told stories. It was the girl's father who suggested that he should take her away with him. They discussed the matter in a friendly fashion, while the girl, nestling against the captain, urged him by the pressure of her hands and her soft, smiling glances. He had taken a fancy to her and he was a domestic man. He was a little dull sometimes at sea and it would be very pleasant to have a pretty little creature like that about the old ship. He was of a practical turn too, and he recognized that it would be useful to have someone around to darn his socks and look after his linen. He was tired of having his things washed by a Chink who tore everything to pieces; the natives washed much better, and now and then when the captain went ashore at Honolulu he liked to cut a dash in a smart duck suit. It was only a matter of arranging a price. The father wanted two hundred and fifty dollars, and the captain, never a thrifty man, could not put his hand on such a sum. But he was a generous one, and with the girl's soft face against his, he was not inclined to haggle. He offered to give a hundred and fifty dollars there and then and another hundred in three months. There was a good deal of argument and the parties could not come to any agreement that night, but the idea had fired the captain, and he could not sleep as well as usual. He kept dreaming of the lovely girl and each time he awoke it was with the pressure of her soft, sensual lips on his. He cursed himself in the morning because a bad night at poker the last time he was at Honolulu had left him so short of ready money. And if the night before he had been in love with the girl, this morning he was crazy about her.

"See here, Bananas," he said to the mate, "I've got to have that girl. You go and tell the old man I'll bring the dough up tonight and she can get fixed up. I figure we'll be ready to sail at dawn."

I have no idea why the mate was known by that eccentric name. He was called Wheeler, but though he had that English surname there was not a drop of white blood in him. He was a tall man, and well-made though inclined to stoutness, but much darker than is usual in Hawaii. He was no longer young, and his crisply curling, thick hair was gray. His upper front teeth were cased in gold. He was very proud of them. He had a

marked squint and this gave him a saturnine expression. The
captain, who was fond of a joke, found in it a constant source
of humor and hesitated the less to rally him on the defect because he realized that the mate was sensitive about it. Bananas,
unlike most of the natives, was a taciturn fellow and Captain
Butler would have disliked him if it had been possible for a
man of his good nature to dislike anyone. He liked to be at sea
with someone he could talk to, he was a chatty, sociable creature,
and it was enough to drive a missionary to drink to live there
day after day with a chap who never opened his mouth. He
did his best to wake the mate up, that is to say, he chaffed
him without mercy, but it was poor fun to laugh by oneself,
and he came to the conclusion that, drunk or sober, Bananas
was no fit companion for a white man. But he was a good sea-
man and the captain was shrewd enough to know the value of
a mate he could trust. It was not rare for him to come aboard,
when they were sailing, fit for nothing but to fall into his bunk,
and it was worth something to know that he could stay there
till he had slept his liquor off, since Bananas could be relied on.
But he was an unsociable devil, and it would be a treat to have
someone he could talk to. That girl would be fine. Besides, he
wouldn't be so likely to get drunk when he went ashore if
he knew there was a little girl waiting for him when he came on
board again.

He went to his friend the chandler and over a peg of gin
asked him for a loan. There were one or two useful things a
ship's captain could do for a ship's chandler, and after a quarter
of an hour's conversation in low tones (there is no object in letting all and sundry know your business), the captain crammed
a wad of notes in his hip pocket, and that night, when he went
back to his ship, the girl went with him.

What Captain Butler, seeking for reasons to do what he had
already made up his mind to, had anticipated, actually came
to pass. He did not give up his drinking, but he ceased to
drink to excess. An evening with the boys, when he had been
away from town two or three weeks, was pleasant enough, but

it was pleasant too to get back to his little girl; he thought of her sleeping so softly, and how, when he got into his cabin and leaned over her, she would open her eyes lazily and stretch out her arms for him: it was as good as a full hand. He found he was saving money, and since he was a generous man he did the right thing by the little girl: he gave her some silver-backed brushes for her long hair, and a gold chain, and a reconstructed ruby for her finger. Gee, but it was good to be alive.

A year went by, a whole year, and he was not tired of her yet. He was not a man who analyzed his feelings, but this was so surprising that it forced itself upon his attention. There must be something very wonderful about that girl. He couldn't help seeing that he was more wrapped up in her than ever, and sometimes the thought entered his mind that it might not be a bad thing if he married her.

Then, one day the mate did not come in to dinner or to tea. Butler did not bother himself about his absence at the first meal, but at the second he asked the Chinese cook:

"Where's the mate? He no come tea?"

"No wantchee," said the Chink.

"He ain't sick?"

"No savvy."

Next day Bananas turned up again, but he was more sullen than ever, and after dinner the captain asked the girl what was the matter with him. She smiled and shrugged her pretty shoulders. She told the captain that Bananas had taken a fancy to her and he was sore because she had told him off. The captain was a good-humored man and he was not of a jealous nature; it struck him as exceedingly funny that Bananas should be in love. A man who had a squint like that had a precious poor chance. When tea came round he chaffed him gaily. He pretended to speak in the air, so that the mate should not be certain that he knew anything, but he dealt him some pretty shrewd blows. The girl did not think him as funny as he thought himself, and afterwards she begged him to say nothing more. He was surprised at her seriousness. She told him he did not know her people. When their passion was aroused they were capable of anything. She was a little frightened. This was so absurd to him that he laughed heartily.

"If he comes bothering round you, you just threaten to tell me. That'll fix him."

"Better fire him, I think."

"Not on your sweet life. I know a good sailor when I see one. But if he don't leave you alone I'll give him the worst licking he's ever had."

Perhaps the girl had a wisdom unusual in her sex. She knew that it was useless to argue with a man when his mind was made up, for it only increased his stubbornness, and she held her peace. And now on the shabby schooner, threading her way across the silent sea, among those lovely islands, was enacted a dark, tense drama of which the fat little captain remained entirely ignorant. The girl's resistance fired Bananas so that he ceased to be a man, but was simply blind desire. He did not make love to her gently or gaily, but with a black and savage ferocity. Her contempt now was changed to hatred and when he besought her he answered him with bitter, angry taunts. But the struggle went on silently, and when the captain asked her after a little while whether Bananas was bothering her, she lied.

But one night, when they were in Honolulu, he came on board only just in time. They were sailing at dawn. Bananas had been ashore, drinking some native spirit, and he was drunk. The captain, rowing up, heard sounds that surprised him. He scrambled up the ladder. He saw Bananas, beside himself, trying to wrench open the cabin door. He was shouting at the girl. He swore he would kill her if she did not let him in.

"What in hell are you up to?" cried Butler.

The mate let go the handle, gave the captain a look of savage hate, and without a word turned away.

"Stop here. What are you doing with that door?"

The mate still did not answer. He looked at him with sullen, bootless rage.

"I'll teach you not to pull any of your queer stuff with me, you dirty, cross-eyed nigger," said the captain.

He was a good foot shorter than the mate and no match for him, but he was used to dealing with native crews, and he had his knuckle-duster handy. Perhaps it was not an instrument that a gentleman would use, but then Captain Butler was not a gentleman. Nor was he in the habit of dealing with gentlemen. Before Bananas knew what the captain was at, his right arm had shot out and his fist, with its ring of steel, caught him fair and square on the jaw. He fell like a bull under the pole-ax.

"That'll learn him," said the captain.

Bananas did not stir. The girl unlocked the cabin door and came out.

"Is he dead?"

"He ain't."

He called a couple of men and told them to carry the mate to his bunk. He rubbed his hands with satisfaction and his round blue eyes gleamed behind his spectacles. But the girl was strangely silent. She put her arms round him as though to protect him from invisible harm.

It was two or three days before Bananas was on his feet again, and when he came out of his cabin his face was torn and swollen. Through the darkness of his skin you saw the livid bruise. Butler saw him slinking along the deck and called him. The mate went to him without a word.

"See here, Bananas," he said to him, fixing his spectacles on his slippery nose, for it was very hot. "I ain't going to fire you for this, but you know now that when I hit, I hit hard. Don't forget it and don't let me have any more funny business."

Then he held out his hand and gave the mate that good-humored, flashing smile of his which was his greatest charm. The mate took the outstretched hand and twitched his swollen lips into a devilish grin. The incident in the captain's mind was so completely finished that when the three of them sat at dinner he chaffed Bananas on his appearance. He was eating with difficulty and, his swollen face still more distorted by pain, he looked truly a repulsive object.

That evening, when he was sitting on the upper deck, smoking his pipe, a shiver passed through the captain.

"I don't know what I should be shiverin' for on a night like this," he grumbled. "Maybe I've gotten a dose of fever. I've been feelin' a bit queer all day."

When he went to bed he took some quinine, and next morning he felt better, but a little washed out, as though he were recovering from a debauch.

"I guess my liver's out of order," he said, and he took a pill.

He had not much appetite that day and towards evening he began to feel very unwell. He tried the next remedy he knew, which was to drink two or three hot whiskies, but that did not seem to help him much, and when in the morning he surveyed himself in the glass he thought he was not looking quite the thing.

"If I ain't right by the time we get back to Honolulu I'll just give Dr. Denby a call. He'll sure fix me up."

He could not eat. He felt a great lassitude in all his limbs. He slept soundly enough, but he awoke with no sense of refreshment; on the contrary he felt a peculiar exhaustion. And the energetic little man, who could not bear the thought of lying in bed, had to make an effort to force himself out of his bunk. After a few days he found it impossible to resist the languor that oppressed him, and he made up his mind not to get up.

"Bananas can look after the ship," he said. "He has before now."

He laughed a little to himself as he thought how often he had lain speechless in his bunk after a night with the boys. That was before he had his girl. He smiled at her and pressed her hand. She was puzzled and anxious. He saw that she was concerned about him and tried to reassure her. He had never had a day's illness in his life and in a week at the outside he would be as right as rain.

"I wish you'd fire Bananas," she said. "I've got a feeling that he's at the bottom of this."

"Damned good thing I didn't, or there'd be no one to sail the ship. I know a good sailor when I see one." His blue eyes, rather pale now, with the whites all yellow, twinkled. "You don't think he's trying to poison me, little girl?"

She did not answer, but she had one or two talks with the Chinese cook, and she took great care with the captain's food. But he ate little enough now, and it was only with the greatest difficulty that she persuaded him to drink a cup of soup two or three times a day. It was clear that he was very ill, he was losing weight quickly, and his chubby face was pale and drawn. He suffered no pain, but merely grew every day weaker and more languid. He was wasting away. The round trip on this occasion lasted about four weeks and by the time they came to Honolulu the captain was a little anxious about himself. He had not been out of his bed for more than a fortnight and really he felt too weak to get up and go to the doctor. He sent a message asking him to come on board. The doctor examined him, but could find nothing to account for his condition. His temperature was normal.

"See here, Captain," he said, "I'll be perfectly frank with you. I don't know what's the matter with you, and just seeing you like this don't give me a chance. You come into the hospital so that we can keep you under observation. There's nothing organically wrong with you, I know that, and my impression is that a few weeks in hospital ought to put you to rights."

"I ain't going to leave my ship."

Chinese owners were queer customers, he said; if he left his ship because he was sick, his owner might fire him, and he couldn't afford to lose his job. So long as he stayed where he was his contract safeguarded him, and he had a first-rate mate. Besides, he couldn't leave his girl. No man could want a better nurse; if anyone could pull him through she would. Every man had to die once and he only wished to be left in peace. He would not listen to the doctor's expostulations, and finally the doctor gave in.

"I'll write you a prescription," he said doubtfully, "and see if it does you any good. You'd better stay in bed for a while."

"There ain't much fear of my getting up, doc," answered the captain. "I feel as weak as a cat."

But he believed in the doctor's prescription as little as did the doctor himself, and when he was alone amused himself by lighting his cigar with it. He had to get amusement out of something, for his cigar tasted like nothing on earth, and he smoked only to persuade himself that he was not too ill to. That evening a couple of friends of his, masters of tramp steamers, hearing he was sick came to see him. They discussed his case over a bottle of whisky and a box of Philippine cigars. One of them remembered how a mate of his had been taken queer just like that and not a doctor in the United States had been able to cure him. He had seen in the paper an advertisement of a patent medicine, and thought there'd be no harm in trying it. That man was as strong as ever he'd been in his life after two bottles. But his illness had given Captain Butler a lucidity which was new and strange, and while they talked he seemed to read their minds. They thought he was dying. And when they left him he was afraid.

The girl saw his weakness. This was her opportunity. She had been urging him to let a native doctor see him, and he had stoutly refused; but now she entreated him. He listened with harassed eyes. He wavered. It was very funny that the American doctor could not tell what was the matter with him. But he did not want her to think that he was scared. If he let a damned nigger come along and look at him it was to comfort *her*. He told her to do what she liked.

The native doctor came the next night. The captain was lying alone, half awake, and the cabin was dimly lit by an oil lamp. The door was softly opened and the girl came in on tiptoe. She held the door open and someone slipped in silently behind her. The captain smiled at this mystery, but he was so weak now, the smile was no more than a glimmer in his eyes. The doctor was a little old man, very thin and very wrinkled, with a completely bald head, and the face of a monkey. He was bowed and gnarled like an old tree. He looked hardly human, but his eyes were very bright, and in the half darkness, they seemed to glow with a reddish light. He was dressed filthily in a pair of ragged dungarees, and the upper part of his body was naked. He sat down on his haunches and for ten minutes looked at the captain. Then he felt the palms of his hands and the soles of his feet. The girl watched him with frightened eyes. No word was spoken. Then he asked for something that the captain had worn. The girl gave him the old felt hat which the captain used constantly and taking it he sat down again on the floor, clasping it firmly with both hands; and rocking backwards and forwards slowly he muttered some gibberish in a very low tone.

At last he gave a little sigh and dropped the hat. He took an old pipe out of his trouser pocket and lit it. The girl went over to him and sat by his side. He whispered something to her, and she started violently. For a few minutes they talked in hurried undertones, and then they stood up. She gave him money and opened the door for him. He slid out as silently as he had come in. Then she went over to the captain and leaned over him so that she could speak in his ear.

"It's an enemy praying you to death."

"Don't talk fool stuff, girlie," he said impatiently.

"It's truth. It's God's truth. That's why the American doctor couldn't do anything. Our people can do that. I've seen it done. I thought you were safe because you were a white man."

"I haven't an enemy."

"Bananas."

"What's he want to pray me to death for?"

"You ought to have fired him before he had a chance."

"I guess if I ain't got nothing more the matter with me than Bananas' hoodoo I shall be sitting up and taking nourishment in a very few days."

She was silent for a while and she looked at him intently.

"Don't you know you're dying?" she said to him at last.

That was what the two skippers had thought, but they hadn't said it. A shiver passed across the captain's wan face.

"The doctor says there ain't nothing really the matter with

me. I've only to lie quiet for a bit and I shall be all right."

She put her lips to his ear as if she were afraid that the air itself might hear.

"You're dying, dying, dying. You'll pass out with the old moon."

"That's something to know."

"You'll pass out with the old moon unless Bananas dies before."

He was not a timid man and he had recovered already from the shock her words, and still more her vehement, silent manner, had given him. Once more a smile flickered in his eyes.

"I guess I'll take my chance, girlie."

"There's twelve days before the new moon."

There was something in her tone that gave him an idea.

"See here, my girl, this is all bunk. I don't believe a word of it. But I don't want you to try any of your monkey tricks with Bananas. He ain't a beauty, but he's a first-rate mate."

He would have said a good deal more, but he was tired out. He suddenly felt very weak and faint. It was always at that hour that he felt worse. He closed his eyes. The girl watched him for a minute and then slipped out of the cabin. The moon, nearly full, made a silver pathway over the dark sea. It shone from an unclouded sky. She looked at it with terror, for she knew that with its death the man she loved would die. His life was in her hands. She could save him, she alone could save him, but the enemy was cunning, and she must be cunning too. She felt that someone was looking at her, and without turning, by the sudden fear that seized her, knew that from the shadow the burning eyes of the mate were fixed upon her. She did not know what he could do; if he could read her thoughts she was defeated already, and with a desperate effort she emptied her mind of all content. His death alone could save her lover, and she could bring his death about. She knew that if he could be brought to look into a calabash in which was water so that a reflection of him was made, and the reflection were broken by hurtling the water, he would die as though he had been struck by lightning; for the reflection was his soul. But none knew better than he the danger, and he could be made to look only by a guile which had lulled his least suspicion. He must never think that he had an enemy who was on the watch to cause his destruction. She knew what she had to do. But the time was short, the time was terribly short. Presently she realized that the mate had gone. She breathed more freely.

Two days later they sailed, and there were ten now before the new moon. Captain Butler was terrible to see. He was nothing but skin and bone, and he could not move without help. He could hardly speak. But she dared do nothing yet. She knew that she must be patient. The mate was cunning, cunning. They went to one of the smaller islands of the group and discharged cargo, and now there were only seven days more. The moment had come to start. She brought some things out of the cabin she shared with the captain and made them into a bundle. She put the bundle in the deck cabin where she and Bananas ate their meals, and at dinner time, when she went in, he turned quickly and she saw that he had been looking at it. Neither of them spoke, but she knew what he suspected. She was making her preparations to leave the ship. He looked at her mockingly. Gradually, as though to prevent the captain from knowing what she was about, she brought everything she owned into the cabin, and some of the captain's clothes, and made them all into bundles. At last Bananas could keep silence no longer. He pointed to a suit of ducks.

"What are you going to do with that?" he asked.

She shrugged her shoulders.

"I'm going back to my island."

He gave a laugh that distorted his grim face. The captain was dying and she meant to get away with all she could lay hands on.

"What'll you do if I say you can't take those things? They're the captain's."

"They're no use to you," she said.

There was a calabash hanging on the wall. It was the very calabash I had seen when I came into the cabin and which we had talked about. She took it down. It was all dusty, so she poured water into it from the water bottle, and rinsed it with her fingers.

"What are you doing with that?"

"I can sell it for fifty dollars," she said.

"If you want to take it you'll have to pay me."

"What d'you want?"

"You know what I want."

She allowed a fleeting smile to play on her lips. She flashed a quick look at him and quickly turned away. He gave a gasp of desire. She raised her shoulders in a little shrug. With a savage bound he sprang upon her and seized her in his arms. Then she laughed. She put her arms, her soft, round arms, around his neck, and surrendered herself to him voluptuously.

When the morning came she roused him out of a deep sleep. The early rays of sun slanted into the cabin. He pressed her to his heart. Then he told her that the captain could not last more than a day or two, and the owner wouldn't so easily find another white man to command the ship. If Bananas offered to take less money he would get the job and the girl could stay with him. He looked at her with lovesick eyes. She nestled up against him. She kissed his lips, in the foreign way, in the way the captain had taught her to kiss. And she promised to stay. Bananas was drunk with happiness.

It was now or never.

She got up and went to the table to arrange her hair. There was no mirror and she looked into the calabash, seeking for her reflection. She tidied her beautiful hair. Then she beckoned to Bananas to come to her. She pointed to the calabash.

"There's something in the bottom of it," she said.

Instinctively, without suspecting anything, Bananas looked full into the water. His face was reflected in it. In a flash she beat upon it violently, with both her hands, so that they pounded on the bottom and the water splashed up. The reflection was broken in pieces. Bananas started back with a sudden hoarse cry and he looked at the girl. She was standing there with a look of triumphant hatred on her face. A horror came into his eyes. His heavy features were twisted in agony, and with a thud, as though he had taken a violent poison, he crumpled up on to the ground. A great shudder passed through his body and he was still. She leaned over him callously. She put her hand on his heart and then she pulled down his lower eyelid. He was quite dead.

She went into the cabin in which lay Captain Butler. There was a faint color in his cheeks and he looked at her in a startled way.

"What's happened?" he whispered.

They were the first words he had spoken for forty-eight hours.

"Nothing happened," she said.

"I feel all funny."

Then his eyes closed and he fell asleep. He slept for a day and a night, and when he awoke he asked for food. In a fortnight he was well.

It was past midnight when Winter and I rowed back to shore and we had drunk innumerable whiskies and sodas.

"What do you think of it all?" asked Winter.

"What a question! If you mean, have I any explanation to suggest, I haven't."

"The captain believes every word of it."

"That's obvious; but you know that's not the part that interests me most, whether it's true or not, and what it all means; the part that interests me is that such things should happen to such people. I wonder what there is in that commonplace little man to arouse such a passion in that lovely creature. As I watched her, asleep there, while he was telling the story I had some fantastic idea about the power of love being able to work miracles."

"But that's not the girl," said Winter.

"What on earth do you mean?"

"Didn't you notice the cook?"

"Of course I did. He's the ugliest man I ever saw."

"That's why Butler took him. The girl ran away with the Chinese cook last year. This is a new one. He's only had her there about two months."

"Well, I'm hanged."

"He thinks this cook is safe. But I wouldn't be too sure in his place. There's something about a Chink, when he lays himself out to please a woman she can't resist him."

From *Trembling of a Leaf,* by W. Somerset Maugham (New York, Doubleday & Company, Inc., 1921).

GWENFREAD ALLEN

# BOMBS FALL ON HAWAII:
# DEC. 7, 1941

An attack on the Hawaiian Islands on December 7, 1941, plunged
America into World War II, and the country was united with
the cry, "Remember Pearl Harbor!".
 Although lacking the full-length scope of Walter Lord's excellent *Day of Infamy,* Gwenfread Allen's brief and authentic
account gives not only the outlines but also a number of striking
sidelights on the events of that exciting day. For her carefully
prepared volume on the impact of World War II on Hawaii,
Miss Allen, a skilled Honolulu journalist, drew upon the docu-
ments in the Hawaii War Records Depository, collected during
the four-year conflict.

AT 3:42 A.M. ON DECEMBER 7, 1941, THE MINESWEEPER *Condor*
sighted a submarine periscope off the entrance to Pearl Harbor.
Since this was an area where no American submarine traveled
submerged, the *Condor* immediately notified the destroyer
*Ward.* Inshore waters were searched for an hour and a half
but without success.

At 6:30 the destroyer answered a similar alert from the
target repair ship *Antares* and this time located the submarine,
apparently trailing the *Antares* into Honolulu Harbor. The
*Ward* fired on the intruder — the first American shots of World
War II — and scored a hit. After the crippled submarine went
down, a Navy patrol plane joined the destroyer in a depth-
charge attack.

The *Ward* reported the action to 14th Naval District headquarters at 6:51 and two minutes later followed with a second message. The information made its way through channels, reaching Rear Admiral Husband E. Kimmel, Commander-in-Chief of the Pacific Fleet, about 7:30. Since unverified submarine contacts were being reported several times a week — none, however, so close to American shores as this — the admiral asked for amplification of the message.

Meanwhile, two Army privates were completing their three-hour training period at an isolated radar station in the hills between Waialua and Kahuku, one of six new mobile radar units which troops in Hawaii were learning to operate. While waiting for an Army truck to pick them up, the pair continued practice. Suddenly the radar screen was covered with markings unlike any they had ever seen before. They checked the set, found that it was functioning properly, and concluded that a large number of planes was approaching Oahu from three degrees east of north at a distance of 132 miles. Since the lookouts were officially off duty after 7:00, they debated whether or not to follow the usual routine of notifying the information center. At 7:20 they decided to phone, but by that time everyone had left the center except the telephone operator and a lieutenant who was serving his second morning of observation. He assumed that the planes were the B-17s which he knew were flying in from the mainland and dismissed the matter.

But no such swarm of American planes was in the air as had filled the radar scope that morning of December 7, 1941. As early as 6:30 A.M., two Japanese reconnaissance planes were over Oahu. They were followed by 360 planes which Japanese carriers two hundred miles to the north had launched in three waves between 6:00 and 7:15 A.M. Most of the planes approached the Pearl Harbor area directly from the sea. A few crossed the Koolau Range, unrecognized above the fleecy clouds, after accomplishing their missions on windward Oahu.

At about 7:57 a score of fighters swooped down from the clouds to within twenty feet of the ground at the Marine Corps Air Station at Ewa, riddling the forty-nine planes closely lined up on the field. Thirty-three aircraft went up in smoke, and the remaining sixteen were too badly damaged to fly. The marines, in desperation, emptied their pistols at the departing Japanese.

At one minute before 8:00, as the preparatory signal for colors was being hoisted over the ninety-four vessels in Pearl Harbor, the real battle began. Japanese dive bombers droned down on Ford Island, in the center of Pearl Harbor, destroying thirty-three of the seventy planes on the field.

Within seconds, torpedo planes and dive bombers swung in from all sides to pummel the heavy vessels in "battleship row" adjacent to Ford Island. Almost simultaneously, Hickam Field, next to Pearl Harbor, and Kaneohe Naval Air Station, on the windward side, were subjected to the Japanese onslaught. Seven minutes later enemy aircraft pounded Wheeler Field, which adjoins Schofield Barracks in central Oahu.

The battleships in the harbor underwent a sustained assault. Within thirty minutes torpedo planes made four separate attacks and dive bombers eight. A lull from 8:25 to 8:40 was followed by a half-hour of dive bombing and horizontal bombing attacks which continued until 9:45.

In the first half-hour, the major damage had been done. All seven battleships had been hit at least once. The *West Virginia* was sinking, the *California* was down by the stern, the *Arizona* was a flaming ruin. During the next half-hour attack, the *Tennessee* received slight additional damage, the *Pennsylvania* took another hit, the *Nevada,* in a gallant effort to sortie, was beached to prevent her sinking in the channel, and the *Oklahoma* capsized with four torpedoes in her hull. As the attacks continued, damage increased. In all, six ships were sunk, twelve were severely damaged, and others suffered minor blows. Dead, wounded, or trapped in the ships were 2,500 men.

Nearby Hickam Field sustained three ten-minute attacks, at approximately 7:55, 8:25, and 9:00. Bombs fell on some of the huge barracks, killing and wounding several hundred men. Bombs landed on the guardhouse, putting the air raid siren out of order, and on the ordnance building, delaying access to ammunition. Bombs also hit machine shops, hangars, the theater, the parade ground, and the post exchange. Bombs even pockmarked the baseball diamond, which was in an area where the outdated maps carried by the Japanese showed gasoline storage. Planes, lined up with only ten feet between wingtips, became a total loss. Luckily, the longest runways in the islands were not damaged.

Kaneohe NAS was first strafed, then strafed again and bombed twenty-five minutes later. The station had thirty-six planes prior to the attack, three of which were in the air on patrol. Of the remainder, twenty-seven were destroyed and the other six damaged. One hangar burned down to its steel skeleton; another crumpled under a direct hit.

At Wheeler Field, twenty-five enemy planes dive-bombed and machine-gunned the hangar lines for a quarter hour, and seven fighters later strafed planes which were being taxied onto the field preparatory to taking off. Forty-two combat planes were totally destroyed and others damaged.

Little Bellows Field, on the windward side near Waimanalo, was unmolested until 8:30, when a lone Japanese fighter opened fire at the tent area. Later, nine fighters machine-gunned the planes on the field, but totally destroyed only three. Damage here was lightest of any installation except the newly established emergency field at Haleiwa, which was not touched, evidently because the Japanese did not know it existed.

At none of the Army fields were planes loaded with bombs or ammunition. Bellows did not get a plane into the air until 8:50; Hickam, not until afternoon. However, five planes took off from unbombed Haleiwa by 8:15 and engaged the enemy in furious dogfights. Six planes took off from Wheeler at 8:30, and eight more within the next forty-five minutes. Army planes made a total of eighty-one take-offs during the day.

The eleven B-17s which arrived from the mainland between 8:00 and 9:00 unwittingly flew into the battle, without ammunition. One landed at Wheeler Field, one at Bellows, two at Haleiwa, one on a golf course at Kahuku, and the others dodged bombs and bullets to land at Hickam as scheduled. One was destroyed in landing and three others were badly damaged.

Twenty-five Navy planes were in the air when the attack

started. Seven were patrol flying boats which had taken off earlier in the morning from Kaneohe and Ford Island, and eighteen were scout bombers which had been launched from the *Enterprise* two hundred miles west of Pearl Harbor. Like the B-17s, they flew into the fight unawares, but they were armed and able to take part in the battle. About half landed on Oahu, one sped away to Kauai, and the others were lost. No Navy planes were able to take off after the attack started.

Within seven to ten minutes after the first bombs fell, all anti-aircraft batteries on ships in Pearl Harbor were in action, even those on ships which had been hit. An Army anti-aircraft detachment at Sand Island shot down two planes about 8:15. Other Army anti-aircraft units needed time to move into position and obtain ammunition, and only three were ready to fire during the attack.

The combined defense of anti-aircraft gunners and American pilots caused Japanese planes to crash at several points on Oahu and at sea. Twenty-nine Japanese planes failed to reach their carriers, a number comparable to the average then being shot down in European raids even when defenses were alerted.

As soon as the Japanese planes accomplished their designated missions, most of them streaked back to their carriers and were taken aboard between 10:30 A.M. and 1:30 P.M. Some official reports say that all enemy planes had retired by 9:45, and certainly most of the action was over by that time. The few planes reportedly seen later in the morning may have been stragglers which failed to return to their carriers.

Five Japanese midget submarines, launched from mother submarines, participated in the attack. One was rammed and sunk inside Pearl Harbor during the action, three were lost at sea, and one was grounded off Bellows Field. The lone survivor of the latter swam ashore and became the only prisoner of war of the day. For a time it was believed that papers in the submarine indicated that it might have been in Pearl Harbor before the attack, but later investigations discredited that interpretation.

The December 7 disaster took the lives of 2,008 Navy men, 109 Marines, and 218 Army men. The injured included 710 sailors, 69 Marines, and 364 soldiers, bringing the casualty total to 3,478. Japan lost less than one hundred men. The United States lost outright 188 planes; Japan lost 29. The United States suffered severe damage to eighteen ships and minor damage to others; Japan lost one full-size submarine and five midget submarines.

While bombs were still falling, rescuers fought through fire and flooded compartments to reach the dead and wounded; sailors blown off their own vessels reported for duty on nearby ships; airmen struggled to reach their planes despite heavy strafing; repairmen toiled in heat, darkness, filth, and danger; telephone operators stuck to their posts to hasten urgent calls.

Honolulu police received the first report of damage in the city at 8:05 A.M. when a resident of Damon Tract, near Hickam Field, telephoned that his kitchen had been hit. After 8:30, reports came in fast succession: from Pacific Heights, Advertiser Square, Fort and School Streets, the Spencer Street home of the Catholic bishop. At 8:45, Lewers and Cooke, a large building-supply house in the heart of downtown Honolulu, suffered several thousand dollars damage from flooding when an anti-aircraft shell went through the roof, exploded on the third floor, and broke the fire-prevention sprinkler system. In upper Nuuanu Valley, a woman was killed; at Kamehameha Schools on Kapalama Heights, a wall was knocked down; at a *saimin* stand at the corner of Nuuanu and Kukui Streets, several widely known amateur boxers were killed and others injured. Four Pearl Harbor workers answering a radio summons to report on the job were killed when their automobile was hit on Judd Street.

At 9:30 A.M., a projectile exploded near the driveway of the governor's residence, at Beretania, near Richards Street, sending splinters whistling through the shrubbery and across the street to kill a pedestrian. Later, after Governor Joseph B. Poindexter had gone to his office at Iolani Palace in downtown Honolulu, a shell burst in the corner of the grounds there.

The Honolulu fire department answered thirty-nine calls

during the day. Three companies rushed to Hickam Field, where all military fire-fighting apparatus had been put out of action. Three Honolulu firemen were killed and seven injured while fighting disastrous blazes in the airfield's barracks and ordnance buildings. Dispatch of these men to Hickam handicapped the department in responding to calls which began to pour in from Honolulans. Fire damage to civilian property, resulting mostly from three fires in the McCully district of Honolulu, totaled in a few hours more than half the loss for the entire year. The three major fires caused $158,000 damage to a block of stores and dwellings occupied by thirty-one families at King and McCully Streets, $40,000 to several classrooms and the library of Lunalilo School on Pumehana Street, and several thousand dollars damage to three small houses at Hauoli and Algaroba Streets. First-aid personnel were forced out of the school building and had to treat eighteen casualties under coconut trees.

It was generally believed at the time that the three McCully fires were caused by incendiary bombs; many persons even reported seeing such bombs fall. But Honolulu fire department officials reached the conclusion that no incendiaries were used in the raid. Evidence indicated that a projectile started the first blaze, sparks from which probably caused the other two. This contention is strengthened by the fact that the Lunalilo roof did not burst into flame until half an hour after the McCully Street fire was reported.

Though most of the other fires in Honolulu on December 7 were comparatively minor, a few were spectacular. Particularly so was a blaze in the industrial district of Iwilei, where a large gas tank flared for two and a half hours in the morning and then broke out in flames again at night.

The Waipahu and Ewa sugar plantations, next to Pearl Harbor, and the two of Wahiawa, adjoining Schofield Barracks, saw even more action than did Honolulu.

At Waipahu, machine-gun bullets, shrapnel, and shells started two cane fires, riddled the sugar mill, hit the plantation hospital in four places, went through the roof of the company store, exploding in an electric-supply warehouse, and narrowly missed many houses. In nearly all of the fields of tall cane, many of which concealed terrified women and children, shells buried themselves — dozens of them in some concentrated areas — blasting holes in the ground the size of barrels and flattening cane for several square yards.

At Ewa, after bombing the nearby Marine airfield, enemy planes machine-gunned the plantation's main street, the mill and power plant and some thirty houses, and started two cane fires.

At Wahiawa, low-flying planes strafed stores and cars, wounding several people. Patients overflowed from Dr. Merton H. Mack's small private hospital into Red Cross headquarters in the rear of the Wahiawa fire station. An enemy plane crash in a pineapple field near the town did little damage, but another started a fire which destroyed five small houses before the blaze could be brought under control by a handful of firemen and a Boy Scout bucket brigade. Bodies of the four crewmen of the downed aircraft were buried in the Wahiawa cemetery.

At Aiea, betwen Honolulu and Pearl Harbor, the plantation's fire department fought a house fire and two cane fires, one of which was caused by the crash of an enemy plane.

Waialua and the north shore were quiet, although at about 10:00 A.M. soldiers from the 21st Infantry searched houses at Mokuleia for reported parachutists. Windward Oahu and the Waianae area suffered no civilian damage, despite reports of bombing and machine-gunning.

Of Oahu's civilian population, at least fifty-seven are known to have been killed, nearly fifty required hospitalization, and about 230 were less seriously injured. An undetermined number later died of injuries, and a few casualties were not listed in available records. Private property valued at $500,000 was destroyed.

Most of the civilian casualties occurred in Honolulu, but at Waipahu two persons were killed and thiry-seven injured; at Ewa seven civilians were injured; at Wahiawa three were killed and nine injured. Waialua plantation hospital received two patients, both of whom had been shot by bullets from enemy planes near Schofield Barracks.

Islanders believed at first that all damage was caused by Japanese bombs, but it has been definitely established that American anti-aircraft action caused almost all the injuries and damage in civilian areas, especially in Honolulu itself. Most civilian casualties in the city resulted from flying splinters from anti-aircraft projectiles, fragments of pavement or other objects thrown by explosions, or merely from concussion. . . .

Realization of the attack came slowly to islanders distant from the scenes of terror and destruction. Remote explosions were muffled. The drone of planes was not unusual. The dark smoke from Pearl Harbor mingled with low-lying clouds.

At seventeen seconds past 8:04 A.M., KGMB interrupted a concert program to recall all Army, Navy, and Marine Corps personnel to duty. This order was repeated at 8:15 and 8:30, and police and firemen were called at 8:32.

At 8:40 came the first reference to actual enemy attack: "A sporadic air attack has been made on Oahu. . . . Enemy airplanes have been shot down. . . . The rising sun has been sighted on the wingtips!"

The word "sporadic" misled many listeners, who confused it with the common Army term "simulated." Simulated attacks were no new thing to maneuver-conscious Oahu residents, and they assumed this was just another Army and Navy exercise. Some telephoned radio stations to ask for details, to the harassment of announcers who were trying to convince listeners of the peril of the morning's events.

"This is no maneuver!" one announcer shouted into the microphone. "This is the real McCoy!"

Announcements became more urgent. By noon, each Honolulu station had broadcast a dozen times the order recalling all service personnel; they summoned doctors, nurses, and volunteer aides, civilian workers of the Army and Navy, and employees of various firms. Trucks and motorcycles were called to first-aid stations. Every few minutes, radios barked orders and warnings. . . .

Governor Poindexter spoke over KGU proclaiming a state of emergency. Then, at 11:41 A.M., the Army ordered the Honolulu commercial broadcasting stations off the air so that their beams could not be used to guide enemy planes.

The ominous silence which resulted, even more nerve-shattering than the announcements, led nearly everyone on Oahu to twist radio dials in search of more information. They heard the police radio ordering patrolmen to investigate a steady stream of alarming reports. Thereafter, for days, many radio sets on Oahu were never turned off. Until commercial stations resumed their regular schedules a week later, residents kept their sets tuned to the police radio, except when it advised them to turn to the commercial stations for special announcements.

KGU and KGMB returned to the air nine times that fateful Sunday for periods varying from forty-five seconds to five minutes. A broadcast of major significance was the announcement at 4:25 P.M. that the islands had been placed under martial law and that the office of Military Governor of Hawaii had been assumed by Major General Walter C. Short, Commanding General of the Hawaiian Department. General Short's statement was repeated twice in English and, for the benefit of aliens, once in Japanese. Later, blackout orders were announced over the air: "Please turn out your lights. . . . Hawaii is observing a complete blackout. Turn out your lights. This means the whole Territory. Turn out your lights and do not turn them on for any purpose whatsoever. Turn off your lights and keep them off."

The final December 7 broadcast, at 8:52 P.M., ordered the employees of all retail firms doing business with the Army Engineers to report for duty immediately.

Islanders sat in their homes in the eerie dark, straining their ears for the expected return of enemy planes. At 7:14 P.M., they heard the police radio broadcast: "Pearl Harbor is being bombed again." They heard firing and saw tracer bullets, falling planes, and the resultant fires. Not until long afterward did they learn of the tragic error which had occurred when tense anti-aircraft gunners at Pearl Harbor were alerted by the roar of planes overhead. Although Pearl Harbor had been informed that some *Enterprise* planes which had been searching for Japanese carriers would land at Ford Island, the arrivals were not recognized on their approach. As the commanding officer of Ford Island testified later, "Somebody let fly and I never saw so many bullets in the air in my life and never expect to. . . . All tracer bullets at night." Four of the six planes coming in for a landing were shot down. One fell on Palm Lodge, a residential hotel on the Pearl Harbor peninsula, killing the pilot and starting a fire which destroyed the building.

Few islanders went to bed that night. Some, fully clothed, dozed fitfully. Outdoors there was silence, broken only occasionally by the rumble of a vehicle on official business, the shot of a gun in the hands of a nervous sentry, the "Halt! Who goes there?" which islanders were to hear often in the ensuing months.

Shortly before midnight, the moon began to rise, and a vivid lunar rainbow, the old Hawaiian omen of victory, arched over the dark city.

From *Hawaii's War Years* by Gwenfread Allen (Honolulu, University of Hawaii Press, 1950).

# JAMES JONES

# THE WAY IT IS

One of the most widely read novels of our time is James Jones' *From Here to Eternity,* set in Hawaii in the year of Pearl Harbor, when the author was an enlisted soldier in the regular army, stationed at Schofield Barracks. Few of his readers, however, are aware of the short stories he published in magazines before the novel made him famous. "The Way It Is," the second to appear, is perhaps the best of these. Commenting on it in a letter to one of the present editors, James Jones says: "I remember it as one of a group of five, all done during a break in the writing of *Eternity.* All five were eventually published. But what strikes me most about them was that in the writing of these stories, during a time when I was very perturbed and worried as to just where to go in the writing of *Eternity,* I at one and the same time — in these five stories — discovered my own way of writing, and realized that the technique of explicit writing, as propounded by Hemingway, would not be sufficient to satisfy my need to express myself. I couldn't say enough within the restrictions of it. *The Way It Is* was the story which led me instinctively to this belief."

Readers of Jones' short novel *The Pistol* (1959) will recognize the setting as identical with that of "The Way It Is."

I SAW THE CAR COMING DOWN THE GRADE AND GOT UP FROM THE culvert. I had to push hard with my legs to keep the wind from sitting me back down. I stepped out into the road to stop him, turning my back to the wind, still holding the mess kit I had been scouring. Some of the slop of sand and grease dripped out of it onto my leg.

Then I saw Mazzioli was on the running board and had his pistol out and aimed at the driver's head. I tossed the mess kit, still full, over against the culvert and got my own pistol out.

I couldn't see the driver. It was hard to see the car in the red air of the dusk against the black of the cliff and with the cold wind pouring against my eyes. It was a foreign make, a runabout with strange lines and the steering wheel on the right-hand side. When it stopped Mazzioli jumped off the running board and motioned with his pistol.

"All right," he said in that thick voice. "Get out of there, you."

I knew that man when he climbed out. He used the road every day. He could have passed for a typical Prussian with his scraped jowls and cropped bullethead. He wore a fine tweed jacket and plus-fours, and his stockings were of ribbed wool and very fine. I looked down at my legging and kicked off the gob of sand and grease. It didn't help much. I hadn't even had my field jacket off for three weeks, since the bombing.

"What's up, Greek?" I said, peering through the deepening dusk. I had to yell to make it heard above the wind.

"I hopped a ride down the hill with this guy," he said woodenly. "All the way down he was asting me questions about the position. How many men? How many guns? Was there a demolition? What was the road-guard for? I mean to find out what's the story." He looked offended.

I walked over to him so I could hear above the wind. He was a little Wop but very meaty. His father ran a grocery store in Brooklyn.

"What do you figure on doing?" I asked. I thought I had seen the Junker before someplace, and I tried hard to make my mind work.

Mazzioli waved his pistol at the standing man. "Git over there, you, and put your back to the cliff," he said ominously. The beefy Junker walked to it slowly, his steps jerky from rage, his arms dangling impotently. He stood against the black, porous cliff and Mazzioli followed him. "Where's the men?" Mazzioli shouted to me above the wind. "I want a man to stand guard over this guy. You git a man and have him . . ."

"There's nobody here but me," I called back. "I let them go up to the top of the hill. Two of them didn't get any chow tonight. They went up to number one hole to listen to the guitar a while." I walked over to him.

I could see him stiffen. "Goddam you. You know there's always supposed to be three men and one noncom here all the time. That's the orders. You're supposed to be second in command. How do you expect to handle these men when you don't follow the orders?"

I stared at him, feeling my jaws tighten. "All right," I shrugged. "I let them go. So what?"

"I'm turning this in to Lieutenant Allison. The orders are orders. If you want to be on this road-guard to do your duty, okay. If you want to be on this road-guard to stop Coca-Cola trucks you can go back upstairs to the position. This road-guard is vital, and as long as I'm in charge of it everybody does like the orders says."

I didn't say anything.

"You're a rotten soldier, Slade," Mazzioli said. "Now look what's happened. I wanted you to help me search this guy's car. Now there's nobody here to guard this guy."

"Okay," I said. "So I'm a rotten soldier. My trouble is I got too many brains." He was making me mad and that always got him. Ever since I went six months to the University downtown in Honolulu.

"Don't start giving me that stuff," he snarled.

The Junker against the cliff stepped forward. "See here," he said. "I demand you stop this bickering and release me. You're being an idiot. I am . . ."

"Shut up, you," Mazzioli snarled. "Shut up! I warned you, now shut up!" He stepped to meet him and jabbed the muzzle of his pistol into the Junker's big belly. The man recoiled and stood back against the cliff, his beefy face choleric.

I stood with my hands in the pockets of my field jacket, my shoulders hunched down against the rawness of the wind and watched the scene. I had put my pistol away.

"All right," Mazzioli said to me. "The question is what're we gonna do now? If there's nobody here but you and me?"

"You're in command," I said.

"I know it. Keep quiet. I'm thinking."

"Well," I said. "You could have the guy drive you up the hill to the lieutenant. You could keep him covered till you turned him over to the lieutenant. Then you would be absolved," I said. Big words always got him.

"No," he said dubiously. "He might try something."

"Or," I said, "you could search the car and have me watch the guy."

"Yeh," he admitted. "I could do that . . . Yet . . . No, I don't want to do that. We may need more men."

It was dark now, as black as the cliff face, and I grinned. "Okay," I said, telling him what I had in my mind all along, "then I could call Alcorn down from up on the cliff and he could watch the guy."

"Yes. That's it. Why didn't I think of that before?"

"I don't know. Maybe you're tired."

"You call Alcorn down," he commanded me.

I walked toward the cliff wall that reared its set black face up and up in the darkness several hundred feet. The wind beat on me with both fists in the blackness.

"Wait a minute," Mazzioli called. "Maybe we shouldn't call Alcorn down. There's supposed to be a man up there all the time."

"Look," I said. "I'll tell you what I think. Before you go ahead, you better get the lieutenant's permission to do anything with this guy. You better find out who this guy is."

"I'm in charge of this road-guard," he yelled into the wind, "and I can handle it. Without running to no lieutenant. And I don't want back-talk. When I give you an order, you do it. Call Alcorn down here like I said."

"Okay," I said. I leaned on the culvert and called loudly, my face turned up to the cliff. There was no answer. I flashed my light covered with blue paper. Still no answer.

For a second I couldn't help wondering if something had got him. The Japanese invasion of Hawaii had been expected every day since Pearl was bombed. It was expected here at Kaneohe Bay on the windward side where the reef was low and there was good beach. Nobody doubted they would get ashore.

"What's the matter?" asked Mazzioli sharply from the darkness. "Is Alcorn asleep?"

"No," I said. "It's the wind; it carries off the sound. The light will get him." I picked up a handful of pebbles and threw them up the cliff with all my strength, trying to make no noise the Greek would hear.

Sixty feet up was a natural niche and the BAR man was stationed there twenty-four hours a day. It was a hidden spot that covered the road and the road-guard. In case of surprise it would prove invaluable. That was Lieutenant Allison's own idea. The road-guard was Hawaiian Department's idea.

Alcorn had stayed up there alone for the first four days after the bombing. In the four days he had one meal before somebody remembered him. Now he and the other man pulled twelve hours apiece.

The road-guard was part of the whole defense plan. It was figured out in November when the beach positions were constructed. The defense was to mine the Pali Road and Kamehameha Highway where it ran up over this cliff at Makapuu Point. It was planned to blow both roads and bottle them up in Kaneohe Valley and force them north, away from Honolulu. They were great demolitions and it was all top secret. Of course, in December they found maps of the whole thing in the captured planes. Still, it was very vital and very top secret.

A rock the size of my fist thumped into the sand at my feet. I grinned. "You missed me," I called up the cliff. "Come down from there, you lazy bastard." I barely caught a faraway, wind-tossed phrase that sounded like "truck, too." Then silence, and the wind.

The machine-gun apertures in the pillboxes up the hill all

faced out to sea. Whoever planned the position had forgot about the road, and all that faced the road was the tunnels into the pillboxes. To cover the road the MG's would have to be carried up into the open, and it was a shame because there was a perfect enfilade where the road curved up the cliff. But they couldn't rebuild the pillboxes we had cut into solid rock, so instead they created the road-guard.

The road-guard was to be five men and a BAR from up above. That was us. We were to protect the demolition when the Jap landed. It was not expected to keep him from getting ashore. We were to hold him off, with our BAR, till the demolition could be blown behind us. After that we were on our own. It was excellent strategy, for a makeshift, with the invasion expected truly every day. And the road-guard was vital, it was the key.

Every man at Makapuu volunteered for the road-guard. The five of us were lucky to get it. The job was to stop and search all vehicles for anything that might be used to blow the demolition. The Coca-Cola trucks and banana trucks and grocery trucks and fruit trucks used this road every day to go to market. We stopped them all, especially the Coca-Cola trucks.

In a couple of minutes I heard a scrambling and scraping and a bouncing fall of pebbles and Alcorn came slouching along the sand at the road edge, blowing on his hands.

"The Greek wants you, Fatso," I said.

He laughed, low and rich and sloppy. "I think I'm deef from this wind, by god," he said and scratched inside his field jacket "What's he want now?"

"Come over here," Mazzioli ordered. We walked over through the blackness and the wind and I felt I was swimming under water against a strong current. The Greek swung his blue light from the Junker onto us. Alcorn's clothes hung from him like rags and on the back of his head was a fatigue hat with the brim turned up that defied the wind. He must have sewed an elastic band on it. Beside him I looked like I was all bucked up for a short-timer parade.

"Where's your helmet?" Mazzioli said. "You're supposed to wear your helmet at all times. That's the orders."

"Aw now, sarge," Alcorn whined. "You know the steel band of them things gives a man a headache. I cain't wear one."

I grinned and gave the brim of my own inverted soup-plate helmet a tug. Alcorn was a character.

"When are you men going to learn to obey orders?" the Greek said. "An Army runs by discipline. If you men don't start acting like soldiers, I'll turn you in."

"Off with his head," I said.

"What did you say?"

"I said, coffee and bed. That's what we need. There's not a man on this position who's had three good hours sleep since this bloody war started. Putting up barbed wire all day and pulling guard all night. And then putting up the same wire next day because the tide washed it out."

Alcorn snickered and Mazzioli said nothing. The Greek had had charge of a wire detail that worked one whole night to put up three hundred yards of double apron wire on the sand beach below the road. In the morning it was gone. Not a single picket left.

"Alcorn," Mazzioli ordered, "get a rifle and keep a bayonet against this guy's belly till I tell you not to."

"I don't know where the rifles are down here," Alcorn said.

"I'll get it," I said.

I walked to the culvert and climbed down around it. The wall made a protection from the wind and I felt I had dropped into a world without breath. The absence of the wind made me dizzy and I leaned my face against the concrete. I felt the way you feel when you look out the window at a blowing rainstorm. All our blankets and stuff were down here. Against the wall of the culvert lay four rifles with bayonets on them, wrapped in a shelter-half. I pulled one out and made myself climb up into the wind again.

Alcorn took the rifle and kept the bayonet against the Junker's paunch. Every time the Junker moved or tried to speak

Alcorn jabbed him playfully in the belly. The Junker was getting madder and madder, but Alcorn was having a fine time.

I knew the lewd nakedness of that scraped face someplace before. I went over in my mind all the people I had seen at the University.

The Greek was doing a bang-up job of searching the car, he even looked under the hood. I sat on the culvert and got my mess kit and put a handful of fresh sand in it from beside the road and rubbed it around and around. The dishwater that got out to us from the CP at Hanauma Bay gave us all the dysentery until we started using the sand.

I tried to think where I'd seen him. It wasn't the face of a teacher, it had too much power. I dumped the greasy mess from the mess kit and poured in a little water from my canteen. I sloshed it around to rinse the sand out, listening vacantly to the Greek cursing and fidgeting with the car.

Just three days ago a two-man sub ran aground off Kaneohe and the second officer swam ashore, preferring capture. It was expected the sub was scouting the invasion that was coming truly any day.

They said he was the first prisoner of the war. I got to see him when they brought him in. He was a husky little guy and grinning humbly. His name was Kazuo Sakamaki. I knew a girl at the University named Harue Tanaka. I almost married her.

It seemed like the wind had blown my mind empty of all past. It had sucked out everything but Makapuu and the black rocks and blue lights and the sand-choked grass. The University with its clear, airy look from the street, its crisp greenness all hidden away in a wind-free little valley at the foot of rocky wooded Tantalus, it was from another life, a life protected from the wind, a life where there were white clouds in the sun but no wind, just gently moving air.

I wiped the mess kit with the GI face towel I kept in it and clamped it together and stuck it back in my pack that lay by the culvert, wanting to go down behind the culvert and light a cigarette.

Maybe the Junker was one of the big boys on the University board. The big boys always sent their kids to Harvard or some school on the mainland, but they were the board. The only white faces you saw were the instructors and the haoles who didn't have the dough to send their kids to the mainland — and an occasional soldier in civvies, looking out of place. Only these and the board. And the tourists.

Then I remembered the scraped face, coming out of the main building on a hot still August day, wiping the sweat from the face with a big silk handkerchief.

"Couldn't find a thing," Mazzioli said, coming up from the car. "I don't know what to do. This guy looks like a German. He even talks like a German."

"Listen," I said. "No German who looks like a German and talks like a German is going to be a spy. Use your head. This guy is some kind of big shot. I seen him at the University."

"To hell with you and your University."

"No," I said. "Listen."

"Why would he ask me questions about the number of men and guns and pillboxes?"

"Hell, I don't know. Maybe he wanted to write an editorial for the *Advertiser*."

"I can't let him go," he said.

"All right. Send Alcorn up for the lieutenant and let him handle it. You worry too much, Greek."

"Yeh, I could do that." But he was dubious. He walked back to the car for a moment and then went over to Alcorn. "Alcorn, you go up and get the lieutenant down here. Tell him we got a suspicious character down here." He turned to me. "Slade, you watch this guy and don't take any chances with him. I'm going over this car again."

Alcorn handed me the rifles and started off up the road. Through the darkness Mazzioli hollered after him. "Double time and jerk the lead," he shouted. The wind carried it away. The wind carried everything away.

To me Mazzioli said, "If he tries anything, shoot the bastard."

"Okay," I said. I set the rifle butt on the ground and leaned on it. "Take it easy, mister," I said. "Remember there's a war on. The lieutenant's coming down, and you'll be on your way home in a little bit."

"I am not accustomed to such treatment," he said, staring at me with flat eyes, "and I intend to see somebody pays for this indignity."

"We're only doing our duty," I said. "We got orders to stop all suspicious persons. This is important to the defense plan."

"I am not a suspicious person," he said, "and you men . . ."

I interrupted; it was probably the only chance I'd ever get to interrupt a big shot. "Well," I said, "you were asking suspicious questions about our position."

". . . and you men should have something better to do than hold up citizens."

Mazzioli, looking harassed, came over from the car. "What's that?" he snarled. "What's your name?"

The Junker stared at him. "My name is Knight," he said, and waited for it to sink in. When Mazzioli's face was blank he added, "Of Knight & Crosby, Limited." His voice was cold with rage and hate.

Above the wind we heard the voices of Lieutenant Allison and Alcorn on the road.

I looked at the Greek but he showed nothing. Nobody could live in Hawaii without knowing Knight & Crosby, Ltd. The Big Five were as well known as Diamond Head.

Lieutenant Allison put one hand on Mazzioli's shoulder and the other on mine. "Now," he said paternally. "What's the trouble?"

Mazzioli told him the whole tale. I went back to the culvert and listened to the wind playing background music to the double tale of woe. After both stories were told, Lieutenant Allison escorted Mr. Knight to his runabout with extreme courtesy.

"You can appreciate, Mr. Knight, our position." Lieutenant Allison put his foot on the running board and rested his hands on the door. "You can understand my sergeant was only doing his duty, a duty conceived to protect you, Mr. Knight."

Mr. Knight did not speak. He sat with his hands gripping the wheel, staring straight ahead.

"I'm sorry you feel that way, Mr. Knight," Lieutenant Allison said. "These men were carrying out orders we have received from Hawaiian Department Headquarters."

Mr. Knight made no sign he had heard. He gave the impression he was suffering this association under duress and was fretting to have done and be gone.

"A soldier's duty is to follow out his orders," Lieutenant Allison said.

"All right," the lieutenant said. He took his foot off the running board and dropped his hands. "You may go, Mr. Knight. You can rest assured such a thing won't happen again, now that my men know who you are."

"It certainly won't," Mr. Knight said. "Bah!" He started his runabout with a roar and he did not look back.

I watched from the culvert and grinned contentedly. "Now there'll be hell to pay," I told Mazzioli.

After Knight was gone, Mazzioli called the lieutenant over to the other side of the road and spoke earnestly. I watched the excited movement of his blue light and grinned more widely.

Lieutenant Allison came over to me with the Greek following close behind. "Alcorn," he called. Alcorn shuffled over from the base of the cliff.

"I've been having bad reports about you two men," Lieutenant Allison began. "Where's your helmet, Alcorn?"

Alcorn shuffled his feet. "It's up the cliff. I cain't wear one of them things more'n a half hour, Lootenant," he said. "I get a turrible headache if I do. When Corporal Slade called me down, I clean forgot all about it."

"You're all through down here," Lieutenant Allison said. "Get back up there and get that helmet on. I'll be coming around inspecting and I don't want to catch you without a helmet. If I do there'll be some damned heavy details around here, and if that don't stop your headache, by god, maybe a court-martial will.

"You're no different than anybody else. If I can wear a helmet all the time, then you can do it. I don't like it any better than you do.

"Now get the hell back up there."

Alcorn saluted and started for the base of the cliff.

"Alcorn!" Lieutenant Allison called after him in the darkness.

"Yessir?"

"You don't ever go to sleep up there, do you?"

"Oh, no sir."

"You'd better watch it. I'll be inspecting tonight."

I could hear the scrambling and falling of pebbles and I thought it was a very lonely sound.

"Come over here, Slade," Lieutenant Allison said. He walked away from Mazzioli and I followed him, pleased the calling-down would be in private instead of in front of the Greek. It was a luxury.

"I'm going back up the hill," Lieutenant Allison said. "You walk part of the way with me. I want to talk to you." The two of us started up the road. "I'm going to send those men back down here when I get to the top," Lieutenant Allison said. "You won't need to go up."

"Thank you, sir," I said.

"Why did you let those men go up the hill tonight, Slade?"

"They didn't get any chow tonight, sir," I said. "I felt sorry for them."

"You're not supposed to feel sorry for anybody. You're a soldier. You enlisted in the Army, didn't you?"

"Yes, sir," I said. "But it was because I couldn't get a job."

"A soldier's job is to feel sorry for nobody."

"I can't help it, sir," I said. "Maybe my environment was wrong. Or maybe I haven't had the proper indoctrinization.

I always put myself in the other guy's place. I even felt sorry for Mr. Knight. And he sure didn't need it."

"What happened with Mr. Knight was the proper action to take. It turned out badly, but he could have been a saboteur with a carload of TNT to blow the demolition."

"What will happen about Knight, sir?" I said.

"Mr. Knight is a big man in Hawaii. The Big Five run the whole territory. There may be some bad effects. I may even get an ass-eating. Nevertheless, Mazzioli acted correctly. In the long run, it will all turn out all right because we did what was right. The Army will take that into account."

"You believe that?" I said.

"Yes," he said. "I believe it. You don't realize how important that road-guard is to the whole war. What if the enemy had made a landing at Kaneohe tonight? They'd have a patrol on you before you knew it. The very thing you did out of kindness might be what lost the war for us. It's not far-fetched: if they took this road and cliff, they'd have this island in a month. From there it'd be the west coast. And we'd be fighting the war in the Rocky Mountains."

"All for the want of a horseshoe nail," I said.

"That's it," he said. "That's why every tiniest thing is so important. You're one of the smartest men in the Company, Slade. There's no reason for me to explain these things to you. There's no reason why you shouldn't make OCS, except for your attitude. I've told you that before. What would you have done? Alone there with the men up on the hill?"

"I knew who he was," I said.

Lieutenant Allison turned on me. "Why in the name of Christ didn't you tell Mazzioli!" He was mad.

"I did," I said. "But he didn't listen. Orders is orders," I said.

Lieutenant Allison stopped. We were half-way up the hill. He looked out over the parapet and down at the sea, vaguely white where it broke on the rocks.

"What's the matter with you, Slade? You don't want to be cynical about this war."

"I'm not cynical about this war," I said. "I may die in this war. I'm cynical about the Army. It's a helluva lot easier to be an idealist if you're an officer. The higher the officer, the higher the ideals." To hell with it, I thought, to hell with all of it.

"Slade," he said, "I'd like for you to buckle down. I wasn't kidding when I said you could make OCS. I'd like to see you go to OCS because you're smart. You could do it if you'd only buckle down."

"I've been an EM too long," I said. "I'm too cynical."

"You know, you could be shot for talking like this in the German Army."

"I know it," I said. "That's why I don't like the German Army, or the Japanese Army, or the British Army, or the Russian Army. I could get ten years in the American Army if you wanted to turn me in."

Lieutenant Allison was leaning on the parapet. "If I didn't like you, by god I would."

"Trouble with me," I said, "I'm too honest. They didn't have indoctrinization courses yet when I enlisted," I said.

"It's not a question of briefing," he said. "It's a question of belief."

"Yes," I said. "And also of who manufactures it."

"We have to be cruel now so we can be kind later, after the war."

"That's the theory of the Communist Internationale," I said. "I hear their indoctrinization courses are wonderful."

"They're our allies," he said. "When the enemy is defeated, why it will all be set."

"I could never be an officer," I said. "I've not been indoctrinated well enough."

He laughed. "Okay, Slade. But you think over what I said, and if you want me to, I'll recommend you. You know, an intelligent man who refuses to use his intelligence to help win the war is a bottleneck. He's really a menace. In Germany he would be shot if he didn't use his intelligence to help win."

"Japan too," I said. "And in Italy and in Russia," I said. "Our country we only lock them up as conchies, as yet."

"Do you think I like being an officer?"

"Yes," I said. "I would like it. At least you get a bath and hot chow."

He laughed again. "Okay. But you think it over."

"I'll think about it," I said. "I'll think about all of it. But I never find an answer. Sometimes I wonder if there is an answer. The Greek is the man you ought to recommend."

"Are you kidding?" he grinned. "Mazzioli is a good sergeant."

"He believes the end justifies the means," I said. "He's been properly indoctrinated. I couldn't turn a man in if I had to."

Lieutenant Allison stood up from the parapet. "Think it over, Slade," he said.

"All right, sir," I said. "But I can tell you one thing. It's damn fine I can talk to you. But I always remember you're not all officers and I'm not all the EM," I said.

"Thanks, Slade," he said.

I walked on back down the road. I stopped every now and then to listen to the sea's attack against the cliff. It would be nice to be an officer. The sea and the wind were like two radio stations on the same dial mark. You could even have a bed-roll and a dog-robber. The old Revolutionists in Russia, I thought, they really had it all figured out; they really had the world saved this time. I kicked a pebble ahead of me down the road.

I must have gone very slow because the three men from the top were on my heels when I reached the bottom.

"Hey, Slade," one of them said. He came up. "I'm sorry we got you in trouble tonight. Nobody guessed this would happen."

"Forget it," I said. "All I got was a ass-eating."

Mazzioli was sitting on the culvert. "I'm going to roll up," he said belligerently.

"Okay, Greek," I said. I sat on the culvert a while, facing the wind. I liked to sit there at night alone, defying the wind. But a man could only do it so long. After a while a man got stupid from its eternal pummeling. A man got punch-drunk from it. Once before it made me so dizzy I fell down on my knees when I got up.

It was a wild place, the roaring sea, the ceaseless wind, the restless sand, the omniscient cliff.

I said good night to the men on post and rolled up myself. When I went under the wall it took my breath again. I lay in my blankets and listened to it howl just over my head.

It was three o'clock when the messenger from up on the hill woke me.

"What?" I said. "What is it? What?"

"Where's the Greek?" he said.

"He's here."

"You gotta wake him up."

"What's up?"

"You're moving back up the hill. Lieutenant's orders."

"Whose orders?" I said. "What about the demolition? What about the road-guard?"

"Lieutenant's orders. The road-guard is being disbanded. Altogether."

"What's the story?" I asked.

"I dunno. We got a call from the Company CP; the cap'n was maddern hell. He just got a call from Department HQ; they was maddern hell. Told the cap'n to disband the road-guard immediately. The orders'll be down in a couple days."

I laughed. "Orders is orders," I said.

"What?"

"Nothing," I said. "Is the lieutenant still up?"

"Yeh. He's in hole number one, with the telephone. Why?"

"I got to see him about something," I said.

"I'm going back," he said. "This wind is freezin' me. You sure you're awake?"

"Yes," I said. "You take off." I got up and woke the rest of the detail. "Get your stuff together, you guys. We're moving out. One of you call Alcorn down."

The Greek sat up, rubbing his eyes. "What is it? what's up? what's wrong?"

"We're moving out," I said. "Back up the hill. The road-guard is disbanded." When I stood up the wind hit me hard. I got my pack and kicked my blankets up into a pile. I slung my rifle and pack and picked up the blankets.

"You mean the *road-guard?*" Mazzioli's voice asked through the darkness and the wind. "For *good?*"

I climbed up around the wall and the wind caught at my blankets and I almost lost them.

"That's the way it is," I said.

From *Harper's Magazine*, June, 1949.

J. P. MARQUAND

# LUNCH AT HONOLULU

New England is his background, but John Phillips Marquand
(1893 — ), Pulitzer Prize-winning novelist, knows Honolulu. He
resided there in the 1930's, when he began writing his "Mr. Moto"
mystery stories, and during World War II he served there as a
naval attaché in the Pacific theater. It was during this latter
period, doubtless, that he met the prototypes of the characters
so brilliantly portrayed in one of his finest short stories — "Lunch
at Honolulu."

This story, says Clifton Fadiman, "is remarkable for the absolute rightness of its dialog . . . , the neat surgery of its satire,
the absence of even a single soft sentence, and the unforced compassion of its conclusion."

THE HOUSE WAS OFF NUUANU, BEYOND THE CEMETERY WHERE
Hawaiian royalty lay with symbolic tabu sticks at the corners of
their burial plots. It was a fine clear day by the sea, but rain was
falling up by the jagged skyline of the mountains. Mr. Huntley
knew that in Honolulu they called it liquid sunshine.

The house where he was invited for lunch was built of coral
stone and redwood, and a porte-cochere covered the drive.
The house might have been in Redlands, California, except for
the ornamental planting. It was said that almost anything could
grow on the Hawaiian Islands. By the time the taxicab had
stopped beneath the porte-cochere, Mr. Huntley had identified
upon the lawns a traveler's palm, an Alexandra palm, a Norfolk Island pine, ginger flowers, hibiscus, and a bed of calla
lilies, snapdragons, and forget-me-nots. There were also some

bamboo and banana. This dizzying combination gave its own horticultural evidence that Honolulu was the melting pot of races and the crossroads of the Pacific.

Even before Mr. Huntley had climbed the steps, a middle-aged Japanese maid had opened the door. Her hair was done in Japanese convention. She wore the kimono and the obi. When she bowed and took his hat, she looked like a part of the chorus of *Madame Butterfly.* Inside, the long living room was cool and shadowy, paneled with some polished dark wood. There were reed mats on the dark, highly polished floor. There were comfortable American upholstered chairs and Chinese lacquered tables. There were Hawaiian calabashes filled with ginger flowers. There was a large Capehart phonograph, and on the walls were Chinese ancestral portraits, an oblong of old tapa cloth, and some Malay weapons.

The Japanese maid smiled. Before she put her hand in front of her mouth, she revealed three black teeth and one brilliant gold one. She drew in her breath politely.

"Mr. Wintertree, he waits, on the back *lanai,* please," she said. "This way, please."

As Mr. Huntley followed her, he had a glimpse of himself in a cloudy ornate Italian mirror. His image was disturbing in that shadowy room that was heavy with the scent of tuberoses. He was a moist, dumpy, middle-aged interloper in a wrinkled Palm Beach suit.

Mr. Wintertree was on the back veranda. The veranda, furnished with wicker chairs, potted ferns and hanging air plants, looked over a deep-green tropical gorge to the darker jagged mountains. To the left, far below, were the streets and houses of Honolulu, and the docks and the Aloha Tower, and the harbor and the sea. Mr. Wintertree was a cadaverous man. He was dressed in an immaculate linen suit. His face was deeply tanned. His hair was as white and as smooth as his coat.

"*Aloha,* Mr. Huntley," he said. "It's very kind of you to come and take potluck. Mrs. Wintertree was dreadfully sorry she couldn't be here. It's her day at the Red Cross, so it will be a stag party — just five of us. Admiral Smedley is coming with Captain Rotch of his staff. Henry D. Smedley — you know the admiral?"

"No, I have never met him," Mr. Huntley answered. "I hope I'm not too early."

"Oh, no, no," Mr. Wintertree said. "They'll be here any minute now. Just the admiral and Captain Rotch, and Lieutenant —" A slight frown appeared on Mr. Wintertree's face. "What the devil is his name? Oh yes, Wright. A Lieutenant Wright. He's just off a carrier. Walter Jones wrote me about him, too. He's a naval aviator. Did you ever hear Walt mention him?"

"No, not that I remember," Mr. Huntley said. "It's very kind of you to have me here."

"It's always a pleasure to see a friend of old Walt's," Mr. Wintertree said. "Maybe he told you, we were together in the class of '08 at Yale. When did you last see Walt?"

"In New York last month," Mr. Huntley told him. "Walt told me to be sure to look you up."

"I wish you could see this place the way it used to be before the war," Mr. Wintertree said. "It's the duty of *kamaainas* to make *malihinis* like the islands, but Honolulu is a madhouse now. Army, Navy — they're into everything. They'll be taking the golf club next."

"What's a *kamaaina?*" Mr. Huntley asked.

Mr. Wintertree smiled.

"That's a Hawaiian word. Roughly translated it means 'old-timer,'" Mr. Wintertree said. "I'm an old-timer and you're a *malihini*. This is a *kamaaina* house. Father built it in 1880. Honolulu was just a small town on a small Pacific island then. My God, how it's changed!"

"You have a beautiful view from this porch," Mr. Huntley said.

"*Lanai,* not porch," Mr. Wintertree told him. "I suppose we're eccentric the way we cling to Hawaiian words. This is a *lanai,* and that couch over there is called a *hikiee*. It's a real

Hawaiian *hikiee,* not just a couple of mattresses the way they make them now. You can see it is made out of *lauhala* mats, the woven leaves of the pandanus tree."

"*Hikiee,*" Mr. Huntley repeated.

"Good," Mr. Wintertree said. "That's the way to say it."

"What do you do with it?" Mr. Huntley asked.

"Why, you lie on it," Mr. Wintertree said. "Do you want to lie on it?"

"No thanks, not now," Mr. Huntley answered. "You do have a beautiful view from here."

"Those light-colored trees that you see on the side of the mountain are kukui trees," said Mr. Wintertree. "They have small round nuts called kukui nuts. In old times the Hawaiians would string those nuts on a reed and use them for candles. My father used to say when he was a child that his father — we come of missionary stock — used to say, 'Children, one more kukui nut and it's bedtime.' "

Mr. Huntley glanced at a low table, hoping to find a cigarette.

"When my father was a boy," Mr. Wintertree said, "he spoke of seeing a little crowd of native Hawaiians on the docks, about where the Aloha Tower is now. We were all friends in those days. Those Polynesian boys were looking at something and laughing — two bluebottle flies. Yes, they had never seen a fly, and now we have everything — flies, Marines, planes, battleships. I suppose you're out here for the government, Mr. Huntley."

"Yes," said Mr. Huntley. "I'm out for the OWI."

"What's the OWI?" Mr. Wintertree asked.

"That's a native American expression," Mr. Huntley said.

"Now, now," Mr. Wintertree told him. "Don't forget that we're just as native American here as any other part of America." He looked at his wrist watch. "I've never known Admiral Smedley to be so late. Wait — I'm wrong, I think I hear him now."

Brisk and somewhat heavy steps sounded on the floor of the living room. It was Admiral Smedley, followed by Captain

Rotch. The admiral's glance was sharp and direct. His face was set in tranquil lines, like the bust of a Roman emperor. His gray hair was cut very short. He was dressed in fresh khaki. He wore two tiny silver stars in his shirt collar. On his finger was a Naval Academy ring.

"We're just waiting for one other guest," Mr. Wintertree said. "A friend of a friend of mine. He is just off a carrier — Lieutenant Wright."

"That must be the *Great Lick*," the admiral said. "She ran into a little difficulty. What did you say the officer's name was?"

"Wright," Mr. Wintertree answered.

"I don't know him," the admiral said. "Rotch, did you ever hear of anybody named Wright?"

"No, sir," the captain said.

"Well, it's a big navy," the admiral said. "And the Pacific's a big ocean."

"We might have something to drink while we're waiting," Mr. Wintertree said. "Would you care for something, Admiral? Sherry or a Martini? — or a little of our island drink, *okolehao?*"

"*Okolehao*, I haven't had any of that since I was stationed here in '32," the admiral said. "We used to call it oke. How about you, Rotch?"

"If the boss falls off the wagon, I guess I can too," the captain said, and he laughed.

"I hope you'll excuse me if I don't join you," Mr. Wintertree said. "I very seldom indulge in the middle of the day, but Taka and Togo will give you anything you want. Would you care for a Martini, Mr. Huntley?"

"Thank you," Mr. Huntley said.

The Japanese maid came through the door on the far end of the porch, which evidently led to the dining room. She carried a large tray of dark wood, upon which were small plates of olives and other appetizers. Behind her came an old Japanese in a white coat, with bottles, ice, and glasses.

"Taka and Togo have been with us for thirty years," Mr. Wintertree said, and he lowered his voice. "They were very unhappy on December 7th."

"So was I," the admiral said. "Do you live out here too, Mr. Huntley?"

"Oh, no," Mr. Huntley said. "I'm with the OWI. I've only been here about a week."

"Oh, a writer, are you?" the admiral asked. "Well, there's a lot to write about."

"You have a beautiful view from this veranda," Mr. Huntley heard Captain Rotch say to Mr. Wintertree.

"Yes, we think it's a very pleasant *lanai*," he heard Mr. Wintertree answer. "You see it faces both *mauka* and *makai*. Those are the old Hawaiian words for the sea and the mountains, Captain Rotch. They form two of the cardinal points on our island's compass. Those light-colored trees on the mountainside are called kukui trees."

"Let's see," the admiral said to Mr. Huntley. "I think I have read something that you have written. Didn't you write an article for the *Saturday Evening Post* about trailers?"

"No, sir, that must have been someone else."

"Yes, maybe it was someone else. Did you fly out, or come by boat?" the admiral asked.

"I flew out," Mr. Huntley told him.

"You can get places flying — anywhere in the world in two days' flying," the admiral said. "It's a great place, Honolulu. We're certainly lifting its face for it. Give us another year and we'll make it look like Pittsburgh. No one's ever going to say again that America can't fight a war. Thank you." He took a glass from the tray the old Japanese was passing.

The Japanese houseman bowed and smiled. He was a very polite old-time Japanese.

"This is like old times," the admiral called. "This is real oke, Wintertree."

"It comes from the big island," Mr. Wintertree answered. "They used to make it in the old days — that was during prohibition — but there were only two kinds of *okolehao*, the right kind and the wrong kind. This is the right kind. It was made from the root of the ti plant. You've seen its leaves on dinner tables, Admiral. In the old days the Hawaiians would break off a ti plant and sit on it and slide down a mountain slope. It was one of the old royal sports."

"Yes, I've heard they did," the admiral said. "In my spare time I've been making a little study of the Polynesians. I've got a dictionary of Hawaiian words."

"It will be useful to you," Mr. Wintertree said. "Hawaiian words still crop up in *kamaainas'* conversations."

"Some of the words are very expressive," the admiral said. "Do you know the word for cat?" But Mr. Wintertree did not answer. He was moving to the living-room door, to shake hands with the last of his guests, Lieutenant Wright. Lieutenant Wright had a piece of adhesive tape above his left eye, but even so he looked very fresh and young. His voice was loud and mellow.

"And how do you do, sir," Lieutenant Wright said. "Thanks for letting me aboard. I hope I'm not too late to snap onto a drink."

"Oh — not too late at all. I am very glad you could come, Lieutenant," Mr. Wintertree told him. "As soon as I heard from your Uncle Walt . . ."

Lieutenant Wright laughed so loudly that Mr. Huntley saw the admiral's forehead wrinkle.

"Uncle Walt would have given me hell if I had passed you up," Lieutenant Wright said. "Uncle Walt told me if I ever hit this rock to look you up, sir, and now I've hit it." He looked at Mr. Huntley's glass. "Is that a Martini I see him drinking?"

"Yes, that's a Martini," Mr. Wintertree said. "And this is Admiral Smedley, Captain Rotch, and Mr. Huntley."

"How do you do, Admiral," Lieutenant Wright said. "Sorry I'm late, but I don't mind catching up." He took a Martini from the tray. "Make me another one, boy," he added gently. "Maybe you better make me two. This is really a nice place you've got here, Mr. Wintertree."

The conversation had died. There was a silence while Lieutenant Wright picked up another Martini. The admiral cleared his throat.

"I hear you're off the *Great Lick,*" the admiral said.

Lieutenant Wright laughed loudly, although there appeared to be no reason for his laughing.

"Yes, sir, the old *Lick* and promise. That's what the kids call her, Admiral, sir," Lieutenant Wright answered. "And she's mostly *Lick*." Lieutenant Wright laughed again. "She really is, sir. She really took them aboard, sir, but we knocked off one of their BBs."

The admiral turned to Captain Rotch. "How many did you say she took?"

"Three of them, sir," the captain said.

"She really took them." Lieutenant Wright laughed again. "Oh, boy! she really took them."

The admiral glanced at Mr. Huntley and then at Mr. Wintertree. He seemed to feel that the occasion compelled him to say something but not too much.

"Occasionally," he said, "in the course of an air battle a Japanese plane crashes on the deck or superstructure of one of our ships — a suicide plane. It naturally causes considerable damage."

Lieutenant Wright whistled. He was on his third Martini, and as far as Mr. Huntley could see, rank did not disturb him.

"Did you say damage, sir?" he asked.

The wrinkles deepened on the admiral's forehead.

"Just one minute, please," he began, but the lieutenant raised his voice.

"It's really rugged when one of them comes in at you," the lieutenant said. "Now this first that hit us — it was about eighteen hundred and thirty hours — he came in from the port side. We gave him everything we had. You could see the 40s going into him like red-hot rivets."

"Just a minute," the admiral said. "Just a minute, son — " but the lieutenant's voice was louder.

"That kid must have been dead, but he still kept coming in. You got the idea there was nothing you could do but stand and take it. It was a very rugged feeling."

"Rotch," the admiral said to the captain. Captain Rotch's manner reminded Huntley of that of a kindly policeman. He rested his hand on Lieutenant Wright's shoulder and whispered something. As he listened, the lieutenant's face looked blank and his thoughts seemed to drift away from him and he was back again where he had started, right on Mr. Wintertree's *lanai*.

"I'm sorry, sir," he said. "I didn't know it was restricted."

"That's all right, son," the admiral told him. "That's all right."

"Down in Noumea we had a song about it," the lieutenant said. "Some of the kids made it up at the club. 'I'm forever whispering secrets.'"

Mr. Wintertree's voice interrupted.

"I think luncheon is ready now," Mr. Wintertree was saying.

"Well, let's skip it," Lieutenant Wright said. "As long as pop here says luncheon's ready."

"If you'll just lead the way, Admiral," Mr. Wintertree said.

In the dining room a narrow dark table was set for lunch. There was a center decoration of breadfruit and green leaves. There were Chinese plates and small wooden bowls filled with a gray pastelike substance, that Mr. Huntley knew was a native food called poi. The admiral was at Mr. Wintertree's right, Mr. Huntley at his left. Captain Rotch was beside Mr. Huntley and the lieutenant was beside the admiral.

"I'm forever whispering secrets," the lieutenant was singing beneath his breath. He lifted up his plate very carefully and set it down. Then Mr. Huntley saw him staring at his bowl of poi. The servants were passing plates of clear consommé.

"I'm sorry there isn't a sixth to balance the table," Mr. Wintertree said. "This is Mrs. Wintertree's day at the Red Cross. I see you looking at the table, Admiral. Do you know what wood it's made from?"

"Yes," the admiral said, "koa wood."

"No, no," Mr. Wintertree said. "It's made from the monkey-pod tree."

"Have they got monkeys on this rock?" the lieutenant asked.

Mr. Wintertree went on without answering.

"Now, the chairs we are sitting on are koa. They are our

best wood, very close to mahogany. The koa is a very handsome tree, Mr. Huntley, long, graceful, curving leaves. You still find specimens in the mountains, but our most beautiful wood came from the kou tree."

"I never heard of the kou tree," the admiral said.

"As long as it isn't the cuckoo tree," Lieutenant Wright said and he began to laugh.

"The old calabashes were all made from the kou," Mr. Wintertree said. "You can see one of them — a very handsome one — on the sideboard, but the kou is nearly extinct. When ants appeared on the island, they ate the kou."

"What did they want to eat it for, pop?" Lieutenant Wright asked.

"They ate the leaves," Mr. Wintertree answered.

"Well, bugs do eat the damndest things on islands," Lieutenant Wright said. "At Hollandia something ate the seat right out of my pants. Maybe it was ants. Ants in my pants, pop."

"Mr. Wintertree," the admiral asked, "do you know the Hawaiian word for cat?"

"Why, yes," Mr. Wintertree said. *"Popoki."*

"I suppose you know how the word was derived?" the admiral asked.

The soup was finished. Mr. Wintertree glanced at the servants and they began to take away the plates.

"Oh, yes," he said. "Of course I know." But the admiral went on telling him.

"Well, Huntley ought to hear it," the admiral said. "Mr. Huntley can write it down sometime. It seems that there didn't use to be any cats in the Hawaiian Islands."

"No cats, no ants," Lieutenant Wright said. The admiral glanced at him sideways.

"And no Naval Reserve officers," the admiral said. "It seems the missionaries brought the cats."

Lieutenant Wright smiled.

"And the Navy brought in the reserve officers, Admiral, sir. They had to, to win this war."

Captain Rotch cleared his throat.

"Perhaps the admiral would like to finish what he is saying," he said gently.

"Sorry, sir," Lieutenant Wright said quickly. "Aye, aye, sir. The missionaries brought the cats ..."

"You see, none of the Kanakas had ever seen a cat. They didn't have a name for it," the admiral went on. Mr. Huntley saw that Mr. Wintertree winced when the admiral used the word "*Kanaka.*" "Then they must have heard one of the white missionary women call her cat 'poor pussy' and that's how you get it — poor pussy — *popoki.*"

"By God, what do you know," the lieutenant said, and he whistled. "You come to an island and it's like every other island and all the native Joes and Marys are just alike. Coral, palm trees, a lagoon, and then out come the canoes — and there you are, like that." He snapped his fingers. "Pretty soon you beat a drum and start singing."

"You have never been to Honolulu before, have you?" It seemed to Mr. Huntley that Mr. Wintertree's voice was sharp. "I think you'll find it different. These fish are mullet. The old kings used to keep them in the royal fishponds."

"There's nothing better than good mullet," Captain Rotch said.

"Back out there" — the lieutenant waved his hand to illustrate out there — "we used to chuck a stick of dynamite in a lagoon and get mullet, and did the natives go for those fish? You ought to have seen them go for them. Once when I was out with a sub over in the Zulu Sea — all right, Admiral, sir, security."

"I'm sorry we can't hear about it," the admiral said.

"This is one-finger poi," Mr. Wintertree told the table. "There's a shortage of good poi, like everything else, but some of my native friends help me."

Mr. Wintertree stopped, because Lieutenant Wright had begun to laugh for no apparent reason.

"You know, they tell a story about me out there, pop," the lieutenant said, and he waved his hand again, to illustrate out there, "and I guess I can tell it to you without breaking security. It's rather a funny story." He laughed again as he remembered it and pushed his plate away. "One of the CPOs who was working with me came up to me one day and he said, 'Lieutenant, sir, I ought to get a little leave. This country here is getting me queer.' Well, I didn't blame him. So I just told him to relax and tell me what was the matter. And he said, 'It's this way, sir. All these dark women begin to look to me as though they were white.' And do you know what I said to him? At least, it's what they say I said to him." The lieutenant paused and beamed at everyone. "I said to him — 'Kid, what dark women?'" The admiral smiled. Mr. Huntley laughed, although he had heard the story several times before.

"We are having papaya for dessert," Mr. Wintertree said. "It isn't quite the season, but I'm proud of my papayas."

They had small cups of very black coffee out on the *lanai*. Mr. Wintertree explained that it was kona coffee, so named because it was grown on the slopes of the Kona coast on the big island of Hawaii. There was an island too big to be spoiled, Mr. Wintertree said. The ghosts of the past still lingered over the Kona coast. You could still see the old burial caves in the cliffs that fringe the bay where Captain Cook was killed. You could still see the black walls of lava rock that marked the compounds of the native villages.

As Mr. Huntley sat listening, he was thinking of the irrational accidents that threw people together. In a few moments this party on the *lanai* would be breaking up. The admiral would return to his office. Mr. Huntley would return to his hotel. He wondered what the lieutenant would find to do. Very little, he imagined, now that Honolulu was a garrison town.

"They still sing the old meles on Hawaii," Mr. Wintertree was saying. "Those old word-of-mouth songs have been passed on for centuries."

The lieutenant looked at his small cup of coffee.

"Would it be out of order to turn this in for something else?" he asked.

"Turn it in?" Mr. Wintertree repeated.

"For a Scotch and soda," the lieutenant said. "If you wouldn't mind, pop."

"Oh, certainly," Mr. Wintertree answered. "A Scotch and soda, Togo."

"Double," the lieutenant said. "If you wouldn't mind."

"Sometime you should hear an old Hawaiian chant — a mele," Mr. Wintertree told the admiral. "It's a living page of history."

The lieutenant clapped his hands together and drummed his foot on the floor.

"Boom-boom," he said. "Yai, yai, boom-boom. One night at Tanga those Joes began singing — Oh, thanks."

Togo was back with a double Scotch and soda, but the lieutenant had grown restless. He prowled back and forth across the *lanai,* withdrawn from the conversation, but Mr. Huntley could still hear him, muttering beneath his breath, "Yai, yai, boom-boom." This must have gone on for several minutes while the rest of them were talking before the Japanese maid appeared. She said some officers in an automobile were calling for Lieutenant Wright. Lieutenant Wright looked very much relieved.

"I thought those boys could wangle some transportation," he said. "You've got to see these rocks when you hit them. Well, I'd better be shoving. Thank you, Mr. Wintertree. Good-by, Admiral, sir. So long, Captain. So long, Mister."

There was a moment's silence when Lieutenant Wright left. They could hear him cross the living room.

"Boom-boom, boom-boom," he was still chanting. "Yai, yai, boom-boom."

The admiral looked at his empty cup, and then he looked at the captain.

"That was a pretty fresh kid," the captain said.

"Yes," the admiral answered. "It's quiet, now he's gone."

"You never can tell about a new guest," Mr. Wintertree said. "I'm sorry."

The wicker chair in which the admiral was sitting creaked as he leaned forward to set his cup on a little table.

"That's all right," he said. "Every now and then they act

that way. You and I would, too." The chair creaked again as the admiral rose. "Will you see if the car is outside, Rotch? It's only that boy was glad — and that's natural — just glad he is still alive."

From *Thirty Years* by J. P. Marquand (Boston, Little, Brown & Co., 1954).

THOMAS D. MURPHY

# THE AJA'S COME HOME

WHEN THE ATTACK STRUCK PEARL HARBOR ON DECEMBER 7, 1941, the Japanese people born in Hawaii proved by many acts to be loyal Americans. The young men, in particular, were eager to show their loyalty. When, after some months, Army authorities decided to call for twelve hundred volunteers among the young "AJA's" — Americans of Japanese Ancestry, as they preferred to be called — no less than ten thousand offered to enlist.

The war record of the 100th Infantry Battalion, later a part of the 442nd Regimental Combat Team, as related in Thomas D. Murphy's volume *Ambassadors in Arms,* captures the imagination. They landed at Salerno in September, 1943, and fought so valiantly in the Italian and French campaigns that by V-E Day they were designated by experts as "probably the most decorated unit in United States military history." Other AJA's served in Pacific engagements from Guadalcanal to Okinawa. Some of these men were interpreters who often risked their lives to obtain information on enemy movements. All in all, more than eighteen thousand Hawaiian AJA's served in the armed forces before the end of World War II.

Professor Murphy is head of the Department of History at the University of Hawaii. One of the more penetrating chapters of his book deals with the return of the AJA's to Hawaii. They had fought the enemy abroad; but there was another enemy — racial intolerance — to overcome at home. Now they faced the problems of adjustment to civilian life and the responsibility of leadership among their people in the rapidly changing patterns of postwar Hawaii.

FOR MOST OF THE MEN OF THE 100TH BATTALION, THE PRIMARY concern in 1945 was their return to Hawaii. What would things

287

be like back home? By V-J day many veterans were already back in the islands on furlough, and after that date the others returned in small batches, so that there never was any formal homecoming, with ceremonies and so on. It mattered little. It was enough, at first, to be home, and to loll in the sun, and to marvel that one still lived.

There were problems, nevertheless. From Camp McCoy to the Po Valley, various members of the battalion had been writing to members of the Emergency Service Committee encouraging them in their leadership of the Japanese community and supporting their campaigns to persuade the Issei * to abandon the "old country" institutions, traditions, and mannerisms. These letters urged that the older folk give up the speaking of Japanese if they could speak English, talk out boldly against the Emperor, follow the leadership of the ESC faithfully, and generally leave no doubt in anyone's mind that they were heart and soul in the war, not only against Germany but also against Japan. Wounded men who returned home said the same things. Just because the AJA soldiers had made a good battle record, the Issei had no right to become complacent. After Germany was finished there would still be the fight to crush Japan, and then people of Japanese ancestry would be more "on the spot" than ever before. The gains that the second generation had made toward first-class American citizenship must not be lost because some of the Issei thought more of their own mental and physical comfort than they did of America.

It was with chagrin, therefore, that returned soldiers heard, during the summer and fall of 1945, that many of the younger Nisei were blown up with pride because of the publicity given their soldier brothers and had become arrogantly disrespectful to persons of other racial ancestries; and that the older folk were reverting quickly to the "old country" ways laid aside during the war. It was even more shocking to learn that a small but fanatical group among the Issei flatly refused to believe that

* The first generation of immigrants, as distinguished from the Nisei, their children, born under the American flag.

"invincible" Japan had been crushed — even insisted among themselves that she had won the war — and were joining recently formed religious-nationalistic organizations within which they gave each other mutual support for their delusions. Angered AJA veterans protested unofficially to the leaders of these movements and officially to federal authorities.

It was developments within the Japanese community such as these which Doc Kometani had in mind as he spoke, an interpreter at his side, to audiences throughout the Territory:

"We who by God's will were permitted to return and you who are fortunate to be here have a challenge — an obligation to those who now peacefully sleep under the white crosses in Italy and France — to build a better Hawaii.

"By the blood and tears of our people we have earned a place for ourselves in this community. We have made tremendous gains in recent years and we must strive to maintain and extend them.

"To the older people, I wish to address a special appeal at this time. We of the second and third generations are Americans by right and choice. Our future is here in America. We ask you to use your influence to help us become better Americans. You have helped to make our position here secure by your admirable conduct and participation in the war effort. If you permit the revival of certain institutions which have placed us 'on the spot,' you will undo the wonderful work of the boys in uniform. We owe you a great debt of gratitude and if you will exert your influence to bring about a greater assimilation of our young people and better relations among Hawaii's people you will earn the everlasting gratitude of posterity. You will thereby be laying a solid foundation for the future of American citizens of Japanese ancestry in Hawaii.

"I have been back only a few weeks but I have observed trends and events which I am afraid might endanger the traditional feeling of racial tolerance in Hawaii. The beauty and greatness of Hawaii we have long cherished to return to lie in our friendly relationships with all the races in Hawaii. That is one of the things we fought this war for. Selfishly speaking, we who are not yet fully accepted as citizens with all the rights and privileges will be the ones who stand to lose most if racial antagonisms spread throughout the territory. I plead with you to exert your utmost to maintain friendly relationships with people of all races. Let us keep the *aloha* spirit alive in Hawaii.

"The highest aspiration of our boys in uniform is to return to a Hawaii where a citizen irrespective of ancestry will share and share equally in the rights as well as the responsibilities of citizenship. We have helped win the war on the battlefront but we have not yet won the war on the home front. We shall have won only when we attain those things for which our country is dedicated, namely, equality of opportunity and the dignity of man.

"This battle for acceptance on a free and equal basis will be a long and tedious one. The important thing is to see that progress is made. There will be times when we will become a bit impatient. It is imperative that we maintain a broad outlook, a historical perspective, if you will. There are some things we can do to hasten our acceptance in this democratic community.

"It is important that we actively participate in the life of the community, especially in those activities that involve people of all races. There are many organizations formed along interest rather than racial lines. It is important that we not only join them but assume the full responsibilities of membership.

"Then, too, I feel that we should do our part in bringing about a greater intermingling of the races on a genuinely social basis. I think it will be an excellent idea for us to cultivate the friendship of at least one person from each racial group in Hawaii.

"All of us need to examine our own prejudices before we condemn others and before we can honestly plead for equal treatment. Our attitude toward other races, toward the haoles, toward certain people in our own race, certainly can be improved. Because of our numerical strength, we can contribute a great deal to make Hawaii a happy and prosperous land.

"We in Hawaii today stand squarely at the crossroads. One road leads to democracy and racial tolerance for which many of our boys paid the supreme sacrifice on the battlefields of this war. The other leads to racial strife, intolerance, and greed which will inevitably breed wars. We who have seen the horrors and tragedies of war hope that our children and children's children will be spared what we have just finished. The men who were laid to rest under the thousands of white crosses all over the world will not rest in peace unless we are able to fulfill their hopes and dreams of creating a better Hawaii, a better world."

It was easy enough to tell those of Japanese ancestry to maintain a calm and broad outlook, but it was sometimes difficult for AJA veterans to maintain it, when they encountered criticism that they had returned home with too "cocky" an attitude. Charlie Hemenway exasperatedly commented that those who made the charge had had, before the war, a concept of the Nisei as a lesser breed of second-class status who were supposed to be properly respectful, submissive, and grateful for all small favors. Now that these boys had come home from the war with a greater degree of self-assurance and a feeling that they had earned first-class citizenship, some of the island people still persisted in treating them as inferiors. The veterans naturally refused to take it, and they were called "cocky."

In an interview with a newsman, Corporal Tad Kanda, a veteran of the 100th, patiently and tactfully explained the situation.

"Some of our old friends think that we are cocky since we have returned to Hawaii. It's regrettable because we aren't. We've done only what millions of other men were doing.

"The trouble is that we have seen how the other side of the world lives. It had broadened our sphere of interest and sometimes our old friends don't understand.

"Most of us feel that we had too much publicity and we

realize the only reason for it was that we . . . were the only unit of our kind. When occasionally some AJA starts to brag, the rest of us quiet him immediately. We have a reputation to live up to, and we are not going to have it spoiled by a few individuals."

Despite such explanation the matter of publicity continued to be a cause of irritation. Many islanders who had never been hostile to the AJA's had found themselves annoyed at the amount of print devoted to the deeds of the 100th and the 442nd. Other Hawaii boys, not of Japanese ancestry, had served in the nation's armed forces, even though not in such large numbers. Why this constant barrage of articles which, by comparison, made the individual services of these other soldiers seem inconsequential? Mainlanders were probably getting the idea that the only servicemen from Hawaii had been the AJA's.

It was a natural reaction. It was easy, now that the Nisei had proved themselves, to forget what things had been like for these young men from 1939 through 1943. It was also easy for some islanders to forget — and for others perhaps difficult to realize — that the achievement of the 100th, the 442nd, and the AJA interpreters was not simply a Hawaiian story, but one which had implications for the whole of the nation. Men of good will, sitting at typewriters in the War Department and in other governmental agencies, in newspaper offices, behind magazine desks, and elsewhere saw the story of the Nisei servicemen from the islands as an American saga. They wanted the contrast between Hawaii's spirit of *aloha* and California's intolerance — and the wartime results which had stemmed from each — to be known to as many Americans as possible. Harry Truman had succinctly expressed this viewpoint when he had reviewed five hundred veterans of the 442nd at the White House. "You fought not only the enemy but you fought prejudice — and you have won. Keep up that fight and we will continue to win — to make this great republic stand for just what the Constitution says it stands for — the welfare of all of the people all of the time. Bring forward the colors."

At the Congressional hearings on statehood held in Hawaii

in 1946 and 1948 a few of the irreconcilables still publicly expressed their doubts as to the matter of loyalty, brought forth the old suspicions, and leveled the new charge of "cockiness." Making reply, an AJA veteran said, in part:

"We AJA's have always been accepted as Americans by our friends of other racial groups in Hawaii. It was a natural pattern that, together with the thousands of other sons of Hawaii, we did, as good Americans, our duty on the battlefronts and on the home front. . . .

"Not by our own doing, but by order of the War Department, many of our group fought as members of the 100th Infantry Battalion and of the 442nd Regimental Combat Team and, because we were a unique group, we made good newspaper copy.

"This, gentlemen, was not of our asking or doing. We simply did our duty as did thousands of other sons of Hawaii, as did millions of other Americans, and we as an ethnic group do not claim credit. If any credit is due us as sons of Hawaii, that credit should go to the entire territory which educated us and had faith in us.

"We fulfilled our duties . . . not so much to prove our loyalty, but more to justify the faith that our friends in Hawaii reposed in us. . . .

"With the few who, in spite of the hundreds of white crosses that mark the graves of our fallen comrades in Italy, France, Germany, and the South Pacific, will still have you believe that we are not Americans, we are not too much concerned. For when a man loves his country so well that he is willing to give his life in service to it, there is certainly nothing further one can do."

There was, in fact, little need to be concerned about the "few." Testimony at both hearings showed an overwhelming feeling that the wartime services of the AJA's had buried the loyalty question for good, and dual citizenship, once such a hot issue, was hardly mentioned. As Hawaii's struggle for statehood continued, it was significant that both overt and secret opponents of that movement shifted their ground, and now concentrated attention on the matter of Communist leadership within Hawaii's union movement.

As the months passed, those fears of a rebirth of racial feeling which Captain Kometani had expressed proved groundless. The mass delusions of the fanatical Issei minority died away, and though the rest of the Japanese aliens gradually sank comfortably back into more and more of the prewar ways, no one seemed to mind much as Japanese speech began to be heard again in public places, the temples were reopened, Japanese-language programs reappeared on the radio, and Japanese movies were again shown in the theaters. The AJA veterans could see that because they had worn the Army uniform and had fought for their native land, their parents had achieved a stronger feeling of "belonging," a greater sense of identification with America. They felt, indeed, that this was one of the greatest results their military service had wrought. As for the return of many of the prewar customs, the veterans gradually came to feel that perhaps the old people should be allowed a little comfort during their declining years. After all, when one came to think of it, now that all the shouting and shooting were over, what real harm had most of the old institutions done, even the language schools, which were gradually being reopened? If lack of public opposition meant consent, the rest of the community seemed to agree.

Veterans had other problems, however, than those of status and community relationships. A man had to eat, and try to make some plans for the future. Most of the boys went back to their old jobs, but there were some significant changes in the vocational pattern. Some of the Big Five companies gave jobs in the executive ranks to AJA officers of the battalion. Other officers and some enlisted men decided to make the Army a career, and were assigned to occupation duty in Japan, where they served as interpreters between the land of their ancestors and that of their birth. Many men took advantage of their GI Bill rights, and either enrolled or re-enrolled at the University of Hawaii or mainland colleges. Some who were already college graduates (notably the public-school teachers) went to mainland universities for graduate work in law, medicine, dentistry, and other presumably more profitable professions.

There was a spate of marriages as men decided to make up for lost years and settle down, and the slow trend toward more matings with girls of other than Japanese stock again showed up in the newspaper announcements. Italian, French, and mainland haole girls who had married members of the battalion came to the islands to join their husbands in a community where interracial marriages offered more promise of happiness than in most other places on the globe. Men again took part in the activities of organizations in which they had been members before the war, and, with a new sense of maturity and a stronger sense of "belonging," participated more actively in the affairs of the community.

In public office, as in other spheres, the new status of the AJA became increasingly evident. In 1952 Sakae Takahashi, former captain in the 100th, once a schoolteacher, now a lawyer, was appointed treasurer of the Territory by the Democratic governor, Oren E. Long. Takahashi, the first AJA in the history of the Territory to receive a post in a governor's cabinet, was shortly joined by Attorney General Michiro Watanabe, another AJA. When Samuel W. King became Republican governor in 1953, he named Howard K. Hiroki, a veteran of the 100th, Territorial auditor, and appointed Doctor Katsumi Kometani and lawyer Jack Mizuha (another former schoolteacher) chairman of the Territory's Board of Commissioners of Public Instruction and member of the Board of Regents of the University of Hawaii respectively. The same pattern was apparent throughout lower echelons of public trust. In ten short years the old order of things had changed considerably.

From *Ambassadors in Arms* by Thomas D. Murphy (Honolulu, University of Hawaii Press, 1954).

WILLIAM MEREDITH

# AN ACCOUNT OF A VISIT
# TO HAWAII

William Meredith, after he was graduated from Princeton, spent
several years in the islands — first as a naval aviator during World
War II and afterwards as an instructor of English at the University of Hawaii. In the following fine-textured poem the poet
confronts a paradox. He finds that Hawaii, in its engaging mildness and its illusiveness, has perils for some of those who go
there, and that
            "It is no easy place to save the soul."
Meredith left Hawaii and returned to active service with the
Navy for two years during the Korean war. He is at present an
assistant professor at Connecticut College, and in summers
teaches at the Bread Loaf School of English. He has written three
volumes of beautifully wrought and intelligent poetry: *Love
Letter from an Impossible Land, Ships and Other Figures,* and
*The Open Sea.*

Snow through the fronds, fire flowing into the sea
At a goddess' will who does not ask belief —
It is hard to reconcile extremities
Of any size, or to find their centers out,
As paradoxes demonstrate, and griefs,
And this old kingdom running sweetly out.
You would not think to say of a custom here
"This is the place itself," as you might elsewhere.

There are no snakes and very little lust;
Many decorums have made life decorous.
Fish stands for food and hospitality,
And the innocence of symbols generally
Is surprising, now that we think absurd
The Noble Savage. *Mildmercy* — one word —
Is perhaps the closest European concept
To name the culture, surely to name the climate

Which has the ocean's powers of deception
When unrippled. The women stringing flowers
To keep the shade describe a slow ellipse
From June to June, like sundials at their hours.
And people have mistaken toy ships
For the ship to take them back across the ocean
And later stayed too long. The practical
Chinese put ripples in the year with catherine wheels.

Mildness can enervate as well as heat.
The soul must labor to reach paradise.
Many are here detained in partial grace
Or partial penalty, for want of force.
The canefields burn in fire that does no harm,
The cataracts blow upward in the Trades,
For all the world as if there were no rules.

And there is danger to the native pride
Of a land where dreams make the economy.
Like tourists, dreams distort the things they buy
And float as easy currency, until
There is no talking to the native heart.
Nightly descending through the baroque cloud
That decorates these hills, riding on air,
Thousands arrive by dream at their desire.

One of the last kings sold the sandalwood
To buy a fleet. For every ship, they filled

An excavation dug to match the hull.
You can see these to this day — volcanic soil
Falls chunk by chunk into the phantom holds.
It rains at night. The trees the old king sold
Do not grow back. The islands have their perils
Which if you do not feel, no one can tell you.

This is another meaning for *aloha,*
A greeting as ambiguous as the place:
Not a promiscuous welcome to all strangers,
But what is more hospitable than that,
Warning of taboos and a hundred dangers —
Whether to you, you must decide alone.
And if it is not safe to come here yet,
One of the things *aloha* means is: wait.

A place to live when you are reconciled
To beauty and unafraid of time.
(They languish, abstract, when no more opposed.)
A place to earn in more chastising climates
Which teach us that our destinies are mild
Rather than fierce as we had once supposed,
And how to recognize the peril of calm,
Menaced only by surf and flowers and palms.

From *The Open Sea and Other Poems* by William Meredith (New York, Alfred A. Knopf, Inc., 1958). This poem first appeared in *Poetry,* March, 1953.

# SUKIYAKI ON THE KONA COAST

May Sarton, poet and novelist, remained in Hawaii for three months during 1957. With her companion, Cora Dubois, a noted social anthropologist, she explored out-of-the-way districts that tourists seldom find and talked with the island people of various races. In the following perceptive article Miss Sarton, besides describing a remarkable dinner, introduces us to an American Japanese family on the Kona Coast of the island of Hawaii. The father and son portrayed, secure in filial regard and confidently in control of their future, are representative citizens of the Fiftieth State.

Born in Belgium in 1912, daughter of George Sarton, the eminent historian of science, May Sarton came to America when her family was driven out by the German invasion of World War I. After a career in the theater she turned to literature, and is the author of several volumes of distinguished poetry and fiction.

THE SINGLE IMAGE THAT WILL BEST BRING BACK FOR ME THE peculiar pleasure of that evening on the Kona coast of the island of Hawaii is an incongruous one — my friend and I trying to climb the wall of a room empty except for us and the lizards we were trying to catch. They gathered round the horizontal light fixture over a great window that might have been plate glass but was actually open onto the Pacific Ocean, and thus we could get leverage on the lintel, placing one foot on the sill. Of course we were trying to capture lightning, as elusive as thought itself.

In the end it was we, hanging precariously there, who were caught by our polite Japanese host, who did not betray the slightest surprise to see two middle-aged haoles, or mainlanders, in this undignified position. He was bringing us coffee, the final ingredients of a remarkable dinner. We got down rather sheepishly and tried to be properly serious, for we had been in the middle of a conversation with him.

Outside we could hear the incessant lapse and fall of the ocean breaking over the reef. Two dilapidated palms were outlined against a sky that was just turning black after a long cloudless red-gold sunset. Every now and then a bard dove gave its plaintive, flutelike trill. Every now and then the palms clattered like paper in the breeze.

We were on the largest of those extinct volcanoes which sit in the middle of the Pacific, the result of quite recent explosions as geologic time goes, and which still pant now and then like whales troubled in sleep, and tremble; and as late as 1955 saw rivers of burning lava run ravaging down to the sea. We had that day walked in forests of huge tree ferns and we had crossed frozen stretches of lava. This sterile substance was the foundation under all we had seen; no single plant, no tree, no bird but had been brought here from somewhere else, far away, the coconuts floated two thousand miles or more, the seed of a flower carried in a bird's craw.

These islands, as they slowly greened over, had attracted human migrants in waves, first the Polynesians bringing taro, dogs, bananas in their canoes and setting up the primitive principalities and powers of what eventually became Hawaiian royalty; the whalers, the sandalwood merchants, the missionaries, the sugar planters and ranchers, the Chinese and Japanese traders and laborers, and finally the tourists. We were among the last to come, and we would not be staying long. But on this evening we felt the enchantment and the peril of living on the island volcano, born in fire, flowering, and slowly dying in an illimitable relentless blue of sea and sky.

An hour before, we had been sitting in the cocktail bar of one of the big hotels, looking out on a swimming pool and at two soft white American men playing shuffleboard. The hotels might be ocean liners, their verandas decks. The same people — or people who seemed interchangeable — inhabited them season after season, changing as little as the sea urchins, purple, white, and black, we had found that morning in a sea pool, making a sort of hotel out of a piece of hole-indented lava. We looked back across the half mile we had just traveled and it seemed a continent away.

It had happened by the merest chance. Driving along the coast that morning, looking for a place to swim, we had noticed a faded sign announcing *sukiyaki* dinners by appointment, and pointing down a rough dirt road in the middle of dense keawe brush. On impulse we turned in, bumping and bumped along till we came to a rough clearing, where we saw a new Ford and a couple of sleeping mongrel dogs. The ocean was hidden by a series of one-story wooden buildings, more like shacks, somehow welded together. A few papaya trees, banana plants, and coconut palms stood about casually among piles of rubbish and the creeping lantana that flows out over every waste place unless the morning-glories have already taken over. There was no sign of anything resembling a restaurant, and no human being appeared when we slammed the car door and walked gingerly past one of the dogs who woke up to growl.

We had to shout "Is anybody home?" a couple of times before a middle-aged Japanese woman came to the door, but she was evidently at a loss in English. She called back into the recesses of the house and finally a young man with black hair standing straight up on his head came out. Yes, they could serve us a dinner at seven that evening, he said, but with such a dead-pan expression that it was impossible to guess whether ours was an exceptional visitation or the routine thing.

At seven that evening we drove back in the fading light, wondering what we had got ourselves in for. This time we were greeted by an older boy, perhaps twenty, in an immaculate pair of khaki pants and bright-flowered Hawaiian shirt. He led us down a passage and around a corner, up some rickety steps, and finally into a bare room, furnished simply with two straight

chairs and a table. One wall was open air, looking out over
the ocean, the sunset, and in the immediate foreground a large
cement platform smoothed down over piles of lava rubble,
standing out to sea like a wharf. The table was set with three
bowls at each place, napkins, chopsticks, a bottle of soy sauce.
That was all.

In this atmosphere, plain to the point of poverty, restful by
its very absence of decoration, we stood in the paneless window
feeling the soft evening air on our faces, and talked with our
host's son, for so he told us he was, introducing his father
proudly as a son should, treating him like a great actor who
would not, of course, appear in the first few moments: "My
father is the chef." As the boy looked out onto the stark landscape of cement and lava he was obviously visualizing a scene
that was vivid in his imagination. The building of the platform, he informed us, represented the first arduous step toward
the creation of a real restaurant here. "And when I get out of
the Army," he said, "we'll be able to go ahead."

The slim line of his body enhanced by bare feet, his relaxed
posture against the lintel, his flowered shirt, and his easy grace
in talking to strangers seemed far from the usual image of a
GI, but these islanders are remarkable for their social ease and
personal dignity. He told us that he was home on furlough
after a "terrible" winter in Maine. "I thought I would die of
the cold, forty below once."

He had paid for the flight home rather than hang around
bumming free rides, for that would have taken nearly a week.
Now the precious month was nearly gone; in a few days he
would have to go back to the mainland and ship out to Japan.
The Army was making a cosmopolitan of him (how casually he
could speak of New York!), but it had given him also, clearly,
a renewed sense of loyalty to his family and of love for this
island. "I could not live anywhere else." I asked if he had
relatives in Japan. "A few cousins perhaps, no one close."

He seemed curiously uneager for this experience ahead, one
for which I myself envied him. His mother, he told us, though

born in Honolulu like his father, had gone back to the home country as a child and thus, he explained, had learned no English, could neither read nor write. His younger brother wanted to be a teacher and perhaps would go to the mainland to study — but they all wanted to stay here, and were involved in life on the island, each in his own way. "I have a little sister, too, seven years old," he said checking a smile, suddenly shy, as if she were a rather particular joy, one perhaps not to be shared. He was an entrepreneur, a man of big dreams who would see that they were realized. He was, one might say, the motive power of the family, and his father was the artist, the man of skills.

"My father will come soon," he announced, as if he sensed that the moment had arrived for the star's entrance onto the stage. As a matter of fact, the bare room was rather like a stage, and our host now stepped onto it with a distinct flourish. He wore a chef's round white cap, and bore in his hands the small stove and utensils for making *sukiyaki;* he was followed at a discreet distance by his wife, who carried various bowls of ingredients. He greeted us with a smile of authority and graciousness and bade us take our places.

The GI son now made a discreet withdrawal, to reappear with a series of dishes which he placed before us. There was a plate of what looked like rather uninteresting noodles but turned out to be a delicious crab-and-noodle salad; our delight was such that our host asked if he might taste it himself. "For that is my wife's doing," he said, "and I myself do not know what she has made for you."

There was a long boat-shaped dish upon which lay dark pink oval slices of raw fish in a basket of shredded green leaves, a delicacy new to me. There was a plate of cucumber salad, and the inevitable bowl of soy sauce with white radish sliced into it. We sat down to this feast, not concealing our pleasure, while our host stood at the end of the table, smiling upon us like a beneficent god.

He had a lean dried-out brown face, thin iron-strong arms

that showed below a short-sleeved cotton shirt, and kind, shrewd eyes. Evidently he regarded the serving of a meal as a performance and our appreciation of it as an accolade.

While we ate he talked, introducing the next scene of this meal that was also a play with a deprecatory description of his fishing that morning. "I got only two small Kona crabs," he said, "but if you would like them . . ." Two crabs appeared on the table as if he had clapped his hands. They were pink and white, about five inches across; we picked them up to admire them and he came over to show us just how to cut them open. They tasted fresh and clear as the day itself. Meanwhile his wife had appeared shyly in the doorway and murmured something in Japanese.

"Perhaps you would like to taste some of my wife's abalone soup as well?"

Indeed we would. Two bowls of soup were added to the congregation of dishes already on the table. Every now and then the little girl, with very bright eyes, made a brief appearance in the doorway, but vanished if one of us noticed her there. Every now and then my friend and I exchanged a look of delight, of complicity, in the occasion. Meanwhile the preparations for *sukiyaki* were going forward at the other end of the table.

"Yes," our host told us proudly, "this is island beef. You will find it very tasty." He lifted the veined red slivers into the sauce, one by one, and added mushrooms and scallions like an alchemist. A delicious fume began to rise from the pan. He looked up with a smile, enjoying our anticipation.

"We usually serve twenty people here in an evening," he said casually. "Clubs make a reservation and often we put the stoves on each table, and let the customers be their own cooks."

"They must be good at it," I ventured.

"They think they are." He smiled the smile of the professional, and moved the various ingredients in the pan deftly around. A big bowl of rice was laid on the table. The great moment, the climax of the play, was drawing near. But we had not as yet mentioned anything to drink. Now that we had established ourselves as connoisseurs (at least my friend could do so, for she has lived in the East and uses chopsticks with agility), we felt we might. Tea, perhaps?

"I thought you might like a little warm sake," he said happily, as if we had picked up the right cue. "I am not supposed to serve liquor, but never mind." And soon the small cups appeared and a pot of the slightly bittersweet drink.

"But you must hold out your cup to me," he told us, realizing that our pouring out for ourselves was a lapse in manners we would not have wished to make had we known better. He filled the cups solemnly, and we drank.

The slight tension of preparing the *sukiyaki* over, our host visibly relaxed while we ate it. "When my boy comes out of the Army we shall get started here, have a real restaurant. You must come back then, when we have twenty tables outside, and an orchestra."

The sun had gone down while we talked, and we looked out into the darkness where the dream grew big. But we did not say how glad we were to be here before it came true and our private play turned into a public performance.

"May I take a little bowl of *sukiyaki* to my daughter?" he asked when he saw that there was far more than we could eat. "She is very fond of it before she goes to bed."

He came back and we talked of the big issue in the air — statehood for the Territory — about to come up again before Congress.

"Twenty years ago, it must have been, when Roosevelt was president, we voted on this question, 'Yes' or 'No.' And everyone voted 'Yes.' A long time," he said.

There had been the war, of course, when the Nisei from these islands volunteered by the hundreds for the Army, and proved once and for all where they stood. They were too large a minority, too closely interwoven with the island economy, to be persecuted, as our Nisei on the mainland had been persecuted after Pearl Harbor. Here the war had left no such scars. It had consolidated all the races on the islands as Hawaiians. And now that the Territory had gone Democratic in the

1954 elections, the Japanese were beginning to come into political power. We thought of these things as we sat talking to this man so fully master of his family and of his fate, so confident of his future, "when my boy comes out of the Army."

The moment of silence had arrived that follows on any really good meal, the silence that is the final applause. We took out cigarettes.

"Tea? Coffee?" he asked.

I longed for a cup of coffee but hesitated; it was hardly in the tradition. But fortunately we did ask for coffee, for our host beamed.

"People like my coffee," he said modestly. It was truly his, for he told us he had grown it himself.

I looked at the thin man standing so proudly before us, smiling, and realized that although he worked in a hotel all day, he also managed to find time to catch the fish and crabs we had just eaten, and to pick, roast, and grind the coffee we were about to taste, as well as to cook meals for twenty of an evening and to rear a loyal family.

Our host went out to brew the coffee, and for the first time we noticed the lizards on the wall. The lights had come on, and the lizards had come to bask in the warmth of their artificial sun, immobile until a shadow came near, then moved lightning-swift, impossible to catch.

"Geckos," our host said when he came back and found us spread-eagled on the wall. "But you'll never catch one!"

We felt like children who have been given a party and now are behaving a bit rowdily at the end. We sat down chastened to taste the home-grown coffee, and found it excellent.

"But how do you find time?" we asked.

"My wife helps," he said, "and the children, when there is nothing else to do." He managed to get enough out of his few acres to take care of all his customers and have plenty to spare.

When we returned to our hotel with its balcony that looked out over the reefs and reverberated each time one of the big combers rolled up and broke in a loud peal of thunder, we felt loath to turn in on the *House Beautiful* studio couches, with a big modern lamp standing between them. We sat on the balcony for a long time, watching the combers, lit up by a spotlight from the hotel garden, rise in a marvelous curve, fall, and break into foam.

From *The Reporter,* June 27, 1957.

KATHRYN HULME

# FATHER DAMIEN'S VILLAGE

Kathryn Hulme, author of the widely read novel *The Nun's Story*, went to Hawaii in 1958 to gather material for a book about her grandfather, who for many years was a captain of ships that plied between San Francisco and Honolulu. Before returning to her home in California Miss Hulme visited Kalaupapa, the isolated leper colony on the island of Molokai. Conditions there, she discovered, have greatly changed since the time of Father Damien, the Belgian priest whose selfless devotion to the lepers and subsequent death from leprosy made him known the world over as the Martyr of Molokai. She found a peaceful New England-like village, where, thanks to modern drugs, many of the patients can now expect a permanent cure.

WHEN I FIRST FLEW OVER MOLOKAI, THE OLD BATTLEGROUND of Father Damien, and heard the airline stewardess say, "The Hansen's disease settlement," as she pointed down to the peninsula of Kalaupapa, I thought she was showing off her medical vocabulary. Most of the passengers gazing momentarily at the surf-fringed peninsula never realized they were flying over the most famous and once most isolated sick colony in the Pacific. Nor did the stewardess explain that Hansen's disease means leprosy. Seen from aloft, the Kalaupapa peninsula on Molokai, home of the lepers since 1865, looked like a scarred thumb thrust into the creamy line of smashing surf.

Although medical opinion now generally concurs in the belief that the Biblical scourge described in the Old Testament is not the Hansen's disease which we know today, it is nevertheless certain that man's first fear of leprosy was crystallized by the thirteenth chapter of Leviticus, wherein the Lord spoke to Moses and Aaron, telling them what to do when "a man shall have in the skin of his flesh a rising, a scab or a bright spot." Segregation was made the law for lepers from that time onward. More than twenty centuries had to wear away before the causative bacillus of the disease was found, in 1874, by a young Norwegian physician named Gerhard Armauer Hansen. Some seventy years later, in the early 1940's, the sulfone drugs were discovered, along with their peculiar properties of clearing up the leper's visible skin ulcerations and, eventually, rendering him noncontagious, therefore free to return to society. In 1949, the Territory of Hawaii, by legislative act, changed the name of leprosy to Hansen's disease, as the medical profession had long been calling it.

I had not planned to visit Molokai when I flew to the Hawaiian Islands. But a letter of introduction which I carried made my detour to Molokai compelling. It was addressed to a noted doctor, scholar, and writer, resident of the islands for more than thirty-five years, who was stationed in the Molokai settlement in the 1920's and knew all of its history before and since. As soon as he learned that I and my traveling companion, a nurse, were interested in leprosy, he fired us up for an immediate trip. He loaned us out-of-print books on leprosy, missionary and medical diaries, memoirs and current pamphlets. Finally he urged us to visit the Hansen's disease institution on the outskirts of Honolulu, Hale Mohalu. There since 1949, when the Navy released this extensive WAVES barracks to the territory, newly discovered cases have been sent for treatment with the new sulfones and for rehabilitation training to prepare them for their certain return to society. They will return after an average stay of five years; less when the disease is detected early.

I read avidly, beginning with Dr. A. A. Mouritz's first great study of the disease in the Pacific, entitled *The Path of the Destroyer;* I read Ernie Pyle's letters written for the Honolulu *Advertiser* in 1937, and Robert Louis Stevenson's letters from his eight-day stay in the settlement and his famous white-heat defense of Father Damien after the ill-judged, inaccurate defamation by the Rev. Dr. McEwen Hyde. I read cool medical pamphlets, Brother Dutton's memoirs and letters, Edward Clifford's account of his long friendship with Father Damien, Charles W. Stoddard's *Diary of a Visit to Molokai in 1884.*

Ernie Pyle wrote in a mood of pity and hopelessness. "Kalaupapa," he said in his first article, "has been dramatized and fictionalized until it is known all over the world today as a spot of veiled mysticism, a cursed place where men are banished to await death and a place where martyrs sacrifice their lives in a beautiful attenuation of human suffering." But Kalaupapa is no longer "a cursed place." In the Hansen's disease institution of Hale Mohalu, a half hour by bus from the center of Honolulu, out where the winds from Pearl Harbor blow fresh in your face, we saw in a small rubber-capped bottle an average daily dose of Promin, the derivative of the sulfone drug that is injected intravenously, and in other small bottles the sulfone tablets, Diasone and Promizole, which are taken by mouth. We were looking at substances, tea-yellow in liquid form, snow-white in tablet form, which had made obsolete such literary expressions as "walking sepulchers."

The medical director of Hale Mohalu is a woman, slight in stature, with blue eyes, wavy brown hair, and serious mouth which pushes dimples into her cheeks when she smiles. She takes up each small bottle and tells you how the medicine is administered daily to every patient, how most respond better to the tablet than to the intravenous form, how within several weeks to six months after a new case is started on the daily dosage the clinical response to it may be seen with your own eyes. Open sores and red spots disappear; lepromatous lumps start to subside. The doctor shows you pictures taken before and after. She talks in the quiet uninflected voice of the dedicated worker, making all this magic sound not only believable but commonplace.

She escorts you through her extensive domain: operating,

dental, and X-ray rooms (during the years while patients are under treatment for Hansen's disease, their other maladies must be cared for as well); through hospital wards and clubrooms, a new movie theater, the kitchens and dining rooms with tables seating four to six persons, each table with its central cluster of sugar, catsup, and mustard containers, all neat as a pin. On one table is a small object folded in a twist of paper. The doctor explains that some patient probably forgot to take his daily tablet during the preceding meal; the patient-waitress had left it at his place where he will find it next time he comes to table. They help each other not to forget.

Vegetable and flower gardens maintained by patients with gardening experience surround the barracks with rows of lettuce, an orchard of papayas, flaming red ti leaves, and taro for their basic poi food. There are workshops to encourage vocational interests: automotive repair, sewing, ceramics, weaving, electrical repair. The habit of working must not be lost during the years of isolation. Every patient in this place will eventually be returned to society to earn his living and pay his taxes. Unless, as the doctor explains, the patient finds the prejudices of "outside" too tough to buck and the baseless skepticism about his uncontagious state too unbearable. This is still a major problem — to educate the outside to receive the permanently released and give them jobs.

The younger released find their way back into normal society more easily than the old. They still have family connections to aid them and, more importantly, they are less blemished when released because the disease was caught early. The disfigured nose, the contracted fingers of a hand with one or more fingers gone are recognized all through the islands for what they once signified, and the age-old recoil works in the beholder like an involuntary reflex. But another modern miracle, the doctor explains, is coming more and more into use to eradicate the telltale signs of the disease — plastic surgery.

The doctor leads you to a visitors' washroom after you have toured her establishment. You wash your hands thoroughly and dry them on paper towels. Decades of research have proved that leprosy is acquired by direct contact either with the diseased person or with the things he has touched, but only after long and intimate contact. "We call it a household disease," the doctor says. The common sleeping mats, the common poi bowl of the Hawaiians were ideal transmitters. We ask her, as she scrubs beside us, if she ever worries about her daily contact with active cases. She gives us a calm glance.

"If I showed fear, I could do nothing with my nurses. No, I'm not afraid. But I have a very healthy respect for *any* disease. I take every reasonable precaution and urge them to do the same." Unobtrusively she teaches you to do likewise. "Please let me open the doors for you on your way out," she says. You don't notice until you have passed through several swinging doors that she has a piece of Kleenex covering the fingers that push them open for you. She accompanies you to the gate which is never locked, remarking in passing that the patients could walk out into the town at any moment, but they never do.

To the left of the unlocked gate was a long porchlike enclosure, roofed, open on the street side and screened on the side facing the isolation grounds. On a table running the length of it five or six fat brown babies were lying on their backs, gurgling over their milk bottles or simply gurgling with contentment as the women beside them patted their stomachs. The women talked with the fathers of the babies who were on the isolation side of the screen. The babies had been removed from the contagion at birth and were being raised outside by their own mothers or by foster mothers if both parents were inside. This is another aspect of Hansen's disease, perhaps the strangest. (Even Father Damien in his time could not believe it possible.) Children born of leprous parents never contract the disease if removed at birth, a positive indication that it is not hereditary.

We had chanced upon the visiting hours when the isolated fathers could view their offspring. Not a finger poked or waggled through the screen as the infants were held up to be admired. The give-and-take from both sides was light and easy, sometimes laced with laughter. The multiple vowels of the Hawaiian tongue made it sound a bit like song.

"Don't forget what you have seen here when you fly to Molokai," the doctor said at parting. "Remember — over there we have many of our older cases, unfortunates whose malady was far advanced before the era of the sulfones. You will see some disfiguring, crippling, blindness, quite different from the average of our patients here."

The plane for Molokai takes off daily at noon from Honolulu airport, flying time twenty-eight minutes. Our pilot was a young man in a flowered sport shirt. He had that day one other passenger besides us, a released patient who sat in the rear seat of the small cabin among stacked cartons of perishables being flown over to Kalaupapa. We passed over Waikiki beach, then Diamond Head, and in no time saw the western tip of Molokai across the channel, flat as its surrounding ocean and discernible, at first, only for the fringe of surf that outlined it. Around the point, on Molokai's northern side, the pali which becomes a two-thousand-foot isolation wall behind the settlement of Kalaupapa began its rise. Back of it we saw the pineapple fields sloping southward to the tourist spots of Molokai: the Halawa Valley waterfalls, the famous stone fish ponds of Hawaiian kings, and Kaunakakai, home of Kamehameha V. Then Kalaupapa was beneath our wings, a finger of brown and green land outlined in black and white by its lava-stone beaches edged with foam.

"I'll be back for you around four thirty," said the pilot. "You'll have a longer visit than the regular tour. There's your car for you at the airport. It takes about two hours to drive around the peninsula, then you'll have the rest of the time for visiting." A church was below us. "Father Damien's," said our pilot. "That's Kalawao below, the first settlement. Nobody living there now." He swung out to sea to come in for the landing. "We're flying right over a basking whale," he said. "Look out my side."

But we were looking at the grassy airstrip below, at the

small open-fronted terminal coming so quickly into focus that we could see the rail running down its middle and read the signs to right and left — "Visitors" on one side, "Patients" on the other. Two lonely-looking figures waited for the plane to taxi back to where they stood — Father Gustave, whom we had asked to meet, and a young Hawaiian man, our driver for the day, a permanently discharged patient who had chosen to remain in the settlement to help sightseers such as ourselves.

On the Father's advice we decided to take the ride around the peninsula first. After lunch we would rejoin him at his house to visit the Franciscan sisters in the infirmary and in the Bishop Home for female patients. Our driver ushered us into a polished blue sedan which, he informed us, was never used to transport patients but was for visitors only. He owned a second car that he used for driving his friends about. The majority of the inhabitants, he said, were car owners and, as we could see, they were also owners of TV sets. Imposing TV aerials were visible among the trees shading the small village of Kalaupapa ahead of us.

Our driver heard our exclamation of surprise. "Oh, we have some radio hams here too," he said. "We often go to their homes to listen to them talking to hams all over the world. Surprising the things you hear. Our hams often handle last-minute communications between the division's medical in Honolulu and here."

"Here" had become abruptly a village street, such as you might expect to find in New England, with small white cottages set back in gardens behind white picket fences, and the sound of the sea just a step away. Only the tropical trees and flowering shrubs in the well-tended gardens — hibiscus, plumeria, oleander, jasmine — belied the New England atmosphere. There were the same tidy appearance of grassy lawns beneath shade trees, the same somnolence undisturbed by children's voices, the same feeling that only old or ill folk lived here now, drowsing behind their shutters while their innumerable cats and dogs drowsed amid the orchid pots on their small private porches. This is the palimpsest. Layers of heartbreak history lie beneath the pleasant surface story, so effectively buried now that only with great force of imagination can you see that Kalaupapa landing as it was in 1873, when Father Damien came to the treeless peninsula.

We drove through the sleepy streets of Kalaupapa to register in the administration building, a verandaed cottage like all the other dwellings of the settlement. Inside was a business office, large and efficient-looking, whose smiling employees were patients. The register showed few visitors from the outside; a public health nurse from Chicago had signed in the day before. A blackboard gave the population figures of the settlement for that day:

| | |
|---|---|
| Registered at Kalaupapa: | 226 |
| Active patients: | male 49, female 28 |
| Arrested cases: | male 95, female 54 |
| In home and infirmary: | 67 |
| In outcottages: | 136 |
| Total present: | 203 |
| Total absent: | 23 |

Some of the absentees we had seen at Hale Mohalu, reporting there for special surgery, optical or dental work. The others, arrested cases, were probably visiting friends on other islands or had "gone topside," our driver informed us. "Topside" was the way the Kalaupapans referred to the plateau of Molokai which lay above their rock-walled pali.

The two-thousand-foot cliff, blue-green with its dense vegetation, dominates every view from the settlement unless you turn your back to it deliberately and look seaward. A perilous foot trail slants up it to where there used to be a locked gate at the top. Clouds seem to spring directly from just behind its stony crest, as if manufactured there in some colossal caldron. The primeval cliff stops all thought of exit from the base of the peninsula as effectively as does the surf breaking against black lava beaches around its other three sides.

In ten minutes you can drive through just about every street in Kalaupapa, but we took it more slowly, stopping often to photograph beautiful little private gardens or public green-swards under curving coco palms. There were so few figures in the landscape that we did not have to worry about the official request that no pictures be taken of patients. The few patients we saw were either working in offices or gardens or motoring about on mysterious errands which could be guessed at only when you saw fish nets hanging from the car windows.

Our driver chatted about the advantages of marrying in the town. Then you could sign up for a cottage of your own and get it, eventually, when its present tenants died or departed. You could do your own housekeeping and cooking instead of living in the unit homes and eating in community dining rooms. Many patients had married, since admission to Kalaupapa, in order to qualify for a private dwelling. He showed us the new-est married couples' homes near the foot of the pali — trim small tract-type houses, each with its own front gate and garden, each with its own landscaping touch. One had brightly painted coconuts suspended all around its view porch, a variation of the painted-gourd decoration popular in certain southern Califor-nia bungalow sections.

Around the unit homes which house unmarried men and women and the more disabled patients, the number of dogs and cats multiplies. "They take the place of children with our peo-ple," said our driver. "You know we have no children here."

The dogs and cats slept side by side, their ancient grudge for-gotten in this village of no visible strife where every need of its slowly diminishing population is taken care of. The driver tells us that deaths are far-spaced nowadays, what with the care the people are receiving. Old age or illnesses natural to old age are the most frequent causes of death. They toll a bell when one of the patients dies, as they used to do in Father Damien's time, when death was a daily visitor.

The driver went slowly past England's rose marble column in memory of Father Damien and past the white marble memor-ial to Mother Marianne, who came with her Franciscan nuns to help Father Damien in his last days and to continue the work for another thirty years until her death in the settlement in

1918. We stopped to look at the government store. Several cars were parked in front of its veranda. The customers — housekeeping patients who may draw ten dollars' worth of provisions each week — came out laughing just like any bargain-happy shoppers from any community store. The illusion of normal living is so pervasive everywhere that it takes a few moments to comprehend an occasional fact the driver gives — as, for example, passing the post office, he tells you that all mail is fumigated before transmission to the outside world.

Work, we learned, was optional for those physically fit; for services to the community, they were paid wages ranging from fifty to seventy cents an hour on jobs averaging from four to six hours daily. The driver estimated that about one hundred were employed at the time of our visit — a bit better than half the total patient population. Considering that all patients are paid a small monthly allowance during their compulsory isolation in Kalaupapa and that they are housed, fed, and clothed at government expense, whether they choose to work or not, these statistics of employment are a triumphant sign of the will of the people to be like other men, able to buy radios, cars, and TV sets if they wish, or better clothing than charity provides. Many are saving against the day when they will be declared medically free of contagion, able to return to normal society.

"We can average about sixty dollars a month," said the driver. "Some of our workers have saved up quite a little sock over the years." He detoured to show us the house of a patient who owns a thousand chickens and supplies the settlement with eggs and fowls. The chickens, I noted, were housed off the ground in wire-floored runs with roofs over them, just as they are in any modern big chicken business. Patients also own the cattle, several hundred head of them, which provide the beef for the settlement. At roundup time all the able-bodied men pitch in to help the cattlemen. The driver then turned into the rural road leading across the peninsula to Kalawao, three miles distant from Kalaupapa.

Kalawao, the site of the first leper settlement on the penin-

sula, is a name to reckon with. It was the dateline address of
Dr. Mouritz's first official medical reports to the Board of
Health in Honolulu on the situation of the leprous outcasts
of Molokai and of Father Damien's voluminous letters to the
Honolulu authorities. Charitable societies all over the world
began to hear of his voluntary exile with his leprous "children"
after the Queen Regent of the islands, Liliuokalani, decorated
him as a Knight of the Royal Order of Kalakaua in September,
1881, eight years after his arrival on Molokai and eight years
before his death from the disease whose devastation he was
trying to alleviate.

Kalawao is now uninhabited, a place of remembrance. Yellow
day lilies grow rampant beside the low lava-stone walls that
once marked the roadway's entrance to the original settlement.
Brown cattle graze in the meadows around the Protestant
church of Siloam, built in 1871, with its gabled porch and
pointed white wood spire diminutive against the rearing background of the pali. Father Damien's church of St. Philomena
lies a few paces nearer to the sea. Its square stone bell tower is
silent these days except twice a year, when memorial Masses are
celebrated there. Beside the black marble cross marking Dami-
en's original grave to the right of his church are a dozen or so
gray sepulchers with headstones all facing out to sea. Here lie his
first helpers in the task that confronted him after his arrival in
May, 1873.

The lava subsoil in which he helped to hack their graves is
covered with lawn now, and coco palms bend over it to make
arched frames for the view of the blue Pacific beyond. The
greensward continues unbroken to the edge of rugged lava
cliffs that drop in rough black chunks to the creaming surf
below. This wide sloping greensward beyond the two churches
is named Baldwin Park. The ambulatory patients of Kalaupapa
come here often on Sundays for special festivals and barbecues.
Church services are held in the small pavilion erected on the
highest point, where Catholic, Protestant, and Mormon clergy
take their turns on the festival days.

The trade winds drive hard upon you as you stand gazing at

the wild and lonely seascape. Imagination strives to revive, and
cannot, the terrible scenes that took place on this land's end
when a thousand hopeless sufferers peopled it. It is all so quiet
now, so exceedingly beautiful with its flowered meadows running down to the sea. In the wooded folds of the towering
cliffs live the only creatures continuous since Father Damien's
time — the wild goats. Nowadays, says our driver, the livelier
citizens of Kalaupapa sometimes climb those cliffs and capture
a baby goat, which they bring back to the settlement and domesticate.

The village of Kalaupapa seemed somehow much busier
when we returned to it from the memory garden of Kalawao.
A maintenance crew of stalwart patients was trimming palm
trees in a shady street. We ate our lunch of hard-boiled eggs
and bananas on the porch of a visitors' cottage near the landing.
There was a noonday hum in the air, and occasionally we heard
the sound of dishes. Behind the screened windows of nearby
cottages the more helpless patients were being fed by their
housemates.

It was wise to leave the visit to the infirmary and the Bishop
Home until the last. Father Gustave received us in his cottage
and told us, by way of introduction, that he was the first
Belgian priest to be assigned to Kalaupapa since 1897. He had
been just two months in his new post and was still learning his
way around the parish, which, apart from its singular location,
had certain health restrictions; he was not, for instance, permitted to enter into any active patient's house. He did, however,
visit every Catholic patient daily in the infirmary and the
Home, bringing them Holy Communion and what spiritual
solace he could.

On the way to the infirmary, we paid our respects to his
church just across the quadrangle of lawn on which his cottage
fronted. It was like any other small well-kept parish church save
for one detail. It had no confession boxes. The confessional was
a frame of wooden lattice set up just behind the communion
rail at the foot of the main aisle. "Easy for the blind to get to it

without needing anyone to lead them," said the Father. Many of his sighted parishioners would have preferred the privacy of a closed confessional, but as long as there were blind among them who knew their way to this familiar old setup, he supposed that it would remain. The racks behind every pew, overflowing with well-thumbed missals, testified to his large and faithful flock. We had no awareness of segregation in his church until the Father caught us kneeling in the regular pews, and gestured to four short rows up front on a side aisle which were reserved for the nuns and for visitors.

Had there been a patient in the church, he explained, that patient would doubtless have done the same thing. It was extraordinary how watchful they were over the healthy who came to visit them. He related an event of his first days when he was making the acquaintance of his people. He was attending a barbecue, playing cards with three patients, of whom one was a temporarily arrested case. This man kept a small pad of wet paper beside his place, on which he moistened his thumb when his turn came to deal the cards. Though he no longer carried the contagion, he took no chances in the presence of a newcomer.

"You've probably noticed their charitable watchfulness over you," said Father Gustave, "when you've impulsively extended your hand upon introduction. They have such gracious ways of avoiding the proffered handshake." We recalled a young woman in the administration building to whom we had been introduced. Now we understood why she had excused herself from taking our hand, remarking that her own was soiled from the mimeograph work she was doing.

In the infirmary, and later in the Home, we visited some of the older patients whose malady was far advanced before the era of the sulfones. These were the living witnesses to what leprosy, long unattended and unchecked, can do to its victims. Some of these advanced cases had been there for a decade or more; most of them would probably die of old age, thanks to the great care given to them now.

For us, their physically devastated bodies were like the liv-

ing artifacts of Kalaupapa's yesterday. They were reminders of
the time when all who were cast upon this island became sightless, fingerless, sometimes throatless (but tracheotomies permit
them to breathe now); when this was the fate of nearly everyone in whom the corruptive Mycobacterium was found. These
cases, I am sure, are not for the average tourist to see; many
indeed would not wish to. But for those who do there comes a
terrific upsurge of faith in the progress of mankind. The true
wonder of the peaceful, unscarred, New England-like village
outside the infirmary windows becomes overwhelmingly apparent here as you see what might have been, had generations
of medical men not had the courage to find a way to conquer
the dread disease.

The quiet nuns who accompanied us spoke up vivaciously in
the presence of their blind patients. Their familiar voices,
describing their visitors, brought to the ruined faces they addressed expressions which you must learn to call smiles here.
Their own smiles, framed in starchy coifs, had by contrast an
unearthly beauty as they bent over their charges to rearrange a
dress collar slightly askew or to pat a crippled hand outstretched
to them. You need see only one of these pre-sulfone-era patients
to understand the battle lines drawn up before so many areas
on our earth today, where — by current census — only some
10 per cent of the estimated four million victims of Hansen's
disease have been brought under care. The statistics of the
great leprosy foundations, national and international, come
alive in these quiet rooms with terrible urgency.

As we took our last walk through the settlement, we seemed
to be seeing it as Father Damien might have at that moment
— with a shock of thankful surprise that it was all so exceedingly peaceful now. The almost total absence of any sign of
suffering on the faces of his erstwhile "children," the sense of
hope pervading the efficient little community, the pride and
the privacy of these set-apart souls — all these things struck
with fresh wonder.

We said our real good-by to Molokai Ahina — Molokai the
Gray — from our plane aloft. There was no gray anywhere on

the Kalaupapa peninsula. The late afternoon sun turned the fronds of the coco palms to clusters of gold swords, which the trade winds seemed to be shaking at the purple pali. The sea around the bright finger of land "where martyrs live forever" was a deep delphinium blue.

From *The Atlantic Monthly*, November, 1958.

# ABRAHAM K. AKAKA

# STATEHOOD SERVICE AT KAWAIAHAO CHURCH, MARCH 13, 1959

News that the Congress of the United States had passed on March 12, 1959, an act enabling Hawaii to become the Fiftieth State was greeted in the islands by a spontaneous wave of joy. Many people gathered to give thanks in the old stone church in downtown Honolulu which had been erected by the early missionaries. Next day its pastor, the Reverend Dr. Abraham Kahikina Akaka (1917 — ) conducted a thanksgiving service in which he expressed so well the feeling of the Hawaiian people toward their new responsibilities that his speech was quickly printed and widely quoted.

Dr. Akaka was born in Honolulu of Chinese-Hawaiian parents, and won his degree at the University of Chicago. He prefers the simple title of *kahu* or "shepherd," which his Hawaiian congregation bestowed upon him when he first entered church work. His linking of the *aloha* spirit with the spirit of God is in keeping with the broad connotation the phrase holds for most Hawaiians.

"ONE NATION UNDER GOD, INDIVISIBLE, WITH LIBERTY AND JUSTICE for all" — these words have a fuller meaning for us all in Hawaii today. And we have gathered in this Mother Church of Hawaii, our Westminster Abbey of Hawaii, to give thanks to God, and to pray for His guidance and protection in the years ahead.

Our newspapers have been full of much valuable historical

data concerning Hawaii's development and growth and aspirations. I will keep the copies of these stories as long as I live, and for my children and grandchildren after them. For they have called to our minds the long train of those whose prayers and hopes and sacrifices through the years were fulfilled yesterday. There remains the formal expression of our people for statehood, and the entrance of our islands into the Union as a full-fledged member.

I would like to speak the message of *self-affirmation* this morning, that in the days ahead we take courage to be ourselves, to be the Aloha State.

On April 25, 1820, one hundred and thirty-nine years ago, the first Christian service of worship was conducted in Honolulu on this very ground. Like our Pilgrim Fathers who arrived at Plymouth, Massachusetts, in 1620, so did the fathers of a new era in Hawaii kneel in prayer to give thanks to God, who had seen them safely on their way after a long and trying voyage.

Gathered around the Reverend Hiram Bingham on April 25, 1820, here at Kawaiahao were a few of our *kupunas* [grandparents, ancestors] who had come out of curiosity. The text for the sermon of that day, though it was April and near Easter time, was from the Christmas story. And there our people heard these words for the first time: *"Mai makau oukou, no ka mea, eia hoi, ke hai aku nei au ia oukou i ka mea maikai, e olioli nui ai e lilo ana no na kanaka a pau. No ka mea, i keia la i hanau ai, ma ke kulanakauhale o Davida, he ola no oukou, oia ka mesia ka haku."* "Fear not, for behold, I bring you good tidings of great joy which shall be to all people. For unto you is born this day in the city of David a savior which is Christ the Lord."

Although our grandfathers did not realize it then, the hopes and fears of all their years through the next century and more were to be met in the meaning and power of those words, for from that beginning a new Hawaii was born. For through those words, our missionaries and people following them under God became the greatest single influence in Hawaii's whole development — politically, economically, educationally, socially, religiously — so that Hawaii's real preparation for statehood can be said to have begun truly on that day one hundred and thirty-nine years ago on this spot.

Yesterday when the first sound of firecrackers and sirens reached my ears, I was with the members of our Territorial Senate in the middle of the opening prayer for the day's session. How strange, and yet how fitting it was that the news should burst forth while we were in prayer together. Things had moved so fast. Our mayor, a few minutes before, asked if the church could be kept open, because he and others wanted to walk across the street to the sanctuary here for prayer when the news came. By the time I got back from the Senate, this sanctuary was well-nigh filled by people who happened to be near when the sirens started ringing — people from our government buildings nearby. And as we sang the great hymns of Hawaii and of our nation, and lifted up our voices in psalms and prayers, it seemed that the very walls of this church spoke of God's dealing with Hawaii in the past, of great events both spontaneous and planned that they had seen here. For the love and power of God has been a refuge and a guide for our people through the past century and more.

There are some of us to whom statehood brings great hopes; and there are some to whom statehood brings silent fears. One might say that the hopes and fears of Hawaii are met in statehood today. There are fears that statehood will motivate economic greed toward Hawaii, that it will turn Hawaii into a great big (as someone has said) spiritual junkyard filled with smashed dreams, worn-out illusions — that it will make us lonely, confused, insecure, empty, anxious, restless, disillusioned — a wistful people.

There is an old mele [chant] that reminds me of fears such as these, and the way God leads out of these fears. *"Haku'i i ka uahi o ka lua, pa i ka lani, haahaa Hawaii, moku o keawe i hanau ia . . . po puna, po hilo, po i ka uahi o kuu aina . . . ola ia kini, ke a mai la ke ahi."* "There is a fire underground, but the fire pit gives forth only smoke, smoke that bursts upward, touching the skies, and Hawaii is humbled beneath its darkness . . . it is night over Hawaii, night from the smoke of my land . . . but there is salvation for the people, for now the land is being lit by a great flame."

We need to see statehood as the lifting of the clouds of smoke, and the opportunity to affirm positively the basic Gospel of the Fatherhood of God and the brotherhood of man. We need to see that Hawaii has potential moral and spiritual contributions to make to our nation and world. The fears Hawaii may have are to be met by men and women who are living witnesses of what we really are in Hawaii, of the spirit of *aloha,* men and women who can help unlock the doors to the future by the guidance and grace of God.

Self-affirmation is the need of the hour. And we can affirm our being, what we really are, as the Aloha State by full participation in our nation and world. For any collective anxiety, the answer is collective courage. And the ground of that courage is God.

We do not understand the meaning of *aloha* until we realize its foundation in the power of God at work in the world. Since the coming of our missionaries in 1820, the name of God to our people has been *aloha.* One of the first sentences I learned from my mother in my childhood was this from Holy Scriptures: *"Aloha ke akua."* In other words, *aloha* is God. *Aloha* is the power of God seeking to unite what is separated in the world — the power that unites heart with heart, soul with soul, life with life, culture with culture, race with race, nation with nation. It is the power that can reunite where quarrel has brought separation; it is the power that reunites a man with himself when he has become separated from the image of God within.

Thus when a people or a person live in the spirit of *aloha,* they live in the spirit of God. And among such a people whose lives so affirm their inner being, we see the working of the

Scripture: "All things work together for good to them who love God. . . . From the *aloha* of God came his son that we might have life and that we might have it more abundantly."

*Aloha* consists of a new attitude of heart, above negativism and legalism. It is the unconditional desire to promote the true good of other people in a friendly spirit, out of a sense of kinship. *Aloha* seeks to do good to a person, with no conditions attached. We do not do good only to those who do good to us. One of the sweetest things about the love and *aloha* of God is that it welcomes the stranger and seeks his good. A person who has the spirit of *aloha* loves even when the love is not returned. And such is the love of God.

This is the meaning of *aloha*. I feel especially grateful that the discovery and development of our islands long ago was not couched in the context of an imperialistic and exploitive national power, but in the context of *aloha*. There is a very deep correlation between the charter under which the missionaries came — namely, "to preach the Gospel of Jesus Christ, to cover these islands with productive green fields, and to lift the people to a high state of civilization" — correlation between this fact, and the fact that Hawaii is not one of the trouble spots in the world today. *Aloha* does not exploit a people and keep them in ignorance and subservience. Rather it shares the sorrows and joys of people; it seeks to promote the true good of others.

Today, one of the deepest needs of mankind is the need to feel a sense of kinship one with another. Truly all mankind belongs together, for from the very beginning all mankind has been called into being, nourished, watched over by the love of God who is *aloha*. The real Golden Rule is *aloha*. This is the way of life we must affirm.

Let us affirm ever what we really are — for *aloha* is the spirit of God at work in you and in me and in the world, uniting what is separated, overcoming darkness and death, bringing new light and life to all who sit in the darkness of fear and the shadow of death, guiding the feet of mankind into the way of peace.

Thus may our becoming a state mean to the nation and world; and may it reaffirm that which was planted in us one hundred and thirty-nine years ago on this ground: "Fear not, for behold I bring you good tidings of great joy, which shall be to *all* people."

# ANCIENT HAWAII

MARTHA BECKWITH
Translator

# THE KUMULIPO

Suggesting comparison with the Hebrew *Genesis*, the Hawaiian
*Kumulipo* is a sacred creation chant and a genealogy of one of
the great *alii* families, traced from the beginning of the world.
An authentic primitive poem of more than two thousand lines,
it was carried in memory by one generation of court reciters to
another.

The selection that follows comprises the opening stanzas and
a refrain. It is from a modern translation, with an analytical
commentary, by Martha Beckwith. As read literally it "seems to
picture the rising of the land out of the fathomless depths of
the ocean. Along its shores the lower forms of life begin to gather,
and these are arranged as births from parent to child." Like most
Hawaiian poetry, however, it has meanings hidden in symbolic
language; and essentially "it is a birth chant, and procreation is
its theme."

Martha Warren Beckwith (1871–1959), who spent her childhood in Hawaii and as a young woman became an acknowledged
authority on Hawaiian folklore, was for many years a teacher
and research professor at Vassar College. Besides her edition of
*The Kumulipo,* she published numerous other studies on native
island literature, including a comprehensive survey of the subject,
*Hawaiian Mythology* (1940).

At the time when the earth became hot
At the time when the heavens turned about
At the time when the sun was darkened
To cause the moon to shine
The time of the rise of the Pleiades

The slime, this was the source of the earth
The source of the darkness that made darkness
The source of the night that made night
The intense darkness, the deep darkness
Darkness of the sun, darkness of the night
  Nothing but night


The night gave birth
Born was Kumulipo in the night, a male
Born was Poʻele in the night, a female
Born was the coral polyp, born was the coral, came forth
Born was the grub that digs and heaps up the earth, came
    forth
Born was his child an earthworm, came forth
Born was the starfish, his child the small starfish came forth
Born was the sea cucumber, his child the small sea cucumber
    came forth
Born was the sea urchin, the sea urchin tribe
Born was the short-spiked sea urchin, came forth
Born was the smooth sea urchin, his child the long-spiked came
    forth
Born was the ring-shaped sea urchin, his child the thin-spiked
    came forth
Born was the barnacle, his child the pearl oyster came forth
Born was the mother-of-pearl, his child the oyster came forth
Born was the mussel, his child the hermit crab came forth
Born was the big limpet, his child the small limpet came forth
Born was the cowry, his child the small cowry came forth
Born was the naka shellfish, the rock oyster his child came
    forth
Born was the drupa shellfish, his child the bitter white
  shellfish came forth
Born was the conch shell, his child the small conch shell came
    forth
Born was the nerita shellfish, the sand-burrowing shellfish his
    child came forth
Born was the fresh-water shellfish, his child the small
  fresh-water shellfish came forth

Born was man for the narrow stream, the woman for the broad
    stream
Born was the ekaha moss living in the sea
Guarded by the ekahakaha fern living on land
Darkness slips into light
Earth and water are the food of the plant
The god enters, man cannot enter
Man for the narrow stream, woman for the broad stream
Born was the tough sea-grass living in the sea
Guarded by the tough land-grass living on land

. . . . . .
*Refrain*
Man for the narrow stream, woman for the broad stream
Born was the hairy seaweed living in the sea
Guarded by the hairy pandanus vine living on land
Darkness slips into light
Earth and water are the food of the plant
The god enters, the man cannot enter

The man with the water gourd, he is a god
Water that causes the withered vine to flourish
Causes the plant top to develop freely
Multiplying in the passing time
The long night slips along
Fruitful, very fruitful
Spreading here, spreading there
Spreading this way, spreading that way
Propping up earth, holding up the sky
The time passes, this night of Kumulipo
    Still it is night

From *The Kumulipo: A Hawaiian Creation Chant,* translated and edited with
a commentary by Martha Warren Beckwith (Chicago, University of Chicago
Press, 1951).

N. B. EMERSON
Translator


# THE WATER OF KANE


One of the most skillful translators of native Hawaiian literature
was Dr. Nathaniel B. Emerson (1839–1915). Born at Wailua,
Oahu, of missionary parents, Emerson spent some years in the
United States as college student, soldier in the Civil War, medical
graduate, and practicing physician. After returning to Hawaii
in 1878 he served as inspector of lepers and devoted much time
to translation of Hawaiian works. Among these was David
Malo's *Hawaiian Antiquities*. Emerson's celebrated volume *Unwritten Literature of Hawaii: The Sacred Songs of the Hula*
(1909) presented the ancient chants in both Hawaiian and English. Another of his books, probably the finest literary treatment
in English of an extended, authentic Hawaiian myth, is *Pele
and Hiiaka* (1915), a retelling of the many legends about the
volcano goddess. He is most brilliant as a translator in "The
Water of Kane," one of the best Hawaiian meles, echoing the
pantheistic mysticism of the old Polynesian religion.


A query, a question,
I put to you:
Where is the water of Kane?
At the eastern gate
Where the sun comes in at Haehae;
There is the water of Kane.

A question I ask of you:
Where is the water of Kane?
Out there with the floating sun,

Where cloud-forms rest on ocean's breast,
Uplifting their forms at Nihoa,
This side the base of Lehua;
There is the water of Kane.

One question I put to you:
Where is the water of Kane?
Yonder on mountain peak,
On the ridges steep,
In the valleys deep,
Where the rivers sweep;
There is the water of Kane.

This question I ask of you:
Where, pray, is the water of Kane?
Yonder, at sea, on the ocean,
In the driving rain,
In the heavenly bow,
In the piled-up mist-wraith,
In the blood-red rainfall,
In the ghost-pale cloud-form;
There is the water of Kane.

One question I put to you:
Where, where is the water of Kane?
Up on high is the water of Kane,
In the heavenly blue,
In the black-piled cloud,
In the black-black cloud,
In the black-mottled sacred cloud of the gods;
There is the water of Kane.

One question I ask of you:
Where flows the water of Kane?
Deep in the ground, in the gushing spring,
In the ducts of Kane and Loa,

A well-spring of water, to quaff,
A water of magic power —
The water of life!
Life! O give us this life!

From *Unwritten Literature of Hawaii: The Sacred Songs of the Hula* translated by N. B. Emerson (Washington, D.C., Smithsonian Institution, Bureau of American Ethnology, Government Printing Office, 1909).

DAVID MALO

# THE ALII AND THE COMMON PEOPLE

The ancient Hawaiians lived under a rigid caste system, with tabus that were strict and often cruelly severe. The *alii*, the noble class, comprised the king and the chiefs of various ranks. They owned the land, even the fish in the sea, and had complete power over their subjects. The mass of common kanakas, the *makaainanas*, cultivated the land and performed all other work; but, it has been estimated, they kept no more than a third of what they produced, the rest being requisitioned by the *alii*. Birth determined the station of a man, and that he might move from one class to another was inconceivable.

All students of ancient Hawaiian culture must rely for information upon the classic work by David Malo, *Moolelo Hawaii*, translated into English under the title *Hawaiian Antiquities*. Born not far from the historic bay of Kealakekua about 1793, Malo during his youth was a retainer of the high chief Kuakini, brother of Queen Kaahumanu. Soon after the missionaries arrived he became a Christian and later attended the missionary high school at Lahainaluna on the island of Maui. Endowed with an alert and inquiring mind, he devoted himself to the study and writing (in the Hawaiian language) of the history and antiquities of his people. He died in 1853 at Kalepolepo, Maui, where he had been pastor of the church.

THE PHYSICAL CHARACTERISTICS OF THE CHIEFS AND THE COMMON people of Hawaii *nei* were the same; they were all of one race, alike in features and physique. Commoners and *aliis* were all descended from the same ancestors, Wakea and Papa. The

337

whole people were derived from that couple. There was no difference between king and plebeians as to origin. It must have been after the time of Wakea that the separation of the chiefs from the people took place.

It is probable that because it was impossible for all the people to act in concert in the government, in settling the difficulties, lifting the burdens, and disentangling the embarrassments of the people from one end of the land to the other that one was made king, with sole authority to conduct the government and to do all its business. This most likely was the reason why certain ones were selected to be chiefs. But we are not informed who was the first one chosen to be king; that is only a matter of conjecture.

The king was set up that he might help the oppressed who appealed to him, that he might succor those in the right and punish severely those in the wrong. The king was over all the people; he was the supreme executive, so long, however, as he did right.

His executive duties in the government were to gather the people together in time of war, to decide all important questions of state, and questions touching the life and death of the common people as well as of the chiefs and his comrades in arms. It was his to look after the soldiery. To him belonged the property derived from the yearly taxes, and he was the one who had the power to dispossess commoners and chiefs of their lands.

From these things will be apparent the supremacy of the king over the people and chiefs. The soldiery were a factor that added to the king's pre-eminence.

It was the policy of the government to place the chiefs who were destined to rule, while they were still young, with wise persons, that they might be instructed by skilled teachers in the principles of government, be taught the art of war, and be made to acquire personal skill and bravery.

The young man had first to be subject to another chief, that he might be disciplined and have experience of poverty, hunger, want, and hardship, and by reflecting on these things learn to care for the people with gentleness and patience, with a feeling of sympathy for the common people, and at the same time to pay due respect to the ceremonies of religion and the worship of the gods, to live temperately, not violating virgins, conducting the government kindly to all.

This is the way for a king to prolong his reign and cause his dynasty to be perpetuated, so that his government shall not be overthrown. Kings that behave themselves and govern with honesty — their annals and genealogies will be preserved and treasured by the thoughtful and the good.

Special care was taken in regard to chiefs of high rank to secure from them noble offspring, by not allowing them to form a first union with a woman of lower rank than themselves, and especially not to have them form a first union with a common or plebeian woman.

To this end diligent search was first made by the genealogists into the pedigree of the woman, if it concerned a highborn prince, or into the pedigree of the man, if it concerned a princess of high birth, to find a partner of unimpeachable pedigree; and only when such was found and the parentage and lines of ancestry clearly established was the young man (or young woman) allowed to form his first union, in order that the offspring might be a great chief.

When it was clearly made out that there was a close connection, or identity, of ancestry between the two parties, that was the woman with whom the prince was first to pair. If the union was fruitful, the child would be considered a high chief, but not of the highest rank or tabu. His would be a *kapu a noho*, that is, the people and chiefs of rank inferior to his must sit in his presence.

A suitable partner for a chief of the highest rank was his own sister, begotten by the same father and mother as himself. Such a pairing was called a *pi'o* (a bow, a loop, a thing bent on itself); and if the union bore fruit, the child would be a chief of the highest rank, a *ninau pi'o*, so sacred that all who came into his presence must prostrate themselves. He was called divine, *akua*. Such an *alii* would not go abroad by day but only at night, because if he went abroad in open day (when people were about their usual avocations), every one had to fall to the ground in an attitude of worship.

Another suitable partner for a great chief was his half sister, born, it might be, of the same mother, but of a different father, or of the same father but of a different mother. Such a union was called a *naha*. The child would be a great chief, *niau pi'o;* but it would have only the *kapu a noho* (sitting tabu).

If such unions as these could not be obtained for a great chief, he would then be paired with the daughter of an elder or younger brother, or of a sister. Such a union was called a *hoi* (return). The child would be called a *niau pi'o* and be possessed of the *kapu moe*.

This was the practice of the highest chiefs that their first-born might be chiefs of the highest rank, fit to succeed to the throne.

It was for this reason that the genealogies of the kings were always preserved by their descendants, that the ancestral lines of the great chiefs might not be forgotten so; that all the people might see clearly that the ancestors on the mother's side were all great chiefs, with no small names among them; also that the father's line was pure and direct. Thus the chief became peerless, without blemish, sacred.

In consequence of this rule of practice, it was not considered a thing to be tolerated that other chiefs should associate on familiar terms with a high chief, or that one's claim of relationship with him should be recognized until the ancestral lines of the claimant had been found to be of equal strength with those of the chief; only then was it proper for them to call the chief a *makamaka* (friend, or intimate — *maka* means eye).

Afterwards, when the couple had begotten children of their own, if the man wished to take another woman — or the woman another man — even though this second partner were not of such choice blood as the first, it was permitted them to do so. And if children were thus begotten they were called *kaikaina*, younger brothers or sisters of the great chief, and would become the backbone, executive officers of the chief, the ministers of his government. . . .

The great chiefs were entirely exclusive, being hedged about with many tabus, and a large number of people were slain for breaking, or infringing upon, the tabus. The tabus that hedged about an *alii* were exceedingly strict and severe. Tradition does not inform us what king established these tabus. In my opinion the establishment of the tabu system is not of very ancient date, but comparatively modern in origin.

If the shadow of a man fell upon the house of a tabu chief, that man must be put to death, and so with anyone whose shadow fell upon the back of the chief, or upon his robe or malo, or upon anything that belonged to the chief. If anyone passed through the private doorway of a tabu chief, or climbed over the stockade about his residence, he was put to death.

If a man entered the *alii*'s house without changing his wet malo, or with his head smeared with mud, he was put to death. Even if there were no fence surrounding the *alii*'s residence, only a mark, or faint scratch in the ground hidden by the grass, and a man were to overstep this line unwittingly not seeing it, he would be put to death.

When a tabu chief ate, the people in his presence must kneel, and if anyone raised his knee from the ground, he was put to death. If any man put forth in a *kioloa* canoe at the same time as the tabu chief, the penalty was death.

If anyone girded himself with the king's malo, or put on the king's robe, he was put to death. There were many other tabus, some of them relating to the man himself and some to the king for violating which anyone would be put to death.

A chief who had the *kapu moe* as a rule went abroad only at night; but if he traveled in daytime a man went before him with a flag calling out *"kapu! moe!"* whereupon all the people prostrated themselves. When the containers holding the water for his bath, or when his clothing, his malo, his food, or anything that belonged to him was carried along, everyone must prostrate himself; and if any remained standing, he was put to death. . . .

Everything went according to the will or whim of the king, whether it concerned land, or people, or anything else — not according to law.

All the chiefs under the king, including the *konohikis* who managed their lands for them, regulated land matters and everything else according to their own notions.

There was no judge, nor any court of justice, to sit in judgment on wrongdoers of any sort. Retaliation with violence or murder was the rule in ancient times.

To run away and hide oneself was the only resource for an offender in those days, not a trial in a court of justice as at the present time.

If a man's wife was abducted from him he would go to the king with a dog as a gift, appealing to him to cause the return of his wife — or the woman for the return of her husband — but the return of the wife, or of the husband, if brought about, was caused by the gift of the dog, not in pursuance of any law. If anyone had suffered from a great robbery, or had a large debt owing him, it was only by the good will of the debtor, not by the operation of any law regulating such matters, that he could recover or obtain justice. Men and chiefs acted strangely in those days.

There was a great difference between chiefs. Some were given to robbery, spoliation, murder, extortion, ravishing. There were few kings who conducted themselves properly as Kamehameha I did. He looked well after the peace of the land.

On account of the rascality of some of the chiefs to the common people, warlike contests frequently broke out between certain chiefs and the people and many of the former were killed in battle by the commoners. The people made war against bad kings in old times.

The amount of property which the chiefs obtained from the people was very great. Some of it was given in the shape of taxes, some was the fruit of robbery and extortion.

Now the people in the out districts were as a rule industrious while those about court or who lived with the chiefs were indolent, merely living on the income of the land. Some of the chiefs carried themselves haughtily and arrogantly, being supported by contributions from others without labor of their own. As was the chief, so were his retainers (kanaka).

On this account the number of retainers, servants and hangers-on about the courts and residences of the kings and high chiefs was very great. The court of a king offered great attractions to the lazy and shiftless.

These people about court were called *puali* or *aialo* (those who eat in the presence), besides which there were many other names given them. One whom the *alii* took as an intimate was called *aikane*. An adopted child was called *keiki hookama*.

The person who brought up an *alii* and was his guardian was called a *kahu;* he who managed the distribution of his property was called a *puuku*. The house where the property of the *alii* was stored was called a *hale papaa* (house with strong fence). The keeper of the king's apparel (master of the king's robes), or the place where they were stored, was called the *hale opeope,* the folding house.

The steward who had charge of the king's food was called an *'aipuupuu,* calloused neck. He who presided over the king's *pot de chambre* was called a *lomilomi,* i.e., a masseur. He who watched over the king during sleep was called *kiaipoo,* keeper of the head. The keeper of the king's idol was called *kahuakua. . . .*

The commoners were the most numerous class of people in the nation, and were known as the *makaainana;* another name by which they were called was *hu* (to swell, multiply, increase like yeast). The people who lived on the windward, that was the back, or *koolau* side of any island, were called *kuaaina* or back-country folks, a term of depreciation, however.

The condition of the common people was that of subjection to the chiefs, compelled to do their heavy tasks, burdened and oppressed, some even to death. The life of the people was one of patient endurance, of yielding to the chiefs to purchase their favor. The plain man (*kanaka*) must not complain.

If the people were slack in doing the chief's work they were expelled from their lands, or even put to death. For such reasons as this and because of the oppressive exactions made upon them, the people held the chiefs in great dread and looked upon them as gods.

Only a small portion of the kings and chiefs ruled with

kindness; the large majority simply lorded it over the people.

It was from the common people, however, that the chiefs received their food and their apparel for men and women, also their houses and many other things. When the chiefs went forth to war some of the commoners also went out to fight on the same side with them.

The *makaainana* were the fixed residents of the land; the chiefs were the ones who moved about from place to place. It was the *makaainanas* also who did all the work on the land; yet all they produced from the soil belonged to the chiefs; and the power to expel a man from the land and rob him of his possessions lay with the chief.

There were many names descriptive of the *makaainanas*. Those who were born in the back districts were called *kanaka nohiikua,* people of the back. The man who lived with the chief and did not desert him when war came was called a *kanaka no luakaua,* a man for the pit of battle.

The people were divided into farmers, fishermen, house builders, canoe makers, etc. They were called by many different appellations according to the trades they followed.

The country people generally lived in a state of chronic fear and apprehension of the chiefs; those of them, however, who lived immediately with the chief were (to an extent) relieved of this apprehension.

After sunset the candles of kukui nuts were lighted and the chief sat at meat. The people who came in at that time were called the people of *lanikae.* Those who came in when the midnight lamp was burning were called the people of *pohokano.* This lamp was merely to talk by; there was no eating being done at that time.

The people who sat up with the chief until daybreak (to carry on, tell stories, gossip, or perhaps play some game, like *konane*) were called *makou* because that was the name of the flambeau generally kept burning at that hour.

There were three designations applied to the *kalaimoku,* or counselors of state. The *kalaimoku* who had served under but one king was called *lanikae.* He who had served under two kings was called a *pohokano,* and if one had served three kings he was termed *makou.* This last class were regarded as being most profoundly skilled in statecraft, from the fact that they had had experience with many kings and knew wherein one king had failed and wherein another had succeeded.

It was in this way that these statesmen had learned — by experience — that one king by pursuing a certain policy had met with disaster, and how another king, through following a different policy, had been successful. The best course for the king would have been to submit to the will of the people.

From *Hawaiian Antiquities (Moolelo Hawaii),* by David Malo, translated by Nathaniel B. Emerson (Honolulu, 1898); a second edition was published by the Bishop Museum, Honolulu, 1951.

# MARY PUKUI and MARTHA BECKWITH

# THE MARCHERS OF
# THE NIGHT

The Hawaiians have an oral literature that is particularly rich
in tales of ghosts and other night spirits. But they are reticent
about telling these stories to haoles, who scoff and are unbelievers,
and so not many of them have found their way into printed
English. The following authentic Hawaiian ghost story was given
in 1930 to Martha Beckwith, the authority on Hawaiian folklore,
by Mrs. Mary Pukui, who as a child had heard it told by her
Hawaiian mother and older relatives in Kau and Puna on the
island of Hawaii. Mrs. Pukui is at present translator and con-
sultant on the staff of the Bishop Museum in Honolulu; she is
the compiler, with Samuel Elbert, of *The Hawaiian-English Dictionary* (University of Hawaii Press, 1957), the standard work in
its field.

EVERY HAWAIIAN HAS HEARD OF THE "MARCHERS OF THE
Night," *Ka huaka'i o ka Po*. A few have seen the procession.
It is said that such sight is fatal unless one had a relative among
the dead to intercede for him. If a man is found stricken by
the roadside a white doctor will pronounce the cause as heart
failure, but a Hawaiian will think at once of the fatal night
march.

The time for the march is between half after seven when
the sun has actually set and about two in the morning before
the dawn breaks. It may occur on one of the four nights of
the gods, on Ku, Akua, Lono, Kane, or on the nights of Kaloa.
Those who took part in the march were the chiefs and warriors

who had died, the *aumakua,* and the gods, each of whom had
their own march.

That of the chiefs was conducted according to the tastes of
the chief for whom the march was made. If he had enjoyed
silence in this life his march would be silent save for the creaking
of the food calabashes suspended from the carrying-sticks, or of
the litter, called *manele,* if he had not been fond of walking.
If a chief had been fond of music, the sound of the drum, nose
flute and other instruments was heard as they marched. Sometimes there were no lights borne, at other times there were
torches but not so bright as for the gods and demigods. A chief
whose face had been sacred, called an *alo kapu,* so that no
man, beast, or bird could pass before him without being killed,
must lead the march; even his own warriors might not pre-
cede him. If on the contrary his back had been sacred, *akua
kapu,* he must follow in the rear of the procession. A chief who
had been well protected in life and who had no rigid tabu
upon face or back would march between his warriors.

On the marches of the chief a few *aumakua* would march
with them in order to protect their living progeny who might
chance to meet them on the road. Sometimes the parade came
when a chief lay dying or just dead. It paused before the door
for a brief time and then passed on. The family might not
notice it, but a neighbor might see it pass and know that the
chief had gone with his ancestors who had come for him.

In the march of the *aumakua* of each district there was music
and chanting. The marchers carried candlenut torches which
burned brightly even on a rainy night. They might be seen even
in broad daylight and were followed by whirlwinds such as
come one after another in columns. They cried *"Kapu o moe!"*
as a warning to stragglers to get out of the way or to prostrate
themselves with closed eyes until the marchers passed. Like
the chiefs, they too sometimes came to a dying descendant and
took him away with them.

The march of the gods was much longer, more brilliantly
lighted and more sacred than that of the chiefs or of the demigods. The torches were brighter and shone red. At the head, at

three points within the line and at the rear were carried bigger torches, five being the complete number among Hawaiians, the *ku a lima*. The gods with the torches walked six abreast, three males and three females. One of the three at the end of the line was Hi'iaka-i-ka-poli-o-Pele, youngest sister of the volcano goddess. The first torch could be seen burning up at Kahuku when the last of the five torches was at Nonuapo. The only music to be heard on the marches of the gods was the chanting of their names and mighty deeds. The sign that accompanied them was a heavy downpour of rain, with mist, thunder and lightning, or heavy seas. Their route the next day would be strewn with broken boughs or leaves, for the heads of the gods were sacred and nothing should be suspended above them.

If a living person met these marchers it behooved him to get out of the way as quickly as possible, otherwise he might be killed unless he had an ancestor or an *aumakua* in the procession to plead for his life. If he met a procession of chiefs and had no time to get out of the way, he might take off his clothes and lie face upward, breathing as little as possible. He would hear them cry "Shame!"as they passed. One would say, "He is dead!" Another would cry, "No, he is alive, but what a shame for him to lie uncovered!" If he had no time to strip he must sit perfectly still, close his eyes and take his chance. He was likely to be killed by the guard at the front or at the rear of the line unless saved by one of his ancestors or by an *aumakua*. If he met a procession of gods he must take off all his clothes but his loincloth and sit still with his eyes tightly closed, because no man might look on a god although he might listen to their talk. He would hear the command to strike; then, if he was beloved by one of the gods as a favorite child or namesake, he would hear someone say, "No! he is mine!" and he would be spared by the guards.

Many Hawaiians living today have seen or heard the ghostly marchers. Mrs. Wiggin, Mrs. Pukui's mother, never got in their way but she has watched them pass from the door of her own mother's house and has heard the Kau people tell of the precautions that must be taken to escape death if one chances to be in their path.

A young man of Kona, Hawaii, tells the following experience. One night just after nightfall, about seven or eight in the evening, he was on his way when of a sudden he saw a long line of marchers in the distance coming toward him. He climbed over a stone wall and sat very still. As they drew near he saw that they walked four abreast and were about seven feet tall, nor did their feet touch the ground. One of the marchers stepped out of the line and ran back and forth on the other side of the wall behind which he crouched as if to protect him from the others. As each file passed he heard voices call out "Strike!" and his protector answered, "No! no! he is mine!" No other sounds were to be heard except the call to strike and the creak of a *manele*. He was not afraid and watched the marchers closely. There were both men and women in the procession. After a long line of marchers four abreast had passed there came the *manele* bearers, two before and two behind. On the litter sat a very big man whom he guessed at once to be a chief. Following the litter were other marchers walking four abreast. After all had passed his protector joined his fellows.

A month later the same young man went to call on some friends and was returning home late at night. Not far from the spot where he had met the marchers before was a level flat of ground and drawing near to the spot he heard the sound of an *ipu* drum and of chanting. He came close enough to see and recognize many of the men and women whom he had seen on the previous march as he had sat behind the stone wall. He was delighted with the chanting and drumming, with the dancing of the *ala'apapa* by the women and the *mokomoko* wrestling and other games of the past by the men. As he sat watching he heard someone say, "There is the grandson of Kekuanoi!" "Never mind! we do not mind him!" said another. This was the name of a grandfather of his who lived on the beach and he knew that he himself was being discussed. For a couple of hours he sat watching before he went home. His grandfather at home had seen it all; he said, "I know that you have been with our

people of the night; I saw you sitting by watching the sports."
Then he related to his grandfather what he had seen on the
two nights when he met the chiefs and warriors of old.

In old days these marchers were common in Kau district, but
folk of today know little about them. They used to march and
play games practically on the same ground as in life. Hence
each island and each district had its own parade and playground
along which the dead would march and at which they would
assemble.

Mrs. Emma Akana Olmsted tells me that when she was told
as a child about the marchers of the night she was afraid, but
now that she is older and can herself actually hear them she is no
longer terrified. She hears beautiful loud chanting of voices,
the high notes of the flute and drumming so loud that it seems
beaten upon the side of the house beside her bed. The voices
are so distinct that if she could write music she would be able to
set down the notes they sang.

From *Kepelino's Traditions of Hawaii,* edited by Martha Warren Beckwith
(Honolulu, Bernice P. Bishop Museum, 1932).

KATHARINE LUOMALA

# MENEHUNES, THE LITTLE
# PEOPLE

Among the most popular of Hawaiian legends are those that
recount the doings of the Menehunes, the mythical little people
of island folk literature. They are a race of dwarflike builders who
work only at night. On the island of Kauai, once a stronghold of
the Menehunes, are many heiaus, roads, fishponds, and water
courses — in particular the famous "Menehune Ditch" near
Waimea — that are pointed out as their constructions. Island
children and others with uninhibited imaginations frequently
report having seen them, even in broad daylight.

The leading authority on legends of the Menehunes is Dr.
Katharine Luomala, research associate at the Bishop Museum and
professor of anthropology at the University of Hawaii. She is author of numerous scholarly studies on the folklore of the Pacific
island area, including *The Menehune of Polynesia and Other
Little People of Oceania* (Bishop Museum, 1951), on which the
following more popularly written account is based.

PARTLY BECAUSE THE MYTHICAL LITTLE PEOPLE OF THE HAWAIIAN
Islands, the Menehunes, are reminiscent of pixies, trolls, and
other little spirits of European folklore, the number of legends
about them has snowballed in modern Honolulu during the last
twenty years. More and more newcomers have arrived and become entranced with the local equivalent of brownies and elves.
Stores now use figures of Menehunes to advertise candy, lingerie,
and automobiles. Commercial artists portray them as wide-
eyed, ingenuous, merry, miniature men and women completely
lost in the task of the moment, whether pounding a native

drum or climbing up a cocktail glass. For a football mascot, the University of Hawaii, located in upper Manoa Valley, a former residential area of the Menehunes, has a figure of a Menehune. He is reminiscent of their chief, Ku of the Loud Voice, who used to bellow for them at sundown to get ready to go to work, for Menehunes work only between sunset and sunrise.

Even though Menehunes are traditionally good and gentle if treated respectfully and not crossed, grade-school children on a sugar plantation near Honolulu told a teacher in 1948 that more than anything else they feared Menehunes, goats, and tidal waves. Children, regardless of racial origin, go through the stage of asking whether Santa Claus, God, and Menehunes are real. Menehunes are the bogeymen used to frighten children who stay out after dark when the Menehunes are prowling. Sometimes, more mature children, high-school age and older, do not outgrow their belief that there are Menehunes. At Waimea, Kauai, a teacher joined the children in hunting for a Menehune which they had glimpsed lurking near the school; the search lasted until the principal arrived and put an end to it.

The wholesome normality which characterizes Menehune life should neither frighten nor fascinate civilized people of today. Then what about the little people does? Perhaps it is the queerness of the idea of spirits, two feet high, who look something like Hawaiians except for their small size, carrying on the old native customs in the midst of modern, industrial Honolulu. It is like having a one-way screen through which self-appointed seers spy on the Menehunes and report to the general public. The thrill of fascinated fear bubbles in the blood when the screen proves defective and the Menehunes watch the modern community and occasionally emerge to poke tiny fingers into its affairs.

Psychologists have analyzed the prelogical attitude which assails even a Freudian when he becomes annoyed at the cussed and ornery way that inanimate objects vanish when needed and suddenly reappear later in an obvious place. Although Menehunes are rarely blamed for lost objects or persons, they are the scapegoats for superstitious workmen who of a morning find their previous day's work mysteriously undone, especially when that work has to do with rocks, for the Menehunes are experts on stonework. Now largely retired from active labor, Menehunes nonetheless linger around construction jobs to act as "sidewalk supervisors" and alter the work at night. In 1951 dismayed workmen moving rocks in Diamond Head Crater quit because, said they, the Menehunes, to show their displeasure about something, tampered every night with what had been done during the day. In order that the workmen would proceed with the job, a foreman experienced with the gremlin habits of Menehunes advised calling in a native Hawaiian seer (kahuna) to find out what was annoying the little people.

Menehunes, if satisfied, are believed to hasten a job by lining up hundreds of their men in a double row to pass stones from hand to hand from a distant quarry to the site, until in one night they have finished their construction. . . . Because they fear daylight and do not want anyone to see them, Menehunes never work more than one night on a job and always quit at dawn. If the work is not finished by then, though this rarely happens, it is left. Of the little people it is said, "No task is difficult. It is the work of one hand"; and "In one night, and by dawn it is finished."

In their heyday, narrators state, Menehunes built in and about Honolulu nine or ten heiaus and two fishponds. On the other islands — Kauai, Maui, Molokai, Hawaii, and Niihau — are twenty-four more temples credited to Menehune workmen, and several fishponds and other stone structures. Only ruins of their stonework remain today, and not a trace is to be found of the wooden canoes which they and their friends of the woodlands built for demigods who wanted to journey in search of lost relatives.

Menehunes average two to three feet in height, although a child of Japanese descent who recently saw one near Foster Gardens in Honolulu said that the little man was about five inches tall. Menehunes are extremely stout, strong, and muscular. Opinions differ as to whether or not they have hairy bodies. Their faces are red and ugly; their noses short and thick; and their hair hangs down over a low, protruding forehead and tangles with their long eyebrows, which hang like crags over large eyes. Their arduous, rigidly disciplined work gives the little people a set, serious, and determined look which Hawaiians say is frightening.

Menehunes, however, are good people who rarely get angry or quarrel without cause. Silent as they are when toiling on a heiau, they make up for it off duty, for they play as hard as they work. They chatter and laugh merrily and endlessly, causing such a racket at times that fish in the sea leap into the air in fright and birds on neighboring islands are terrified. The little people know all the games that the Hawaiians play, and occasionally they organize a festival, when — like the Hawaiians at their *makahiki* celebrations — they spin tops, throw darts, box, wrestle standing up and lying down, race around the island, slide down grassy hillsides on ti leaves, and play "hide the pebble." Their musicians imitate the Hawaiians by playing bamboo nose flutes, ti-leaf trumpets, mouth harps, and hollow-log drums. Yet Menehunes most enjoy the simpler, less organized, impromptu diversions, like carrying rocks from the mountains to throw into the sea and diving after them. They love to roll down hills, especially when the sea is at the bottom and they can splash into the water.

The little people lead a very simple life. When the shrimps and poi which their employers give them as pay are eaten, they pluck wild fruits and berries. Sometimes between jobs they suffer from hunger. Their clothing is so inconsequential that no one has described it; and when the rain falls or they get sleepy they crawl into caves, tree trunks, or under banana leaves. Hawaiians say that Menehunes are invisible to everyone but their own descendants, although others can sometimes hear the hum of their chatter, which sounds like the "low growl of a dog." They are always ready to help relatives, friends, and those who have adopted them as their guardian gods. Their supernatural power enables them to do remarkable things. Their kindness is illustrated by the care they showed Eternal

Fire, a Hawaiian girl who had been abandoned as a baby and adopted by a poor couple. Although Menehunes dislike people who carelessly despoil the woodlands of trees and flowers, they protected Eternal Fire when she wandered in the forests to pick flowers. When a Hawaiian chief's overseer saw her and fell in love with her, the Menehunes provided her with a fine dowry.

They are shy of anyone who is not a relative; but when their affections chance to be fastened on a Hawaiian, their intense devotion tends to make them forget their own band. It is not surprising that their leaders discourage intimate contact with outsiders, for Menehune survival as a distinctive and efficient group depends upon the close unity and loyalty of the members to each other. Long ago, when there were more than five hundred thousand Menehunes on Kauai (nine hundred and two per square mile), their king became dismayed by the increasing number of marriages between Menehune men and Hawaiian women despite the number of offenders he had turned to stone as a punishment. Assembling his people, he ordered them to prepare for an exodus from the island to an undisclosed destination, leaving behind their Hawaiian wives and all children except first-born sons. Only Mohikia dared protest (that is why his name is one of the few Menehune names known) and beg that he be left behind with his Hawaiian wife. He was scolded for putting a woman before his king, but no other punishment was meted out to him.

A few Menehunes managed to hide successfully, it is clear, for reports of their living on Kauai still continue. Also, sometime during the end of the eighteenth century or the early part of the nineteenth, a census taker for Kaumualii, last Hawaiian king of Kauai, energetically and conscientiously carried his search for residents into the very heart of Kauai. He went to the head of Wainiha Valley within ten miles of Mount Waialeale. There he found a community well known to narrators which is called Forest, or Laau, and counted sixty-five Menehune residents. Later commentators have disputed not his figure but his identification, and have declared that the residents were probably

Mus, not Menehunes. However, Mus are close relatives and look much like Menehunes, the major difference being that in side view "the abdomens of the Menehunes are very distended while those of the Mus are round." A jokester who in 1951 sent a photograph of what he claimed were Menehunes to a Honolulu newspaper made the error of showing some of the figures in side view. The shape of the abdomens revealed that they were neither Mus nor Menehunes but probably Hawaiian children. If the little people are carrying rocks in their hands, they are Menehunes, whereas Mus would have bananas. They are known as the "banana-eating bugs."

Although Menehunes have built many canoes of stone or wood for other people, they require no canoes when they travel. When a band of them immigrated to Oahu from mythical Kahiki to work for a chief there, his overseer, a magician said to have "stretching power," lay on the ocean with arms outstretched, and the Menehunes marched single file up one arm and down the other until they stepped off his fingertips onto Oahu, where the chief assigned them lands in the valleys now traditionally associated with them. Their Kauai relatives required no canoe either, because their divine leader owned Kuaihelani, the beautiful island which floats at night in the clouds or on the sea and is a former home of Pele, Hiiaka, and their kinfolk. Its name comes from its shouldering the sky or seeming at times even to support it. When the little people had work on the other islands, the island would gently fall from the atmosphere to the surface of the ocean and draw near shore for them to disembark. Then it would receive them at dawn if they did not care to go to the land they owned in the depths of the valleys.

Little is said about Menehune girls and women; but Analike, who is one of the few mentioned, was a beautiful and very petite Menehune maid of Kuaihelani who married a Hawaiian chief who had been lost at sea and rescued by the residents of the floating island. He tried for a year to domesticate Analike by teaching her to make fire and cook food, knowledge lacked by her people; but he finally gave up, and when Kuaihelani floated near Hawaii, he deserted Analike and took their son, Firelight, and waded ashore. The non-Menehune princess of Kuaihelani has also been remembered because she refused to marry Ola, a high chief of Kauai, who fell in love with her beauty while he was arranging to employ some of her Menehune artisans.

Bands of Menehunes, Oahu narrators claim, formerly lived in the foothills of Honolulu on Punchbowl and in Manoa and Nuuanu Valleys, with a few scattered elsewhere. The different valley bands used to struggle with each other over unusually desirable rocks, as is obvious from the marks resembling tiny fingerprints on a boulder near Oahu Country Club. The Nuuanu Menehunes are infamous because they violated a tabu of silence when a tree equipped to furnish an unending supply of cooked fish and poi was being transported over the Pali, the precipice at the head of their valley. Fearing that Nuuanu was being invaded, the Menehunes shouted in terror and thus broke the tabu and the spell, with the result that the tree crashed down the steep sides of the Pali and its mana vanished forever.

The most courageous and energetic Oahu band lived in Manoa and was last heard from about A.D. 1700 when a non-Menehune band drove them from their fort and heiau to an unknown new home. Between the lines of the two brief references to the event can be read the fact that Menehunes stubbornly resisted to the last all attempts to evict them. One reference names their conqueror as none other than a chief famous for his passion for war and his success in it. This was Kualii, the chief whose reputation today is largely based on a chant composed by two ambitious flatterers who likened him to a god and ascribed to him mastery of the land, the sea, the sun, the stars, and the rains. Only such a chief, it seemed to the narrators, had enough mana to dispossess the little Menehunes. The other reference is just as much, if not more, of a tribute to Menehune courage and patriotism. It is known that they particularly fear owls and dogs, probably because they too are wanderers in the night. Their enemy, using psychological warfare, imported owls from Kauai, which is traditionally the major

Menehune stronghold in the Hawaiian Islands. The Kauai owls, therefore, were more experienced than the Oahu owls in frightening Menehunes. Furthermore, by using an army of owls, the chief was employing the spiritual guardians of Hawaiian warriors, because to a warrior or to any person in danger, an owl spirit is the most effective protector and guide to be had. The shrewd leader was able to command Kauai support because he was king of the owls. . . .

It would be hard to find on Kauai a single stone of any size or a group of rocks, whether assembled by nature or man, that is not named and linked with the Menehunes. Many single rocks represent Menehune men who were transformed by their leaders into stones for malingering on the job, for stealing, for boasting about being able to catch the legs of the moon and failing to do so, or for falling in love with a Hawaiian woman. Rocks at the seashore are said to have been dragged from the valleys by Menehunes and used as slides and diving boards. Any hollowed-out boulder may be a Menehune food dish or canoe. The little people are also believed to have constructed walls, roads, ditches, fishponds, and causeways; excavated caves; and made many perishable things like wooden canoes.

Their most famous job on Kauai is a watercourse, an irrigation ditch with low stone walls, best known now as the "Menehune Ditch" although earlier Hawaiians called it "Ola's Water Lead" to honor the chief for whom the stories say the little people worked. The ditch diverts water from Waimea River to taro patches around the nearby mountainside. Sightseers will find the ruins of the ditch at the end of an unmarked country road leading from the town of Waimea past small rice paddies. Part of the side of the modern road is formed by a length of the low stone wall of the ditch, the rectangular stones of which are dressed and shaped with a jogged end to fit together in order that the top of the wall will be level. Though the Society Islanders, Marquesans, Easter Islanders, and Tongans had a number of constructions made of dressed and fitted stone, work of this type is either absent or uncommon elsewhere in Polynesia. In the Hawaiian Islands are but two examples, a temple of refuge on Hawaii and the Menehune Ditch on Kauai. . . .

Hawaiian narrators state that Chief Ola of Waimea got the Menehunes to work for him after his own people had failed to progress on the construction program which he had planned for the improvement of living conditions. For him, the Menehunes built the dam and the watercourse, a heiau, a fishpond, roads, and an earth oven. They even planted taro patches, although they themselves never practiced agriculture.

According to one narrator, the Hawaiians were building very slowly and with much difficulty a stone wall around an excavation to be used either for fish or for wet taro. One of the workmen, Pi, a man from the village of Hulaia, was lazy and slept all day. Naturally, the chief's overseer refused to give him the fish and poi that the other artisans received. Soon the nagging of his hungry wife and children became so intolerable that Pi had to bestir himself and go to work for the first time in his life. This is what he did. He made up many little leaf-wrapped packages of fish and poi and fastened them to the branches of a candlenut tree, which he then uprooted and set near the unfinished wall where the Menehunes would find it when they came at night to inspect the Hawaiians' work. When the Menehunes arrived and saw the gifts and heard from Pi, who was there too, that he was a relative of theirs, they immediately lined up and began to pass stones from hand to hand until the job was done before dawn. Then they sat down to feast, each with his own package, for Pi had considerately provided one for each of the little gods, as the storyteller calls them. Strangely enough, he had made a mistake about their taste in fish, although everyone knows that Menehunes love shrimp. But the little people, delighted with the poi, forgave him for the error about the fish and found enough shrimp in a nearby stream to give one to each artisan.

The next day Pi's happy chief sent quantities of food and tapa mats to him, and High Chief Ola of Waimea asked him to bring his Menehune relatives to work on the watercourse and other projects which Ola had planned for the welfare of his people. Pi agreed but requested that a strict tabu be established on the night chosen for the work. Everyone must stay indoors and be silent, the dogs must be muzzled, and the chickens must be shut in calabashes to keep them quiet. Then Pi called those of his Menehune relatives who lived near a place called Puukapele to come to work. All night long they passed stones down a double line of workmen for a distance of five or six miles to the site chosen for the dam and the watercourse. By dawn the work was done and the Menehunes sat down to enjoy the feast of shrimp which Ola had provided. One storyteller says that Pi became Ola's principal magician. . . .

Hawaiian mythology has besides the Mus and the Menehunes other mysterious bands of little people, among whom are the Was, the Waos, and the Eepas. The different bands have supernatural and human attributes in varying degrees, specialized magical talents and departments of activity, and certain localities as their homes. All the bands, however, have tended to merge into each other and to acquire each other's attributes, duties, and stories. Thus the Mus and the Menehunes may work together or compete with each other or unite against the Was and the Waos, who are experts in forest activities.

While these little spirits can be helpful, they can also be so malignant and crotchety that a human being who has offended a high-ranking god would seem to have a better chance at success in his aspirations or survival than if he had angered a little imp. Even gods like Kane had trouble with the Mus, and the Eepas were the bane of everyone except those sorcerers who had cajoled one into becoming a familiar spirit. Peculiarly adept at shape-shifting, many Eepas originated, like Maui-of-a-thousand-tricks, from misbirths. (The mentally incompetent and insane were also called Eepas.) A band of them, who lived in Waolani in Nuuanu Valley, stole Chief Kiha's conch shell which he used to blow to control the "myriad gods," as the various bands of little people are collectively known. The Eepas blew the stolen, weird-sounding shell so much at night that the residents of their valley began to complain. A valley chieftain told a thief whom he had captured with his yellow

dog, also an expert thief, that he would spare the lives of both
if they removed the trumpet from the Eepas. The man and his
dog succeeded, although in escaping with their trophy they
chipped the shell a little. It is now in Bishop Museum. The
human teeth set into the shell are said to have been extracted
by Kiha from chiefs he slew in battle.

To avoid insulting even a single one of the innumerable little
gods by unintentionally overlooking him in their invocations,
Hawaiians add a formula which refers to them by ritual numbers involving the number four:

> O the four hundred gods,
> The four thousand gods,
> The four hundred thousand gods,
> The assembly of gods,
> The rows of gods,
> The groups of gods,
> O come! Here is work.

From *Voices on the Wind: Polynesian Myths and Chants* by Katharine Luomala
(Honolulu, Bishop Museum Press, 1955).

# GLOSSARY OF HAWAIIAN WORDS

*akua,* god, divine

*alii,* chief

*aloha,* greeting, affection, farewell

*aole,* no

*aumakua,* ancestral spirit

*auwe,* alas

*haole,* white man, stranger

*hapa,* half

*hau,* island tree or vine

*heiau,* temple platform

*hikiee,* settee

*huhu,* angry

*hula,* dance

*kahuna,* sorcerer, priest

*kahili,* feathered pole used as an ensign of a chief

*kalo,* taro

*kamaaina,* old-timer

*Kanaka,* man, commoner

*kapu,* tabu, forbidden

*kava,* awa, drink made of root

*keawe,* algarroba tree

*kihei,* native shawl

*koa,* island tree

*kona,* a muggy equatorial wind

*konane,* game like checkers

*konohiki,* overseer of chief's estate

*koolau,* windward side

*kou,* island tree

*kukui,* candlenut tree

*kupuna,* grandparent, ancestor

*lanai,* veranda

*lauhala,* pandanus leaf

*lehua,* low, flowering tree

*lei,* garland, necklace

*lomi-lomi,* native massage

*luau,* Hawaiian feast

*maile,* fragrant plant

*maka,* eye

*makahiki,* harvest season

*makai,* toward the sea

*malihini,* newcomer

*manele,* litter

*marai,* temple platform, *heiau*

*maro,* malo, loincloth

*mauka,* toward the mountains

*mele,* song, chant

*menehune,* legendary dwarf

*nei,* old-time

*nuhou,* gossip

*okolehao,* liquor distilled from ti root

*pali,* precipice

*paniolo,* cowboy

*pau,* finished

*pa-u,* voluminous riding skirt

*pepa,* paper, book

*pilikia,* trouble

*poha,* Cape gooseberry

*poi,* foodstuff from taro

*popoki,* cat

*pulu,* fuzzy fiber from tree fern

*tapa,* beaten bark cloth

*taro,* food plant with starchy root

*ti,* leafy shrub

# TALES OF THE PACIFIC

## JACK LONDON

**Stories of Hawaii by Jack London**
Thirteen yarns drawn from the famous author's love affair
with Hawaii Nei.
$4.95                                    ISBN 0-935180-08-7

**The Mutiny of the "Elsinore," by Jack London**
Based on a voyage around Cape Horn in a windjammer
from New York to Seattle in 1913, this romance between
the lone passenger and the captain's daughter reveals
London at his most fertile and fluent best. The lovers are
forced to outface a rioting band of seagoing gangsters in
the South Pacific.
$4.95                                    ISBN 0-935180-40-0

**Captain David Grief by Jack London**
Captain David Grief, South Sea tycoon, came to the
Pacific at the age of twenty, and two decades later he protected a vast trading empire. Eight long tales of daring and
adventure by the famous American storyteller who did
some of his best writing in that region.
$3.95                                    ISBN 0-935180-34-6

**South Sea Tales by Jack London**
Fiction from the violent days of the early century, set
among the atolls of French Oceania and the high islands of
Samoa, Fiji, Pitcairn, and "the terrible Solomons."
$4.95                                    ISBN 0-935180-14-1

## HAWAII

**A Hawaiian Reader**
Thirty-seven selections from the literature of the past
hundred years including such writers as Mark Twain,
Robert Louis Stevenson and James Jones.
$4.95                                    ISBN 0-935180-07-9

**The Spell of Hawaii**
A companion volume to A Hawaiian Reader. Twenty-four
selections from the exotic literary heritage of the islands.
$4.95                                    ISBN 0-935180-13-3

**Kona by Marjorie Sinclair**
The best woman novelist of post-war Hawaii dramatizes
the conflict between a daughter of Old Hawaii and her
straitlaced Yankee husband. Nor is the drama resolved in
their children.
$4.95                                    ISBN 0-935180-20-6

### *The Golden Cloak* by Antoinette Withington
The romantic story of Hawaii's monarchs and their friends, from Kamehameha the Great, founder of the dynasty, to Liliuokalani, last queen to rule in America's only royal palace.
$3.95                                ISBN 0-935180-26-5

### *Teller of Tales* by Eric Knudsen
Son of a pioneer family of Kauai, the author spent most of his life on the Garden Island as a rancher, hunter of wild cattle, lawyer, and legislator. Here are sixty campfire yarns of gods and goddesses, ghosts and heroes, cowboy adventures and legendary feats aong the valleys and peaks of the island.
$4.95                                ISBN 0-935180-33-8

### *The Wild Wind* a novel by Marjorie Sinclair
On the Hana Coast of Maui, Lucia Gray, great-grand-daughter of a New England missionary, seeks solitude but embarks on an interracial marriage with a Hawaiian cowboy. Then she faces some of the mysteries of the Polynesia of old.
$ 4.95                               ISBN 0-935180-3-3

### *Myths and Legends of Hawaii* by Dr. W.D. Westervelt
A broadly inclusive, one-volume collection of folklore by a leading authority. Completely edited and reset format for today's readers of the great prehistoric tales of Maui, Hina, Pele and her fiery family, and a dozen other heroic beings, human or ghostly.
$.4.95                               ISBN 0-935180-43-5

### *Claus Spreckles, The Sugar King in Hawai* by Jacob Adler
Sugar was the main economic game in Hawaii a century ago, and the boldest player was Claus Spreckels, a California tycoon who built a second empire in the Islands by ruthless and often dubious means.
$3.95                                ISBN 0-935180-76-1

### *Remember Pearl Harbor* by Blake Clark
An up-to-date edition of the first full-length account of the effect of the December 7, 1941 "blitz" that precipitated America's entrance into World War II and is still remembered vividly by military and civilian survivors of the airborne Japanese holocaust.
$4.95                                ISBN 0-935180-49-4

**Russian Flag Over Hawaii: The Mission of Jeffery Tolamy,** a novel by Darwin Teilhet
A vigorous adventure novel in which a young American struggles to unshackle the grip held by Russian filibusters on the Kingdom of Kauai. Kamehameha the Great and many other historical figures play their roles in a colorful love story.
$3.95                                    ISBN 0-935180-28-1

**The Betrayal of Liliuokalani: Last Queen of Hawaii 1838-1917** by Helena G. Allen
A woman caught in the turbulent maelstrom of cultures in conflict. Treating Liliuokalani's life with authority, accuracy and details, *Betrayal* also is a tremendously informative concerning the entire period of missionary activity and foreign encroachment in the islands.
$6.95                                    ISBN 0-935180-89-3

**Rape in Paradise** by Theon Wright
The sensational "*Massie Case*" of the 1930's shattered the tranquil image that mainland U.S.A. had of Hawaii. One woman shouted "Rape!" and the island erupted with such turmoil that for twenty years it was deemed unprepared for statehood. A fascinating case study of race relations and military-civilian relations.
$4.95                                    ISBN 0-935180-88-5

**Hawaii's Story by Hawaii's Queen** by Lydia Liliuokalani
The Hawaiian kingdom's last monarch wrote her biography in 1897, the year before the annexation of the Hawaiian islands by the United States. Her story covers six decades of island history told from the viewpoint of a major historical figure.
$6.95                                    ISBN 0-935180-85-0

**The Legends and Myths of Hawaii** by David Kalakaua
Political and historical traditions and stories of the pre-Cook period capture the romance of old Polynesia. A rich collection of Hawaiian lore originally presented in 1888 by Hawaii's "merrie monarch."
$6.95                                    ISBN 0-935180-86-9

**Mark Twain in Hawaii: Roughing It in the Sandwich Islands**
The noted humorist's account of his 1866 trip to Hawaii at a time when the islands were more for the native than the tourists. The writings first appeared in their present form in Twain's important book. *Roughing It* includes an introductory essay from *Mad About Islands* by A. Grove Day.
$4.95                                    ISBN 0-935180-93-1

# SOUTH SEAS

**Best South Sea Stories**
Fifteen writers capture all the romance and exotic adventure of the legendary South Pacific including James A. Michener, James Norman Hall, W. Somerset Maugham, and Herman Melville.
$4.95                              ISBN 0-935180-12-5

**Love in the South Seas by Bengt Danielsson**
The noted Swedish anthropologist who served as a member of the famed **Kon-Tiki** expedition here reveals the sex and family life of the Polynesians, based on early accounts as well as his own observations during many years in the South Seas.
$4.95                              ISBN 0-935180-25-7

**The Trembling of a Leaf by W. Somerset Maugham**
Stories of Hawaii and the South Seas, including "Red," the author's most successful story, and "Rain," his most notorious one.
$4.95                              ISBN 0-935180-21-4

**Rogues of the South Seas by A. Grove Day**
Eight true episodes featuring violent figures from Pacific history, such as the German filibuster who attempted to conquer the Hawaiian Islands for the Russian Czar; "Emma, Queen of a Coconut Empire"; and "The Brothers Rorique: Pirates De Luxe." Forward by James A. Michener.
$3.95                              ISBN 0-935180-24-9

**Horror in Paradise: Grim and Uncanny Tales from Hawaii and the South Seas,** edited by A. Grove Day and Bacil F. Kirtley
Thirty-four writers narrate "true" episodes of sorcery and the supernatural, as well as gory events on sea and atoll.
$4.95                              ISBN 0-935180-23-0

**The Blue of Capricorn** by Eugene Burdick
Stories and sketches from Polynesia, Micronesia, and Melanesia by the co-author of The Ugly American and The Ninth Wave. Burdick's last book explores an ocean world rich in paradox and drama, a modern world of polyglot islanders and primitive savages.
$3.95                              ISBN 0-935180-36-2

**The Book of Puka Puka** by Robert Dean Frisbie
Lone trader on a South Sea atoll, "Ropati" tells charmingly of his first years on Puka-Puka, where he was destined to rear five half-Polynesian children. Special foreword by A. Grove Day.
$3.95                              ISBN 0-935180-27-3

*Coronado's Quest: The Discovery of the American Southwest* by A. Grove Day

The story of the expedition that first entered the American Southwest in 1540. A pageant of exploration with a cast of dashing men and women—not only Hispanic adventurers and valient Indians of a dozen tribes, but gray-robed friars like Marcos des Niza—as well as Esteban, the black Moorish slave who was slain among the Zuni pueblos he had discovered.

$3.95                          ISBN 0-935180-37-0

*A Dream of Islands: Voyages of Self-Discovery in the South Seas* by A. Gavan Daws

The South Seas . . . the islands of Tahiti, Hawaii, Samoa, the Marquesas . . . the most seductive places on earth, where physically beautiful brown-skinned men and women move through a living dream of great erotic power. *A Dream of Islands* tells the stories of five famous Westerners who found their fate in the islands: John Williams, Herman Melville, Walter Murray Gibson, Robert Louis Stevenson, Paul Gauguin.

$4.95                          ISBN 0-935180-71-2

## How to Order

Send check or money order with an additional $2.00 for the first book and $1.00 thereafter to cover mailing and handling to:

Mutual Publishing

1127 11th Ave., Mezz. B, Honolulu, HI 96816

For airmail delivery add $2.00 per book.